THE PRINCETON REVIEW

CRACKING THE
NEW SAT®
& PSAT

1995 EDITION

Other books in The Princeton Review Series

Cracking the New SAT and PSAT with Sample Tests on Computer Disk
Cracking the ACT
Cracking the LSAT
Cracking the LSAT with Sample Tests on Computer Disk
Cracking the GRE
Cracking the GRE with Sample Tests on Computer Disk
Cracking the GMAT
Cracking the GMAT with Sample Tests on Computer Disk
Cracking the MCAT
Cracking the SAT II: Biology Subject Test
Cracking the SAT II: Chemistry Subject Test
Cracking the SAT II: English Subject Tests
Cracking the SAT II: French Subject Test
Cracking the SAT II: History Subject Tests
Cracking the SAT II: Math Subject Tests
Cracking the SAT II: Physics Subject Test
Cracking the SAT II: Spanish Subject Test
Cracking the TOEFL with audiocassette
How to Survive Without Your Parents' Money
Grammar Smart
Math Smart
Study Smart
Student Access Guide to America's Top 100 Internships
Student Access Guide to College Admissions
Student Access Guide to the Best Business Schools
Student Access Guide to the Best Law Schools
Student Access Guide to the Best Medical Schools
Student Access Guide to Paying for College
Student Access Guide to the Best 306 Colleges
Word Smart: Building a Better Vocabulary
Word Smart II: How to Build a More Educated Vocabulary

Also available on cassette from Living Language

Grammar Smart
Word Smart
Word Smart II

THE PRINCETON REVIEW

CRACKING THE NEW SAT® & PSAT

1995 EDITION

BY ADAM ROBINSON AND JOHN KATZMAN
with a foreword by David Owen

VILLARD BOOKS  NEW YORK 1994

ISSN 1049-6238
ISBN 0-679-75338-9

The SAT questions listed below were selected from the following publications of the College Entrance Examination Board: *5 SATs, 1981; 6 SATs, 1982; 5 SATs, 1984; 10 SATs, 1983.* These questions, as well as test directions throughout the book, are reprinted by permission of Educational Testing Service, the copyright owner of the sample questions. Permission to reprint the above material does not constitute review or endorsement by Educational Testing Service or the College Board of this publication as a whole or of any other sample questions or testing information it may contain.

SAT questions: p. 30, #25; p. 31, #1; p. 44, #15; p 92, Passage; p 92, #16–18; p. 93 #20, #21; p. 99, #16; p. 108, #17; p. 51, #7; p. 53, #1, #2, #3; p. 54, #1, #2, #3; p. 55, #9; p. 57, #8; p. 146, #25; p. 148, #24; p. 151, #24; p. 198, #11; p. 199, #18; p. 201, #3; p. 202, #17; p. 203, #17; p. 204, #25; p. 207, #15; p. 210, #12; p. 211, #20; p. 239, #10; p. 240, #13; p. 241, #19; p. 249, #25; p. 256, #24; p. 269, #13; p. 272, #11; p. 380, Passage; p. 381, #25; p. 390, Passage; p. 392, #34; pp. 402–3, Passage; p. 403, #3;

All other questions in the book were created by the authors.

The passage on p. 378 was reprinted from *Memoirs of an Anti-Semite* by Gregor von Rezzori with kind permission of Viking Penguin.

SAT and Scholastic Assessment Test are registered trademarks of the College Entrance Examination Board.

Book Designers: Michael Freedman, Julian Ham, and Andrea Paykin

FOREWORD

The publishers of the Scholastic Assessment Test don't want you to read this book. For nearly sixty years they have claimed that the SAT cannot be coached, and this book proves that it can be.

Cracking the New SAT & PSAT contains information that could help you raise your SAT scores substantially and improve your chances of being admitted to the college of your choice. It also contains information that should make you think twice before boasting about a high SAT score or becoming depressed about a low one. The SAT, you will discover, is not the test that your teachers, guidance counselors, parents, and friends may have led you to believe. Despite its reputation as an "objective" examination, the SAT doesn't measure much more than your ability to take the SAT.

Unfortunately, though, your ability to take the SAT could have a significant impact on the course of your life. Virtually all the nation's most selective colleges—and a great many less selective ones—require their applicants to submit SAT scores. (Many other schools require scores from the SAT's chief competitor, the ACT, published by the American College Testing Program.) Most admissions officers won't understand how to interpret the scores you send them, but this won't keep them from speculating freely about your intelligence and even your personality on the basis of how you do. Where you spend the next four years of your life may be determined in part by what they decide. The test's effect can even carry over into the years beyond college. More than a few employers require recent college graduates to submit their high school SAT scores when applying for jobs. This practice is illegal, but some companies do it anyway. For the time being, anyway, you're probably stuck with the SAT.

Since you are, you owe it to yourself to learn as much as you can about the test. If you're like most of the 1.3 million high school students who will take it this year, you probably don't have a very clear idea of what you're in for. You may have glanced at an SAT preparation book or even taken a coaching course. But most coaching materials don't have much to do with the real SAT. Partly because most available materials are so bad, many teachers and guidance counselors believe that it is impossible for students to improve their SAT scores through coaching. Another reason they believe this is that the test's publishers have always told them coaching doesn't work. The College Board, which sponsors the test, has claimed that score gains resulting from coaching "are always small regardless of the coaching method used or the differences in the students coached." The Educational Testing Service (ETS)—which has written and administered the SAT for the College Board since 1947—says the same thing: "The abilities measured by the SAT develop over a student's entire academic life, so coaching—vocabulary drill, memorizing facts, or the like—can do little or nothing to raise the student's scores."

Despite all the official denial, though, the SAT can very definitely be coached. The only "aptitude" you need to make your scores go up is your aptitude for understanding how ETS's question writers think.

Cracking the New SAT & PSAT is different from other coaching guides because it contains strategies that really work on the SAT. These strategies are taught at a new coaching school called The Princeton Review. The school is based in New York City and has branches in a growing number of other cities. The strategies were developed by Adam Robinson, formerly a private SAT tutor, and John Katzman, the founder of the school. Although The Princeton Review is just a few years old, it has already become legendary among many high school and college students. A guidance counselor at an exclusive private academy in New York once told me that most of her juniors were enrolled at The Princeton Review and that their SAT scores had risen so much that she was no longer certain how to advise them about where they ought to apply to college. At Harvard not long ago, a freshman was overheard saying, "Yeah, he got a 750 on the verbal, but it was only a Princeton Review 750."

If you read this book *carefully,* you will have a huge advantage when you actually take the SAT. In fact, students who take the test without knowing these strategies are, in effect, taking it blindfolded.

ETS often refers to the SAT as an "objective" test, meaning that the score you receive on it isn't just one person's judgment (the way a grade in a course is) but is arrived at "scientifically." Few people stop to think that the word *objective* in this case applies only to the mechanical grading process. Every question still has to be written—and its answer determined—by highly subjective human beings. The SAT isn't really an "objective" test. Banesh Hoffman, a critic of standardized testing, once suggested that a better term for it would be "child-gradable," because marking it doesn't require any knowledge or intelligence. The principal difference between the SAT and a test that can't be graded by a child is that the SAT leaves no room for more than one correct answer. It leaves no room, in other words, for people who don't see eye to eye with ETS.

In 1962, Banesh Hoffman wrote a wonderful book called *The Tyranny of Testing*. It begins with a letter reprinted from the *Times* of London:

Sir, —— Among the "odd one out" type of questions which my son had to answer for a school entrance examination was: "Which is the odd one out among cricket, football, billiards, and hockey?"

I said billiards because it is the only one played indoors. A colleague says football because it is the only one in which the ball is not struck by an implement. A neighbour says cricket because in all the other games the object is to put the ball into a net; and my son, with the confidence of nine summers, plumps for hockey, "because it is the only one that is a girl's game." Could any of your readers put me out of my misery by stating what is the correct answer?

Yours Faithfully,

T. C. Batty

Other answers were suggested in Hoffman's book: billiards, because it's the only one that's not a team sport; football, because it's the only one played with a hollow ball; billiards, because it's the only one in which the color of the ball matters; hockey, because it's the only one whose name ends in a vowel.

The "odd one out" problem is an "objective" question: A grading machine will mark it the same way every time, whatever the answer really is. But you won't be able to answer it correctly unless you know what the testers had in mind when they wrote it. If you aren't on the same wavelength they were on, you won't come up with the answer they wanted.

The same is true with the SAT. In order to do well, you need to understand how the test makers at ETS were thinking when they sat down to write the questions. This book will teach you how to do precisely that.

— David Owen,
author of None of the Above:
Behind the Myth of Scholastic Aptitude

ACKNOWLEDGMENTS

An SAT course is much more than clever techniques and powerful computer score reports; the reason our results are great is that our teachers care so much about their kids. Many of them have gone out of their way to improve the course, often going so far as to write their own materials, some of which we have incorporated into our course manual as well as into this book. The list of these teachers could fill this page, but special thanks must be given to Lisa Edelstein, Thomas Glass, Len Galla, Rob Cohen, Fred Bernstein, and Jayme Koszyn.

For production and editing help, thanks to Andrea Paykin, Mike Freedman, Andy Lutz, Lee Elliott, Cynthia Brantley, Julian Ham, Andrew Dunn, Clayton Harding, Kathleen Standard, Jefferson Nichols, Joshua Shaub, Ramsey Silberberg, Matthew Clark, Illeny Maaza, Meher Khambata, and Maria Quinlan.

The Princeton Review would never have been founded without the advice and support of Bob Scheller. Many of the questions on our diagnostic tests are the result of our joint effort. Bob's program, Pretest Review, provides the best sort of competition; his fine results make us work all the harder.

Finally, we would like to thank the people who truly have taught us everything we know about the SAT: our students.

CONTENTS

INTRODUCTION

Welcome to the 1994 edition of *Cracking the New SAT & PSAT*. This book is for anyone planning to take the SAT in the spring of 1994, or anyone taking the 1993 PSAT. If you are planning to take the SAT in fall of 1993, stop.

Until 1994, the SAT will be given in its old format. If you're taking the fall test, you need our book *Cracking the SAT and PSAT 1993–1994*. Go exchange this book wherever you bought it before you bend the cover or crinkle a page. *If you've recently bought this book, and you've already crinkled a page, send the book (with receipt) to us at TPR Publishing, 2315 Broadway, New York, NY 10024, and we'll swap it for you.*

Back in the early 1980s, when we started preparing students for the SAT with our revolutionary methods, invariably they would say things like, "Wow! These techniques are amazing! But won't ETS change the SAT once everyone finds out about this?" We were a small company back then, so we reassured our students that ETS was highly unlikely to change the test just because a few hundred students each year showed seemingly miraculous score improvements.

By the mid-1980s, however, several hundred students had grown to several thousand. And in 1986, when we revealed our methods to the general public in the first edition of the book you're holding — a book that became a *New York Times* bestseller — our students threw up their hands. "Now you guys have done it. You've let the secrets out of the bag. For sure ETS is going to change the SAT now to stop your techniques."

Well, seven years and tens of thousands of students later, it finally happened. ETS changed the test. And the question all our students and readers ask us now is "Do your techniques still work?"

Yes! If anything, they work even better now. So what's the big deal about these changes, anyway?

The changes themselves are pretty trivial. First, ETS (the Educational Testing Service, which writes and administers the SAT) and the College Board (which sponsors the test) have finally admitted that the SAT doesn't measure intelligence, so they've changed its name from the Scholastic Aptitude Test to the Scholastic Assessment Test I.

Some schools ask you to take a few one-hour Achievement tests in addition to the SAT; these Achievements will be renamed the Scholastic Assessment Test II.

Inside the SAT, antonym items will be dropped from the verbal section. Both the sentence completions and reading comprehension sections will include more questions that test vocabulary.

In the math section, students will be permitted to use calculators. Also, ETS and the College Board will include ten questions in which students will fill in their answers in a little grid. ETS suspected that this format would be confusing, and they were right. According to their own statistics, 20,000 students a year will answer these questions incorrectly because they don't understand the format.

You may have heard that the new, improved SAT would have an essay section, but it won't. Finally, the odious Test of Standard Written English will be dropped. We've never felt that this so-called placement test belonged on the SAT, anyway. Now it appears that ETS and the College Board have come around to our point of view.

The Princeton Review spends almost a million dollars every year improving our materials. We send fifty teachers into each test administration to make sure nothing slips by us. *Cracking the New SAT & PSAT* incorporates our observations, giving you the most up-to-date information possible.

The Princeton Review has grown from 15 kids in 1981 to 50,000 in 1991 because we do what almost no one else does: raise scores. Students in our SAT course improve their test scores a lot (independent studies show an average improvement of 110 to 160 points).

Our approach involves more than great techniques. Classes are small (eight to twelve in a group), and they're grouped by shared ability, so each student receives personal attention. When students don't understand something in class, we work with them in even smaller groups, and then one-on-one in tutoring.

We realize, however, that many kids can't get to our courses. That's why we wrote *Cracking the New SAT & PSAT*. Although the book is no substitute for small classes and great teaching, it can help you improve your score. Make sure you take your time and do the drills carefully. The techniques are too complex to try them out the week before the SAT, so give yourself four or five weeks to practice our suggestions. We recommend that you devote six to ten hours a week to studying our techniques.

Furthermore, this is *not* a textbook; anyone charging you for a course that uses this book is ripping you off. You're better off just buying the book in a bookstore.

So relax. Work hard and get the SAT scores that the colleges you care about will love. And if you need more intense work than a book can offer, give us a call at 1-800-995-5585. Whatever you do, we wish you good luck.

John Katzman
President and Co-founder

Adam Robinson
Co-founder

PART 1

Orientation

WHAT IS THE SAT-I REASONING TEST?

SAT-I—from now on, we'll refer to it simply as the SAT—is a three-hour multiple-choice test that is divided into seven sections:

1. two thirty-minute verbal sections

2. one fifteen-minute verbal section

3. two thirty-minute math sections

4. one fifteen-minute math section

5. one thirty-minute experimental section, either math or verbal

The fifteen-minute verbal section consists of one double critical reading passage followed by thirteen questions. The fifteen-minute math section consists of ten multiple-choice math questions.

Only the verbal and math sections will count toward your SAT scores. The experimental section on your SAT may look just like a verbal section or a math section, but it won't be scored; ETS uses it only to try out new SAT questions and to determine whether the test you are taking is harder or easier than ones that have been given in the past.

The verbal SAT contains three types of questions:

1. sentence completions

2. analogies

3. critical reading

The math SAT also contains three types of questions:

1. regular multiple-choice math (arithmetic, algebra, and geometry)

2. quantitative comparisons

3. grid-ins

Each of these question types will be dealt with in detail later in the book.

THE PSAT

All of the techniques discussed in this book also apply to the PSAT, or Preliminary Scholastic Assessment Test, which is usually administered in eleventh grade. The PSAT is arranged a little differently from the SAT. It contains two thirty-minute verbal sections and two thirty-minute math sections. (There is no experimental section on the PSAT.) As in the past, the PSAT is a sort of retirement home for worn-out SAT questions. Questions on the PSAT are taken directly from old SATs, and all the same techniques apply.

WHERE DOES THE SAT COME FROM?

The SAT is published by the Educational Testing Service (ETS) under the sponsorship of the College Entrance Examination Board (College Board). ETS and the College Board are both private companies. We'll tell you more about them in chapter 1.

HOW IS THE SAT SCORED?

Four or five weeks after you take the SAT, you will receive a report from ETS containing a verbal score and a math score. Each score will be reported on a scale that runs from 200 to 800, with 800 the best possible score and 450 approximately average. The third digit of an SAT score is always a zero, which means that scores can go up or down only ten points at a time. In other words, you might receive a 490, a 500, or a 510 on the verbal; you could never receive a 492, a 495, or a 507. Every question on the SAT is worth about ten points. (Easy questions are worth the same as hard ones.)

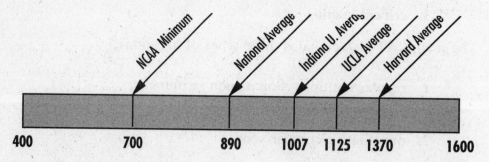

PSAT scores are reported on a scale that runs from 20 to 80. This is exactly like the SAT scale, except that the final zero has been removed. If you think this sounds needlessly complicated, you're right.

RAW SCORES AND PERCENTILES

You may hear about two other kinds of scores in connection with the SAT: raw scores and percentile scores. Here's what they mean:

1. Your raw score is simply the number of questions you answered correctly, minus a fraction of the number of questions you answered incorrectly. It is used in calculating your final "scaled" score. We'll tell you more about raw scores in chapter 2.

2. A percentile score tells you how you did in relation to everyone else who took the test. If your score is in the 60th percentile, it means you did better on the test than 60 percent of the people who took it. People who are disappointed by their SAT scores can sometimes cheer themselves up by looking at their percentile scores.

HOW IMPORTANT ARE SAT SCORES?

The SAT is an important factor when you apply to colleges, but it is not the only one. A rule of thumb: the larger the college, the more important the SAT. Small liberal arts colleges will give a good deal of weight to your extracurricular activities, your interview, your essays, and your recommendations. Large state universities often admit students based on formulas consisting of just two ingredients: SAT scores and grade point average.

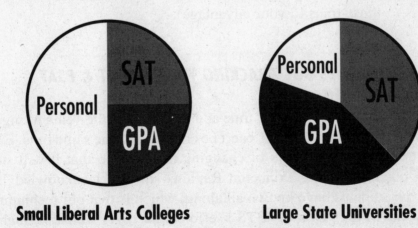

Small Liberal Arts Colleges　　**Large State Universities**

Even at a small liberal arts college, though, SAT scores can be the deciding factor. If your scores fall below a school's usual range, admissions officers will look very critically at the other elements in your application folder. For most college applicants, an SAT score is the equivalent of a first impression. If your scores are good, an admissions officer will be more likely to give you the benefit of the doubt in other areas.

WHAT IS THE PRINCETON REVIEW?

The Princeton Review is the nation's fastest-growing test-preparation school. We have conducted courses in roughly 500 locations around the country, and we prepare more students for the SAT and PSAT than anyone else. We also prepare students for the ACT, GRE, GMAT, LSAT, and MCAT.

The Princeton Review's techniques are unique and powerful. We developed them after scrutinizing dozens of real SATs, analyzing them with computers, and proving our theories with real students. Our methods have been widely imitated, but no one else achieves our score improvements.

This book was drawn from our extensive experience in the classroom. Our techniques for cracking the SAT will help you improve your SAT scores by teaching you to

1. think like the test writers at ETS.

2. take full advantage of the limited time allowed.

3. find the answers to questions you don't understand by guessing intelligently.

4. avoid the traps that ETS has laid for you (and use those traps to your advantage).

WHY ETS EXECUTIVES BUY *CRACKING THE NEW SAT & PSAT* FOR THEIR CHILDREN

ETS has spent a great deal of time and money over the years trying to persuade people that the SAT can't be cracked. At the same time, ETS has struggled to find ways of changing the SAT so that it will stop being cracked by The Princeton Review—in effect acknowledging what our students have known all along, which is that our techniques really do work. Despite ETS's efforts, the SAT remains highly vulnerable to our techniques. In fact, recent changes in the test have made it more coachable than ever.

A NOTE ABOUT SCORE IMPROVEMENTS

We have found in our courses that students' scores usually don't improve gradually. Instead, they tend to go up in spurts, from one plateau to another. Our students typically achieve score gains of 100 points or more after mastering the initial concepts of the course. Their scores then often level off, only to take another jump a few weeks later when more course material has been assimilated.

If you work steadily through this book, you, too, will feel yourself moving from plateau to plateau. But you will have to work. You won't have one of our teachers standing over you, reminding you to review what you have learned.

The Princeton Review's techniques are the closest thing there is to a shortcut to the SAT. But there is no shortcut to The Princeton Review.

A WARNING

Many of our techniques for beating the SAT are counterintuitive. That is, using them will sometimes require you to violate what you think of as common sense. In order to get the full benefit from our techniques, you must *trust* them. The best way to develop this trust is to practice the techniques and convince yourself that they work.

But you have to practice them *properly*. If you try our techniques on the practice questions in most popular SAT coaching books, you will probably decide that they don't work.

Why?

Because the practice questions in those books are very little like the questions on real SATs. There may be "analogies" and "quantitative comparisons" in those books, but if you compare them with the questions on real SATs you will discover that they are different. In fact, studying the practice questions and techniques in some of those other books could actually hurt your SAT score. (The practice questions on the diagnostic test in the back of this book, in contrast, are created with the same writing and testing processes that ETS uses, and they are tried out ahead of time on real students to ensure that they are as much like real SAT questions as they can possibly be.)

We strongly recommend that you purchase *10 SATs*. This book is put out by the College Board and ETS, the companies that publish the SAT, and it contains copies of real tests that were actually given. If you don't find it in your local bookstore, you can order it directly from the College Board (see page 293 for ordering information). As you practice with *10 SATs* be aware that the actual SAT you take will be different from the tests in the book. The SAT will change in 1994, but *10 SATs* hasn't caught up yet. ETS and the College Board won't release more than a few real copies of the new SAT for quite some time. But practicing on the old SATs in *10 SATs* won't hurt you. In fact, it will help a lot, since the bulk of the test hasn't changed. If you time yourself correctly, the scores you earn on the tests in *10 SATs* will come very close to the scores you will earn on the SAT that is currently being administered. And by practicing our techniques on real SATs, you will be able to prove to yourself that they work and increase your confidence when you actually take the test.

You should also ask your guidance counselor for free copies of "Taking the SAT" and "A Guide to the New SAT." These are booklets published by the College Board. "Taking the SAT" contains a full-length practice test, and "A Guide to the New SAT" explains the changes that were implemented in spring of 1994.

Chapter 1

How to Think About the SAT

ARE YOU A GENIUS OR AN IDIOT?

If you're like most high school students, you think of the SAT as a test of how smart you are. If you score 800 on the verbal you'll probably think of yourself as a "genius"; if you score 200 you may think of yourself as an "idiot." You may even think of an SAT score as a permanent label, like your Social Security number. The Educational Testing Service (ETS), the company that publishes the test, encourages you to think this way by telling you that the test measures your ability to reason and by claiming that you cannot improve your score through special preparation.

But this is wrong.

THE SCHOLASTIC ASSESSMENT TEST IS NOT A TEST OF REASONING

The SAT isn't a test of how well you reason, and it isn't a test of how smart you are. More than anything else, it is a test of how good you are at taking ETS tests.

Can you learn to be better at taking the SAT? Of course you can. That's what this book is all about. You can improve your SAT score in exactly the same way you would improve your grade in chemistry: by learning the material you are going to be tested on.

YOU MUST LEARN TO THINK LIKE ETS

If your teacher gave you a D on a chemistry test, what would you do? You'd probably say to yourself, "I should have worked harder" or "I could have done better if I'd studied more." This is exactly the attitude you should have about the SAT. If you were disappointed by your score on the PSAT, you shouldn't say, "I'm stupid"; you should say, "I need to get better at taking this test."

You also need to get better at thinking like the people at ETS who write the questions. In your chemistry class, you know how your teacher thinks and that he or she tends to ask certain kinds of questions. You also know what sorts of answers will win you points, and what sorts of answers won't.

You need to learn to think of the SAT in exactly the same terms. The test writers at ETS think in very predictable ways. You can improve your scores by learning to think the way they do and by learning to anticipate the kinds of answers that they think are correct.

WHAT IS ETS?

ETS is the Educational Testing Service, a big company. It sells not only the SAT but also about 500 other tests, including ones for CIA agents, golf pros, travel agents, firefighters, and barbers. ETS is located outside Princeton, New Jersey, on a beautiful 400-acre estate that used to be a hunting club. The buildings where the SAT is written are surrounded by woods and hills. There is a swimming pool, a goose pond, a baseball diamond, lighted tennis courts, jogging trails, an expensive house for the company's president, a chauffeured motor pool, and a private hotel where single rooms cost more than $200 a night.

You may have been told that ETS is a government agency, or that it's a part of Princeton University. It is neither. ETS is just a private company that makes a lot of money by selling tests. The company that hires ETS to write the SAT is called the College Entrance Examination Board, or the College Board.

WHO WRITES THE SAT TODAY?

Many people believe the SAT questions are written by famous college professors or experts on secondary education. But this is not true. Virtually all questions are written by ordinary company employees or by college students and others who are hired part-time from outside ETS. Sometimes the questions are even written by teenagers. Frances Brodsky, the daughter of an ETS vice president, spent the summer after she graduated from high school writing questions for ETS tests.

THE SAT IS NOT WRITTEN BY GENIUSES; YOU DON'T HAVE TO BE A GENIUS TO EARN A HIGH SCORE

Right now, the real person in charge of writing questions for the verbal half of the SAT is Pamela Cruise. She's a woman who has worked at ETS for several years. The walls of her small office are covered with pictures of the New York Rangers ice hockey team. She's a nice enough person, but, like most of us, she probably isn't a genius. Writing verbal questions for the SAT is just her job.

The person in charge of writing math questions is James Braswell. He's older than Pamela Cruise. He is a soft-spoken man who wears glasses with black plastic frames.

Why are we telling you who these people are? Because you should always remember that the test you are going to take was written by real people. The Wizard of Oz turned out not to be a wizard at all; he was just a little man behind a curtain. The same sort of thing is true about the SAT.

FORGET ABOUT THE "BEST" ANSWER

The instructions for the SAT tell you to select the "best" answer to every question. What does "best" answer mean? It means the answer that ETS believes to be correct. Specifically, it means the answer that Pamela Cruise and James Braswell selected when the questions were written in the first place.

For that reason, we're not going to talk about "best" answers in this book. Instead, we're going to talk about "Pam's answer" and "Jim's answer." These are the only answers that will win you points. Your job on the verbal SAT is to find Pam's answer to every question; your job on the math SAT is to find Jim's.

HOW TO CRACK THE SYSTEM

In the following chapters we're going to teach you our method for cracking the SAT. Read each chapter carefully. Some of our ideas may seem strange at first. For example, when we tell you that it is sometimes easier to answer hard SAT questions without looking at the questions, but only at the answer choices, you may say, "That's not the way I'm taught to think in school."

THE SAT ISN'T SCHOOL

We're not going to teach you math. We're not going to teach you English. We're going to teach you SAT.

Why do you need to know the SAT? Because knowledge of the SAT is what the SAT tests.

In the next chapter we're going to lay down a few basic principles. We're going to show you that it is possible to

1. find a correct answer by eliminating incorrect ones even if you don't know *why* your answer is correct.

2. take advantage of the SAT's "guessing reward."

3. earn partial credit for partial information.

Chapter 2
Cracking the SAT: Basic Principles

A GEOGRAPHY LESSON

What's the capital of Malawi?

Give up?

Unless you spend your spare time reading an atlas, you probably don't even know that Malawi is a tiny country in Africa, much less what its capital is. If this question came up on a test, you'd have to skip it, wouldn't you?

WELL, MAYBE NOT

Let's turn this question into a multiple-choice question—the only kind of question you'll find on the verbal SAT, and virtually the only kind of question you'll find on the math SAT—and see if you can't figure out the answer anyway.

> The capital of Malawi is
>
> (A) Washington, D.C.
> (B) Paris
> (C) Tokyo
> (D) London
> (E) Lilongwe

THE QUESTION DOESN'T SEEM HARD ANYMORE, DOES IT?

Of course, we made our example extremely easy. (By the way, there won't actually be any questions about geography on the SAT.) But you'd be surprised at how many people give up on SAT questions not much more difficult than this one just because they don't know the correct answer right off the top of their heads. "Capital of Malawi? Oh no! I've never *heard* of Malawi!"

These students don't stop to think that they might be able to find the correct answer simply by eliminating all the answers they know are wrong.

YOU ALREADY KNOW ALMOST ALL THE ANSWERS

If someone offered to give you the answers to the SAT before you took it, you'd probably be shocked. But the fact is that every student who takes the test gets to see virtually all of the answers ahead of time.

There's nothing strange or suspect about this. All but ten of the questions on the SAT are multiple-choice questions, and every multiple-choice question is followed by five (or, in a few cases, four) answer choices. On every single multiple-choice question, one of those choices, and only one, will be the correct answer to the question. You won't have to come up with that answer from scratch. You only have to identify it.

How will you do that?

BY LOOKING FOR WRONG ANSWERS INSTEAD OF FOR RIGHT ONES

Why? *Because wrong answers are usually easier to find.* Remember the question about Malawi. Even though you didn't know the answer off the top of your head, you figured it out easily by eliminating the four obviously incorrect choices. You looked for wrong answers first.

In other words, you used the *process of elimination*, which we'll call *POE* for short. This is an extremely important concept, and one that we'll come back to again and again. It's one of the keys to improving your SAT score. When you finish reading this book, you will be able to use POE to answer many questions you don't understand.

The great artist Michelangelo once said that when he looked at a block of marble, he could see a statue inside it. All he had to do to make a sculpture, he said, was to chip away everything that wasn't part of it. You should approach difficult SAT multiple-choice questions in the same way, by chipping away everything that's not correct. By first eliminating the *most obviously incorrect* choices on difficult questions, you will be able to focus your attention more effectively on the smaller number of truly tempting choices that remain.

THIS ISN'T THE WAY YOU'RE TAUGHT TO THINK IN SCHOOL

In school, your teachers expect you to work carefully and thoroughly, spending as long as it takes to understand whatever it is you're working on. They want you to prove not only that you know the answer to a question but also that you know how to derive it. When your algebra teacher gives you a test in class, he or she wants you to work through every problem, step by logical step. You probably even have to show your work. If you don't know all the steps required to arrive at the solution, you may not receive full credit, even if you somehow manage to come up with the correct answer.

But the SAT is different. It isn't like school. You don't have to prove that you know why your answer is correct. The only thing ETS's scoring machine cares about is the answer you come up with. If you darken the right space on your answer sheet, you'll get credit, even if you didn't quite understand the question.

WHAT'S THE CAPITAL OF QATAR?

There won't be many questions on the SAT in which incorrect choices will be as easy to eliminate as they were on the Malawi question. But if you read this book carefully, you'll learn how to eliminate at least one choice on virtually any SAT multiple-choice question, and two, three, or even four choices on many.

What good is it to eliminate just one or two choices on a four- or five-choice SAT item?

Plenty. In fact, for most students, it's an important key to earning higher scores.

Here's another example:

The capital of Qatar is

(A) Paris
(B) Dukhan
(C) Tokyo
(D) Doha
(E) London

On this question you'll almost certainly be able to eliminate only three of the five choices by using POE. That means you still can't be sure of the answer. You know that the capital of Qatar has to be either Doha or Dukhan, but you don't know which.

Should you skip the question and go on? Or should you guess?

CLOSE YOUR EYES AND POINT

You've probably heard a lot of different advice about guessing on multiple-choice questions on the SAT. Some teachers and guidance counselors tell their students never to guess and to mark an answer only if they're absolutely certain that it's correct. Others tell their students not to guess unless they are able to eliminate two or three of the choices.

Both of these pieces of advice are completely incorrect.

Even ETS is misleading about guessing. Although it tells you that you *can* guess, it doesn't tell you that you *should*. And you certainly should. In fact, if you can eliminate even *one* incorrect choice on an SAT multiple-choice question, guessing blindly from among the remaining choices will most likely improve your score. And if you can eliminate two or three choices, you'll be even more likely to improve your score.

DON'T PAY ATTENTION TO ETS

ETS tries to discourage students from guessing on multiple-choice questions by telling them that there is a "guessing penalty" in the way the test is scored. But this is not true. There is no penalty for guessing on the SAT. Even if you can't eliminate any of the choices, random guessing isn't going to hurt your score in the long run.

THERE IS NO GUESSING PENALTY ON THE SAT

Your raw score is just the number of questions you got right, minus a fraction of the number you got wrong (except on the ten grid-ins, which are scored a little differently). Every time you answer an SAT question correctly, you get one raw point. Every time you leave an SAT question blank, you get zero raw points. Every time you answer an SAT question incorrectly, ETS subtracts one fourth of a raw point (if the question had five answer choices), one third of a raw point (if it had four), or nothing (if it was a grid-in).

It is the subtracted fraction—one fourth or one third, depending on the type of question—that ETS refers to as the "guessing penalty."

But it's nothing of the sort. An example should help you understand. Raw scores are a little confusing, so let's think in terms of money instead.

For every question you answer correctly on the SAT, ETS will give you a dollar. For every multiple-choice question you leave blank, ETS will give you nothing. For every multiple-choice question you get wrong, you will have to give twenty-five cents back to ETS. That's exactly the way raw scores work.

Now, suppose you have five SAT multiple-choice questions that you can't answer and you decide to guess blindly on them. What will happen? Each of the questions has five choices: A, B, C, D, and E. On each question, therefore, you will have one chance in five of selecting the right answer by guessing. This means that, when you guess on all five questions, on average you can expect to pick the correct answer on one and incorrect answers on four. (If this seems confusing, ask your math teacher to give you a quick explanation of the laws of probability.)

GUESSING WON'T HURT YOU

What happens to your score if you select the correct answer on one question and incorrect choices on four questions? Remember what we said about money: ETS gives you a dollar for the one answer you guessed correctly; you give ETS a quarter for each of the four questions you missed. Four quarters equal a dollar, so you end up exactly where you started, with nothing—which is the same thing that would have happened if you had left all five questions blank.

Guessing blindly didn't leave you any better off on these five problems than leaving them blank would have. But it didn't leave you any worse off, either. You guessed five times in a row, and you were wrong four times, and there still wasn't any guessing penalty.

IN FACT, THERE'S A GUESSING REWARD

What if you had been able to eliminate one incorrect choice on each of those questions? In that case, guessing blindly from among the remaining choices would have been most likely to *raise* your score. In other words, there would have been a guessing *reward*. All you have to do to earn this reward is eliminate one choice, close your eyes, and take a shot.

Still, guessing makes a lot of people very uncomfortable, so we're going to give you yet another way to think about it. Even if you're already convinced, keep reading.

One of the most common misconceptions about the SAT is that you're better off leaving a multi-choice question blank than "taking a chance" on getting it wrong. Some students even believe that they could earn a perfect score on the test by answering just four or five questions correctly and leaving all the others blank. They think that they won't lose any points unless they give an answer that is actually wrong.

Nothing could be farther from the truth.

In order to earn an 800 on the SAT you have to mark an answer for every question, and every answer you mark has to be correct. If you leave one question blank, the best you can hope to score is 780 or 790; leave forty blank and your maximum possible score is about 400.

In other words, you literally lose points for every question on the SAT that you don't answer correctly—*even if you just leave it blank*. And once those points are gone, they're gone forever. You can't get them back by doing better on some other part of the test.

WHY THIS IS TRUE

Here's another way to think about what we just told you. When you take the SAT, you start off each half of the test with the equivalent of $800 in the bank. If you answer all the questions on each half correctly, you get to keep all $800.

For every question you answer incorrectly, though, you lose $10. Now, here's the important part: For every question you leave blank, *you still lose $8*.

Because of the way ETS calculates raw scores on the SAT, an incorrect answer is only a tiny bit worse than a blank. The one thing you can be certain of is that if you leave a question blank, you are *definitely* going to lose $8, whereas if you guess you have a possibility of keeping $10. If you guess incorrectly, you'll lose just $2 more than you would have if you hadn't guessed at all. And if you guess correctly, you'll get to keep your money. That's not much of a gamble, is it? Remember, you *might* get it right.

PARTIAL CREDIT FOR PARTIAL INFORMATION

We hope we've been able to persuade you that guessing on multiple-choice questions isn't going to hurt you and that, if you learn to do it well, it will help you raise your score. If you're like most people, though, you probably still feel a little funny about it. Your teachers may even explicitly forbid you to guess in class. They want you to prove that you understand what they've been trying to teach you, not trick them into thinking you know something you don't. Earning points for a guess probably seems a little bit like cheating, or like stealing: You get something you want, but you didn't do anything to earn it.

This is not a useful way to think on the SAT. It also doesn't happen to be correct. Here's an example that should help you understand what we mean.

The sun is a

(A) main-sequence star
(B) meteor
(C) asteroid
(D) white dwarf star
(E) planet

If you've paid any attention at all in school for the past ten years or so, you probably know that the sun is a star. (Don't worry; there won't be any questions about astronomy on the SAT, either.) You can easily tell, therefore, that the answer to this question must be either A or D. You can tell this not only because it seems clear from the context that "white dwarf" and "main-sequence" are kinds of stars—as they are—but also because you know for a fact that the sun is not a planet, a meteor, or an asteroid. Still, you aren't sure which of the two possible choices is correct. (It's choice A, by the way.)

HEADS YOU WIN A DOLLAR; TAILS YOU LOSE A QUARTER

By using POE you've narrowed your choice down to two possibilities. If you guess randomly you'll have a fifty-fifty chance of being correct—like flipping a coin. Those are extremely good odds on the SAT: heads you win a dollar, tails you lose a quarter. But let's say that, in spite of everything we've told you so far, you just can't bring yourself to guess. It feels wrong to you to put down an answer when you aren't sure, so you decide to leave the question blank.

DON'T YOU DARE LEAVE IT BLANK!

Before you decide to throw away points on this question, consider the case of another student—your best friend, let's say. Now, your best friend is a good guy and an okay friend, but he's not, to put it politely, a genius. When he comes to this question he has no idea *at all* what the sun is. Planet, asteroid, meteor—he doesn't have a clue. So he leaves it blank, too.

You know more about the sun than your friend does. You know that it's a star and he doesn't. But the two of you are going to earn exactly the same score on this question: zero. According to the SAT, you don't know any more about the sun than he does.

If you were in class, that probably wouldn't happen. Your teacher might give you credit for knowing that the sun is *some* kind of star. In math class your teacher probably gives you partial credit on a difficult algebra problem if you follow all the right steps but make a silly subtraction error and come up with an answer that's slightly off. This happens all the time in school. Your teachers very often give you partial credit for partial information.

GUESSING INTELLIGENTLY WILL INCREASE YOUR SCORE

Guessing makes it possible to earn partial credit for partial information on the SAT. You won't know everything about every question on the test. But there will probably be a lot of questions about which you know *something*. Doesn't it seem fair that you should be able to earn some sort of credit for what you do know? Shouldn't your score be higher than the score of someone who doesn't know anything?

THE ONLY WAY TO MAKE THIS HAPPEN IS TO GUESS

How does guessing give you partial credit for partial information?

Simple. Every time you use POE to eliminate an obviously incorrect answer choice, you tilt the odds a little bit more in your favor: you give yourself an edge. Over the course of the entire test, these edges add up. You won't guess correctly on *every* question—but you will guess correctly on some. If you're 50 percent sure of the answer on each of ten questions, then the odds say you'll be most likely to guess correctly 50 percent of the time. You'll only earn half as many points as you would have earned if you'd been 100 percent certain of the answers—but that's completely fair, because you only knew half as much.

Guessing is unfair only if you don't do it. Unfair to *you*, that is. Your SAT score won't be a fair indication of what you know unless you guess and earn partial credit for partial information. You'd get that partial credit if you were in class. Why shouldn't you get it on the SAT?

A WORD BEFORE WE BEGIN

At school you probably aren't allowed to write in your textbooks, unless your school requires you to buy them. You probably even feel a little peculiar about writing in books you own. Books are supposed to be read, you've been told, and you're not supposed to scrawl all over them.

Because you've been told this so many times, you are going to be very reluctant to write in your test booklet when you take the SAT. Your proctor will tell you that you are supposed to write in it—the booklet is the only scratch paper you'll be allowed to use; it says so right in the instructions from ETS—but you'll still feel bad about marking it up. When you come to a math problem that you can't solve in your head, you'll use your very tiniest handwriting to work it out in the most inconspicuous sliver of the margin. When you've finished, you may even erase what you've written.

THIS IS COMPLETELY RIDICULOUS!

Your test booklet is just going to be thrown away when you're finished with it. No one is going to read what you wrote in it and decide that you're stupid because you couldn't remember what 2 + 2 is without writing it down. Your SAT score won't be any higher if you don't make any marks in your booklet. In fact, if you don't take advantage of it, your score will probably be lower than it should be.

YOU PAID FOR YOUR TEST BOOKLET; ACT AS THOUGH YOU OWN IT

Scratch work is *extremely* important on the SAT. Don't be embarrassed about it. Writing in your test booklet will help you keep your mind on what you're doing.

- When a problem asks you about a certain geometrical figure but doesn't provide a drawing, make one yourself. *Don't simply try to imagine it.* Unless you have a photographic memory, you won't be able to keep track of all the different angles, sides, and vertices, and you'll end up wasting valuable time.

- When you work on a geometry problem that does provide a drawing, *don't hesitate to draw all over it yourself.* Many times you will find it helpful to pencil in information that is supplied in the question but not in the drawing.

- When you've used POE to eliminate an obviously wrong answer choice, *cross it out.* Don't leave it there to confuse you. If you have to come back to the question later on, you don't want to redo all the work you did the first time.

- When you answer a question but don't feel entirely certain of your answer, *circle the question* or put a big question mark in the margin beside it. That way, if you have time later on, you can get back to it without having to search through the entire section.

All this applies just as much to the verbal SAT as it does to the math. You probably think of scratch paper as something that is useful only in arithmetic. But you'll need scratch paper on the verbal SAT, too. The verbal sections of your booklet should be just as marked up as the math ones.

TRANSFER YOUR ANSWERS AT THE END OF EACH GROUP

Scratch work isn't the only thing we want you to do in your test booklet. We also want you to mark your answers there. When you take the SAT, you should mark all your answers in your test booklet, with a big letter in the margin beside each problem, and then transfer them later onto your answer sheet. You should transfer your answers when you come to the end of each group of questions. (For example, when you answer a group of analogy items, you should transfer all your answers together after you come to the end of the group.)

Doing this will save you a great deal of time, because you won't have to look back and forth between your test booklet and your answer sheet every few seconds while you are taking the test. You will also be less likely to make mistakes in marking your answers on the answer sheet.

The only exception to this is the grid-ins, the ten non-multiple-choice math questions. You will need to grid each answer as you find it. We'll tell you how to grid your answers later in the book.

SUMMARY

1. When you don't know the right answer to a multiple-choice question, look for wrong answers instead. They're usually easier to find.

2. When you find a wrong choice, eliminate it. In other words, use POE, the process of elimination.

3. ETS doesn't care if you understand the questions on the SAT. All it cares about is whether you darken the correct space on your answer sheet.

4. Despite what you've probably heard, there is no guessing penalty on the SAT. In fact, there is a guessing *reward*. If you can eliminate just one incorrect choice on an SAT multiple-choice question, you will most likely improve your score by guessing blindly from among the remaining choices.

5. Leaving a question blank costs you almost as many points as answering it incorrectly.

6. Intelligent guessing on multiple-choice questions enables you to earn partial credit for partial information. You get credit for this in school. Why shouldn't you get it on the SAT?

7. Do not hesitate to use your test booklet for scratch paper.

8. Transfer your answers to your answer sheet *all at once* when you reach the end of each group of questions, except for the grid-in questions.

Chapter 3

Cracking the SAT: Advanced Principles

PUTTING THE BASIC PRINCIPLES TO WORK

In the preceding chapter, we reviewed some basic principles about the SAT. We showed you that it is possible to

1. find correct answers by using POE, the process of elimination, to get rid of incorrect ones.

2. take advantage of the SAT's "guessing reward."

3. earn partial credit for partial information.

But how will you know which answers to eliminate? And how will you know when to guess? In this chapter, we'll begin to show you. We will teach you how to

1. take advantage of the order in which questions are asked.

2. make better use of your time by scoring the easy points first.

3. use the Joe Bloggs principle to eliminate obviously incorrect choices on difficult questions.

4. find the traps that ETS has laid for you.

5. turn those traps into points.

To show you how this is possible, we first have to tell you something about the way the SAT is arranged.

ORDER OF DIFFICULTY

If you've already taken the SAT once, you probably noticed that the questions got harder as you went along. You probably didn't think much of it at the time. But it's always true on the SAT. Every group of questions starts out easy and then gets hard.

When you take the SAT, the first scored verbal section will begin with a group of ten sentence completions. The first of these questions will be so easy that you and virtually everyone else will almost certainly be able to answer it correctly. The second will be a little bit harder. The eighth will be very, very hard. And the tenth will be so hard that most of the people taking the test will be unable to answer it.

IS THIS ALWAYS TRUE? YES

All standardized tests are arranged this way. They always have been, and they always will be. It isn't too hard to see why. If your gym teacher wanted to find out how high the people in your gym class could jump, she wouldn't start out by setting the high-jump bar at 7 feet. She'd set it at a height that almost everyone could clear, and then she'd gradually raise it from there.

Questions on the SAT work the same way. If they were arranged differently, many students would become discouraged and give up before finding questions they were able to answer.

EASY, MEDIUM, DIFFICULT

Every group of questions on the SAT can be divided into three parts according to difficulty:

1. *The easy third:* Questions in the first third of each group are easy.

2. *The medium third:* Questions in the middle third are medium.

3. *The difficult third:* Questions in the last third are difficult.

In a ten-item sentence completion group as mentioned, questions 1 through 3 are easy, questions 4 through 7 are medium, and questions 8 through 10 are difficult. Then, if the next group of questions is a set of eleven analogies, questions 1 through 4 are easy questions, 5 through 7 are medium, and questions 8 through 11 are difficult.

THE PRINCETON REVIEW DIFFICULTY METER

Before you attack any SAT question, then, it is important to check out how difficult the question is. To remind you to do this, we will precede each SAT question in this book with The Princeton Review Difficulty Meter.

The difficulty meter icon divides each group of questions into thirds. In one of the verbal sections, for example, the first group of questions consists of ten sentence completions. The second group of questions consists of eleven analogies. The third group of questions consists of nine critical reading questions.

Here's how the difficulty meter for the sentence completions of this section would look:

KNOWING THE ORDER OF DIFFICULTY CAN HELP YOU IMPROVE YOUR SCORE

Knowing that SAT questions are presented in order of difficulty can help you in several ways. First, it enables you to make the best use of your limited time. You should never waste time wrestling with the last (and therefore hardest) question in the sentence completion group if you still haven't answered the first (and therefore easiest) in the analogies group, which follows it. Hard questions aren't worth more than easy ones. Why not do the easiest one first? Smart test takers save hard questions for last, after they've scored all the easy points.

We can state this as a simple rule:

> **Answer easy questions first; save hard questions for last.**

KNOWING THE ORDER OF DIFFICULTY CAN HELP YOU IN MORE IMPORTANT WAYS AS WELL

Knowing how questions are arranged on the SAT can help you make the most efficient use of your time. But it can also help you find Jim's and Pam's answers on questions you don't understand.

To show you why this is true, we need to tell you something about how most people take the SAT and other standardized tests.

CHOOSING ANSWERS THAT "SEEM" RIGHT

Most of us, when we take the SAT, don't have time to work out every problem completely, or to check and double-check our answers. We just go as far as we can on every problem and then choose the answer that *seems* correct, based on what we've been able to figure out. Sometimes we're completely sure of our answer. Other times we simply do what we can and then follow our hunch. We may pick an answer because it "just looks right," or because something about it seems to go naturally with the question.

Whether you're a high scorer or a low scorer, this is almost certainly the way you approach the SAT. You figure out as much of each problem as you can and then choose the answer that seems right, all things considered. Sometimes you're fairly positive that your answer is correct. But other times—on hard problems—all you can do is follow your hunch and hope you're right.

WHICH ANSWERS SEEM RIGHT?

That depends on who the students are, and on how hard the questions are.

Specifically, here's what happens:

1. On easy multiple-choice questions, Jim's or Pam's answers seem right to virtually everyone: high scorers, average scorers, and low scorers.

2. On medium questions, Jim's or Pam's answers seem wrong to low scorers, right to high scorers, and sometimes right and sometimes wrong to average scorers.

3. On hard questions, Jim's or Pam's answers seem right to high scorers and wrong to everyone else.

What we've just said is really true by definition. If the correct answer to a difficult question *seemed* correct to almost everyone, the question couldn't really be difficult, could it? If the answer seemed right to everyone, everyone would pick it. That would make it an easy question.

This is an extremely important concept. Here's a rule to help you remember it:

> *Easy questions have easy answers; hard questions have hard answers.*

For the average student, an "easy" solution to a hard question will always be wrong.

MEET JOE BLOGGS

We're going to talk a lot about "the average student" from now on. For the sake of convenience, let's give him a name: Joe Bloggs. Joe Bloggs is just the average American high school student. He has average grades and average SAT scores. There's a little bit of him in everyone, and there's a little bit of everyone in him. He isn't brilliant. He isn't dumb. He's exactly average.

HOW DOES JOE BLOGGS APPROACH THE SAT?

Joe Bloggs, the average student, approaches the SAT just like everybody else does. Whether the question is hard or easy, he always chooses the answer that *seems* to be correct.

Here's an example of a very hard question from a real SAT:

25 A woman drove to work at an average speed of 40 miles per hour and returned along the same route at 30 miles per hour. If her total traveling time was 1 hour, what was the total number of miles in the round trip?

(A) 30

(B) $30\frac{1}{7}$

(C) $34\frac{2}{7}$

(D) 35
(E) 40

This was the last problem in a 25-problem math section. Therefore, according to the order of difficulty, it was the hardest problem in that section. Why was it hard? *It was hard because most people answered it incorrectly.* In fact, only about one student in ten got it right. (Don't bother trying to work it out. The correct answer—Jim's answer—is choice C.)

HOW DID JOE BLOGGS DO ON THIS QUESTION?

Joe Bloggs—the average student—got this question wrong.

Why?

Because if the *average* student had gotten it right, it wouldn't have been a hard problem, would it?

WHICH ANSWER DID JOE BLOGGS PICK ON THIS QUESTION?

Joe picked choice D on this question; 35 just *seemed* like the right answer to him. Joe assumed that the problem required him to calculate the woman's average speed, and 35 is the average of 30 and 40.

But Joe *didn't* realize that he needed to account for the fact that the woman's trip didn't take the same amount of time in each direction. Her trip *to* work didn't last as long as her trip *home*. The answer could be 35 only if the woman had driven for a half hour at 40 miles an hour and a half hour at 30 miles an hour, and she did not.

Choice D was a trap: Jim Braswell included it among the answer choices because he knew that it would *seem* right to the average student. He put a trap among the choices because he wanted this problem to be a *hard* problem, not an *easy* one.

COULD JIM HAVE MADE THIS AN EASY QUESTION INSTEAD?

Yes, by writing different answer choices.

Here's the same question with choices we have substituted to make the correct answer obvious:

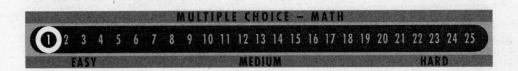

1   A woman drove to work at an average speed of 40 miles per hour and returned along the same route at 30 miles per hour. If her total traveling time was 1 hour, what was the total number of miles in the round trip?

(A)   1 million

(B)   1 billion

(C) $34\frac{2}{7}$

(D)   1 trillion

(E)   1 zillion

When the problem is written this way, Joe Bloggs can easily see that Jim's answer has to be C. It *seems* right to Joe because all the other answers seem obviously wrong.

Remember:

1. An SAT question is easy if the correct answer *seems* correct to the average person—to Joe Bloggs.

2. An SAT question is hard if the correct answer *seems* correct to almost no one.

THE JOE BLOGGS PRINCIPLE

When you take the SAT a few weeks or months from now, you'll have to take it on your own, of course. But suppose for a moment that ETS allowed you to take it with Joe Bloggs as your partner. Would Joe be any help to you on the SAT?

YOU PROBABLY DON'T THINK SO

After all, Joe is wrong as often as he is right. He knows the answers to the easy questions, but so do you. You'd like to do better than average on the SAT, and Joe earns only an average score (he's the average person, remember). All things considered, you'd probably prefer to have someone else for your partner.

But Joe might turn out to be a pretty helpful partner, after all. Since his hunches are *always* wrong on difficult multiple-choice questions, couldn't you improve your chances on those questions simply by finding out what Joe wanted to pick, and then picking something else?

If you could use the Joe Bloggs principle to *eliminate* one, two, or even three obviously incorrect choices on a hard problem, couldn't you improve your score by *guessing* among the remaining choices?

HOW TO NAVIGATE WITH A BROKEN COMPASS

If you were lost in the woods, would it do you any good to have a broken compass? You probably don't think so. But it would depend on *how* the compass was broken. Suppose you had a compass that always pointed south instead of north. Would you throw it away? Of course not. If you wanted to go north, you'd simply see which way the compass was pointing and then walk in the opposite direction.

JOE BLOGGS IS LIKE THAT BROKEN COMPASS

On difficult SAT questions, he always points in the wrong direction. If Joe Bloggs were your partner on the test, you could improve your chances dramatically just by looking to see where he was pointing, and then going a different way.

We're going to teach you how to make Joe Bloggs your partner on the SAT. When you come to difficult questions on the test, you're going to stop and ask yourself, "How would Joe Bloggs answer this question?" And when you see what *he* would do, *you* are going to do something else. Why? Because you know that on hard questions Joe Bloggs is *always* wrong.

WHAT IF JOE BLOGGS IS RIGHT?

Remember what we said about Joe Bloggs at the beginning. He is the average person. He thinks the way most people do. If the right answer to a hard question seemed right to most people, the question wouldn't be hard, would it?

Joe Bloggs *is* right on some questions: the easy ones. But he's *always* wrong on the hard questions.

SHOULD YOU ALWAYS JUST ELIMINATE ANY ANSWER THAT SEEMS TO BE CORRECT?

No!

Remember what we said about Joe Bloggs:

1. His hunches are *correct* on easy questions.

2. His hunches are *sometimes correct* and *sometimes incorrect* on medium questions.

3. His hunches are *always wrong* on difficult questions.

On easy multiple-choice questions, you want to pick the choice that Joe Bloggs would pick. On hard questions, you want to eliminate the choices that Joe Bloggs would pick.

PUTTING JOE BLOGGS TO WORK FOR YOU

In the chapters that follow, we're going to teach you many specific problem-solving techniques based on the Joe Bloggs principle. The Joe Bloggs principle will help you

1. use POE to eliminate incorrect answer choices.

2. make up your mind when you have to guess.

3. avoid careless mistakes.

The more you learn about Joe Bloggs, the more help he'll be on the test. If you make him your partner on the SAT, he'll help you find Pam's and Jim's answers on problems you never dreamed you'd be able to solve.

BECAUSE THIS IS SO IMPORTANT, WE'RE GOING TO SAY IT AGAIN

Here's a summary of how Joe Bloggs thinks:

QUESTION TYPE	JOE BLOGGS LOOKS FOR	JOE BLOGGS SELECTS	TIME JOE SPENDS	HOW JOE DOES
Easy	the answer	the one that seems right	very little	mostly right
Medium	the answer	the one that seems right	not much more	so-so
Difficult	the answer	the one that seems right	too much	all wrong!

YOU SHOULD PROBABLY SKIP SOME QUESTIONS

There are some very difficult questions on the SAT that most test takers shouldn't even bother to read. On the difficult third of every group of questions, there are some items that almost no one taking the test will understand. Rather than spend time beating your head against these items, you should enter a guess quickly and focus your attention on items that you have a chance of figuring out.

> *Any test taker shooting for a score below 700 on either the math section or the verbal section will hurt his or her score by attempting every item.*

Since most test takers try to finish every section ("I had two seconds left over!"), almost every test taker hurts his or her score. The solution, for almost anyone scoring less than 700 on a section, is to slow down.

> *Most test takers could improve their scores significantly by attempting fewer items and devoting more time to items they have a chance of answering correctly.*

YOU HAVE TO PACE YOURSELF

It's very important to set realistic goals. If you're aiming for a 500 on the verbal section, your approach to the SAT is going to be different from that of someone who is aiming for an 800. The following charts will give you some idea of what you realistically need to know in order to score at various levels on the SAT. Use the chart to gauge your progress as you work through the practice tests in *10 SATs*.

VERBAL PACING CHART

If, on your last practice exam, you scored between:	Your target score is:	In the Analogies section you should answer only:	In the Sentence Comp section you should answer only:	In the 2-passage (30Q) section you should answer only:	In the 1-passage (35Q) section you should answer only:	In the dual-passage (13Q) section you should answer only:
200–290	350	All	All	Short passage	None	First passage
300–390	450	All	All	Short passage	1/2 Passage	1–10
400–490	550	All	All	1 1/2 Passages	All	1–10
500–590	650	All	All	All	All	All
600–690	750	All	All	All	All	All
700–790	800	All	All	All	All	All

MATH PACING CHART

If, on your last practice exam, you scored between:	Your target score is:	In the 25-question section, you should answer only:	In the Quant Comp section, you should answer only:	In the Grid-in section you should answer only:	In the 10-question section you should answer only:
200–280	350	1–10	1–6	1–3	1–3
290–350	400	1–13	1–9	1–4	1–4
360–400	450	1–15	1–9	1–4	1–5
410–450	500	1–18	1–11	1–5	1–6
460–500	550	1–20	1–12	1–7	1–8
510–550	600	1–22	1–14	1–8	1–9
560–600	650	1–24	All	1–9	All
610–650	700	All	All	All	All
660–up	800	All	All	All	All

SUMMARY

1. The problems in most every group of questions on the SAT start out easy and gradually get harder. The first question in a group is often so easy that virtually everyone can find Pam's or Jim's answer. The last question is so hard that almost no one can.

2. Because this is true, you should never waste time trying to figure out the answer to a hard question if there are still easy questions that you haven't tried. All questions are worth the same number of points. Why not do the easy ones first?

3. Most every group of questions on the SAT can be divided into thirds by difficulty, as follows:

   • On the easy third of each group of questions, the average person gets all the answers right. The answers that *seem* right to the average person actually *are* right on these questions.

   • On the medium third of each group, the average person's hunches are right only some of the time. Sometimes the answers that *seem* right to the average person really *are* right; sometimes they are wrong.

   • Finally, on the difficult third, the average person's hunches are always wrong. The average person only picks the correct answer on the hardest questions by accident. The answers that *seem* right to the average person on these questions invariably turn out to be wrong.

4. Almost everyone approaches the SAT by choosing the answer that *seems* correct, all things considered.

5. Joe Bloggs is the average student. He earns an average score on the SAT. On easy SAT questions, the answers that seem correct to him are always correct. On medium questions, they're sometimes correct and sometimes not. On hard questions, they're always wrong.

6. The correct answer to a hard question could never seem right to most people. If it did, the question would be easy, not hard.

7. Most test takers could improve their scores significantly by attempting fewer items and devoting more time to items they have a chance of answering correctly.

8. It's very important to set realistic goals. If you're aiming for a 600 on the verbal, your approach to the SAT is going to be very different from that of someone who is aiming for an 800.

9. After each practice exam, go back to the pacing chart. You may need to answer more questions on the next exam to earn the score you want.

PART 2

How to Crack the Verbal SAT

A FEW WORDS ABOUT WORDS

The SAT contains seven sections. Three of these will be verbal, or "English," sections. There may be a fourth verbal section on your test, but it will be experimental and so it won't count toward your score. Don't worry about trying to identify the experimental section. Just work at your normal pace.

Each of the three scored verbal sections on the SAT contains groups of questions drawn from the following categories:

1. sentence completions

2. analogies

3. critical readings

If you practice with *10 SATs* or with other released copies of pre-1994 SATs, you will notice that each verbal section starts with a group of antonyms (opposites). This item type does not appear on the new SAT. That's good news for most test takers. Antonym items were straight vocabulary items. You either knew them or you didn't. Now it won't matter whether you know them or not. (Even so, the vocabulary words tested in old SAT antonym items are exactly the kind of vocabulary words you need to know to do well on the new SAT, so these are good items to practice on anyway.)

WHAT DOES THE VERBAL SAT TEST?

ETS says that the verbal SAT tests "verbal reasoning abilities" or "higher order reasoning abilities." But this—whatever it means—is not true. The verbal SAT is mostly a test of your vocabulary. Even critical reading questions often test nothing more than your familiarity with certain words. If you have a big vocabulary, you'll probably do well on the exam. If you have a small vocabulary, you're going to be in trouble no matter how many techniques we teach you.

For this reason, it's absolutely essential that you get to work on your vocabulary *now!* The best way to improve your vocabulary is by reading. Any well-written book is better than television. Even certain periodicals—*The New York Times*, *The Wall Street Journal*, *The New Yorker*, *The Atlantic*—can improve your verbal performance if you read them regularly. Always keep a notebook and a dictionary by your side as you read. When you encounter words whose meanings you don't know, write them down, look them up, and try to incorporate them into your life. The dinner table is a good place to throw around new words.

Building a vocabulary this way can be slow and painful. Most of us have to encounter new words many times before we develop a firm sense of what they mean. You can speed up this process a great deal by taking advantage of the vocabulary section (part 5) in the back of this book. It contains a short list of words that are highly likely to turn up on the SAT, a section on roots, and some general guidelines about learning new words. If you work through it carefully between now and the time you take the test, you'll have a much easier time on the verbal SAT. The more SAT words you know, the more help our techniques will be.

Before you go on, turn to Part 5 on page 299 for a few minutes. Read through it quickly and sketch out a vocabulary-building program for yourself. You should follow this program every day, at the same time you are working through the other chapters of this book.

The techniques described in the three verbal chapters that follow are intended to help you take full advantage of your growing vocabulary by using partial information to attack hard questions. In a sense, we are going to teach you how to get the maximum possible mileage out of the words you do know. Almost all students miss SAT questions that they could have answered correctly if they had used POE to extend their knowledge.

Study our approach carefully and practice it in the drills we provide. If possible, you should also purchase a copy of *10 SATs*, which is available in bookstores. If you can't find your own copy, check your public library, school library, or guidance counselor's office. This book contains real SATs that were given to students in recent years. Even though the test has changed, these tests are great practice for the SAT. Your guidance counselor may also have copies of *Taking the SAT-I Reasoning Test,* which has tests in the new format. You can never get too much practice on real SATs.

Chapter 4

Joe Bloggs and the Verbal SAT

JOE BLOGGS AND THE VERBAL SAT

Joe Bloggs will be a big help to you on the verbal SAT. By keeping him in mind as you take the test, you will substantially improve your score. Joe will help you identify and eliminate incorrect answer choices before you have a chance to be tempted by them, and he will help you zero in on Pam's answer.

JOE BLOGGS AND THE ORDER OF DIFFICULTY

The verbal sections of SAT contain three item types: sentence completions, analogies, and critical reading questions. The analogies and sentence completions are arranged in order of increasing difficulty. That is, in a group of ten sentence completions, the first three or four will be easy, the next three or four will be medium, and the last three or four will be hard. Critical reading questions are not arranged in order of difficulty. They follow the structure of the passage they refer to. We'll tell you more about that later.

How does Joe Bloggs do on verbal questions? As always on the SAT, he gets the easy ones right, does so-so on the medium ones, and crashes and burns on the hard ones. When you take the SAT, you must constantly be aware of where you are in each group of questions. Knowing where a question falls in the order of difficulty will tell you how much faith you can put in your hunches, and will help you avoid making careless mistakes. In addition, your knowledge of Joe's test-taking habits will enable you to eliminate incorrect choices on the hardest questions, thus greatly improving your odds of guessing Pam's answer.

HOW JOE THINKS

When Joe looks at a verbal SAT question, he is irresistibly attracted to choices containing easy words that remind him of the question. On easy questions, this tendency serves Joe very well. On hard questions, though, it gets him into trouble every time. On easy questions, the answers that seem right to Joe really are right; on hard questions, the answers that seem right to Joe are always wrong.

Here's an example. This is a very difficult analogy question. Don't worry if you don't know how to answer a question like this; we'll deal with the SAT analogies thoroughly in another chapter. For now, all you have to do is look at the words.

15 FLORID:SPEECH::

    (A) harsh:voice
    (B) fluid:style
    (C) vivid:image
    (D) fertile:soil
    (E) ornate:design

ANALYSIS

This is a very hard question from a real SAT. Only about 8 percent of test takers answered it correctly. Two and a half times as many of them would have answered it correctly if they had simply closed their eyes and picked one of the choices at random. Why did the vast majority of these test takers—including, of course, Joe Bloggs—do so poorly on this question? Because they all fell into a trap. Like Joe, they didn't know what "florid" means, so they focused their attention on "speech," an easy word. Then they looked for an answer choice containing something similar. Like Joe, they were immediately drawn to choice A. "Speech" and "voice" seem similar. Joe quickly marked A on his answer sheet, confident that he was one step closer to Harvard.

Was Joe (along with several hundred thousand test takers) correct? No, of course not. Joe *never* picks the right answer on hard SAT questions.

What does that mean for you?

It means that on hard questions like this one, you can simply eliminate any answer choice or choices that you know will be attractive to Joe. Joe is irresistibly drawn to easy answer choices containing words that remind him of the question. Therefore, on hard verbal questions, you can eliminate such choices. We'll tell you more about how to do this as we go along. (Incidentally, Pam's answer to this question is E. Florid means "flowery" or "heavily embellished." Florid speech is speech that is filled with big, fancy, hundred-dollar words. An ornate design is a fancy, heavily embellished one.)

PUTTING JOE TO WORK ON THE VERBAL SAT

Generally speaking, the Joe Bloggs principle teaches you to

1. trust your hunches on easy questions.

2. double-check your hunches on medium questions.

3. eliminate Joe Bloggs attractors on difficult questions.

The next few chapters will teach you how to use your knowledge of Joe Bloggs to add points to your SAT score.

Chapter 5

Sentence Completion

Before we begin, take a moment to read the following set of instructions and to answer the sample question that comes after it. Both appear here exactly as they do on real SATs. Be certain that you know and understand these instructions before you take the SAT. If you learn them ahead of time, you won't have to waste valuable seconds reading them on the day you take the test.

> Each sentence below has one or two blanks, each blank indicating that something has been omitted. Beneath the sentence are five lettered words or sets of words labeled A through E. Choose the word or set of words that, when inserted in the sentence, best fits the meaning of the sentence as a whole.
>
> Example:
>
> Medieval kingdoms did not become constitutional republics overnight; on the contrary, the change was ----.
>
> (A) unpopular
> (B) unexpected
> (C) advantageous
> (D) sufficient
> (E) gradual

Pam's answer to this sample question is E.

SAT SENTENCE COMPLETIONS: CRACKING THE SYSTEM

It's important to know the instructions printed before each group of sentence completions on the SAT, but it's vastly more important to understand what those instructions mean. ETS's instructions don't tell you everything you need to know about SAT sentence completions. The rest of this chapter will teach you what you do need to know.

Your SAT will contain two scored verbal sections. Each will contain one group of sentence completions. One group will have ten sentence sompletions, the other nine. In each group, the items will be arranged in order of increasing difficulty. That is, the first item in each group of sentence completions will be the easiest in the group; the last item in each group will be the hardest.

Because our techniques vary depending on the difficulty of the question, we have placed a difficulty meter before each example. Look at the meter to determine how hard the example is.

YOUR JOB IS TO FIND CLUES

Sentence completions are sentences from which one or two words have been removed. Your job is to find what is missing. You will do this by looking for clues in the sentence and using those clues to eliminate obviously incorrect choices. Our techniques will enable you to

1. anticipate what is missing by learning to recognize what has been given.

2. use contextual clues.

3. use structural clues.

4. eliminate Joe Bloggs attractors.

THINK OF YOURSELF AS AN ARCHAEOLOGIST

Archaeologists sometimes discover stone tablets covered with ancient writing. Very often the tablets are in fragments, with many pieces missing. Yet the archaeologists can sometimes translate the writing on the tablets anyway.

How do they do it? By looking for clues among the words that are there and then using clues to make educated guesses about the words that are missing.

CATCH THE DRIFT

When an archaeologist tries to fill in the missing words on a stone tablet, she doesn't merely plug in any word that fits; she plugs in only words that "catch the drift" of the rest of the tablet. If the tablet as a whole is about methods of planting corn, she won't fill in the blanks with words about digging wells.

You must do the same thing on the SAT. Many students try to find Pam's answer on sentence completions by immediately plugging in the answer choices. The trouble with this method is that very often *all* of the choices will sound sort of possible. Instead of trying all the choices haphazardly, you must anticipate what Pam is looking for and then find the one choice that catches the drift of the rest of the sentence and completes the thought Pam was trying to convey. Here's an example:

SENTENCE COMPLETIONS
1 2 3 **4** 5 6 7 8 9 10
EASY   MEDIUM   HARD

4   Some developing nations have become remarkably ----, using aid from other countries to build successful industries.

(A) populous
(B) dry
(C) warlike
(D) prosperous
(E) isolated

HERE'S HOW TO CRACK IT

Every one of the five choices is a word that could plausibly be used to describe a developing nation. Yet only one can be Pam's answer. Which one is it? The clue is in the phrase: "using aid . . . to build successful industries." What kind of countries would build successful industries? *Prosperous* ones. This is Pam's answer.

LOOK FOR THE DOCTOR

Consider the following two sentence completions:

    I. The banker told the woman, "You're very ----."

      (A) rich
      (B) correct
      (C) preposterous
      (D) cloistered
      (E) sick

    II. The doctor told the woman, "You're very ----."

      (A) rich
      (B) correct
      (C) preposterous
      (D) cloistered
      (E) sick

ANALYSIS

Questions I and II are identical, with the exception of a single word. And yet that single word makes a great deal of difference. It changes Pam's answer from A in number I to E in number II. *Banker* is the key word in question I; *doctor* is the key word in question II. In each case, it is this key word that determines Pam's answer.

Every SAT sentence completion contains a key word or phrase that will provide the clue to solving it—we call this phrase "the doctor." In approaching a sentence completion, you should always ask yourself, "Where's the doctor? Where's the key to the solution?"

COVER THE ANSWERS

"Finding the doctor" in each sentence completion will enable you to develop an idea of Pam's answer before you even look at the answer choices. In fact, the best way to do well on sentence completions is to ignore the answer choices until you have arrived at a good idea of what Pam's answer is likely to be. And we really mean ignore. As you attack each sentence completion, you should cover the answer choices with your answer sheet. Uncover them only after you have developed a solid sense of what you are looking for.

Covering the answer choices on sentence completions will force you to anticipate Pam's answer. Anticipating is the key to doing well on sentence completions. You must form an idea of what Pam's answer will be *before* you look at the answer choices. If you look at the choices first, your thinking will be influenced by them, and you will run the risk of losing the drift of the sentence. You will be more likely to fall for a Joe Bloggs attractor, or to carelessly settle for a choice that is only partially correct.

Covering the answer choices actually makes sentence completions easier. You have a sentence with a blank in it, and you need to fill it with a word that makes sense, given the drift of the sentence. Doing that will enable you to zero in on the answer without cluttering your mind ahead of time with tempting possibilities.

PICK YOUR OWN WORD

The word you select to fill the blank doesn't have to be an elegant word, or a hard word, or the perfect word. It doesn't even have to be a word; instead, it can be a phrase—even a clunky phrase—as long as it captures the correct meaning. Then you can uncover the choices and eliminate those that mean something different. Each choice you eliminate will bring you closer to Pam's answer. If you have anticipated carefully, you will find the correct answer with ease.

In an episode of *The Simpsons*, a lawyer couldn't think of the word *mistrial* and so asked the judge to declare a "bad court thing." *Bad court thing* would be a perfectly good substitute for *mistrial* if you were attempting to anticipate Pam's answer on a sentence completion in which *mistrial* was the missing word. With *bad court thing* in mind, you would spot *mistrial* immediately when you uncovered the answer choices. Anticipation doesn't have to be elegant in order to work.

Here's an example that's not from *The Simpsons*. To force you to anticipate, we won't even show you the answer choices right away.

> **7** The people were tired of reform crusades; they wanted no part of an idea that might turn into a ----.

ANALYSIS

If this sentence consisted *only* of the part after the semicolon, you wouldn't have any idea of what the blank might be: *The people wanted no part of an idea that might turn into a ----.* The doctor—the important clue—must therefore be in the first part of the sentence. What did the people want no part of? Why, it says right there: "reform crusades." Those two words are the doctor. Plugging them into the blank doesn't yield a very well-written sentence, but it conveys Pam's general intention. It catches the drift. The answer we are looking for, therefore, will be a word that means (or could mean) something like reform crusade.

Now we can look at the choices:

(A) respite
(B) reality
(C) necessity
(D) mistake
(E) cause

HERE'S HOW TO CRACK IT

Go through the choices one by one:

(A) Could a respite be the same thing as a reform crusade? No. *Respite* means "rest," as in a respite from labor. Eliminate.

(B) Could reality be the same thing as a reform crusade? No. That doesn't make any sense. Eliminate.

(C) Could a necessity be the same thing as a reform crusade? No. This doesn't make sense, either, especially if you try to plug it into the sentence. Eliminate.

(D) Could a mistake mean the same thing as a reform crusade? A reform crusade could be a mistake, but this doesn't make any sense, either. Eliminate. (Be careful! This is a Joe Bloggs attractor. Joe doesn't pay attention to the clue in the first part of the sentence. He just knows he doesn't want any part of an idea that could turn into a mistake, so he selects this answer. This is a hard question—a number 4—so his hunch is incorrect.)

(E) Could a cause be the same thing as a reform crusade? Yes. For example, attempting to reform laws regarding chemical wastes would be a cause. This is Pam's answer.

The following drill contains sentences from real SATs. We've left out the answer choices, so you'll have to use only the clues in the sentences to help you anticipate what the answers might be.

DRILL 1

Look for the doctor in each sentence; when you find it, circle it. Then try to think of three possible choices for each blank. Don't worry if you can't think of a single, perfect word for each blank; you can use a phrase if you need to, *as long as it catches the drift*. When you've finished these questions, go on to Drill 2 and use your notes to help you select answers from among the actual choices. Then check all your answers on page 357.

1. Although the critics agreed that the book was brilliant, so few copies were sold that the work brought the author little ---- reward.

   x publicity

   financial

   economic

2. Sadly, many tropical rain forests are so ---- by agricultural and industrial overdevelopment that they may ---- by the end of the century.

   ✓ destroyed, non exsistant

3. My plea is not for drab and ---- technical writing about music but for pertinent information conveyed with as much ---- as possible.

   boring, intrest

DRILL 2

Here are the same questions, this time with answer choices provided. Refer to your notes from Drill 1 and make a choice for each question. Remember POE, the process of elimination. Pam's answers are on page 357.

1. Although the critics agreed that the book was brilliant, so few copies were sold that the work brought the author little ---- reward.

   (A) theoretical
   (B) thoughtful
   (C) financial
   (D) abstract
   (E) informative

2. Sadly, many tropical rain forests are so ---- by agricultural and industrial overdevelopment that they may ---- by the end of the century.

   (A) isolated. .separate
   (B) threatened. .vanish
   (C) consumed. .expand
   (D) augmented. .diminish
   (E) rejuvenated. .disappear

3. My plea is not for drab and ---- technical writing about music but for pertinent information conveyed with as much ---- as possible.

   (A) repetitive. .redundancy
   (B) obscure. .felicity
   (C) inscrutable. .ambivalence
   (D) euphonious. .harmony
   (E) provocative. .exhilaration

BEYOND THE DOCTOR

Finding the doctor and anticipating answers should always be your first steps in solving SAT sentence completions. But on some questions, especially the harder ones, you'll need more help. We have several techniques that should enable you to rule out obviously incorrect answers and zero in on Pam's answer. These techniques will enable you to

1. eliminate Joe Bloggs attractors.

2. use the good word/bad word method for finding Pam's answers.

3. take advantage of the order of difficulty.

4. look for trigger words.

5. crack two-blank sentences.

TECHNIQUE 1: ELIMINATE JOE BLOGGS ATTRACTORS

In each group of sentence completions on your SAT, the last few questions will be quite difficult. On these hard questions, you will find it useful to remember the Joe Bloggs principle and eliminate choices that you know would attract Joe. Here's an example:

9 The phenomenon is called viral ---- because the presence of one kind of virus seems to inhibit infection by any other.

(A) proliferation
(B) mutation
(C) interference
(D) epidemic
(E) cooperation

HERE'S HOW TO CRACK IT

Joe Bloggs is attracted to choices containing easy words that remind him of the subject matter of the sentence. The words in the sentence that Joe notices are *virus* and *infection*—words related to medicine or biology. Which answers attract him? Choices B and D. You can therefore eliminate both.

(Where's the doctor in this sentence? It's the word *inhibit*. By rewording the sentence a little, you can catch the drift and anticipate Pam's answer: "The phenomenon is called viral *inhibition* because the presence of one kind of virus seems to inhibit infection by any other." Which answer choice could mean something similar to inhibition? Interference. Pam's answer is C.)

IMPORTANT NOTE

Eliminating Joe Bloggs attractors should always be the first thing you do in considering answer choices on a hard sentence completion. If you don't eliminate them immediately, you will run a strong risk of falling for them as you consider the various choices.

HOWEVER

You should never eliminate a choice unless you are dictionary-sure of its meaning.

Eliminating choices without justification is the most common mistake students make when they learn to apply POE to sentence completions. One example of this is eliminating a choice because it "doesn't sound right." Remember that this is *exactly* what Joe Bloggs does. On difficult sentence completions, a choice that "doesn't sound right" may very well be Pam's answer.

Some students prefer to use POE in stages, eliminating first the choices that are obviously incorrect, then eliminating the ones that are doubtful, and finally selecting an answer.

TECHNIQUE 2: USE THE GOOD WORD/BAD WORD METHOD FOR FINDING PAM'S ANSWERS

On many sentence completions, the wording of the sentence will give you general clues that will enable you to eliminate bad choices and zero in on Pam's answer. An extremely useful technique is to look at each blank and ask yourself whether, based on the context, the missing word is probably a "good" word (that is, one with positive connotations) or a "bad" word (one with negative connotations).

Using this technique is a bit like anticipating Pam's answer, except that all you are trying to do is determine what *sort* of word the missing word is. It's a technique to try when direct anticipation doesn't make you think of anything.

Here's an example:

SENTENCE COMPLETIONS

1 2 3 4 5 6 7 (8) 9 10

EASY   MEDIUM   HARD

8   Ruskin's vitriolic attack was the climax of the ---- heaped on paintings that today seem amazingly ----.

(A) criticism. .unpopular
(B) ridicule. .inoffensive
(C) praise. .amateurish
(D) indifference. .scandalous
(E) acclaim. .creditable

HERE'S HOW TO CRACK IT

A vitriolic attack is something bad (so is just a plain attack, if you don't know what *vitriolic* means). Therefore, the climax of a vitriolic attack must also be bad, and the first blank must be a bad word. Already we can eliminate choices C and E (and possibly also choice D).

Now look at the second blank. The first part of the sentence says that Ruskin thought the paintings were very bad; today, "amazingly," they seem—what? Bad?

No! This has to be a good word. If the paintings were still regarded as bad, Ruskin's attack wouldn't seem amazing today. The second blank must be a good word. Choices C and E are already crossed out. We can now also eliminate choices A and D. The only choice left is B—Pam's answer. We've earned 10 points on a very hard item whose meaning we don't understand. Not bad!

The good word/bad word method is also helpful when you have anticipated Pam's answer but haven't found a similar word among the choices. Simply decide whether your anticipated answer is positive or negative, then determine whether each of the answer choices is positive or negative. Eliminate the choices that are different, and you'll find Pam's answer.

> As always on the SAT, your aim should be to eliminate incorrect answers. Get rid of as many bad choices as you can, guess from among the remaining choices, and move on.

TECHNIQUE 3: TAKE ADVANTAGE OF THE ORDER OF DIFFICULTY

Let's assume you've tried everything: You've looked for the doctor, you've tried to anticipate Pam's answer, you've eliminated the Joe Bloggs attractors, you've used the good word/bad word technique. But you still can't find Pam's answer. What should you do?

In chapter 4 we taught you that easy questions generally have easy answers and hard questions have hard answers. Joe Bloggs tends to avoid choices containing words whose meaning he doesn't understand. As a result, we can be fairly certain that on easy questions (which Joe gets right) Pam's answer will contain easy words, and on hard questions (which Joe gets wrong) her answer will contain hard words.

What does this mean in terms of strategies for the SAT? It means two things:

1. On easy questions, you should be very suspicious of hard choices.

2. On hard questions, you should be very suspicious of easy choices.

To put it another way, a hard word will usually not be Pam's answer on an easy question. And an easy word will usually not be Pam's answer on a hard question.

We've said it before, and we'll say it again: Easy questions on the SAT have easy answers; hard questions have hard answers. It's important to try to get the drift first and anticipate the blank. Then, when you come down to the wire and need to guess on the hardest couple of sentence completions in each group, simply pick the hardest choice—the one with the weirdest, most difficult words. Eliminate any choice whose word or words you *can* define, and guess from among what's left. No problem!

How easy is easy? How hard is hard? The following drill should help give you a sense of the range of difficulty in the vocabulary tested on the SAT.

DRILL 3

Each group contains three sentence completion answer choices. Rearrange each group in increasing order of difficulty. Just put a 1 beside the easiest choice, a 2 beside the medium choice, and a 3 beside the most difficult choice. You can check your answers on page 357.

GROUP A
- interrupted
- inevitable. .mitigates
- force. .lacking

GROUP B
- postulate. .explore
- detect. .overlook
- paradigm

GROUP C
- certitudes. .elusive
- vague. .traditions
- represent. .diversity

GROUP D
- gullible..distant
- parsimony. .chary of
- increased. .inadequate

TECHNIQUE 4: LOOK FOR TRIGGER WORDS

Very often on SAT sentence completions, the most important clue to Pam's answer is a single revealing word or expression that lets you know exactly where Pam is heading. We call these revealing words *trigger* words. About half of all SAT sentence completions contain trigger words. If you learn how to notice and take advantage of them, your score will improve.

Some trigger words are negative, and some are positive. The most important negative trigger words are *but, though,* and *although.* These are words that "change the direction" of a sentence. The most important positive trigger words are *and* and *because.* These are words that *maintain* the direction of a sentence.

Negative trigger words are more common on the SAT than positive trigger words. Both provide terrific clues that you can use to find Pam's answer. To see what we mean, take a look at the following incomplete sentences. In place of the blank in each one, fill in a few words that complete the thought in a plausible way. There's no single correct answer.

Just fill in something that makes sense in the context of the entire sentence:

I   really   like   you,   *but*
_____.

I   really   like   you,   *and*
_____.

Here's how one of our students filled in the blanks:

I really like you, *but* <u>I'm going to kill you</u>.

I really like you, *and* <u>I'm going to hug you</u>.

ANALYSIS

In the first sentence, the word *but* announces that the second half of the sentence will contradict the first half. Because the first half of the sentence is positive (good word), the second half must be negative (bad word). I *like* you, but I'm going to *kill* you. The sentence "changes direction" after the negative trigger word *but*.

In the second sentence, the word *and* announces that the second half of the sentence will confirm or support the first half. Because the first half of the sentence is positive (good word), the second half must be positive as well. I *like* you, and I'm going to *hug* you. In this case, the sentence continues in the same direction after the positive trigger word *and*.

In the first sentence, the word *but* announces that the direction of the sentence is about to change. In the second sentence, the word *and* announces that the direction of the sentence is going to stay the same. If you pay attention to trigger words, you will find it easier to catch the drift and anticipate Pam's answer on sentence completions.

TECHNIQUE 5: DIVIDE AND CONQUER TWO-BLANK SENTENCE COMPLETIONS

Some sentence completions on your test will contain two blanks. Many students fear these items, because they look long and intimidating. But two-blank sentence completions are more difficult than single-blank items *only* if you insist on trying to fill in both blanks at the same time. The key to cracking these items is to concentrate on one blank at a time. (Incidentally, this is true of all complex questions on the SAT. The best way to attack a difficult question is to break it into manageable parts and keep track of where you are by making use of your scratch paper—your test booklet.)

Here's how to crack these items: attack two-blank questions as you would any sentence completion, by reading the sentence and attempting to anticipate the missing words as you read the item. But don't linger over the entire sentence. Focus immediately on whichever blank seems easier to anticipate, and concentrate on that part of the sentence alone. Once you've anticipated a word for that blank, look at the choices and eliminate any that do not work for it.

All our usual sentence completion techniques apply. Look for the doctor, use good word/bad word, look for trigger words, and so on. But apply these techniques to only one blank at a time.

You won't need to anticipate both blanks at the same time in order to eliminate choices. Why? Because if the second word in an answer choice won't work in the second blank of the sentence, then it doesn't matter at all whether the first word works. Don't waste time by wrestling with answer choices that can't possibly be Pam's answer.

If the second word of a choice doesn't work in the second blank, you even don't need to glance at the first word. If the second word is impossible, it doesn't matter that the first word works; one strike and a choice is out. As always, be sure to cross out each eliminated choice immediately, so that you don't waste time or become confused.

SENTENCE COMPLETION SUMMARY

1. Never simply plug in the answer choices on sentence completions. You must catch the drift of the sentence before you can find Pam's answer.

2. Always look for the doctor—the key word or words that give you the most important clue you need to catch the drift.

3. Learn to anticipate Pam's answer by mentally filling in each blank before you look at the answer choices. If you look at the answer choices first, you will often be misled.

4. Eliminate Joe Bloggs attractors. On difficult questions, Joe is attracted to answers containing easy words that remind him of the subject matter of the sentence. Learn to recognize these words and be extremely suspicious of the answer choices in which they appear.

5. Never eliminate a choice unless you are dictionary-sure of its meaning.

6. When you have trouble finding the doctor or anticipating Pam's answer on a hard sentence completion, use the good word/bad word method of catching the general drift of the sentence, and then use POE to eliminate obviously incorrect choices.

7. Take advantage of the order of difficulty. Easy sentence completions tend to have easy answers, hard ones tend to have hard answers. Only if you can do nothing else on a hard sentence completion, simply pick the choice containing the hardest or weirdest words.

8. Look for trigger words—revealing words or expressions that give you important clues about the meanings of sentences. The most important negative trigger words are *but, though,* and *although.* These are words that "change the direction" of a sentence. The most important positive trigger words are *and* and *because.*

9. Attack two-blank sentence completions by focusing on one blank at a time. Use the same techniques you would use on one-blank items. If you can eliminate either word in an answer choice, you can cross out the entire choice. A choice can't be Pam's answer if either word is wrong.

Chapter 6
Analogies

This chapter is about analogies, the second of the three types of verbal SAT questions. There will be at least two groups of analogy questions on the SAT you take, one in each of the two scored thirty-minute verbal sections (and possibly one in the experimental section, if it's a verbal section).

Before we begin, take a moment to read the following instructions and to answer the sample question that comes after it. Both appear here exactly as they do on real SATs. Be certain that you know and understand these instructions before you take the SAT. If you learn them ahead of time, you won't have to waste valuable seconds reading them on the day you take the test.

> Each question below consists of a related pair of words or phrases, followed by five pairs of words or phrases labeled A through E. Select the pair that best expresses a relationship similar to that expressed in the original pair.
>
> Example:
>
> CRUMB:BREAD::
> (A) ounce:unit
> (B) splinter:wood
> (C) water:bucket
> (D) twine:rope
> (E) cream:butter

Pam's answer to this sample question is choice B. A crumb is a small piece of bread just as a splinter is a small piece of wood. The two pairs of words are related in the same way.

SAT ANALOGIES: CRACKING THE SYSTEM

It's important to know the instructions printed before each analogy group on the SAT, but it is vastly more important to understand what those instructions mean. ETS's instructions don't tell you everything you need to know about SAT analogies. The rest of this chapter will teach you what you do need to know.

One of your two scored thirty-minute verbal sections will contain a group of six analogies; the other will contain a group of thirteen. Each group of analogies will be arranged in order of increasing difficulty, from very easy to very hard.

In each group of analogies

1. the first third will be easy.

2. the middle third will be medium.

3. the final third will be difficult.

Because our techniques vary depending on the difficulty of the question, the examples we use in this chapter will always be preceded by a difficulty meter. Always pay attention to where you are on the test when answering SAT questions.

Our techniques work very well on SAT analogies. For this reason, you must never leave an analogy question blank on the SAT. If you learn our techniques, you should be able to eliminate at least one obviously incorrect choice even on the hardest questions. Even on some hard questions, you will be able to find Pam's answer even though you don't know several of the words. Every time you leave an analogy blank you'll be throwing away points.

WHAT IS AN ANALOGY?

Every analogy question on the SAT begins with a pair of capitalized words. Your task is to determine how these words are related to each other and then select another pair of words that are related to each other in exactly the same way.

There is only one kind of word relationship that counts on SAT analogy questions. We call this kind of relationship *a clear and necessary* one. What is a clear and necessary relationship? It is a tight, solid, logical relationship that is based on the meanings of the words. To put it somewhat differently: *A clear and necessary relationship is the kind of relationship that exists between a word and its dictionary definition.* The easiest way to understand what we mean is to look at an example.

Take the words *dog* and *kennel*. Is there a clear and necessary relationship between them? Yes, there is. A kennel is a shelter for a dog. If you look up *kennel* in the dictionary, that's exactly what you'll find. The relationship between the two words is clear (you don't have to rack your brain to think of a way in which you can sort of make it work, sort of). It is also necessary—dogs and kennels have to go together.

Want an example of an *un*clear and *un*necessary relationship? How about *dog* and *garage*. You have a dog, let's say, and it always sleeps in the garage. For your dog, the garage is a shelter. But you can easily see that the two words don't necessarily have anything to do with each other. Garages are for cars, not dogs. If you look up *garage* in the dictionary, you won't find it defined as "a structure where cars are parked; also, some people's dogs sleep there." You might be able to come up with a complicated justification for your answer, but it wouldn't win you any points with Pam. Remember, your job on the SAT is to find Pam's answer, not yours. And Pam's dog sleeps in a kennel.

The SAT is a little bit like the television show *Family Feud*. On *Family Feud*, contestants don't get any points for clever or funny answers; they only get points for the answers that were given by "the 100 people in our survey." The SAT works the same way. The only "good answer" on the SAT is Pam's answer.

THE BASIC APPROACH

How can you determine what the clear and necessary relationship is between the two words in capital letters? The best way is to construct a brief sentence using them. This sentence must use both words and it must state their relationship clearly. You will make it easier on yourself if you keep your sentence as short and specific as possible. In other words, no creative writing.

A good sentence will start with one of the words in capital letters and end with the other. If the pair is APPLE:FRUIT, a good sentence would be "An apple is a type of fruit." Notice that this sentence actually defines the word apple: it is a type of fruit. A bad sentence would be "I bought an apple because you need to eat fruit." This sentence is too long. It would be worthless to you on the SAT.

When possible, in making your sentence you should use the word *is* or *means* to connect the words in capital letters, as we did in the sentence above. These words keep you focused on definitions. If *is* or *means* doesn't work, you should try to use an action word to connect the words in capital letters. If the pair is CAR:MOTOR, a good sentence would be "A car is run by a motor," or (inverting the order) "A motor runs a car." A good sentence would *not* be "A car has a motor." The word *has* tells you nothing about what a motor does in a car. It tells you nothing about the relationship between the definitions of the two words.

FIRST, FORM A SENTENCE
Let's try this approach on an easy question.

ANALOGIES
10 11 12 13 14 15
EASY MEDIUM HARD

10 COMPANY : PRESIDENT ::

    (A) team : athlete
    (B) hospital : patient
    (C) airline : passenger
    (D) library : reader
    (E) army : general

HERE'S HOW TO CRACK IT
First we form a sentence: "A president is the head of a company." Then we plug in the answer choices:

    (A) Is an athlete the head of a team? Well, an athlete is a part of a team, but the head of a team would be a captain. Eliminate. This could not be Pam's answer.

    (B) Is a patient the head of a hospital? No. Eliminate.

    (C) Is a passenger the head of an airline? No. Eliminate.

    (D) Is a reader the head of a library? No. A reader might use a library, but a library's head would be called something like chief librarian. Eliminate.

    (E) Is a general the head of an army? Yes. That's exactly what a general is. This is Pam's answer.

Let's try another one.

11 APPLE : FRUIT ::

   (A) meal : restaurant
   (B) macaroni : cheese
   (C) dessert : vegetable
   (D) beef : meat
   (E) crust : pizza

HERE'S HOW TO CRACK IT

First, we form a sentence: "An apple is a kind of fruit." Now we plug in the choices.

(A) Is a meal a kind of restaurant? No. These two words are related, but not like this. Eliminate.

(B) Is macaroni a kind of cheese? No. Eliminate.

(C) Is dessert a kind of vegetable? No. Eliminate.

(D) Is beef a kind of meat? Yes. A possibility.

(E) Is crust a kind of pizza? No. Eliminate.

Pam's answer has to be choice D. It's the only one we weren't able to eliminate.

Notice that even though D looked good immediately, we still checked choice E. You should always do this on the SAT. If you answer too quickly, you may end up with a choice that sounds all right to you but not as good as *another* choice that you haven't seen yet. *You can never be certain of your answer on an analogy until you have considered all the choices.*

Sometimes, after plugging the choices into your sentence, you may find yourself with two or more answers that seem possible. In such cases, you'll have to go back and make your sentence more specific, then try again.

Here's an example:

12 TIGER : ANIMAL ::

    (A) pigeon : hawk
    (B) dinosaur : fossil
    (C) shark : fish
    (D) colt : horse
    (E) tulip : flower

Suppose that, in approaching this question for the first time, we form our sentence as "A tiger is a kind of animal." Now we plug in the choices:

    (A) Is a pigeon a kind of hawk? No. Eliminate.

    (B) Is a dinosaur a kind of fossil? Not really, although some people might think so. We won't eliminate it yet, although it isn't a very good possibility.

    (C) Is a shark a kind of fish? Yes, a possibility.

    (D) Is a colt a kind of horse? Yes, in a way. Another possibility.

    (E) Is a tulip a kind of flower? Yes. Yet another possibility.

Our problem is that we have made our sentence too loose and vague.

HERE'S HOW TO CRACK IT

We need to make our sentence more specific. How do we do that? By keeping in mind what the words really *mean*. The important fact about a tiger is not simply that it is a certain kind of animal, but that it is a ferocious one, or a dangerous one, or a meat-eating one. The only answer choice that fulfills this requirement is C.

> *The very best sentence is a short and specific one that defines one word in terms of the other. Pam only selects one answer on each question. If you come up with more than one, you've done something wrong. And always keep in mind that the verbal SAT is a vocabulary test. Virtually all the relationships tested on SAT analogies are between the definitions of words.*

PAM'S FAVORITE RELATIONSHIPS

Not all analogy relationships are equal in Pam's eyes. Certain kinds of relationships tend to crop up again and again on the SAT. Here are the two most popular types.

RELATIONSHIPS OF DEGREE

These are relationships in which one of the words is an extreme degree of the other. That is, one of the words means roughly the same thing as the other, only more so or less so. Here are some examples:

POUR : DRIP

BREEZE : GALE

FAMISHED : HUNGRY

Pour is an extreme form of drip. A gale is an extremely strong breeze. Famished means extremely hungry.

"WITHOUT" OR "LACK OF" RELATIONSHIPS

These are Pam's second favorite analogy relationships. In them, one word means a lack of the other. Here are three examples:

SHALLOW : DEPTH

JUVENILE : MATURITY

RANDOM : PATTERN

Shallow means without depth. Juvenile means without maturity. Random means without pattern.

DRILL 1

The following drill will give you practice in making good sentences. Link each of the following pairs of words in a short, specific sentence that emphasizes the clear and necessary relationship between the meanings of the two words. If you aren't absolutely certain about the meaning of any word, look it up, add it to your word list, and make sure you know it before you take the SAT.

ARCHITECT : BUILDING ::_____

WARDEN : PRISON ::_____

LEGIBLE : WRITING ::_____

AQUATIC : WATER ::_____

CALLOUS : SENSITIVITY ::_____

GENEROUS : PHILANTHROPIST ::_____

SOME IMPORTANT FACTS TO REMEMBER ABOUT CLEAR AND NECESSARY RELATIONSHIPS

As you try to determine the clear and necessary relationships in SAT analogies keep the following points in mind:

PART OF SPEECH

1. Roughly *half* of all SAT analogies have to do with the relationships between nouns:

    NOUN : NOUN ::

    (A) noun : noun
    (B) noun : noun
    (C) noun : noun
    (D) noun : noun
    (E) noun : noun

2. Other analogies have to do with the relationships between adjectives and nouns (ADJECTIVE : NOUN or NOUN : ADJECTIVE), verbs and nouns (VERB : NOUN or NOUN : VERB), or, less frequently, verbs and adjectives (VERB : ADJECTIVE or ADJECTIVE : VERB). Adverbs are almost never used in SAT analogies.

3. Parts of speech are always consistent within individual analogies. If the words in capital letters are ADJECTIVE : NOUN, then *all* the choices will be adjective:noun. ETS *never* violates this rule. For example:

> ADJECTIVE : NOUN ::
>
> (A) adjective : noun
> (B) adjective : noun
> (C) adjective : noun
> (D) adjective : noun
> (E) adjective : noun

DON'T GET CONFUSED

4. Some words (such as *run*, *laugh*, *jump*, and many others) can be used as both verbs and nouns. Don't get confused. If the first word in choice E is *laugh*, and all the other first words are nouns, then you know that *laugh* is being used as a noun.

5. When it is not immediately obvious whether one of the words in capital letters is being tested as a noun, an adjective, or a verb, ETS will almost always "establish the part of speech" in choice A. If you can't tell which category a word in capital letters belongs to, look at the first answer choice. It should clear up your confusion:

> CLASP : TIE ::
>
> (A) shoe : foot

Although *clasp* could be used as either a verb or a noun, you can tell from choice A that it is being tested as a noun.

BEWARE

6. Beware of answer choices that are catch phrases or words that are often used together such as *fleeting:thought*, *risky:business*, *happy:birthday*, *good:morning*. Because such pairs of words sound so familiar, you may be led to think that they contain a clear and necessary relationship. But they almost never do. When you encounter such a pair of words, split it apart, define each word separately, and make certain they are really related in a clear and necessary way. Virtually all such pairs can be eliminated.

FINDING PAM'S ANSWER WITH YOUR EYES CLOSED

You should now have a good understanding of the sort of relationship that must exist between the words in capital letters in SAT analogy items. You just used this understanding to write sentences in Drill 1. Now we're going to show you how to use this same concept to eliminate incorrect answer choices, and thus improve your guessing odds, even if you don't know the meaning of the words in capital letters.

SOUND IMPOSSIBLE?

You may think this is impossible. But it's not. Here's how it works.

You already know two important rules about SAT analogy items:

> **Rule 1.** **The words in capital letters are always related to each other in a clear and necessary way.**

> **Rule 2.** **The words in Pam's answer must be related to each other in exactly the same way as the words in capital letters.**

From these two rules we can easily deduce a third:

> **Rule 3.** **The words in Pam's answer must be related to each other in a clear and necessary way.**

This is a very simple idea. Since the relationship between the words in Pam's answer has to be exactly the same as the relationship between the words in capital letters, the relationship between the words in Pam's answer must also be clear and necessary. From this we can deduce a fourth rule—the most important rule of all:

Rule 4. Any answer choice containing words that are not related to each other in a clear and necessary way could not possibly be ETS's answer and can therefore be eliminated.

This rule will enable you to eliminate incorrect choices even when you don't know the words in capital letters.

The following drill will give you a better idea of what sort of relationship is tested on the SAT. Link each of the following pairs of words in a short, specific sentence that emphasizes the clear and necessary relationship (if any) between the two words. The best such sentence is one that defines one of the words in terms of the other. If you aren't *absolutely* certain of the meaning of any word, look it up, add it to your word list, and make sure you know it before you take the SAT. Warning: Some of these pairs are unrelated. If you find such a pair, don't try to turn it into a sentence; just put an X beside it. We've answered the first three questions for you. Be sure to check your answers against the key on page 358.

1. acorn : nut   *An acorn is a type of nut*

2. cardiologist : operations   *X*

3. counselor : advice   *A counselor's job is to give advice*

4. solar : sun

5. sticky : glue

6. purr : hunger

7. grateful : thanks

8. morsel : quantity

9. equine : horse

10. speculation : profit

11. preach : exhortation

12. dive : cliff

13. alias : identity

ELIMINATING UNRELATED PAIRS

Keeping in mind Rule 4, try your hand at the following analogy. Notice that we've left out the words in the stem:

12 ____ : ____ ::

    (A) plentiful : resource
    (B) wealthy : money
    (C) voluntary : result
    (D) neutral : activity
    (E) humorous : movie

HERE'S HOW TO CRACK IT

We have no idea what the words in capital letters are, so we ignore them and study the choices. Let's look at them one at a time:

(A) Is there a clear and necessary relationship between plentiful and resource? No. A resource might be plentiful, but it also might be scarce. The two words don't necessarily go together.

(B) Is there a clear and necessary relationship between wealthy and money? Yes. Wealthy means something like "having a lot of money." A possibility.

(C) Is there a clear and necessary relationship between voluntary and result? No. Eliminate.

(D) Is there a clear and necessary relationship between neutral and activity? No. Eliminate.

(E) Is there a clear and necessary relationship between humorous and movie? No. Movies don't have to be humorous.

We've eliminated everything but B. That means B has to be Pam's answer. We were able to find it even if we didn't know the words in capital letters. (The missing words were MASSIVE:SIZE.)

> *Don't make the mistake of being too clever on analogies. Pam isn't trying to see how ingenious you are. You won't win any points with her for coming up with a brilliant justification for an incorrect answer. Pam thinks of the analogy section as being fairly straightforward. If you can't find the relationship between two words after looking at them for five seconds (assuming you know the meanings of both words), then you should probably assume that there is no relationship.*

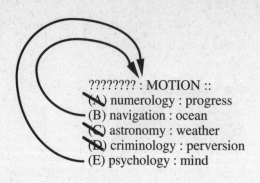

???????? : MOTION ::
(A) numerology : progress
(B) navigation : ocean
(C) astronomy : weather
(D) criminology : perversion
(E) psychology : mind

WORKING BACKWARD FROM THE CHOICES

You won't find many SAT analogy items in which it is possible to eliminate all four incorrect choices. On any item where eliminating unrelated pairs doesn't take you all the way to Pam's answer, you'll need to use other techniques. Perhaps the most powerful of these other techniques is working backward.

Working backward is most useful when you are uncertain about the meaning of one of the words in capital letters. It is a method of testing an answer choice by determining whether the relationship between the words in it could possibly be the same as the relationship between the words in capital letters.

How does this work? Remember that when you knew both words in capital letters, you looked for Pam's answer by constructing a sentence and then plugging in the words from each choice. Since you now know only one of the words in capital letters, you cannot construct a sentence using them. However, you may be able to construct a sentence from a choice and then apply it to the words in capital letters.

Here's an example. Assume that you don't know the first word in capital letters and that you have already eliminated three unrelated pairs from among the choices. You are left with two choices that contain clear and necessary relationships. You must decide which one is Pam's answer.

12   ——— : YEAST ::

    (A) lubricant : oil
    (B) [eliminated]
    (C) detergent : dirt
    (D) [eliminated]
    (E) [eliminated]

HERE'S HOW TO CRACK IT

Is there a clear and necessary relationship between *lubricant* and *oil*? Of course there is. "Oil is a kind of lubricant." Now go back to the words in capital letters. Could yeast be a kind of ———? Yes, that's possible. Yeast could certainly be a kind of something. You don't have to think of an actual word to go in the blank. All you have to do is decide whether such a word is likely to exist.

Now try the same thing on choice C. Is there a clear and necessary relationship between *detergent* and *dirt*? Yes, definitely. "Detergent cleans away dirt." Now go back to the words in capital letters. Could ——— clean away yeast? No, that doesn't seem plausible. Even though you don't know what the first word in capital letters means, you can see that it probably couldn't mean what it would have to mean in order for C to be Pam's answer. Therefore, you can eliminate it. Pam's answer must be A. (It is. The missing word is *leaven*. Leaven is a substance that makes dough rise, and yeast is a kind of leaven, just as oil is a kind of lubricant.)

When you're trying to figure out whether there is a clear and necessary relationship between the words in an analogy choice, you'll often find it useful to ask yourself, "Could either of these words appear in the dictionary definition of the other?" Sometimes Pam's answers on analogy questions won't quite pass this test. But keeping the dictionary in mind will always help you. Remember, the verbal SAT is a vocabulary test. Pam uses analogy questions to test your understanding of the meanings of words. She isn't interested in whether you know that Shakespeare wrote *The Tempest*. All she cares about is whether you know that a tempest is a violent windstorm.

WHEN YOU DON'T KNOW WORDS IN THE ANSWER CHOICES

Decoding words in the answer choices can be tricky, since you can't be certain that the words in a choice are clearly and necessarily related. Assuming you know both words in capital letters, you can still ask yourself whether *any* word could create a relationship in the choice identical to the relationship between the words in capital letters. If not, you can eliminate the choice. Here's an example:

12   INNOVATOR : CREATE ::

(A) patient : cure
(B) ——— : give
(C) scientist : describe
(D) president : elect
(E) prisoner : confess

HERE'S HOW TO CRACK IT

Let's say we don't know the meaning of the first word in choice B. What should we do? We should simply follow our usual procedure. First we form a sentence: "An innovator is someone who creates." Then we plug in the choices.

(A) Is a patient someone who cures? No. A patient is someone who is (or is not) cured. Eliminate.

(B) Could ——— mean someone who gives? Possibly. We don't know the word, so we have to hang on to this choice.

(C) Is a scientist someone who describes? Well a scientist might describe something, but this isn't a good definition of *scientist*. Eliminate. There is no clear and necessary relationship between these two words.

(D) Is a president someone who elects? No. A president is someone who is elected. Eliminate.

(E) Is a prisoner someone who confesses? No. A prisoner might have made a confession, but many prisoners don't confess, and many people who confess aren't prisoners. There is no clear and necessary relationship. Eliminate.

We've eliminated everything except choice B, so it must be Pam's answer. We pick it even though we don't know what one of the words is. (The missing word is *benefactor,* a benefactor is someone who gives.)

JOE BLOGGS AND SAT ANALOGIES

As is always true on the SAT, Joe Bloggs finds some answer choices much more appealing than others on analogy items. Most of all, Joe is attracted to choices containing words that

1. remind him of one or both of the words in capital letters.

2. "just seem to go with" the words in capital letters.

3. are easy to understand.

ELIMINATING JOE'S ANSWERS ON THE DIFFICULT THIRD

The Joe Bloggs principle is most useful in helping you eliminate incorrect answer choices on the difficult third. To do this you first have to know how to spot choices that seem right to Joe.

What makes a choice *seem* right to Joe on an analogy question? Almost always an answer choice will seem right to Joe if one of the words in it reminds him of one of the words in the question. If a word in a choice "just seems to go with" one of the words in capital letters, Joe will be attracted to that choice. Here's an example:

ANALOGIES
10 11 12 13 14 15
EASY MEDIUM HARD

12 SONG : VERSES ::

(A) moon : phases
(B) tree : roots
(C) battle : soldiers
(D) poem : stanzas
(E) newspaper : reporters

HERE'S HOW TO CRACK IT

Which choice attracts Joe Bloggs on this question? Choice D. Songs and verses just seem to go with poems and stanzas. Does that mean choice D is wrong? *No!* Look at the number of this question. It's a number 10, the easiest in its group. Joe Bloggs gets the easy ones right, and D is Pam's answer.

But Joe's impulse to pick answers that "just seem to go with" the words in capital letters will get him in trouble on hard questions. After all, if Joe knew the answer to a hard analogy, it wouldn't be hard, would it? On the hardest analogy questions, therefore, you can safely eliminate choices that you know would seem attractive to Joe Bloggs. *Before you do anything else on a hard question, look for Joe's answers and cross them out.*

Here's an example:

15   INFINITESIMAL : SIZE ::

    (A) trifling : significance
    (B) distant : galaxy
    (C) cacophonous : music
    (D) lucid : behavior
    (E) enormous : mountain

HERE'S HOW TO CRACK IT

Which choices attract Joe on this question? Choice E definitely does, because enormous and mountain "just seem to go with" size. What does that mean? It means that E is wrong, because this is a hard question and Joe doesn't get the hard ones right.

Joe is probably also attracted to choice B: galaxies are large, which makes that choice "just seem to go with" the words in capital letters. You can also eliminate choice B.

(Pam's answer on this question is A. *Infinitesimal* means extremely small, or lacking in size; *trifling* means lacking in significance.)

Once you've learned to eliminate choices containing words that attract Joe Bloggs, we'll teach you other techniques for eliminating even more incorrect choices.

THE JOE BLOGGS PRINCIPLE: ELIMINATING ATTRACTORS

We have a name for answers that seem right to Joe Bloggs. We call them "attractors." You must look at hard analogy questions—the last three or four questions in a ten-analogy group—through Joe's eyes, find the attractors, and eliminate them.

Here's another example:

14 DESTITUTION : MONEY ::

    (A) budget : options
    (B) sobriety : inebriation
    (C) opulence : wealth
    (D) deficit : finance
    (E) pollution : factory

HERE'S HOW TO CRACK IT

This is the next to last question in its group, which means it's the second hardest. Joe Bloggs will definitely get it wrong.

Destitution is a very hard word. Most people, including Joe Bloggs, don't know what it means. *Money*, however, is an easy word. Joe looks through the choices for a word that seems to go with *money*. He finds three attractors: *budget* in choice A, *wealth* in choice C, and *finance* in choice D. Joe will weigh these three choices and then pick one of them.

Once again, since this is an extremely difficult question, we know that Joe must certainly be wrong. We can therefore eliminate all three choices. If Joe's hunch were correct, this would be an easy question, not a hard one.

(Pam's answer on this question is B. If you guessed blindly after eliminating the three Joe Bloggs answers, you would have a fifty-fifty chance of picking it—good odds! Later in this chapter, you'll learn other techniques that may enable you to eliminate the other incorrect choice.)

NOW WHAT?

Your first step in approaching the *hardest* three or four questions in each analogy group should always be to eliminate Joe's attractors. You'll seldom find three, and you sometimes find none, but you'll usually find at least one. When you find it, cross it out in your test booklet. If it's Joe's answer, it can't be Pam's.

> *When you eliminate an incorrect choice on an analogy or any other SAT question, draw a line through it in your test booklet. On harder questions, you may have to go back several times before you settle on an answer. If you cross out choices you've eliminated, you won't waste time looking at them over and over again.*

HARD QUESTIONS, HARD ANSWERS

Joe Bloggs is lazy. He doesn't like problems that look too hard, and he doesn't like complicated solutions. This means that he has a very strong tendency to select choices containing words that he understands and is familiar with. He is very unlikely to select a choice if it contains words he's never heard of (unless there is something else about that choice that attracts him, such as an easy word that reminds him of one of the words in capital letters). When Joe takes a stab at a question, he picks something easy and familiar.

This can be a big help for you. Because Joe is so irresistibly drawn to easy choices, one of the best places to look for Pam's answer on a hard analogy question is in a hard choice—a choice containing words that Joe doesn't understand. When you find yourself stumped on a hard analogy item, simply eliminate what you can and then select the remaining choice that contains the hardest and weirdest words.

This same principle can help you on easy items as well. Since Joe gets the easy analogy items right, and since he avoids choices containing hard words, you don't need to worry about hard weird choices, either. On easy items, trust your hunches instead.

How easy is easy? How hard is hard? The following drill should help give you a sense of the range of difficulty in the vocabulary tested on the SAT.

Each group contains five pairs of words. Rearrange the pairs in increasing order of difficulty. The easiest way to do this might be to look for the easiest pair in each group and mark a 1 beside it; then look for the hardest pair and mark a 5 beside it; then look for the easiest pair of the remaining three and mark a 2 beside it; and so on. (The answers are on page 359.)

Remember: You must gauge difficulty from Joe Bloggs's point of view. A word isn't necessarily easy just because *you* know what it means. A word is only easy if *Joe* knows what it means.

GROUP A
scribble : penmanship
banality : bore
urban : city
striped : lines
preamble : statute

GROUP B
taste : connoisseur
mural : painting
trees : forest
mendicant : beggar
finale : opera

GROUP C
word : sentence
arson : conflagration
garrulous : speaker
reflex : involuntary
mirror : reflection

GROUP D
threadbare : clothing
novel : literature
fins : aquatic
loyal : devotion
insurrectionist : docile

As we have said several times, you need to use different techniques for the easy, medium, and hard thirds of each analogy group. The following lists should help you remember how to approach each third, as well as the order in which you should apply the techniques.

EASY THIRD

1. Remember: Joe Bloggs gets these questions right. The choices that *seem* right *are* right. Trust your hunches, but be careful to consider *all* the choices.

2. Form a short, specific sentence that expresses the clear and necessary relationship between the two words in capital letters. The best such sentence should *define* one of the words in terms of the other. Therefore, use "is" or "means" in your sentence.

3. Plug each answer choice into your sentence. If you find more than one choice that works, go back and make your sentence more specific.

4. Don't worry too much about hard words among the choices (Joe doesn't know them either). If you get stuck, go with something obvious.

5. Eliminate unrelated pairs.

MIDDLE THIRD

1. Remember: Joe Bloggs gets some of these questions right, and some of these questions wrong. Don't automatically distrust your hunches, but be very careful about selecting an answer. Be especially careful to consider *all* the choices.

2. Form a short, specific sentence that expresses the clear and necessary relationship between the two words in capital letters. The best such sentence should *define* one of the words in terms of the other. Therefore, use "is" or "means" in your sentence.

3. Eliminate unrelated pairs.

4. If you don't know one of the words in capital letters, work backward from the choices.

DIFFICULT THIRD

1. Remember: Joe Bloggs gets these questions wrong. Before you do anything else, eliminate answers that would appeal to Joe Bloggs. Answers that *seem* right to Joe Bloggs in this third can't possibly be right.

2. If you know the word in the stem, form a sentence and plug it in.

3. Eliminate unrelated pairs.

4. If you don't know one of the words in capital letters, work backward from the choices.

5. When all else fails, pick the choice with the hardest, weirdest words for Joe.

Chapter **7**
Critical Reading

This chapter is about critical reading, the third of the three item types on the verbal SAT. Critical reading used to be called reading comprehension. It accounts for half of all the points that can be scored on the verbal SAT, so this chapter is important.

Before we begin, take a moment to read the following set of instructions, which appears exactly as it does on real SATs.

> Each passage below is followed by questions based on its content. Answer the questions following each passage on the basis of what is stated or implied in that passage and in any introductory material that may be provided.

Be sure that you know and understand these instructions before you take the SAT. If you learn them ahead of time, you won't have to waste valuable seconds reading them on the day you take the test.

SAT CRITICAL READING: CRACKING THE SYSTEM

It's important to know the instructions printed before each group of critical reading passages in the SAT, but it's vastly more important to understand what those instructions mean. ETS's instructions don't tell you everything you need to know about critical reading. The rest of this chapter will tell you what you do need to know.

Our techniques will enable you to

1. read quickly and efficiently.

2. eliminate answer choices that could not possibly be correct.

3. take advantage of outside knowledge.

4. take advantage of inside knowledge (about how Pam thinks).

5. use proven strategies to find Pam's answers.

6. find Pam's answer in some cases *without reading the passages.*

7. make better use of your limited time by skipping (in some cases) a difficult passage.

BASIC QUESTION TYPES

Believe it or not, the passage is the least important part of every critical reading group. Far more important than the passage are the questions. There are just two basic types: general and specific. General questions ask you about the passage as a whole. ("What is the author's main idea?") Specific questions ask you about particular details presented in the passage. ("What is the meaning of the word *tedious* in line 7?") The strategies for answering general questions are different from the strategies for answering specific questions. Keeping these differences firmly in your mind is one of the keys to doing well on critical reading.

BASIC PASSAGE TYPES

Critical reading passages on the SAT are drawn from four broad subject areas:

1. Science: These passages may concern discoveries, controversies, or other topics in physics, chemistry, astronomy, biology, medicine, botany, zoology, and the other sciences.

2. Humanities: These passages may be excerpts from essays about art, literature, music, philosophy, or folklore, or they may concern an artist, a novelist, a historical figure, or some other real person.

3. Social sciences: These passages may discuss a topic in politics, economics, sociology, or history.

4. Narrative: These passages are usually excerpts from novels, short stories, or humorous essays. (We have yet to see a poem on the SAT.)

One of the passages on your SAT will probably deal with the members of an ethnic or minority group. This *ethnic passage,* as we call it, will usually be either a social science passage or a humanities passage. The ethnic passage has its own techniques and rules, so we will deal with it separately.

ORDER OF DIFFICULTY, LOGICAL ORDER

Critical reading questions are the only questions on the SAT that are *not* presented in order of difficulty. When there are two critical reading *passages*, however, they are generally presented in order of difficulty.

Although critical reading questions are not presented in order of difficulty, they are presented in a logical order that closely follows the structure of the passage. That is, a question about the first paragraph will come before a question about the second paragraph, which will come before a question about the third paragraph, and so on. ETS always follows this pattern. Later in the chapter, we'll tell you how to use this fact to your advantage.

SAVE CRITICAL READING FOR LAST

The most important fact to remember about SAT critical reading passages is that they are extraordinarily time-consuming. Critical reading questions are worth the same number of points as analogies, but they take much, much longer to answer. Critical reading passages come last in each verbal section, and last is when you should tackle them. Do all sentence completions and analogies *before* you do the passages. (If you were offered a job that paid $10 an hour and another that paid $10 a minute, which one would you choose?)

SAT CRITICAL READING QUESTIONS HAVE NOTHING TO DO WITH CRITICAL READING

If you actually tried to comprehend the reading passages on the SAT—by critically reading and rereading them until you understood each one thoroughly—you wouldn't have any time left for the rest of the test.

You will never do well on SAT critical reading unless you keep one central fact in mind: Your goal is to earn points, not to understand the passages. The questions cover no more than 10 or 20 percent of the material in each passage. We'll teach you how to identify the important 10 or 20 percent and ignore most of the rest. The less time you have to spend looking at the passage, the more time you'll have for earning points.

THINK OF CRITICAL READING AS A TREASURE HUNT

If we told you that we had hidden $50,000 somewhere in your hometown, and then handed you an envelope filled with clues, would you search every inch of your hometown before you opened the envelope and looked at the clues?

Of course not.

You'd look at the clues first and use them to help you eliminate places where the treasure could not possibly be hidden.

THE SAME IS TRUE WITH THE SAT

Every reading passage contains a hidden treasure of at least 50 points. Your job is to find the treasure. There are a number of clues that will help you. Some of these clues are located in the passages; others are located in the questions and answers. In this chapter, we will help you learn to identify these clues and use them to earn a higher SAT score.

SAMPLE PASSAGE AND QUESTIONS

In the discussion that follows we will occasionally refer to the sample passage that begins on the next page and the questions that follow.

Questions 16–21 are based on the following passage.
The following passage is a summary of a sociological study concerning groups of Mexican-American women.

The subject of my study is women who are initiating social change in a small region in Texas. The women are Mexican-Americans who are, or
Line were, migrant agricultural workers. There is more
(5) than one kind of innovation at work in the region, of course, but I have chosen to focus on three related patterns of family behavior.

The pattern I lifestyle represents how migrant farm workers of all nationalities lived in the past
(10) and how many continue to live. I treat this pattern as a baseline with which to compare the changes represented by patterns II and III. Families in pattern I work on farms year round, migrating for as many as ten months each year.
(15) They work and travel in extended kin units, with the eldest male occupying the position of authority. Families are large—eight or nine children are not unusual—and all members are economic contributors in this strategy of family
(20) migration. The children receive little formal schooling.

Families in pattern II manifest some differences in behavior while still maintaining aspects of pattern I. They continue to migrate but
(25) on a reduced scale, often modifying their schedules of migration to allow children to finish the school year. Parents in this pattern often find temporary local jobs as checkers or clerks to offset lost farming income. Pattern II families
(30) usually have fewer children than do pattern I families, and the children make a far smaller contribution to the economic welfare of the family.

The greatest amount of change from pattern I,
(35) however, is found in pattern III families, who no longer migrate at all. Both parents work full time in the area, and they have an average of three children. The children attend school for the entire year. In pattern III, the women in particular
(40) create new roles for themselves for which no local models exist. They not only work full time but may, in addition, return to school. They also assume a greater responsibility in planning family activities, setting household budgets, and making
(45) other domestic decisions than do women in the other patterns. Although these women are in the minority among residents of the region, they serve as role models for others, causing ripples of change to spread in their communities.
(50) New opportunities have continued to be determined by preexisting values. When federal jobs became available in the region, most involved working under the direction of female professionals such as teachers or nurses. Such
(55) positions were unacceptable to many men in the area because they were not accustomed to being subordinate to women. Women therefore took the jobs, at first, because the income was desperately needed. But some of the women decided to stay at
(60) their jobs after the family's distress was over. These women enjoyed their work, its responsibility, and the companionship of fellow women workers. The steady, relatively high income allowed their families to stop migrating.
(65) And, as the efficaciousness of these women became increasingly apparent, they and their families became even more willing to consider changes in their lives that they would not have considered before.

16 Which of the following titles best reflects the main focus of the passage?

(A) A Study of Three Mexican-American Families at Work in Texas
(B) Innovative Career Women: Effects on Family Unity
(C) Changes in the Lifestyles of Migrant Mexican-American Families
(D) Farming or Family: The Unavoidable Choice for Migrant Farm Workers
(E) Recent Changes in Methods of Farming in Texas

17 According to the passage, pattern I families are characterized by which of the following?

(A) Small numbers of children
(B) Brief periods of migrant labor
(C) Female figures of family authority
(D) Commercial as well as agricultural sources of income
(E) Parents and children working and traveling together

18 All of the following statements about pattern II children express differences between them and pattern I children EXCEPT:

(A) They migrate for part of each year.
(B) They have fewer siblings.
(C) They spend less time contributing to family income.
(D) They spend more months in school.
(E) Their parents sometimes work at jobs other than farming.

19 The word <u>domestic</u> in line 39 most nearly means

    (A) crucial
    (B) native
    (C) unspoken
    (D) imported
    (E) household

20 According to the passage, which of the following is NOT true of women in pattern III families?

    (A) They earn a reliable and comparatively high income.
    (B) They continue to work solely to meet the urgent needs of their family.
    (C) They are more involved in the deciding of family issues than they once were.
    (D) They enjoy the fellowship involved in working with other women.
    (E) They serve as models of behavior for others in the region.

21 The author's attitude toward the three patterns of behavior mentioned in the passage is best described as one of

    (A) great admiration.
    (B) grudging respect.
    (C) unbiased objectivity.
    (D) dissatisfaction.
    (E) indifference.

BASIC PRINCIPLES: HOW TO CRACK CRITICAL READING

We said earlier that the questions are far more important than the passages. We really meant it. Did you ever finish reading a passage only to look up and ask yourself, "What did I just read?" Since the questions will test only a tiny fraction of the information in the passage, you don't want to waste a lot of time trying to memorize (or understand) details that you won't need to know to answer questions.

In fact, we don't want you really to read the passage at all. We want you to treat the passage like an article in an encyclopedia. Each time Pam asks you a question, you will turn to your encyclopedia to find the answer.

HERE'S OUR STEP-BY-STEP GAME PLAN
FOR CRACKING CRITICAL READING

We have a step-by-step game plan for reading SAT critical reading passages and answering the questions about them. We'll outline the plan first and then discuss each step in detail.

1. Find the main idea of the passage, using the method we will describe.

2. Find and answer the first *general* question. The very first question asked is often a general question. General questions are usually the easiest; answering them first also makes the specific questions easier, because answering the general questions will force you to solidify your initial idea of what the passage is about and how it is organized. Especially if you don't have time to answer all the questions following a passage, answer the general questions first. Remember POE.

3. After you have answered the general questions, find the first *specific* one. See if any of the answer choices can be eliminated immediately. When you find a choice that can be eliminated, cross it out in your answer booklet. *POE is very important on critical reading questions.* We'll talk about this more in a minute.

4. Go back to the passage and find Pam's answer. If you don't know immediately where to find it, skim quickly until you zero in.

5. When you have answered the first specific question, move on to the second. *Look for the answer to one question at a time. If you try to keep more than one question in your mind, you will get bogged down and waste valuable time.* Don't think about the second question until you have answered the first. Don't read all the questions before you look for the answer to any.

6. Don't waste time. If you find yourself in a rut on a hard question, quickly eliminate as many choices as you can, guess, and move on.

STEP ONE: FIND THE MAIN IDEA

Virtually every SAT reading passage has the same basic structure: The author has a main idea. Her primary purpose is to develop or explain this idea. She does this by stating her main idea and then supporting it with details, facts, examples, metaphors, and secondary ideas. The author also has an attitude toward her subject (she may be for something, against something, or neutral), which she conveys in her tone or style.

The first thing you will do with every reading passage is to find its main idea. Knowing the main idea will make it easier for you to find Pam's answers. It may even give you one of Pam's answers outright (if the passage is followed by a main idea question, as it often is).

Think of an SAT reading passage as a house. The main idea of the passage is like the overall plan of the house. Finding the main idea of the passage is like walking quickly through the house. As you walk, you don't want to waste your time by memorizing every detail of every room; you want to develop a general sense of the house as a whole. If you tried to memorize every detail, you'd never get through the house. Later on, when Pam asks you what was sitting on the table beside the chair in the master bedroom, you won't know the answer off the top of your head, but you will know where to look for it. And you will be able to answer more questions in less time than someone who has tried to memorize every detail.

The main idea of an SAT reading passage is usually fairly easy to find. Pam tends to put the main idea in predictable places. Once you know these places, you'll be able to find the main idea quickly without wasting valuable time.

Here's what you should read in your search for the main idea:

1. The italicized introductory paragraph, which serves the same function as a headline on a newspaper story and helps you focus on what the passage is about

2. The first two sentences of the first paragraph of the passage itself

3. The first sentence of each additional paragraph

4. The final sentence of the passage

In our classrooms we call this reading strategy "2-1-1-F," which stands for "2 sentences, 1 sentence, 1 sentence, final sentence." As you begin each critical reading group, remember 2-1-1-F to remind yourself that you shouldn't initially read very much of the passage at all. You may sometimes find that it makes sense to read another sentence or two—perhaps finishing the entire first paragraph, if it's short—but years of experience have shown us that 2-1-1-F is enough.

Incidentally, when we say *read* we don't mean *memorize*. You are trying to identify the main idea of the passage, nothing more. Don't get hung up on details. The idea is to get to the questions as fast as you can.

FINDING THE MAIN IDEA: A TEST DRIVE

Now that you know how to look for the main idea of a passage, let's try the method on our sample passage, which begins on page 92.

First, read the italicized introductory paragraph:

> *The following passage is a summary of a sociological study concerning groups of Mexican-American women.*

This sets you on the right track. Now read the first two sentences of the passage:

> The subject of my study is women who are initiating social change in a small region in Texas. The women are Mexican-Americans who are, or were, migrant agricultural workers.

As you read quickly, the following phrases ought to attract your attention: "women who are initiating social change"; "Mexican-American"; "migrant agricultural workers." The main idea, or most of it, is right here. The main idea might be stated quickly as "Mexican-American migrant women workers initiating social change," or something similar. Don't fret about the details. Move on.

The structure of this passage is so straightforward that you aren't going to have to read even so much as the entire first sentence of any succeeding paragraph. A glance at the first sentence of the second paragraph tells you "pattern I lifestyle"; a glance at the first sentence of the third paragraph tells you "pattern II"; a glance at the fourth paragraph tells you "pattern III." Remember: *you aren't looking for details right now.* You're looking for the main idea, and you're getting a sense of how the passage is put together. The author is writing about lifestyles, and each of these paragraphs is dealing with a different one.

The last paragraph is full of details and sociological jargon. Don't get bogged down on big words. Focus on the final sentence. In the future, the women and their families will be "even more willing to consider changes." That's all you need to notice for now.

STEP TWO: ATTACK THE GENERAL QUESTIONS

Now that you have found the main idea of the passage, you should head directly to the questions. As we mentioned earlier, the questions closely follow the organization of the passage. In other words, a question about the first paragraph will come before a question about the second paragraph. (In the fifteen-minute double-passage critical reading group, the first few questions will concern the first passage only, the next few questions will concern the second passage only, and the last couple of questions will concern the two passages together. We'll have more to say about this in a while.) Furthermore, virtually every critical reading passage will include at least one question that refers to a specific line number in the passage. You can use these line references as guideposts in your search for Pam's answers. For example, if the fourth question refers to line 30 in the passage, you can be certain that Pam's answers to the first three questions will be found in lines 1 through 29, and that Pam's answers to the fifth and succeeding questions will be found in line 31 and beyond. Line reference questions enable you to set helpful boundaries in your search for answers.

As we mentioned earlier, there are two main types of questions: general and specific. You want to attack the general questions first, saving the specific questions for last.

There are two main types of general questions—main idea and tone. We'll cover them one at a time.

MAIN IDEA QUESTIONS

The most common type of general question is the main idea or main purpose question. These questions seek to test whether you understand what the passage is about or why the author wrote it. Main idea questions can be phrased in a number of ways:

"What is the best title for the passage?"

"The passage is primarily concerned with . . ."

"Which of the following best describes the content of the passage?"

"The author's main purpose is . . ."

"Which of the following questions does the passage answer?"

Pam's answer to a main idea question will usually be the main idea of the passage (which you have already found) stated in a slightly different way. Main idea questions usually have general answers. Therefore, you can eliminate any choice that is too specific. The incorrect choices on a main idea question are usually statements that are partly true, or statements that are true of part of the passage, but that don't tell the whole story. At the same time, though, Pam's will never be *so* general that it could describe the main idea of virtually any passage.

If the question asks for the main purpose of the passage, make sure that the purpose you choose is something that could possibly be accomplished in the course of a few paragraphs. The author's purpose in writing a 250-word passage could never be "to describe the nature of the universe" or "to discuss the role of Europe in world affairs."

Similarly, if the main purpose of a passage concerns a particular person or thing, make sure that person or thing is mentioned in the answer you choose. If the main purpose of a factual passage is to describe some part of the life of Emily Dickinson, you can eliminate any answer choice that does not contain Emily Dickinson's name. To put the same point another way, if the main focus of the passage is on Emily Dickinson, the main purpose of the passage will *not* be "to discuss the role of women in American poetry." Joe Bloggs often falls for this sort of answer. He knows that Emily Dickinson is a poet and a woman, and he focuses immediately on what seems to him to be a winning combination. In this case, "the role of women in American poetry" is far too broad an idea to be the theme of a passage that is really about one particular American woman poet.

MAIN IDEA QUESTIONS: A TEST DRIVE

Let's try our approach to main idea questions by tackling the first question following the sample passage on page 92. Here's the question:

> **16** Which of the following titles best reflects the main focus of the passage?
>
> (A) A Study of Three Mexican-American Families at Work in Texas
> (B) Innovative Career Women: Effects on Family Unity
> (C) Changes in the Lifestyles of Migrant Mexican-American Families
> (D) Farming or Family: The Unavoidable Choice for Migrant Farm Workers
> (E) Recent Changes in Methods of Farming in Texas

HERE'S HOW TO CRACK IT

Questions that ask you to pick a title for the passage are main idea questions. As is often true on the SAT, this main idea question is the first following our passage. Remember the main idea you uncovered at the outset, and study the answer choices. Refer back to the passage as needed. Here are the choices:

(A) This is a Joe Bloggs attractor. It could be a correct answer if it were worded slightly differently: "A Study of Three *Kinds of* Mexican-American Families at Work in Texas." Don't get careless. Pam will always offer you tempting choices that sound almost right, but not quite. Eliminate.

(B) A possibility, perhaps, except that the passage doesn't really mention anything about family unity, and the women in the paper are not really "career women."

(C) Pam's answer.

(D) Eliminate. The women in the passage don't have to choose one or the other.

(E) For Joe Bloggs only. The passage is not about farming methods.

It is very important on questions like this to cross out choices as you eliminate them. As you go through the choices, you should have a definite sense of zeroing in on Pam's answer by using POE. If you don't cross out eliminated choices, you'll just be spinning your wheels. You'll keep reading and rereading the same choices over and over again, and you'll spend too much time on each question. Remember: you've only read a teeny bit of the passage, so Pam's answer is unlikely to leap right off the page at you. But you have enough knowledge to eliminate some choices right off the bat, and you know where to look (2-1-1-F) to get the information you need to choose between the last couple of tempting possibilities. High-scoring students do this automatically, without really being aware that they are doing it. You can learn to do it automatically, too.

QUESTIONS ABOUT TONE, ATTITUDE, OR STYLE

The other common general questions are ones about the author's tone, attitude, or style. These are often the easiest general questions to crack. There are usually one or two of these questions on every SAT. They are short and usually easy to answer without doing much more than glancing at the passage. *Even on a hard passage that you intend to skip, you may want to take a stab at a tone, style, or attitude question if there is one.* These questions are easy to spot, because they usually contain very few words.

The main thing to remember when attacking questions about tone, attitude, or style is that Pam uses passages by authors she feels good about. These authors are usually optimistic, reflective, objective, instructive, descriptive, or something similar. They are never desperate, disgusted, cynical, bitter, or apathetic. "Resigned" is about as low on the emotional scale as they go. (In a fiction or humor passage, the author's attitude may be satirical or ironic—like the tone of Mark Twain in one of his humorous essays—but these are the only types of passages in which the attitude is likely to be in any sense negative.)

Similarly, the style or tone of a passage will never be apologetic, apathetic, irrational, pompous, condescending, or anything similarly negative. If the passage is about a topic in science, for example, the author's style and tone will almost certainly be objective, unbiased, analytical. When Pam picks passages for the SAT, she looks for thoughtful, careful, uncontroversial passages written by thoughtful, careful, uncontroversial people. The tone of such a passage would never be ambivalent, dogmatic, or indifferent.

Using this information, you can almost always eliminate one or two answer choices on an attitude, style, or tone question without even looking at the passage. Because you know that Pam only uses certain types of passages, you are able to spot choices that don't sound like Pam at all.

ADVANCED PRINCIPLES: RESPECT FOR PROFESSIONALS AND ARTISTS

One key to doing well on questions of tone, attitude, and style is understanding Pam's very predictable feelings about certain types of people. Pam is deeply respectful of doctors, lawyers, scientists, writers, scholars, artists, and other such serious citizens. SAT reading passages treat such people with dignity and respect. You would be exceedingly unlikely to find an SAT reading passage about uncaring doctors, ruthless lawyers, or unscrupulous scientists. Nor would you be likely to find a passage about a bad writer or an untalented artist.

Here is an example:

27 The author views the work of modern astrophysicists with

(A) angry skepticism
(B) apologetic confusion
(C) admiring approval
(D) amused antagonism
(E) ambivalent condescension

HERE'S HOW TO CRACK IT

Without even reading the passage, you know that Pam believes that astrophysicists, like all scientists, ought to be admired. Science is good, so scientists are good, too. Pam's answer can only be C. All the other choices are at least partly negative. You don't need to see the passage to know that Pam's answer is C.

The same will be true of any passage concerning a professional, an artist, or a writer. The author's attitude will be admiration, approval, appreciation, respect. It will never be apathy, disdain, puzzlement, exasperation.

On the very rare occasion when a passage is somewhat critical of a group of professionals or artists, this criticism will be mild, like a gentle slap on the wrist. In fact, most such criticism is really veiled praise.

Here is an example:

18 The author believes that federal judges can
    sometimes be criticized for

   (A) failing to consider the meaning of the law
   (B) ignoring the rights of defendants
   (C) letting their personal opinions influence
      the outcomes of trials
   (D) slowing the flow of court cases by caring
      too much about the requirements of
      justice
   (E) forgetting that the Constitution is the
      foundation of the American legal
      system

HERE'S HOW TO CRACK IT

Choices A, B, C, and E all contain very serious criticisms of judges. Pam could never agree with any of them, because in her view judges and our legal system are honorable. If a judge can be criticized, in Pam's view, it can only be for "caring too much," as in choice D. This is Pam's answer.

In general, Pam's opinions are pretty much exactly the same as those of a kindly junior high school teacher. Like such a teacher, Pam invariably admires judges, lawyers, scientists, poets, novelists, and artists. Also like such a teacher, she doesn't think much of people who are controversial (unless they are members of a minority group—about whom we'll have more to say shortly), and she doesn't think much of people who are not as respectful as she is of the leaders of our culture and our society. Remember the kindly old junior high school teacher when you are stumped on one of these questions.

ADVANCED PRINCIPLES: NO STRONG EMOTIONS

Also like a kindly junior high school teacher, Pam avoids strong, unqualified emotions. The author of a reading passage selected by Pam may be "admiring" or "somewhat skeptical," but he would never be "irrational" or "wildly enthusiastic." On critical reading questions about the attitude, style, or tone of a passage or its author, you can simply eliminate answer choices containing emotions that are too positive or too negative.

For example:

19 As revealed in the passage, the author's
attitude toward Parliament is one of

(A) angry consternation
(B) unrestrained amusement
(C) gentle criticism
(D) reluctant agreement
(E) sneering disrespect

HERE'S HOW TO CRACK IT

Let's consider each choice in turn.

(A) This is much too strong an emotion for ETS. Pam is almost
never angry (especially about such a venerable institution as Parliament). Eliminate.

(B) Pam is sometimes amused, but her amusement is never unrestrained. That would be much too strong an emotion. (Can you
picture your kindly old junior high school teacher rolling on the floor?)
Eliminate.

(C) A possibility. *Criticism* is a fairly strong and negative word,
but it is softened by *gentle*.

(D) This is also a possibility: a positive word and a negative word
more or less cancel each other out.

(E) This is much too strong an emotion to be Pam's answer.
Eliminate.

We've eliminated choices A, B, and E. If we guess now, we have
a fifty-fifty chance of being correct. (Pam's answer is C—the better of
the two possible answers.)

ETS only uses reading passages that it believes to be well written
and intelligent. Pam would never select a passage whose tone was
hysterical or whose author was stupid or irrational. In answering
critical reading questions, therefore, you can always eliminate answer
choices that describe passages or their authors in clearly negative
terms.

For example:

23 The author's approach in this passage can best be described as which of the following?

(A) Condescending to the reader in an effort to strengthen a dubious thesis
(B) Presenting only those points that support the author's personal beliefs
(C) Emphasizing certain details in order to mask the weakness of the central argument
(D) Making a thoughtful case in a confident, objective tone
(E) Neglecting to account for the opinions of distinguished critics

HERE'S HOW TO CRACK IT

Let's consider each choice in turn.

(A) Eliminate. Pam's favorite authors would never condescend to the reader or put forth a dubious thesis. (To condescend is to talk down to or patronize.)

(B) Eliminate. Pam's favorite authors don't leave out points simply in order to support their personal beliefs.

(C) Eliminate. Pam's favorite authors don't have weak central arguments.

(D) This is the best guess so far. (It's also Pam's answer.)

(E) Eliminate. Pam's favorite authors don't neglect the opinions of their critics (especially their distinguished ones).

Pam almost never uses negative words to describe an author's tone or attitude *unless she is describing the author's attitude toward people who do not agree with the author or with Pam*. An author's attitude toward a famous painter will almost always be positive: it will likely be one of "admiration" or "respect"; but the author will have a *negative* attitude toward people who don't also appreciate the work of that artist.

Here is an example:

28   The author's attitude about people who believe that Mandel's paintings "are just pretty pictures" (lines 34–36) can be described as one of

(A) apathy
(B) amusement
(C) disapproval
(D) fury
(E) agreement

HERE'S HOW TO CRACK IT

The author likes Mandel's paintings; therefore, he must disapprove of people who think they "are just pretty pictures." Choice E is therefore easy to eliminate. Choice D is much too strong an emotion to be a likely ETS answer. Choices A and B should also be easy to eliminate. Pam's answer is C.

What is the author's attitude toward those who don't think Emily Dickinson was much of a poet? It might be disapproval, gentle mockery, respectful disagreement. This may seem like a negative attitude, but it's really just the flip side of Pam's respectful attitude towards professionals, authors, scientists, and so on. Her attitude toward such accomplished people is positive; her attitude toward people who don't share her opinions is mildly negative.

TONE, ATTITUDE, AND STYLE QUESTIONS: A TEST DRIVE

The last question following the sample passage on page 92 is a question about "the author's attitude."

Take another look, and give it a try:

21 The author's attitude toward the three patterns of behavior mentioned in the passage is best described as one of

(A) great admiration
(B) grudging respect
(C) unbiased objectivity
(D) dissatisfaction
(E) indifference

HERE'S HOW TO CRACK IT

The passage is clearly an excerpt from some sort of serious academic research study. Choices D and E can be eliminated immediately; no scholar or sociologist quoted by Pam would exhibit such negative feelings. Like the kindly junior high school teacher, Pam believes that professors and academic researchers are deserving of the highest respect. Choices A and B are also at least generally positive, but they, too, can be eliminated. It would be unprofessional of a scholar to exhibit "great admiration" for a subject—scholars are supposed to be objective—and "grudging respect" both is unprofessional and doesn't make sense in the context of the passage. Pam's answer is C; scholars are supposed to be unbiased and objective.

STEP THREE: ATTACK THE SPECIFIC QUESTIONS

Most of the critical reading questions on your SAT will be specific. These questions will require you to find a particular piece of information in the passage. You will attack them one at a time. First you will read the question carefully. Then you will jump back to the passage to find the answer. As you study the relevant part of the passage, you will use POE to eliminate choices that cannot possibly be correct. As always, you will cross out eliminated choices in your test booklet so that they don't come back to haunt you.

How will you know where to look for the information you need? You will have several important clues. First, your quick search for the main idea of the passage will have given you a general sense of how the passage is put together. So will the information you've turned up in answering the general questions. Second, you will know that Pam does not arrange critical reading questions in random order. The answer to the first specific question will be found near the first part of the passage; the answer to the last specific question will be found in the last part of the passage; the answers to the other specific questions will be found near the middle. As you work through the questions, you will have a definite sense that you are moving through the passage. Line reference questions (those that refer to specific line numbers) will give you specific guideposts along the way. If you just found Pam's answer to a specific question in the second paragraph, you won't find Pam's answer to the next specific question in the first.

Specific questions may give you other clues as well. For example, if the question concerns a particular person, focus your attention on the places in the passage where that person's name appears.

There are three main types of specific questions—explicit, inferential, and line reference. We'll cover them one at a time.

EXPLICIT QUESTIONS

Explicit questions are about information that is directly stated in the passage. An explicit question is one that requires you to find a particular piece of information in the passage—Do bats eat fruit? Is aluminum an export of Brazil? In the passage, you will find a sentence or series of sentences that tell you exactly what you need to know. Explicit questions are often phrased like this:

"The passage states that . . ."

"According to the author . . ."

"According to the passage . . ."

To find Pam's answer, head back to the passage and use your clues to find the information she has asked for directly.

EXPLICIT QUESTIONS: A TEST DRIVE

Take another look at question 17 following the sample passage that begins on page 92.

17 According to the passage, pattern I families are characterized by which of the following?

(A) Small numbers of children
(B) Brief periods of migrant labor
(C) Female figures of family authority
(D) Commercial as well as agricultural sources of income
(E) Parents and children working and traveling together

HERE'S HOW TO CRACK IT

This question is asking you for specific information about pattern I families. Where will you find it? We know that because this is the second question, its answer will be found near the beginning of the passage. We also know (as a result of glancing over the passage in search of its main idea) that the second paragraph concerns pattern I families. That's exactly where we should look for Pam's answer to this question.

Attack each choice in order and use POE to eliminate obviously incorrect choices, being careful to cross them out in your test booklet. *Remember: You should always consider just one choice at a time, and you should cross out each choice that you eliminate.* Some students read all the choices, then go back to the passage and hope they come across the answer. That's a terrible strategy for anyone who doesn't have a photographic memory. Instead, attack the question one step at a time. Look at each choice, refer back to the passage, and either cross out or save. Then go on to the next choice.

(A) Eliminate. The paragraph says pattern I families "are large—eight or nine children are not unusual."

(B) Eliminate. Pattern I families migrate "for as many as ten months each year."

(C) Eliminate. In pattern I families, "the eldest male" is the figure of family authority.

(D) Eliminate. Pattern I families "work on farms year round."

(E) This is Pam's answer. The paragraph says that pattern I families "work and travel in extended kin units." (Besides, we've eliminated everything else.)

INFERENTIAL QUESTIONS

Some questions asks you to make an *inference* or *deduction* based on what you have read. These questions are really just like explicit questions—they require you to go back to the passage to find particular information—except that Pam's answer to such a question will almost always be a *paraphrase* of an explicit statement in the passage. That is, it will use different words to say something that is said in the passage.

Here is an example of the difference between an explicit and an inferential question: if the author states that he is a vegetarian, his statement is explicit. You can *infer* from this that the author would feel out of place at a traditional Thanksgiving feast. When you *infer* something, you draw an independent conclusion based on the *explicit* information that you have been given.

An inferential question will be phrased something like this:

"It can be inferred from the passage that . . ."

"The author would most likely agree with which of the following statements?"

"The passage suggests that . . ."

Pam's answer to an inferential question usually won't contain more information than is stated directly in the passage. But the information will be stated in a different way.

LINE REFERENCE QUESTIONS

A line reference question is one that refers you back to a specific point in the passage. You won't need clever clues to tell you where to look for Pam's answers to these questions. Focus your attention immediately on the line or lines that are mentioned in the question. To be sure you understand the context, also read a few lines before and a few lines after.

ETS also uses line reference questions to test vocabulary. For example, a question may simply ask you for the meaning of the word "stupefying" in line 12. Attack these questions aggressively, handling them in exactly the same way we've taught you to handle sentence completions. Even if you don't know the meaning of the word, the context should enable you to eliminate several incorrect choices using POE. Here's our step-by-step strategy:

1. Cover the answer choices with your answer sheet, so that you won't be influenced by them.

2. Go to the passage and read the sentence that the line number refers to. Find the word that you have been asked to define.

3. Pretend that the word is a blank in a sentence completion. Lightly draw a line through it with your pencil. Then read the sentence again and (using our anticipation technique on page 50, as described in the chapter on sentence completions) come up with your own word for the blank. If you don't come up with a word on your first try, read one sentence before and one sentence after, so that the context will give you clues.

4. Once you've settled on your own word for the blank, uncover the answer choices and use POE to eliminate those choices that are not like your word.

It is very important to use this method in answering these questions. If you simply plug in the choices—Joe Bloggs's favorite technique—you may fall into a trap. Pam's answer will often be a secondary meaning of the word she has asked you to define. If you go straight to the choices, you may be irresistibly attracted to one that might be correct in a different context, but is dead wrong in this one. Covering up the answer choices will eliminate temptation. Don't get careless.

LINE REFERENCE QUESTIONS: A TEST DRIVE

Take another look at question 19 in the sample passage that begins on page 92. This is a standard ETS line reference question, in which you are asked to choose the best definition for a vocabulary word based on its context in the passage. Here's the question:

19 The word *domestic* in line 45 most nearly
means

(A) crucial
(B) native
(C) unspoken
(D) imported
(E) household

HERE'S HOW TO CRACK IT

Cover up the answer choices. Then find the word in the passage and lightly draw a line through it. Now proceed as though trying to anticipate Pam's answer for a sentence completion problem. Here's the problem you are trying to solve:

> They also assume a greater responsibility in
> planning family activities, setting household
> budgets, and making other _____ decisions
> than do women in the other patterns.

The "decisions" in question are "other" decisions, meaning that making them is like "planning family activities" or "setting household budgets." As a result, the word that belongs in the blank means something like "family" or "household." Now look at the choices.

(A) Nothing like the word you anticipated. This may be a tempting choice for a test taker who doesn't have any idea what *domestic* means. Joe is drawn to this choice, because he figures that the women's new decisions must be important. Eliminate.

(B) Nothing like the word you anticipated. This is one meaning of *domestic*, but it is not Pam's answer. "Domestic" in the context of the passage does not mean "native" or "from one's own country" (as it might if the paragraph were discussing the difference between domestic and foreign cars).

(C) Nothing like the word you anticipated.

(D) Nothing like the word you anticipated. This is the opposite of a meaning of *domestic* that doesn't apply in this context.

(E) Here's one of the words you anticipated. This is Pam's answer.

ADVANCED PRINCIPLES: ARGUING WITH PAM

The answer to an SAT critical reading question must be so absolutely correct that no one would want to argue with Pam about it. If even 1 percent of the 1.5 million students who take the SAT each year were able to raise a plausible objection to Pam's answer to a question, Pam would have to spend all her time arguing with students. In order to keep this from happening, she tries to make her answers impossible to argue with.

How does she do that? Let's look at an example:

> Which of the following statements is impossible to argue with?
>
> A.   The population of the world is 4.734 billion people.
> B.   The population of the world is quite large.

ANALYSIS

Statement A sounds precise and scientific; statement B sounds vague and general. Which is impossible to argue with?

Statement B, of course! Does anyone know exactly what the population of the world is? What if some experts say that the population of the world is 4.732 billion people? Doesn't the population of the world change from minute to minute? A number that is correct today will be wrong tomorrow. It's easy to think of dozens of reasons that statement A could be wrong.

Statement B, on the other hand, is so vague and general no one could argue with it. Anyone can see easily that it is true. If it were Pam's answer to an SAT critical reading question, no one would be able to quibble with her.

Pam and the other question writers at ETS understand the same thing. They understand that the more detailed and specific a statement it is, the easier it is for someone to quibble with it or raise an objection to it. And they understand that the more general and vague a statement is, the harder it is for someone to quibble with it or raise an objection to it.

From this fact, we are able to derive two extremely useful principles:

1.   Answer choices that say something is *always* true are usually incorrect.

2. Answer choices that say something is *sometimes* true are usually Pam's answer.

We call the first (incorrect) type of answer choice a *must* choice. We call the second (Pam's answer) type a *may* choice. Thus, we can restate and simplify our two principles:

1. *Must* choices are usually wrong.

2. *May* choices are usually right.

These principles are hard for some students to accept. Such students, in trying to choose between two possible answers to a critical reading question, may think something like: "Well, the earth's population certainly is large, but that seems so vague. I guess the answer must be the one with the big number in it."

This is often wrong. Pam's answer *must* be true. If there is even one exception to it, she won't be able to defend it. Pam's answer doesn't have to be (and usually isn't) profound. Do *not* look for subtle reasons when deciding between competing choices.

Let's look at an example of what we mean. We'll assume that you've already been able to eliminate some of the choices. You don't need to read the passage:

CRITICAL READING

16 17 18 19 20 21 22 23 24 25 26 **27** 28 29 30

MEDIUM

27 With which of the following statements would the author of the passage probably agree?

(A) No useful purpose is served by examining the achievements of the past.
(B) A fuller understanding of the present can often be gained from the study of history.
(C) [eliminated]
(D) [eliminated]
(E) Nothing new ever occurs.

HERE'S HOW TO CRACK IT

Which of these statements are *must* statements? Choices A and E. Choice A says that studying the past has no useful purpose, meaning none at all. This statement is absolute. All we would have to do to prove it false would be to find one tiny exception to it. Therefore, the author of the passage probably wouldn't be any more likely to agree with it than we would.

Similarly, choice E says that nothing new ever occurs. This, too, is a *must* statement. Therefore, it's easy to raise objections to it. Nothing at all that is new ever occurs? Not even once in a while? Surely there must be an exception somewhere. This statement is easy to attack. If we find a single small exception, we have proven the statement wrong.

Choice B, however, is so general and vague that no one could argue with it. It is a *may* statement. A single example would be enough to prove it correct. It must be Pam's answer.

Here's another example:

29 The author of the passage apparently believes that modern techniques are

    (A) totally worthless
    (B) [eliminated]
    (C) in need of further improvement
    (D) [eliminated]
    (E) [eliminated]

HERE'S HOW TO CRACK IT

Choice A is highly specific and intense, and therefore very easy to argue with. *Totally* worthless? Never the least bit valuable? Not even as an example of what not to do? Surely there must be one case in which they might be *somewhat* useful. You should attack this choice aggressively. If you can find even one small example in the passage that suggests modern techniques have some value, then this choice cannot be correct. Choice C, on the other hand, is extremely vague and therefore much harder to argue with. Isn't *everything* in need of further improvement? (This is also Pam's answer.)

Here's a silly example that makes the same point.

20 With which of the following statements would the weather forecaster probably agree?

(A) It will begin raining tomorrow at 3:36.
(B) Tuesday's low temperature will be 38 degrees.
(C) Next year's snowfall will total 45 inches.
(D) Tomorrow may be cooler than today.
(E) Next month will be the wettest month of the year.

HERE'S HOW TO CRACK IT

This question and the answer choices don't refer to an actual reading passage, of course. But even without seeing a passage (or knowing a weather forecaster), you ought to be able to tell that D is the only statement with which our imaginary weather forecaster, or anyone else, would probably agree. "Tomorrow may be cooler than today" is vague enough to be true no matter what. It may be cooler tomorrow, or it may not. All the bases are covered. The other four statements, by contrast, are so specific and absolute that no weather forecaster would make them. If a television weather forecaster said, "It will begin raining tomorrow at 3:36," your reaction would be, "Oh, yeah? How do you know?"

> *The vague choice is not always correct—although it usually is. And the specific choice is not always incorrect—although it usually is. But when you are trying to decide between two choices, both of which seem good, the more specific choice will be much easier to poke holes in. AND A CHOICE THAT IS EASIER TO POKE HOLES IN WILL BE EASIER TO ELIMINATE, IF IT IS WRONG.*

SPOTTING *MUST* CHOICES

Must isn't the only word that signals choices that are easy to argue with and therefore likely to be wrong. Here are several other such words:

> each
> all
> will
> totally
> always
> only
> solely

All of these words are absolute. If a statement says that something is *always* true, then you need to find only one exception in order to prove it wrong. If a statement says that *each* child ordered a hot dog, then you need to find only one child with a hamburger to prove it wrong. All of the words in the list above are highly specific, and therefore they make the choices that contain them easier for you to attack and, very likely, to eliminate. The following drill will help you practice this technique.

DRILL 1

Each of the following statements is an incorrect answer choice. Read each one and circle the word or phrase in it that makes it highly specific and therefore highly unlikely to be correct. Answers can be found on page 359.

(A) leads politicians to place complete reliance upon the results of opinion polls
(B) Baker's ideas had no influence on the outcome.
(C) Foreign languages should never be studied.
(D) All financial resources should be directed toward improving the work environment.
(E) the belief that nature is inscrutable and cannot be described

---

SPOTTING *MAY* CHOICES

May isn't the only word that signals choices that are hard to argue with and therefore likely to be correct. Here are several other such words:

can
some
most
sometimes
might
suggest

If a statement says that something is sometimes true, then you need to find only one example in order to prove it correct. If a statement says that some families own encyclopedias, you need to find only one family with a *World Book* to prove it correct. All of the words in the list above are vague, and therefore they make the choices that contain them harder for you to attack. Answer choices containing these words are good bets to be Pam's answer. The following drill will help you practice this technique.

DRILL 2

Each of the following statements is a correct answer choice. Read each one and circle the word or phrase in it that makes it vague and therefore hard to argue with. Answers can be found on page 360.

(A) New research may lead to improvements in manufacturing technology.
(B) Not all workers respond the same way to instruction.
(C) Improved weather was but one of the many factors that led to the record crop.
(D) Most scientists believe that continued progress is possible.
(E) Everyone cannot expect to be happy all the time.

ATTACKING *MUST* STATEMENTS: A TEST DRIVE

Take a look at question 20 from the sample passage that begins on page 92.

20 According to the passage, which of the following is NOT true of women in pattern III families?

(A) They earn a reliable and comparatively high income.
(B) They continue to work solely to meet the urgent needs of their family.
(C) They are more involved in the deciding of family issues than they once were.
(D) They enjoy the fellowship involved in working with other women.
(E) They serve as models of behavior for others in the region.

HERE'S HOW TO CRACK IT

The wording of this question is a little tricky. You are being asked to find an *untrue* statement about pattern III families. (We'll have more to say about this type of question later in the chapter.)

The easiest way to make a statement untrue is to make it highly specific by using one of the words we just discussed. Take a quick look at the answer choices. The word *solely,* in choice B, should jump right out at you. Attack this choice first. Looking back at the fifth paragraph, you find that pattern III women continued to work "after the family's financial distress was over." It is *not* true, therefore, that pattern III women worked *solely* to meet urgent needs. That means that choice B is untrue and that it is Pam's answer.

A word like *solely* is a red flag. Pam very often adds a word like this to an answer choice for the sole purpose of making the choice untrue, and in this case you were looking for an untrue choice. A choice containing a word like this is a good starting point for your attack on a question. All you need to do to prove the statement untrue is to find one teeny exception to it. Train yourself to notice signal words like this.

ADVANCED PRINCIPLES: USE OUTSIDE KNOWLEDGE

ETS says you should never use "outside knowledge" in answering critical reading questions—that is, you are supposed to answer the questions only on the basis of the material in the reading passages. This is very bad advice. Outside knowledge can be a big help on SAT critical reading. Why? *Because Pam's answer to a critical reading question will never contradict an established, objective fact.* In writing this chapter we analyzed hundreds of SAT reading passages; *not once* did outside knowledge mislead us. In fact, outside knowledge can enable you to eliminate many choices as absurd or disputable, without reading a word of the passage.

Here's an example:

CRITICAL READING

16 17 18 19 20 21 22 23 24 25 26 27 28 29 30

◄───── MEDIUM ─────►

16 According to the passage, all of the following are true of living organisms EXCEPT

(A) they are able to reproduce themselves.
(B) they are past the point of further evolution.
(C) they are capable of growth.
(D) they respond to stimuli.
(E) they are characterized by a capacity for metabolism.

HERE'S HOW TO CRACK IT

If you know even a little about biology, you will probably be able to answer this question without reading the passage. (Remember that on this question you are asked to look for a statement that is *not* true.) Now let's consider each choice in turn.

(A) The ability to reproduce is one of the obvious differences between living things and nonliving things. Eliminate.

(B) Have living organisms stopped evolving? Of course not. This must be Pam's answer.

(C), (D), and (E) These choices are all part of the standard biological definition of life. Eliminate.

ADVANCED PRINCIPLES: EXCEPT/LEAST QUESTIONS

As in the previous example, Pam will often ask questions that require you to determine which of five choices is LEAST likely to be true, or she will offer five choices and say that all are true EXCEPT the "correct" answer. (These questions can be worded in several ways. Sometimes, for example, you will be asked to find a choice that is NOT true.) These questions can be confusing to answer, because they require you to select an answer that is incorrect—exactly the opposite of what you are used to doing.

These questions are very difficult for most students, but they respond beautifully to POE, and we have a technique that gives our students a big advantage on them. Here's what we teach them to do:

1. Cross out and ignore the capitalized negative word (EXCEPT, LEAST, NOT) in the question.

2. Read each choice in turn, and determine whether it is true or false. If it is true, write Yes beside it in your test booklet. If it is false, write No beside it.

3. After you have gone through the choices, you'll have four Yes's and one No. Select the one marked No as your answer. That's all there is to it. (On some especially tricky LEAST/EXCEPT questions, you may find that you have four No's and one Yes. No problem. Your answer is always the odd man out—in this case, the Yes. Just eliminate the four that are the same, and select the one that's left.)

There are two LEAST/EXCEPT questions following the sample passage that begins on page 92. We've already looked at one of them (question 20, a NOT question) in order to demonstrate a different technique. But take a look at it again.

20 According to the passage, which of the following is NOT true of women in pattern III families?

   (A) They earn a reliable and comparatively high income.

   (B) They continue to work solely to meet the urgent needs of their family.

   (C) They are more involved in the deciding of family issues than they once were.

   (D) They enjoy the fellowship involved in working with other women.

   (E) They serve as models of behavior for others in the region.

HERE'S HOW TO CRACK IT

Cross out the NOT and forget about it. Go right to the choices and give them the Yes/No test.

   (A) Do pattern III families earn a reliable and comparatively high income? Yes. It says so in the final paragraph.

   (B) Do they continue to work solely to meet the urgent needs of their family? No. The final paragraph says they stay in their jobs after the family's distress is over.

   (C) Are they more involved in deciding family issues than they once were? Yes. It says so in the next to last paragraph.

   (D) Do they enjoy the fellowship involved in working with other women? Yes. It says so in the final paragraph.

   (E) Do they serve as models of behavior for others in the region? Yes. It says so in the next to last paragraph.

   The only No—the odd man out—is choice B. This is Pam's answer.

   Now try the other LEAST/EXCEPT question in the sample. Its wording is significantly trickier.

18 All of the following statements about pattern II children express differences between them and pattern I children EXCEPT:

(A) They migrate for part of each year.
(B) They have fewer siblings.
(C) They spend less time contributing to family income.
(D) They spend more months in school.
(E) Their parents sometimes work at jobs other than farming.

HERE'S HOW TO CRACK IT

Cross out the EXCEPT and forget about it. Now look at the choices. This question is asking about differences between pattern I and pattern II families. As you check each choice, you have to ask yourself whether the choice describes a difference between pattern I and pattern II. A quick glance at the passage will tell you that the answer can be found in the second and third paragraphs. Now go to the choices.

(A) Is migration a difference between pattern I and pattern II children? No. Both migrate.

(B) Is number of siblings a difference? Yes. Pattern II children have fewer siblings than pattern I children.

(C) Is this a difference? Yes. Pattern II children spend less time than pattern I children contributing to family income.

(D) Is this a difference? Yes. Pattern II children spend more time in school than pattern I children.

(E) Is this a difference? Yes. The parents of pattern II children sometimes work at jobs other than farming

Pam's answer must be A. It's the only No. It's the odd man out.

Notice that you still would have found Pam's answer if you had posed the question a little differently. Suppose that, in considering each choice, you had asked yourself, "Is this true of both pattern I and pattern II?" In that case you would have had one Yes and four No's. Choice A still would have been the odd man out, because it would be the only Yes. You still would have found Pam's answer. The confusion arises because the question is really asking you to determine which choice is *not* an example of something that is *not* true. It's almost a double negative. That's very hard for Joe Bloggs to keep track of. But it's no problem for you if you use the Yes/No test. Our technique eliminates the source of Joe's confusion by ignoring it altogether.

ADVANCED PRINCIPLES: I, II, III QUESTIONS

Occasionally on the SAT, you will find a question like the following:

29 According to the author, which of the following characteristics is common to both literature and biology?

   I. They are concerned with living creatures.
  II. They enrich human experience.
 III. They are guided by scientific principles.

  (A) I only
  (B) II only
  (C) III only
  (D) I and III
  (E) I, II, and III

We call these "I, II, III questions." We could also call them "triple true/false questions," because you are really being asked to determine whether each of three separate statements is true or false. These questions are very time-consuming, and you will receive credit only if you answer all three questions correctly. Therefore, you should save them for last. Still, these questions are excellent for educated guessing, because you can improve your odds dramatically by using POE.

As is usually true on the SAT, the key to success is taking one step at a time. Consider each of the numbered statements individually. If you discover that it's true, you can eliminate any choice that does not contain it. If you discover that it is false, you can eliminate any choice that does contain it.

For example, suppose you know from reading the passage that statement II is false. That means you can eliminate two choices, B and E. Since B and E both contain II, neither can be correct. (Similarly, if you know that one of the statements is correct, you can eliminate any answer choice that does *not* contain it.) Incidentally, Pam's answer in this case is C.

ADVANCED PRINCIPLES: THE ETHNIC PASSAGE

For many years, members of minority groups have complained—justifiably—that the SAT is unfair to them. A number of years ago, ETS responded to their criticism by adding an "ethnic passage" to each SAT. This ethnic passage is always one of the critical reading passages on the test. It is a passage that has to do with African-Americans, Latinos, Asian-Americans, or some other ethnic group. Its purpose is to make members of these groups feel better about taking a test that is fundamentally unfair to them.

The ethnic passage doesn't make the SAT any fairer to minorities, but it does make the test easier to crack. Why? Because the ethnic passage is extremely predictable. Its tone is invariably *positive* or *inspirational*. Answer choices that express negative or unflattering opinions about minorities, therefore, can always be eliminated.

> *You must never skip the ethnic passage. It is the most predictable passage on the SAT, and you will be able to answer at least some of the questions even if you don't have time to read the passage.*

Here is an example. You don't need to read the passage in order to answer it.

24 The author views African-American literature with

(A) apathy
(B) confusion
(C) despair
(D) distaste
(E) admiration

HERE'S HOW TO CRACK IT

Pam's answer to this question, E, ought to jump right off the page. The purpose of the ethnic passage is to demonstrate that ETS admires minorities. ETS would never use a passage in which the author expressed negative or unflattering opinions about minorities. *Apathy, confusion, despair,* and *distaste* are all negative words; none of them could be Pam's answer. The only possible answer is *admiration.*

Let's look at another example, from another ethnic passage:

23 The passage implies that Professor Anderson [an African-American] received less credit than he deserved because

(A) he failed to publish his results.
(B) his findings were soon disproved by other scientists.
(C) he was a frequent victim of racial discrimination.
(D) his work was too complex to be of widespread interest.
(E) he had no interest in the accolades of his colleagues.

HERE'S HOW TO CRACK IT

Once again, Pam's answer, C, ought to be obvious. ETS added an ethnic passage to the SAT because it had been accused of racial discrimination. The purpose of the passage is to demonstrate that ETS thinks racial discrimination is a bad thing. Choices A, B, D, and E are all serious criticisms of a man who is an African-American. They could never be Pam's answer.

Pam's admiration for minorities even takes precedence over her admiration for the other people. The ethnic passage is the only place where she will say something negative about, for example, a government official—if that official is white and has discriminated against a member of a minority.

ADVANCED PRINCIPLES: TRIGGER WORDS

Critical reading questions test only a tiny percentage of the material contained in the passages. Some of your most useful clues as to what these questions will cover are provided by what we call "trigger" words. (You learned about trigger words in the chapter on sentence completions as well. Critical reading trigger words are similar, although there are important differences in how you use them. Read on.) Sentences that contain trigger words contain answers to questions nearly 70 percent of the time.

> *You shouldn't focus on trigger-word sentences as you look for the main idea of the passage. Rather, when you come to a hard question and are stuck among several choices, you should be on the lookout for trigger words in the part of the passage where you are looking for Pam's answer. They will help you make up your mind.*

Here are the trigger words. You *must* memorize this list:

> but
> although (while, even though)
> however
> yet
> despite (in spite of)
> nevertheless
> nonetheless
> notwithstanding
> except (unless)

HOW DO TRIGGER WORDS WORK?

Trigger words are words that signal a change in the meaning of a sentence, paragraph, or passage. Here's a simple example:

Sentence:

> Mr. Jones loves insects, but he doesn't think much of ants.

Question:

> Which of the following statements is true?
>
> (A) Mr. Jones loves all insects
> (B) Mr. Jones is not particularly fond of some insects.

ANALYSIS

The trigger word in the sentence is *but*. It signals that the meaning of the sentence is about to change. When Joe Bloggs looks at the sentence to find the answer to the question, he doesn't read past the *but*. He reads the words "Mr. Jones loves insects" and chooses answer choice A. *But* choice A *is incorrect*. Mr. Jones does not love *all* insects. Ants are a kind of insect, and Mr. Jones doesn't like ants;

therefore, he is not particularly fond of *some* insects. The correct answer to the question is choice B.

The answer to the question, in effect, was hiding behind the trigger word.

> *Pam uses critical reading questions to determine how carefully you read. She will try to trip you up by asking questions that seem to have one answer but actually have another. Very often the real answer will be hiding behind a trigger word. In writing her questions, Pam looks for places in the passage where the meaning changes. She thinks of each of these changes as a trap for a careless reader—as a trap for Joe Bloggs. If you learn to pay attention to the trigger words, you will be able to avoid many of Pam's traps.*

DRILL 3

Go back to the sample reading passage at the beginning of this chapter. Skim through it looking for trigger words. When you find one, circle it and then underline the sentence in which it appears. You'll find answers on page 360.

Note: Pam's answers to questions 16, 18, and 20 in the sample passage are contained in trigger-word sentences.

ADVANCED PRINCIPLES: DOUBLE PASSAGES

On your SAT, there will be a fifteen-minute verbal section that will contain a pair of related critical reading passages followed by thirteen questions. This double passage may look intimidating, but it doesn't have to be. Our strategy for attacking it is the same as our strategy for attacking a single passage, with a couple of modifications.

As is true on single passages, the questions following double passages follow the structure of the passages. In a typical example, the first five or six questions will concern the first passage alone, the next five or six questions will concern the second passage alone, and the last two or three questions will concern both passages. Your key to doing well on double passages is to think of them as two single passages. Here's what you should do:

1. Find the main idea of the first passage, using the methods we have described.

2. Attack any general questions that are based on the first passage alone.

3. Attack any specific questions that are based on the first passage alone.

4. Find the main idea of the second passage. Because the second passage will always be related in some way to the first passage, finding its main idea should be fairly simple. Very often, the second passage will comment on an argument made in the first passage, or raise an objection to it. It will never simply repeat the main idea of the first passage, but it will be related to it in some way. Use your knowledge of the first passage to help you zero in on the main idea of the second.

5. Attack any general questions that are based on the second passage alone.

6. Attack any specific questions that are based on the second passage alone.

7. Attack the remaining two or three questions, which will require you to consider the two passages together. By now you should have enough information to enable you to zero in on Pam's answer.

The main point is not to look at the second passage until you absolutely have to. Treat the second passage as a separate passage as long as you can. The great majority of the questions won't require you to think of any connection whatsoever between the two passages. Don't waste time by trying to figure out in advance something that you won't need to know at all.

If you get stuck on these last questions, ignore them and focus your efforts instead on any earlier questions that you may have left unanswered. Your last few minutes will be better spent attacking a question that relates to only one of the passages, because you won't have to cover as much ground to find Pam's answer. Similarly, you should be careful not to waste time by permitting yourself to get hung up on a hard question that relates only to the first passage if you have not yet tackled any easy questions that relate only to the second. Pacing is straightforward on the fifteen-minute double-passage section; you have a bit more than a minute per question, and there are no other item types to worry about. But you still need to pay careful attention to the clock.

ADVANCED PRINCIPLES: SKIPPING A PASSAGE

Most test takers will run out of time on critical reading, in all three verbal sections. That's okay. If you're working at the proper pace, the questions you don't have time to tackle are almost certainly questions you would have missed anyway. In fact, if you're aiming for a score of less than 550, it may make sense for you to skip one passage entirely. The time you would have spent on that passage would be better spent doing something else. You'll have to take some timed practice tests to decide if this strategy really makes sense for you.

CRITICAL READING SUMMARY

1. Critical reading accounts for half of all the points that can be scored on the verbal SAT.

2. The passage is the least important part of every critical reading group. Far more important than the passage are the questions. There are just two basic types: general and specific. General questions ask you about the passage as a whole. Specific questions ask you about particular details presented in the passage.

3. There are four types of subject matter that occur on the SAT: science, humanities, social sciences, and narrative.

4. Critical reading questions are the only questions on the SAT that are not presented in order of difficulty. Critical reading *passages*, however, *are* generally presented in order of difficulty. In addition, double passages are generally harder than single passages.

5. You should always save critical reading for last in each verbal section of the SAT. These problems take a great deal of time to read and answer, but the questions aren't worth any more points than ones that can be answered quickly.

6. Most test takers will run out of time on critical reading. That's okay. If you are working at the proper pace, the questions you don't have time to tackle are questions you would have missed anyway.

7. If you're aiming for a score of less than 550, it may make sense for you to skip one passage entirely.

8. SAT critical reading has nothing to do with comprehending reading. The name of the game is scoring points.

9. Every SAT reading passage and the questions that follow it contain clues that will enable you to eliminate obviously incorrect answers and increase your chances of choosing Pam's answer. Your job is to find these clues.

10. Reading slowly will improve neither your critical reading nor your SAT score. Treat the passage like an article in an encyclopedia. When Pam asks you a question, turn to your encyclopedia to find the answer.

11. Every passage has a main idea or central theme. Your first task is to find it. Knowing the main idea will make it easier for you to find Pam's answers. Do not clutter your brain by trying to memorize details.

12. After you have found the main idea, attack the general questions following the passage. Begin with the first general question, and proceed one question at a time.

13. After you have attacked all the general questions, attack the specific ones. Begin with the first specific question, and proceed one question at a time.

14. It is very important on questions like this to cross out choices as you eliminate them. You should have a definite sense of zeroing in on Pam's answer. If you don't cross out eliminated choices, you'll just be spinning your wheels.

15. Pam is deeply respectful of doctors, lawyers, scientists, writers, scholars, artists, and other such serious citizens. SAT reading passages treat such people with dignity and respect.

16. Pam avoids strong, unqualified emotions on the SAT.

17. Attack *must* statements. The answer to an SAT critical reading question is most likely a *may* answer. In trying to decide between competing choices on a questions, you should concentrate on the choice that seems more SPECIFIC and ATTACK that choice. If you can find any reason to dispute that choice, you should eliminate it and select the other.

18. Take advantage of outside knowledge in choosing your answers. Pam's answer will never contradict an established, objective fact.

19. Be careful on LEAST/EXCEPT and NOT questions. On these tricky items, Pam's answer is the choice that is *not* true. Use the yes/no technique.

20. I, II, III questions are very time-consuming and should therefore be saved for last. Still, they are excellent for educated guessing, because eliminating choices is easy and straightforward.

21. The tone of the ethnic passage is invariably positive or inspirational.

22. You must never skip the ethnic passage. It is the most predictable passage on the SAT, and you will be able to answer at least some of the questions even if you don't have time to read the passage.

23. When you are stuck among several choices on a hard question, you should be on the lookout for trigger words in the part of the passage where you are looking for Pam's answer.

24. Treat double passages as two separate passages. Don't even look at the second passage until you absolutely have to. The great majority of the questions won't require you to think of any connection whatsoever between the two passages.

PART 3

How to Crack the Math SAT

A FEW WORDS ABOUT NUMBERS

The SAT contains seven sections, six of which are scored. Three of the six scored sections will be math sections. Two of the scored math sections will last thirty minutes each; the third will last fifteen minutes. There may be a fourth, thirty-minute math section on your test, but it won't count toward your score. Don't waste time trying to figure out which sections are the scored ones. Just work at your normal pace.

The math questions on your SAT will be drawn from the following five categories:

1. arithmetic

2. basic algebra

3. geometry

4. quantitative comparisons

5. grid-ins

Quantitative comparisons and grid-ins are formats rather than branches of mathematics. Quant comps are questions in which you are asked to compare two values and determine whether one is greater than the other. Grid-ins are the only nonmultiple-choice questions on the SAT; instead of selecting Jim's answer from among several choices, you will have to find Jim's answer independently and mark it in a grid. The quant comps and grid-ins on your test will be drawn from arithmetic, algebra, and geometry, just like regular SAT math questions. But because these formats have special characteristics, we will treat them separately.

WHAT DOES THE MATH SAT MEASURE?

ETS says that the math SAT measures "mathematical reasoning abilities" or "higher-order reasoning abilities." But this is not true. The math SAT is merely a brief test of arithmetic, first-year algebra, and a bit of geometry. By a "bit" we mean just that. You won't have to know how to figure the volume of a sphere or the cross-section of a cone. You also won't have to know calculus, trigonometry, or the quadratic formula. The principles you'll need to know are few and simple. We'll show you which ones are important.

ORDER OF DIFFICULTY

As was true on the verbal SAT, questions on the math SAT are arranged in order of difficulty. The first question in each math section will be the easiest in that section, and the last will be the hardest. In addition, the questions within the quantitative comparison and grid question groups will also be arranged in order of difficulty. You must always pay attention to the difficulty of a problem in determining how to attack it.

SLOW DOWN

Most test takers would do considerably better on the math SAT if they slowed down and spent less time even thinking about the hardest problems. Haste causes careless errors, and careless errors can decimate your score. Most students would be better off ignoring the hardest problems and using the time they save to check their work on easy and medium problems. If you're shooting for an 800, you'll have to answer every question correctly, but if your target is 500, you should simply ignore the hardest five or six questions in each section. Use your limited time wisely.

THE PRINCETON REVIEW APPROACH

The average student will have little trouble with easy math questions, a fair amount of trouble with medium ones, and very little luck at all with difficult ones. For this reason, the focus of our approach is on techniques that are most useful in solving medium problems. This is where most students stand to benefit the most. If you learn to handle these problems well, you can expect a score of 600 or so.

This doesn't mean that the average student should not attempt the difficult problems; nor does it mean that we have no techniques for these problems. All we mean is that unless you expect to score above 600 or so, concentrating on easy and medium questions will be the best use of your time. If you finish these satisfactorily and have time remaining, you can turn your attention to the hardest problems, focusing on the types that are most susceptible to our techniques or that are familiar to you from math class.

Generally speaking, each chapter in this part will begin with the basics and then gradually move into more advanced principles and techniques. If you find yourself getting lost toward the end of a chapter, don't worry. Concentrate your efforts on principles you can understand but have yet to master.

DON'T THROW AWAY YOUR MATH BOOK

Although we will show you which mathematical principles are most important to know for the SAT, this book cannot take the place of a basic foundation in math. For example, if you discover as you read this book that you have trouble adding fractions, you'll want to go back and review the appropriate chapter in your math book or ask your math teacher for an explanation. Our drills and examples will refresh your memory if you've gotten rusty, but if you have serious difficulties with the following chapters, you should consider getting extra help. This book will enable you to see where you need the most work. Always keep in mind, though, that the math tested on the SAT is different from the math taught in class. If you want to raise your score, don't waste time studying math that ETS never tests.

CALCULATORS

Students are now permitted (but not required) to use calculators on the SAT. You should definitely bring a calculator to the test. It will be extremely helpful to you, as long as you know how and when to use it and don't get carried away. We'll tell you more about calculators as we go along.

BASIC INFORMATION

Before moving on to the rest of this part, you should be certain that you are familiar with some basic terms and concepts that you'll need to know for the math SAT. This material isn't at all difficult, but you must know it cold. If you don't, you'll waste valuable time on the test and lose points that you easily could have earned.

INTEGERS

Integers are the numbers that most of us are accustomed to thinking of simply as "numbers." They can be either positive or negative. The positive integers are

1, 2, 3, 4, 5, 6, 7, and so on

The negative integers are

–1, –2, –3, –4, –5, –6, –7, and so on

Zero (0) is also an integer, *but it is neither positive nor negative.*

Note that positive integers get bigger as they move away from 0, while negative integers get smaller. In other words, 2 is bigger than 1, but −2 is smaller than −1. This number line should give you a clear idea of how negative numbers work.

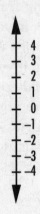

DIGITS

There are ten digits:

0, 1, 2, 3, 4, 5, 6, 7, 8, 9

All integers are made up of digits. In the integer 3,476, the digits are 3, 4, 7, and 6. Digits are to numbers as letters are to words.

The integer 645 is called a "three-digit number" for obvious reasons. Each of its digits has a different name:

5 is called the units digit
4 is called the tens digit
6 is called the hundreds digit

Thus the value of any number depends on which digits are in which places. The number 645 could be rewritten as follows:

$$
\begin{array}{rcr}
6 \times 100 & & 600 \\
4 \times 10 & = & 40 \\
+\ 5 \times 1 & & +\ \underline{5} \\
& & 645
\end{array}
$$

645
hundreds tens units

POSITIVE AND NEGATIVE

There are three rules regarding the multiplication of positive and negative numbers:

1. pos × pos = pos
2. neg × neg = pos
3. pos × neg = neg

ODD OR EVEN

Even numbers are integers that can be divided evenly by 2. Here are some examples of even numbers:

-4, -2, 0, 2, 4, 6, 8, 10, and so on

You can always tell at a glance whether a number is even: *It is even if its final digit is even.* Thus 999,999,999,992 is an even number because 2, the final digit, is an even number.

Odd numbers are integers that *cannot* be divided evenly by 2. Here are some examples of odd numbers:

-5, -3, -1, 1, 3, 5, 7, 9, and so on

You can always tell at a glance whether a number is odd: *It is odd if its final digit is odd.* Thus, 222,222,222,229 is an odd number because 9, the final digit, is an odd number.

Several rules always hold true with odd and even numbers:

even + even = even	even × even = even
odd + odd = even	odd × odd = odd
even + odd = odd	even × odd = even

REMAINDERS

If a number cannot be divided evenly by another number, the number left over at the end of the division is called the remainder. For example, 25 cannot be divided evenly by 3. Twenty-five divided by 3 is 8 with 1 left over. The 1 is the remainder.

Don't try to figure remainders on your calculator. (On your calculator, 25 divided by 3 is 8.3333333, but .3333333 is not the remainder.)

CONSECUTIVE INTEGERS

Consecutive integers are integers listed in increasing order of size without any integers missing in between. For example, –1, 0, 1, 2, 3, 4, and 5 are consecutive integers; 2, 4, 5, 7, and 8 are not. Nor are –1, –2, –3, and –4 consecutive integers, because they are *decreasing* in size. The formula for consecutive integers is $n, n + 1, n + 2, n + 3$, and so on, where n is an integer.

PRIME NUMBERS

A prime number is a number that can be divided evenly only by itself and by 1. For example, the following are *all* the prime numbers less than 30: 2, 3, 5, 7, 11, 13, 17, 19, 23, 29. *Note: 0 and 1 are not prime numbers.*

DIVISIBILITY RULES

You may be called upon to determine whether one number can be divided evenly by another. To do so, use your calculator. If the result is an integer, the number is evenly divisible. Is 4,569 divisible by 3? Simply punch up the numbers on your calculator. The result is 1,523, which is an integer, so you have determined that 4,569 is indeed divisible by 3. Is 2,789 divisible by 3? The result on your calculator is 596.33333, which is not an integer, so 2,789 is not divisible by three. (Integers don't have decimal points with digits after them.)

STANDARD SYMBOLS

The following standard symbols are used frequently on the SAT:

SYMBOL	MEANING
=	is equal to
≠	is not equal to
<	is less than
>	is greater than
≤	is less than or equal to
≥	is greater than or equal to

FINALLY, THE INSTRUCTIONS

Each of the three scored math sections on your SAT will begin with the same set of instructions. These instructions include a few formulas and other information that you may need to know in order to answer some of the questions. The mathematical information in them is repeated from the basic principles we have just discussed. You must learn these instructions ahead of time. You should never have to waste valuable time by referring to them during the test.

Still, if you do suddenly blank out on one of the formulas while taking the test, you can always refresh your memory by glancing back at the instructions. Be sure to familiarize yourself with them thoroughly ahead of time, so you'll know which formulas are there.

Following are the instructions as they will appear on your test. (Several abbreviations are used in the formulas: *A* means area, *r* means radius, *C* means circumference, and *V* means volume.)

Time—30 Minutes 25 Questions	This section contains two types of questions. You have 30 minutes to complete both types. You may use any available space for scratchwork.

Notes:

(1) The use of a calculator is permitted. All numbers used are real numbers.

(2) Figures that accompany problems in this test are intended to provide information useful in solving the problems. They are drawn as accurately as possible EXCEPT when it is stated in a specific problem that the figure is not drawn to scale. All figures lie in a plane unless otherwise indicated.

Reference Information

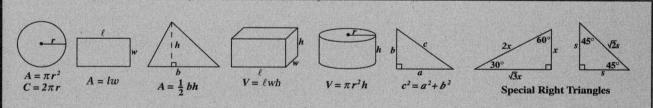

$A = \pi r^2$
$C = 2\pi r$

$A = lw$

$A = \frac{1}{2}bh$

$V = lwh$

$V = \pi r^2 h$

$c^2 = a^2 + b^2$

Special Right Triangles

The number of degrees of arc in a circle is 360.
The measure in degrees of a straight angle is 180.
The sum of the measures in degrees of the angles of a triangle is 180.

Chapter 8

Joe Bloggs and the Math SAT

YO, JOE!

Joe Bloggs should have been a big help to you on the verbal SAT questions. By learning to anticipate which answer choices would attract Joe on difficult questions, you taught yourself to avoid careless mistakes and eliminate obviously incorrect answers.

You can do the same thing on the math SAT. In fact, Joe Bloggs attractors are often easier to spot on math questions. Jim is quite predictable in the way he writes incorrect answer choices, and this predictability will make it possible for you to zero in on his answers to questions that would have seemed impossible to you before.

HOW JOE THINKS

As was true on the verbal SAT, Joe Bloggs gets the easy questions right and the hard questions wrong. In chapter 3, we introduced Joe by showing you how he approached a particular math problem. That problem, you may remember, involved the calculation of an average speed. Here it is again:

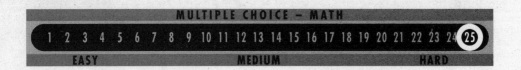

MULTIPLE CHOICE — MATH

1 2 3 4 5 6 7 8 9 10 11 12 13 14 15 16 17 18 19 20 21 22 23 24 **25**

EASY   MEDIUM   HARD

25 A woman drove to work at an average speed of 40 miles per hour and returned along the same route at 30 miles per hour. If her total traveling time was 1 hour, what was the total number of miles in the round trip?

(A) 30

(B) $30\frac{1}{7}$

(C) $34\frac{2}{7}$

(D) 35

(E) 40

When we showed this problem the first time, you were just learning about Joe Bloggs. Now that you've made him your invisible partner on the SAT, you ought to know a great deal about how he thinks, at least on the verbal SAT. What you need to do now is extend your knowledge of Joe's thought processes to include math.

HERE'S HOW TO CRACK IT

This problem was the last in a 25-item math section. Therefore, it was the hardest problem in that section. Therefore, Joe got it wrong.

The answer choice most attractive to Joe on this problem is D. The question obviously involves an average of some kind, and 35 is the average of 30 and 40, so Joe picked it. Choice D just *seemed* like the right answer to Joe. (Of course, it *wasn't* the right answer; Joe gets the hard ones wrong.) From this fact we can derive a general rule:

> *Joe Bloggs is attracted to easy solutions arrived at through methods that he understands.*

Because this is true, we know which answers we should avoid on hard questions: answers that *seem* obvious or that can be arrived at simply and quickly. If the answer really were obvious, and if finding it really were simple, the question would be easy, not hard.

Joe Bloggs is also attracted to answer choices that simply repeat numbers from the problem. From this fact we can derive a second general rule:

> **On difficult math problems, Joe Bloggs is attracted to answer choices that simply repeat numbers from the problem.**

This means, of course, that you should avoid such choices. In the problem about the woman traveling to work, it means that you can also eliminate choices A and E, because 30 and 40 are numbers repeated directly from the problem. Therefore, they are extremely unlikely to be Jim's answer.

Having now eliminated three of the five choices, you shouldn't have much trouble in seeing that Jim's answer has to be C. (If you can't choose between the two remaining choices, guess and go on; you'll have a fifty-fifty chance of being right—heads you win a dollar, tails you lose a quarter.)

PUTTING JOE TO WORK ON THE MATH SAT

Generally speaking, the Joe Bloggs principle teaches you to

1. trust your hunches on easy questions.

2. double-check your hunches on medium questions.

3. eliminate Joe Bloggs attractors on difficult questions.

The rest of this chapter will be devoted to using Joe Bloggs to zero in on Jim's answers on difficult questions. The other math chapters will help you deal with medium questions, and you're on your own with the easy ones. (Quantitative comparisons will be treated separately in chapter 12: Grid-in questions will be treated in chapter 14; there are special Joe Bloggs rules for them.)

BASIC TECHNIQUES

HARD QUESTIONS = HARD ANSWERS

As we've just explained, hard questions on the SAT simply don't have answers that are obvious to the average person. Avoiding the "obvious" choices will take some discipline on your part, but you'll lose points if you don't. Even if you're a math whiz, the Joe Bloggs principle will keep you from making careless mistakes.

Here's an example:

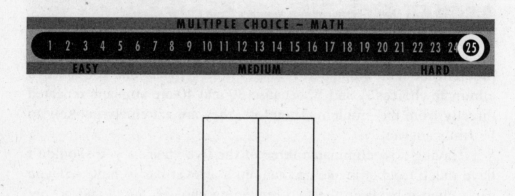

MULTIPLE CHOICE – MATH

1 2 3 4 5 6 7 8 9 10 11 12 13 14 15 16 17 18 19 20 21 22 23 24 **25**

EASY   MEDIUM   HARD

25   The figure above is a square divided into two nonoverlapping regions. What is the greatest number of nonoverlapping regions that can be obtained by drawing any two additional straight lines?

(A) 4
(B) 5
(C) 6
(D) 7
(E) 8

HERE'S HOW TO CRACK IT

This is the last question from its section. Therefore, it's extremely difficult. One reason it's so difficult is that it is badly and confusingly written. (Jim's strengths are mathematical, not verbal.) Here's a clearer way to think of it: The drawing is a pizza cut in half; what's the greatest number of pieces you could end up with if you make just two more cuts with a knife?

The *most obvious* way to cut the pizza would be to make cuts perpendicular to the center cut, dividing the pizza into six pieces, like this:

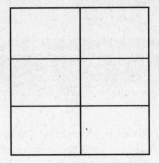

There, that was fast and easy. Which means? Which means that 6 can't possibly be correct and that choice C can be eliminated. If finding Jim's answer were that simple, Joe Bloggs would have gotten this question right and it would have been an easy question, not a difficult one.

Will this fact help you eliminate any other choices? Yes. Because you know that if you can divide the pizza into at least six pieces, neither five nor four could be the greatest number of pieces into which it can be divided. Six is a greater number than either 5 or 4; if you can get six pieces you can also get five or four. You can thus eliminate choices A and B as well.

Now you've narrowed it down to two choices. Which will you pick? You shouldn't waste time trying to find the exact answer to a question like this. It isn't testing any mathematical principle, and you won't figure out the trick unless you get lucky. If you can't use another of our techniques to eliminate the remaining wrong answer, you should just guess and go on. Heads you win a dollar, tails you lose a quarter. (Jim's answer is D. Our third technique, incidentally, will enable you to zero in on it exactly. Keep reading.)

In case you're wondering, here's how Jim divides the pizza:

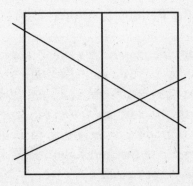

Here's another example:

24   A 25-foot ladder is placed against a vertical wall of a building with the bottom of the ladder standing on concrete 7 feet from the base of the building. If the top of the ladder slips down 4 feet, then the bottom of the ladder will slide out how many feet?

(A) 4 ft
(B) 5 ft
(C) 6 ft
(D) 7 ft
(E) 8 ft

HERE'S HOW TO CRACK IT

Which answer seems simple and obvious? Choice A, of course. If a ladder slips down 4 feet on one end, it *seems* obvious that it would slide out 4 feet on the other.

What does that mean? It means that we can eliminate choice A. If 4 feet were Jim's answer, Joe Bloggs would get this problem right and it would be an easy one, not among the hardest in its section.

Choice A also repeats a number from the problem, which means we can be doubly certain that it's wrong. Which other choice repeats a number? Choice D. So we can eliminate that one, too.

If you don't know how to do this problem, working on it further probably won't get you anywhere. You've eliminated two choices; you should guess and move on. (Jim's answer is E. Finding it would require you to use the Pythagorean theorem—see chapter 10.)

> *No matter how thoroughly you prepare yourself, when you actually take the SAT you may find that you are irresistibly attracted to an "obvious" choice on a hard SAT math question. You'll look at the problem and see no other possible solution. If this happens, you will probably say to yourself, "Aha! I've found an exception to the Joe Bloggs rule!" Trust us: Don't be tempted. Eliminate and guess.*

SIMPLE OPERATIONS = WRONG ANSWERS ON HARD QUESTIONS

Since Joe Bloggs doesn't understand most difficult mathematical operations, he is attracted most to solutions that use very simple arithmetic. Therefore, all such solutions should be eliminated on hard SAT questions.

Here's an example:

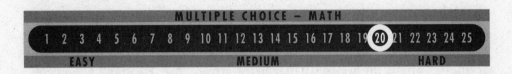

20 A dress is selling for $100 after a 20 percent discount. What was the original selling price?

(A) $200
(B) $125
(C) $120
(D) $80
(E) $75

HERE'S HOW TO CRACK IT

When Joe Bloggs looks at this problem he sees "20 percent less than $100" and is attracted to choice D. Therefore, you must eliminate it. If finding the answer were that easy, Joe Bloggs would be on his way to Harvard. Joe is also attracted to choice C, which is 20 percent more than $100. Again, eliminate.

With two attractors out of the way, you ought to be able to solve this problem quickly. The dress is on sale, which means that its original price must have been more than its current price. That means that Jim's answer has to be greater than $100. Two of the remaining choices, A and B, fulfill this requirement. Now you can ask yourself:

(A) Is $100 20 percent less than $200? No. Eliminate.

(B) Is $100 20 percent less than $125? Could be. This must be Jim's answer. (It is.)

> *Once you have eliminated the Joe Bloggs attractors, look at the problem again. With the attractors out of the way, you can often find Jim's answer quickly by using common sense to eliminate less attractive but equally obvious incorrect choices. Eliminating an attractor is getting rid of a temptation. Once it's gone, the correct answer is often apparent.*

LEAST/GREATEST

Hard SAT math problems will sometimes ask you to find the least (or greatest) number that fulfills certain conditions. On such problems, Joe Bloggs is attracted to the answer choice containing the least (or greatest) number. You can therefore eliminate such choices. (ETS sometimes uses similar words that mean the same thing: most, maximum, fewest, and so on. The same rules apply to problems containing all such terms.)

Look back at the square problem on page 146. The question asks you for the greatest number of regions into which the square can be divided. Which choice will therefore attract Joe Bloggs? Choice E. Eight is the greatest number among the choices offered, so, it will seem right to Joe. Therefore, you can eliminate it.

Here's another example:

17   If 3 parallel lines are cut by 3 nonparallel lines, what is the maximum number of intersections possible?

(A)   9
(B)   10
(C)   11
(D)   12
(E)   13

HERE'S HOW TO CRACK IT

The problem asks you for the maximum, or greatest number. What is the maximum number among the choices? It is 13; therefore, you can eliminate choice E.

By the simple operations = wrong answers rule that we just discussed, you can also eliminate choice A. Joe's preference for simple arithmetic makes him tend to think that the answer to this problem can be found by multiplying 3 times 3. The simple operation leads quickly to an answer of 9, which must therefore be wrong.

Jim's answer is D. Here's how he gets it:

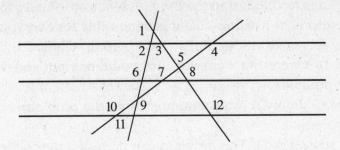

"IT CANNOT BE DETERMINED"

Once or twice on every math SAT, the fifth answer choice on a problem will be

> (E) It cannot be determined from the information given.

The Joe Bloggs principle makes these questions easy to crack. Here's why:

Joe Bloggs can *never* determine the correct answer on difficult SAT problems. Therefore, when Joe sees this answer choice on a difficult problem, he is greatly attracted to it.

What does this mean?

It means that if "cannot be determined" is offered as an answer choice on a difficult problem, it is almost certainly wrong. In fact, if "cannot be determined" is offered as an answer choice on one of the last problems in a math section, you should eliminate it.

Here's an example:

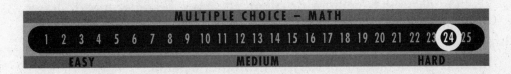

MULTIPLE CHOICE – MATH

1 2 3 4 5 6 7 8 9 10 11 12 13 14 15 16 17 18 19 20 21 22 23 **24** 25

EASY   MEDIUM   HARD

24 If the average of x, y, and 80 is 6 more than the average of y, z, and 80, what is the value of $x \_ z$?

(A) 2
(B) 3
(C) 6
(D) 18
(E) It cannot be determined from the information given.

HERE'S HOW TO CRACK IT

This problem is next to last in a section. It looks absolutely impossible to Joe. Therefore, he assumes that it is impossible for everyone, and he selects E as his answer. Naturally, he is wrong. Choice E should be eliminated. If it were Jim's answer, Joe would be right and this would be an easy problem.

Choice C simply repeats a number from the problem, so you can also eliminate that.

Jim's answer is D. The problem can be restated as follows:

$$\frac{x + y + 80}{3} - 6 = \frac{y + z + 80}{3} \text{ , which means that}$$

$$\frac{x}{3} + \frac{y}{3} + \frac{80}{3} - 6 = \frac{y}{3} + \frac{z}{3} + \frac{80}{3}$$

Subtracting common terms from both sides of the equation yields

$$\frac{x}{3} - 6 = \frac{z}{3}$$

Multiplying both sides by 3 to eliminate the fractions yields

$$x - 18 = z \text{, or}$$
$$x - z = 18$$

Should "cannot be determined" always be eliminated as an answer choice?

No!

On easy and medium problems, "cannot be determined" has a very good chance of being Jim's answer. Specifically, "cannot be determined" has about one chance in two of being Jim's answer if it is offered as a choice in an easy or medium question.

What this means is that if you are stuck on an easy or medium problem and "cannot be determined" is one of the choices, you should pick it and move on. You will have one chance in two of being correct.

> *Quantitative comparisons (which offer "cannot be determined" as a choice on every problem) are a special case and will be dealt with separately.*

JOE BLOGGS MATH SUMMARY

1. Joe Bloggs gets the easy math SAT questions right and the hard ones wrong.

2. On difficult problems, Joe Bloggs is attracted to easy solutions arrived at through methods he understands. Therefore, you should eliminate obvious, simple answers on difficult questions.

3. On difficult problems, Joe Bloggs is also attracted to answer choices that simply repeat numbers from the problem. Therefore, you should eliminate any such choices.

4. On difficult problems that ask you to find the least (or greatest) number that fulfills certain conditions, you can eliminate the answer choice containing the least (or greatest) number.

5. On difficult problems, you can eliminate any answer choice that says "It cannot be determined from the information given."

Chapter 9
The Calculator

THE CALCULATOR

You are allowed (but not required) to use a calculator when you take the SAT. You should definitely do so. A calculator can be enormously helpful on certain types of SAT math problems. This chapter will give you general information about how to use your calculator. Other math chapters will give you specific information about using your calculator in particular situations.

You'll need to bring your own calculator when you take the SAT. If you don't own one now, you can buy one for under ten dollars, or you can ask your math teacher about borrowing one. If you can possibly buy one, you should do it, and you should buy it far enough ahead of time to practice with it before you take the test. Even if you now use a calculator regularly in your math class at school, you should still read this chapter and the other math chapters carefully and practice the techniques we describe.

You don't need a fancy calculator for the SAT. A plain old inexpensive calculator with four functions (add, subtract, multiply, divide) is plenty. Such a calculator will probably also have a square root key, which may help you once or twice. If you have a fancier calculator, such as a scientific calculator, you can still use it, but the extra functions won't help you. You will be less likely to make careless errors if you use a calculator that has a relatively large screen and relatively large keys.

The only danger in using a calculator on the SAT is that you may be tempted to use it in situations where it won't help you. Joe Bloggs thinks his calculator will solve all his difficulties with math. It won't. Occasionally, it may even cause him to miss a problem that he might have answered correctly on his own. But if you practice and use a little caution, you will find that your calculator will help you a great deal.

WHAT A CALCULATOR IS GOOD AT

Here is a complete list of what a calculator is good at on the SAT:

1. Arithmetic computation

2. Converting fractions to decimals

3. Comparing fractions

4. Square roots

5. Percentages

6. Nothing else

We'll discuss the calculator's role in most of these areas in the next chapter, which is about SAT arithmetic, and in other chapters.

CALCULATOR ARITHMETIC

Adding, subtracting, multiplying, and dividing integers and decimals is easy on a calculator. The only thing you need to be careful with is keying in the numbers. A calculator will give you an incorrect answer to an arithmetic calculation only if you don't press the correct keys. Here are two things to watch out for:

1. Be sure to check each number on the display as you key it in

2. Be sure to press the on/off or clear-all key after you finish each problem or each separate step

The main thing to remember about a calculator is that it can't help you find the answer to a question you don't understand. If you wouldn't know how to solve a particular problem using pencil and paper, you won't know how to solve it using a calculator, either. Your calculator will help you, but it won't take the place of a solid understanding of basic SAT mathematics.

USE YOUR PAPER FIRST

When you use your calculator, you must be sure to set up the problem or equation on paper first. By doing so, you will eliminate the possibility of getting lost or confused. This is especially important when solving the problem involves a number of separate steps. The basic idea is to use your scratch paper to make a plan, and then use your calculator to execute it.

Using scratch paper will also give you a paper record of what you have done if you change your mind or run into trouble. If you suddenly find that you need to try a different approach to a problem, you may not have to go all the way back to the beginning. Having a paper record will also make it easier for you to check your work, if you have time to do so.

Avoid using the memory function on your calculator (if it has one). Because you can use your test booklet as scratch paper, you don't need to juggle numbers within the calculator itself. Instead of storing the result of a calculation in the calculator, write it on your scratch paper, clear your calculator, and move to the next step of the problem. A calculator's memory is fleeting; scratch paper is forever.

ORDER OF OPERATIONS

In the next chapter, we will discuss the proper order of operations when solving equations in which several operations must be performed. Be sure you understand this information, because it applies to calculators as much as it does to pencil and paper computations. (In the next chapter, we will teach you a mnemonic device that will enable you to remember this easily.) You must always perform calculations in the proper order.

SUMMARY

1. You should definitely use a calculator on the SAT.

2. You need to bring your own calculator when you take the test. You don't need a fancy one.

3. Even if you already use a calculator regularly, you should practice with it before the test.

4. Be careful when you key in numbers on your calculator. Check each number on the display as you key it in. Clear your work after you finish each problem or each separate step.

5. The main thing to remember about a calculator is that it can't help you find the answer to a question you don't understand. If you wouldn't know how to solve a particular problem using pencil and paper, you won't know how to solve it using a calculator, either.

6. When you use your calculator, you must be sure to set up the problem or equation on paper first. By doing so, you will eliminate the possibility of getting lost or confused.

7. Avoid using the memory function on your calculator (if it has one). Scratch paper works better.

8. Whether you are using your calculator or paper and a pencil, you must always perform calculations in the proper order.

Chapter 10
Arithmetic

ARITHMETIC OPERATIONS
THERE ARE ONLY SIX OPERATIONS

There are only six arithmetic operations that you will ever need to perform on the SAT:

1. addition $(3 + 3)$

2. subtraction $(3 - 3)$

3. multiplication $(3 \times 3 \text{ or } 3 \cdot 3)$

4. division $(3 \div 3)$

5. raising to a power (3^3)

6. finding a square root or a cube root $(\sqrt{3} \text{ or } \sqrt[3]{3})$

If you're like most students, you probably haven't paid much serious attention to these topics since junior high school. You'll need to learn about them again if you want to do well on the SAT. By the time you take the test, using them should be automatic. All the arithmetic concepts are fairly basic, but you'll have to know them cold. You'll also have to know when and how to use your calculator, which will be quite helpful.

In this chapter, we'll deal with each of these six topics.

WHAT DO YOU GET?

You should know the following arithmetic terms:

1. The result of addition is a *sum* or *total*.

2. The result of subtraction is a *difference*.

3. The result of multiplication is a *product*.

4. The result of division is a *quotient*.

5. In the expression 5^2, the 2 is called an *exponent*. The entire expression is an example of *exponential notation*.

THE SIX OPERATIONS MUST BE PERFORMED IN THE PROPER ORDER

Very often solving an equation on the SAT will require you to perform several different operations, one after another. These operations must be performed in the proper order. In general, the problems are written in such a way that you won't have trouble deciding what comes first. In cases where you are uncertain, you only need to remember the following sentence:

Please Excuse My Dear Aunt Sally

That's **PEMDAS**, for short. The acronym PEMDAS stands for **P**arentheses, **E**xponents, **M**ultiplication, **D**ivision, **A**ddition, **S**ubtraction. First you clear the parentheses; then you take care of the exponents; then you multiply, divide, add, and subtract. (We'll have more to say about exponents in a little while.)

The following drill will help you learn the order in which to perform the six operations. First set up the equations on paper. Then use your calculator for the arithmetic. Make sure you perform the operations in the correct order.

Solve each of the following problems by performing the indicated operations in the proper order. Answers can be found on page 360.

$$107 + (109 - 107) = \underline{\hspace{2cm}}$$

$$(7 \times 5) + 3 = \underline{\hspace{2cm}}$$

$$6 - 3(6 - 3) = \underline{\hspace{2cm}}$$

$$2 \times [7 - (6 \div 3)] = \underline{\hspace{2cm}}$$

$$10 - (9 - 8 - 6) = \underline{\hspace{2cm}}$$

PARENTHESES CAN HELP YOU SOLVE EQUATIONS

Using parentheses to regroup information in SAT arithmetic problems can be very helpful. In order to do this you need to understand two basic laws that you may have forgotten since the days when you last took arithmetic: the associative law and the distributive law. You don't need to remember the name of either law, but you do need to know how each works. Let's look at them one at a time.

THE ASSOCIATIVE LAW

There are really two associative laws, one for addition and one for multiplication. But both laws say basically the same thing, so we can combine them into one: *When you are adding or multiplying a series of numbers, you can group or regroup the numbers any way you like.* For example:

$$a + (b + c) = (a + b) + c = b + (a + c)$$
$$a(bc) = (ab)c = b(ac)$$

THE DISTRIBUTIVE LAW

This is one of the most important principles on the SAT. You must be absolutely certain that you know it:

$$a(b + c) = ab + ac$$
$$a(b - c) = ab - ac$$

This law is so important that you must *always* apply it whenever you have a chance. If a problem gives you information in "factored form"—$a(b + c)$—then you should multiply through or *distribute* the first variable before you do anything else. If you are given information that has already been distributed—$ab + ac$—then you should factor out the common term, putting the information back in factored form. Very often on the SAT, simply doing this will enable you to spot Jim's answer.

NOTE

Earlier we told you that you should perform all operations within parentheses first. The distributive law is something of an exception to that rule. It gives you a different route to the same result.

For example:

Distributive: $2(3 + 4) = 2(3) + 2(4) = 6 + 8 = 14$
Parentheses first: $2(3 + 4) = 2(7) = 14$

You get the same answer each way. But whenever you see a chance to apply the distributive law, you should do it.

The following drill illustrates the distributive law.

DRILL 2

Simply rewrite each problem by either distributing or factoring, whichever is called for. Then use your calculator to solve questions 1 and 2. Questions 3, 4, and 5 have no numbers in them. Therefore, they can't be solved with a calculator. Answers can be found on page 361.

1. $6(57 + 18) =$ _____

2. $51(52) + 51(53) + 51(54) =$ _____

3. $a(b + c - d) =$ _____

4. $xy - xz =$ _____

5. $abc + xyc =$ _____

FRACTIONS

A FRACTION IS JUST ANOTHER WAY OF EXPRESSING DIVISION

The expression $\frac{x}{y}$ is exactly the same thing as $x \div y$. The expression $\frac{1}{2}$ means nothing more than $1 \div 2$. In the fraction $\frac{x}{y}$, x is known as the *numerator* and y is known as the *denominator*. (You won't need to know these terms on the SAT, but you will need to know them to follow the explanations in this book.)

ADDING AND SUBTRACTING FRACTIONS WITH THE SAME DENOMINATOR

To add two or more fractions that all have the same denominator, simply add up the numerators and put the sum over one of the denominators. For example:

$$\frac{1}{100} + \frac{4}{100} = \frac{1+4}{100} = \frac{5}{100}$$

Subtraction works exactly the same way:

$$\frac{4}{100} - \frac{1}{100} = \frac{4-1}{100} = \frac{3}{100}$$

MULTIPLYING ALL FRACTIONS

Multiplying fractions is easy. Just multiply the numerators and put their product over the product of the denominators. (If you need to, you can easily do this on your calculator, as long as you set up the problem on paper first, so that you don't get confused.) Here's an example:

$$\frac{4}{5} \times \frac{5}{6} = \frac{20}{30}$$

Always look vertically or diagonally to see if two vertical or diagonal numbers can be cancelled out. When you multiply fractions, all you are really doing is performing one multiplication example on top of another.

> *In any problem involving large or confusing fractions, try to reduce the fractions, before you do anything else.*

For example, you should never multiply two fractions before looking to see if you can reduce either or both. If you reduce first, your final answer will be in the form that ETS is looking for.

$$\frac{12}{60} = \frac{2 \times 2 \times 3}{2 \times 2 \times 3 \times 5}$$

$$= \frac{2^1 \times 2^1 \times 3^1}{2^1 \times 2^1 \times 3^1 \times 5}$$

$$= \frac{1}{5}$$

Another way to do this is to divide both the numerator and the denominator by the largest number that is a factor of both. In the preceding example, 12 is a factor of both 12 and 60. Dividing numerator and denominator by 12 also yields the reduced fraction $\frac{1}{5}$.

REDUCING FRACTIONS

When you add or multiply fractions, you will very often end up with a big fraction that is hard to work with. You can almost always *reduce* such a fraction into one that is easier to handle.

To reduce a fraction, divide both the numerator and the denominator by the largest number that is a factor of both. For example, to reduce $\frac{12}{60}$, divide both the numerator and the denominator by 12, which is the largest number that is a factor of both. Dividing 12 by 12 yields 1; dividing 60 by 12 yields 5. The reduced fraction is $\frac{1}{5}$.

If you can't immediately find the largest number that is a factor of both, find *any* number that is a factor of both and divide both the numerator and denominator by that. Your calculations will take a little longer, but you'll end up in the same place. In the previous example, even if you don't see that 12 is a factor of both 12 and 60, you can no doubt see that 2 is a factor of both. Dividing numerator and denominator by 2 yields $\frac{6}{30}$. Doing the same thing again yields $\frac{3}{15}$. You can't divide by 2 again, but you can divide by 3. Doing so yields $\frac{1}{5}$.

Once again, you have arrived at Jim's answer.

ADDING AND SUBTRACTING FRACTIONS WITH DIFFERENT DENOMINATORS

Before you can add or subtract two or more fractions that don't all have the same denominator, you have to give them the same denominator. The way to do this is to multiply each fraction by a number that will change its denominator without changing the value of the fraction. What number will do this? *The number 1, when it is expressed as the denominator of the other fraction over itself.*

That's a mouthful, but it's easy to see with an example:

$$\frac{1}{3} + \frac{1}{2} =$$

$$\left(\frac{1}{3}\right)\left(\frac{2}{2}\right) + \left(\frac{1}{2}\right)\left(\frac{3}{3}\right) =$$

$$\frac{2}{6} + \frac{3}{6} =$$

$$\frac{5}{6}$$

ANALYSIS

All we've done here is multiply both fractions by 1 ($\frac{2}{2}$ and $\frac{3}{3}$ both equal 1). This doesn't change the value of either fraction, but it does change the form of both.

DIVIDING ALL FRACTIONS

To divide one fraction by another, invert the second fraction and multiply. To *invert* a fraction is to stand it on its head—to put its denominator over its numerator. Doing this is extremely easy, as long as you remember how it works. Here's an example:

$$\frac{2}{3} \div \frac{3}{4} =$$
$$\frac{2}{3} \times \frac{4}{3} =$$
$$\frac{8}{9}$$

Be careful not to cancel or reduce until *after* you dlip the second fraction. You can even do the same thing with fractions whose numerators and/or denominators are fractions. These problems look quite frightening but they're actually easy if you keep your cool. Here's an example:

$$\frac{4}{\frac{4}{3}} =$$

$$\frac{\frac{4}{1}}{\frac{4}{3}} =$$

$$\frac{4}{1} \div \frac{4}{3} =$$

$$\frac{4}{1} \times \frac{3}{4} =$$

$$\frac{\cancel{4}}{1} \times \frac{3}{\cancel{4}} =$$

$$\frac{3}{1} =$$
$$3$$

CONVERTING MIXED NUMBERS TO FRACTIONS

A mixed number is a number like $2\frac{3}{4}$. It is the sum of an integer and a fraction. When you see mixed numbers on the SAT, you should usually convert them to ordinary fractions. You can do this easily by using a combination of the techniques we've just outlined. Here's how:

1. Convert the integer to a fraction with the same denominator as the fraction in the mixed number. With $2\frac{3}{4}$, in other words, you would convert the 2 to the fraction $\frac{8}{4}$. Note that $\frac{8}{4}$ equals 2 and has the same denominator as $\frac{3}{4}$.

2. Now that you have two fractions with the same denominator, you can simply add them:

$$\frac{8}{4} + \frac{3}{4} = \frac{11}{4}$$

ANALYSIS

The mixed number $2\frac{3}{4}$ is exactly the same as the fraction $\frac{11}{4}$. We converted the one to the other because fractions are easier to work with than mixed numbers.

COMPARING FRACTIONS

The SAT sometimes contains problems that require you to compare one fraction with another and determine which is larger. Many students have trouble with these problems, but there is nothing difficult about them. To compare two fractions, simply use your calculator to convert each fraction to a decimal. Then compare the decimals. For example, a problem might require you to determine which fraction is bigger, $\frac{9}{10}$ or $\frac{10}{11}$. All you have to do is use your calculator to convert each fraction to a decimal by performing the division problem that it stands for. That is, convert $\frac{9}{10}$ to a decimal by dividing 9 by 10 on your calculator, yielding 0.9. Now divide 10 by 11, yielding 0.9090909. Which is bigger? Clearly 0.9090909 is. That means that $\frac{10}{11}$ is bigger than $\frac{9}{10}$.

COMPARING MORE THAN TWO FRACTIONS

If you are asked to compare more than two fractions, convert all the fractions into decimals and line them up. See page 173 for how to compare decimals.

FRACTIONS BEHAVE IN PECULIAR WAYS

Joe Bloggs has trouble with fractions because they don't always behave the way he thinks they ought to. For example, because 4 is obviously greater than 2, Joe Bloggs sometimes forgets that $\frac{1}{4}$ is *less than* $\frac{1}{2}$. He becomes especially confused when the numerator is some number other than 1. For example, $\frac{2}{6}$ is less than $\frac{2}{5}$.

Joe also has a hard time understanding that when you multiply one fraction by another, you will get a fraction that is smaller than either of the first two. For example:

$$\frac{1}{2} \times \frac{1}{4} = \frac{1}{8}$$

$$\frac{1}{8} < \frac{1}{2}$$

$$\frac{1}{8} < \frac{1}{4}$$

One way to make fractions seem less peculiar is to use your calculator to convert them to decimals.

REMEMBERING EVERYTHING AT ONCE

Very often on problems dealing with fractions, you will have to apply several of the rules we've just given you in order to find an answer. For example, you may have to convert a mixed number to a fraction, then reduce that fraction, then find a common denominator with another fraction, and so on. Your goal in doing all this is to express the problem in the simplest form possible. The simpler a problem is, the less likely you will be to make an error.

> *The most common source of mistakes on word problems involving fractions is misreading. Read fraction word problems carefully.*

The following drill will give you practice with handling fractions.

If you have trouble on any of these problems, go back and review the information just outlined. Answers can be found on page 361.

1. Reduce $\dfrac{18}{6}$ as far as you can.

2. Convert $6\dfrac{1}{5}$ to a fraction.

3. $2\dfrac{1}{3} - 3\dfrac{3}{5} =$

4. $\dfrac{5}{18} \times \dfrac{6}{25} =$

5. $\dfrac{3}{4} \div \dfrac{7}{8} =$

6. $\dfrac{\dfrac{2}{5}}{5} =$

7. $\dfrac{\dfrac{1}{3}}{\dfrac{3}{4}} =$

DECIMALS

A DECIMAL IS JUST ANOTHER WAY OF EXPRESSING A FRACTION

Every fraction can be expressed as a decimal. To find a fraction's decimal equivalent, simply divide the numerator by the denominator. (You can do this easily with your calculator.) For example:

$$\frac{3}{5} =$$

$$3 \div 5 =$$

$$5\overline{)3.0}^{\,0.6}$$
$$\underline{3.0}$$

$$= 0.6$$

NOT ALL DECIMALS HAVE (VISIBLE) DECIMAL POINTS

How many of these numbers are decimals?

$$0.6 \quad 56 \quad -12$$

Answer: They all are. It's just that we usually don't bother to note the decimal point on a number like 56 or −12. But these numbers could easily be written with decimal points, like this:

$$56.0 \quad\quad -12.0$$

Keep this in mind as you read what follows.

THE POSITION OF THE DECIMAL POINT DETERMINES THE VALUE OF THE DIGITS

The following table will show you how the value of a number is determined by the placement of the decimal point:

$$1,420 \quad\quad = 1,000 + 400 + 20 + 0$$

$$142.0 \quad\quad = 142 = 100 + 40 + 2$$

$$14.20 \quad\quad = 14.2 = 10 + 4 + \frac{2}{10}$$

$$1.420 \quad = 1.42 = 1 + \frac{4}{10} + \frac{2}{100}$$

$$0.1420 \quad = 0.142 = \frac{1}{10} + \frac{4}{100} + \frac{2}{1,000}$$

$$0.01420 = 0.0142 = \frac{0}{10} + \frac{1}{100} + \frac{4}{1,000} + \frac{2}{10,000}$$

ADDING, SUBTRACTING, MULTIPLYING, AND DIVIDING DECIMALS

Manipulating decimals is easy with a calculator. Simply punch in the numbers—being especially careful to get the decimal point in the right place every time—and read the result from the display. A calculator makes these operations easy. In fact, working with decimals is one area on the SAT where your calculator will regularly prevent you from making careless errors. You won't have to line up decimal points or remember what happens when you divide. The calculator will keep track of everything for you, as long as you punch in the correct numbers to begin with. Just be sure to practice carefully before you go to the test center.

Here are some examples to practice on:

DRILL 4

$$0.43 \times 0.87 = \underline{\hspace{2cm}}$$

$$\frac{43 + .731}{0.03} = \underline{\hspace{2cm}}$$

$$3.72 \div 0.02 = \underline{\hspace{2cm}}$$

$$0.71 - 3.6 = \underline{\hspace{2cm}}$$

COMPARING DECIMALS

Some SAT problems will ask you to determine whether one decimal is larger or smaller than another. Many students have trouble doing this. It isn't difficult, though, and you will do fine as long as you *remember to line up the decimal points and fill in missing zeros.*

Here's an example:

Problem: Which is larger, 0.0099, or 0.01?

Solution: Simply place one decimal over the other with the decimal points lined up, like this:

        0.0099
        0.01

To make the solution seem clearer, you can add two zeros to the right of 0.01. (You can always add zeros to the right of a decimal without changing its value.) Now you have this:

        0.0099
        0.0100

Which decimal is larger? Clearly, 0.0100 is, just as 100 is larger than 99. (Remember that $0.0099 = \frac{99}{10,000}$, while $0.0100 = \frac{100}{10,000}$. Now the answer seems obvious, doesn't it?)

ANALYSIS

Joe Bloggs has a terrible time on this problem. Because 99 is obviously larger than 1, he tends to think that 0.0099 must be larger than

0.01. But it isn't. Don't get sloppy on problems like this! Jim loves to trip up Joe Bloggs with decimals. In fact, any time you encounter a problem involving the comparison of decimals, you should stop and ask yourself whether you are just about to make a Joe Bloggs mistake.

MONEY!

If you get confused about decimals, remember dollars and cents. $3.35 is a decimal. It means 3 dollars plus $\frac{35}{100}$ of a dollar. $4.20 equals 4 dollars plus $\frac{2}{10}$ of a dollar. $0.50 equals half of a dollar.

> *When you get stuck on a decimal problem, convert the decimal into its money equivalent to clear your head and remind yourself what decimals are all about.*

RATIOS

A RATIO IS A FRACTION

Many students get extremely nervous when they are asked to work with ratios. But there's no need to be nervous. In fact, you just finished working with some ratios: every fraction is a ratio. Furthermore, every ratio can be expressed as a fraction. The fraction $\frac{1}{2}$ is just another way of expressing "the ratio of 1 to 2" or, in the customary ratio notation, 1:2. Thus, there are three ways of denoting a ratio:

1. $\frac{x}{y}$

2. the ratio of x to y

3. $x:y$

IF YOU CAN DO IT TO A FRACTION, YOU CAN DO IT TO A RATIO

Since a ratio is a fraction, it can be converted to a decimal or a percentage. All the following are methods of expressing the ratio of 1 to 2:

1. $\frac{1}{2}$

2. 1:2

3. 0.5

4. 50 percent

The ratio of 2 to 1 can be expressed as follows:

1. $\frac{2}{1}$

2. 2:1

3. 2

4. 200 percent

You can also do everything else that you've learned to do with fractions: cross-multiply, find common denominators, reduce, and so on.

THINK OF A RATIO AS A NUMBER OF PARTS

If a class contains 3 students and the ratio of boys to girls in that class is 2:1, how many boys and how many girls are there in the class? Of course: There are 2 boys and 1 girl.

Now, suppose a class contains 24 students and the ratio of boys to girls is still 2:1. How many boys and how many girls are there in the class? This is a little harder, but the answer is easy to find if you think about it. There are 16 boys and 8 girls.

How did we get the answer? We added up the number of "parts" in the ratio (2 parts boys plus 1 part girls, or 3 parts altogether) and divided it into the total number of students. In other words, we divided 24 by 3. This told us that the class contained 3 equal parts of 8 students each. From the given ratio (2:1), we knew that two of these parts consisted of boys and one of them consisted of girls.

An easy way to keep track of all this is to use a tool we call the ratio box. Every time you have a ratio problem, set up a ratio box with the information provided in the problem and use it to find Jim's answer. Here's how it works.

Let's go back to our class containing 24 students, in which the ratio of boys to girls is 2:1. Quickly sketch a table that has columns and rows, like this:

	Boys	Girls	Whole
Ratio (parts)	2	1	3
Multiply By			
Actual Number			24

This is the information you have been given. The ratio is 2:1, so you have 2 parts boys and 1 part girls, for a total of 3 parts altogether. You also know that the actual number of students in the whole class is 24. You start by writing these numbers in proper spaces in your box.

Your goal is to fill in the two empty spaces in the bottom row. To do that, you will multiply each number in the parts row by the same number. To find that number, look in the last column. What number would you multiply by 3 to yield 24? You should see easily that you would multiply by 8. Therefore, write an 8 in all three blanks in the multiply-by row. (The spaces in this row will *always* contain the same number, although of course it won't always be an 8.) Here's what your ratio box should look like now:

	Boys	Girls	Whole
Ratio (parts)	2	1	3
Multiply By	8	8	8
Actual Number			24

The next step is to fill in the empty spaces in the bottom row. You do that the same way you did in the last column, by multiplying. First, multiply the numbers in the boys column ($2 \times 8 = 16$). Then multiply the numbers in the girls column ($1 \times 8 = 16$). Here's what your box should look like now:

	Boys	Girls	Whole
Ratio (parts)	2	1	3
Multiply By	8	8	8
Actual Number	16	8	24

Now you have enough information to answer any question that ETS might ask you. For example:

- What is the ratio of boys to girls? You can see easily from the ratio (parts) row of the box that the ratio is 2:1.

- What is the ratio of girls to boys? You can see easily from the ratio (parts) row of the box that the ratio is 1:2.

- What is the total number of boys in the class? You can see easily from the bottom row of the box that it is 16.

- What is the total number of girls in the class? You can see easily from the bottom row of the box that it is 8.

- What fractional part of the class is boys? There are 16 boys in a class of 24, so the fraction representing the boys is $\frac{16}{24}$, which can be reduced to $\frac{2}{3}$.

As you can see, the ratio box is an easy way to find, organize, and keep track of information on ratio problems. And it works the same no matter what information you are given. Just remember that all the boxes in the multiply-by row will always contain the same number.

Here's another example:

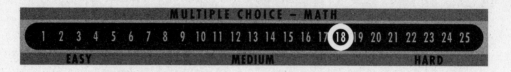

18 In a jar of red and green jelly beans, the ratio
of green jelly beans to red jelly beans is 5:3.
If the jar contains a total of 160 jelly beans,
how many of them are red?

(A) 20
(B) 36
(C) 45
(D) 60
(E) 100

HERE'S HOW TO CRACK IT

First, sketch out a ratio box:

	Green	Red	Whole
Ratio (parts)	5	3	8
Multiply By			
Actual Number			160

Now find the multiplier. What to you multiply by 8 to yield 160?
You multiply 8 by 20. Now write 20 in each box on the multiply-by
row:

	Green	Red	Whole
Ratio (parts)	5	3	8
Multiply By	20	20	20
Actual Number			160

The problem asks you to find how many red jelly beans there are. Go to the red column and multiply 3 by 20. The answer if 60. Jim's answer is D. Notice that you would have set up the box in exactly the same way if the question had asked you to determine how many jelly beans were green. (How many are green? The answer is 5×20, which is 100.)

HERE'S ANOTHER WAY TO CRACK IT
The ratio is 5:3 in this problem, which means there are 8 parts altogether. How many jelly beans are in a part? To find out all we have to do is *divide the total number of jelly beans by the total number of parts:* 160 divided by 8 equals 20. That means each part consists of 20 jelly beans. How many parts contain red jelly beans? Three. That means there are 60 red jelly beans and Jim's answer is D.

PROPORTIONS ARE EQUAL RATIOS
Very often on SAT math problems you will be given a problem containing two proportional, or equal, ratios from which one piece of information is missing.

Here's an example:

MULTIPLE CHOICE – MATH

1 2 3 4 5 6 7 8 9 10 11 12 13 14 15 16 17 18 19 20 21 22 23 24 25
EASY   MEDIUM   HARD

7 If 2 packages contain a total of 12 doughnuts, how many doughnuts are there in 5 packages?

(A) 12
(B) 24
(C) 30
(D) 36
(E) 60

HERE'S HOW TO CRACK IT
This problem simply describes two equal ratios, one of which is missing a single piece of information. Here's the given information represented as two equal ratios:

$$\frac{2 \text{ (packages)}}{12 \text{ (doughnuts)}} = \frac{5 \text{ (packages)}}{x \text{ (doughnuts)}}$$

Since ratios are fractions, we can treat them exactly like fractions. To find the answer all you have to do is figure out what you could plug in for x that would make $\frac{2}{12} = \frac{5}{x}$. One way to do this is to cross-multiply:

$$\frac{2}{12} \diagdown\diagup \frac{5}{x}$$

$$\text{so, } 2x = 60$$
$$x = 30$$

Jim's answer is C.

PERCENTAGES

PERCENTAGES AREN'T SCARY

There should be nothing frightening about a percentage. It's just a convenient way of expressing a fraction whose denominator is 100.

Percent means "per 100" or "out of 100." If there are 100 questions on your math test and you answer 50 of them, you will have answered 50 out of 100, or $\frac{50}{100}$, or 50 percent. Or, to think of it another way:

$$\frac{part}{\text{whole}} = \frac{x}{100} = x \text{ percent}$$

MEMORIZE THESE PERCENTAGE-DECIMAL-FRACTION EQUIVALENTS

$$0.01 = \frac{1}{100} = 1 \text{ percent} \qquad 0.25 = \frac{1}{4} = 25 \text{ percent}$$

$$0.1 = \frac{1}{10} = 10 \text{ percent} \qquad 0.5 = \frac{1}{2} = 50 \text{ percent}$$

$$0.2 = \frac{1}{5} = 20 \text{ percent} \qquad 0.75 = \frac{3}{4} = 75 \text{ percent}$$

CONVERTING PERCENTAGES TO FRACTIONS

To convert a percentage to a fraction, simply put the percentage over a denominator of 100 and reduce. For example $80 \text{ percent} = \frac{80}{100} = \frac{8}{10} = \frac{4}{5}$.

CONVERTING FRACTIONS TO PERCENTAGES

Since a percentage is just another way of expressing a certain kind of fraction, you shouldn't be surprised that it is easy to convert a fraction to a percentage. To do so, simply divide the numerator by the denominator and move the decimal point in the result two places to the *right*. Here's an example:

Problem: Express $\frac{3}{4}$ as a percentage.

Solution: $\frac{3}{4} = 4\overline{)3.00} = 0.75$ or 75 percent

$$
\begin{array}{r}
0.75 \\
4\overline{)3.00} \\
\underline{28} \\
20 \\
\underline{20}
\end{array}
$$

Converting fractions to percentages is easy with your calculator.

CONVERTING PERCENTAGES TO DECIMALS

To convert a percentage to a decimal, simply move the decimal point two places to the *left*. For example: 25 percent can be expressed as the decimal 0.25; 50 percent is the same as 0.50 or 0.5; 100 percent is the same as 1.00 or 1.

CONVERTING DECIMALS TO PERCENTAGES

To convert a decimal to a percentage just do the opposite of what you did in the preceding instruction. All you have to do is move the decimal point two places to the *right*. Thus, 0.5 = 50 percent; 0.375 = 37.5 percent; 2 = 200 percent.

The following drill will give you practice working with fractions, decimals, and percentages.

Fill in the missing information in the following table. Answers can be found on page 361.

	Fraction	Decimal	Percent
1.	$\dfrac{1}{2}$		
2.		3.0	
3.			0.5
4.	$\dfrac{1}{3}$		

WHAT PERCENT OF WHAT?

Problem:

What number is 10 percent greater than 20?

Solution:

We know that 10 percent of 20 is 2. So the question really reads: What is 2 greater than 20? The answer is 22.

ANALYSIS

Joe Bloggs gets confused on questions like this. You won't if you take them slowly, and solve them one step at a time. The same holds true for problems that ask you what number is a certain percentage *less* than another number. What number is 10 percent less than 500? Well, 10 percent of 500 is 50. The number that is 10 percent less than 500, therefore, is 500 – 50, or 450.

WHAT PERCENT OF WHAT PERCENT OF WHAT?

On harder SAT questions, you may be asked to determine the effect of a *series* of percentage increases or reductions. The key point to remember on such problems is that each *successive* increase or reduction is performed on the result of the *previous* one. Here's an example:

18   A business paid $300 to rent a piece of office equipment for one year. The rent was then increased by 10 percent each year thereafter. How much will the company pay for the first three years it rents the equipment?

    (A) $920
    (B) $960
    (C) $990
    (D) $993
    (E) $999

HERE'S HOW TO CRACK IT

You are being asked to find a business's total rent for a piece of equipment for three years. The easiest way to keep from getting confused on a problem like this is to take it one step at a time. First, make a sort of outline of exactly what you have to find out.

         Year 1:
         Year 2:
         Year 3:

Actually write this down in the margin of your test booklet. There's one slot for each year's rent; Jim's answer will be the total.

You already know the number that goes in the first slot: 300, because that is what the problem says will be paid for the first year.

What number goes in the second slot? 330, because 330 equals 300 plus 10 percent of 300.

Now, here's where you have to pay attention. What number goes in the third slot? *Not 360!* The rent goes up 10 percent each year. This increase is calculated from the *previous* year's rent. That means that the rent for the third year is $363, because 363 equals 330 plus 10 percent of *330*.

Now you are ready to find Jim's answer:

         Year 1:   300
         Year 2:   330
         Year 3:
                  <u>363</u>
                  993

Jim's answer is thus choice D, $993.

> *Never try to solve a problem like this by rewriting it as an equation: $x = y + (y + 0.1y) + [(y + 0.1y) + 0.1(y + 0.1y)]$ or something like that. You may eventually end up with the right answer, but you'll spend too much time doing it and you'll stop enjoying life.*

WHAT PERCENT OF WHAT PERCENT OF YIKES!

Sometimes you may find successive percentage problems in which you aren't given actual numbers to work with. In such cases you need to plug in some numbers.

Here's an example.

21 A number is increased by 25 percent and then decreased by 20 percent. The result is what percent of the original number?

    (A)   80
    (B) 100
    (C) 105
    (D) 120
    (E) 125

HERE'S HOW TO CRACK IT

Using the Joe Bloggs principle, you ought to be able to eliminate three choices right off the bat: A, D, and E. Joe loves easy answers. Choices A, D, and E are all equal to 100 plus or minus 20 or 25. All three choices *seem* right to Joe for different reasons. This is a difficult question, so answers that seem right to Joe must be eliminated. Get rid of them.

A somewhat more subtle Joe Bloggs attractor is choice C. Joe thinks that if you increase a number by 25 percent and then decrease by 20 percent, you end up with a net increase of 5 percent. He has forgotten that in a series of percentage changes (which is what we have here), each successive change is based on the result of the previous one.

We've now eliminated everything but choice B, which is Jim's answer.

Could we have found it without Joe's help? Yes. Here's how:

You aren't given a particular number to work with in this problem—just "a number." Rather than trying to deal with the problem in the abstract, you should immediately plug in a number to work with. What number would be easiest to work with in a percentage problem? Why, 100, of course:

1. 25 percent of 100 is 25, so 100 increased by 25 percent is 125.

2. Now you have to decrease 125 by 20 percent, 20 percent of 125 is 25, so 125 decreased by 20 percent is 100.

3. 100 (our result) is 100 percent of 100 (the number you plugged in), so Jim's answer, once again, is B.

> *Beware of percentage change problems in the difficult questions. The answers to these problems almost always defy common sense. Unless you are careful, you may fall for a Joe Bloggs attractor.*

AVERAGES

WHAT IS AN AVERAGE?

Three different types of averages are used in math problems on the SAT. The three types are arithmetic mean, median, and mode. We'll deal with each type separately.

WHAT IS THE MEAN?

The mean of a set of n numbers is simply the total of the numbers divided by n. In other words, if you want to find the mean of three numbers, you add them up and divide by 3. For example, the mean of 1, 2, and 3 is $\frac{(1 + 2 + 3)}{3}$, or $\frac{6}{3}$, or 2. Here are some other examples.

The mean of -4 and 2 is $\frac{(-4 + 2)}{2}$, or -1

The mean of $\frac{1}{2}$ and $\frac{1}{4}$ is $\frac{\left(\frac{1}{2} + \frac{1}{4}\right)}{2}$, or $\frac{3}{8}$

The mean of 0.1 and 0.2 is $\frac{(0.1 + 0.2)}{2}$, or 0.15

MEANS, TOTALLY

> **The key to solving any problem involving a mean is to find the total of the items before you do anything else.**

This is absolutely crucial. For example, if a problem states that the mean of three test scores is 70, the first thing for you to note is that the total of the three scores is 210 (70×3). If you are then told that one of the three scores is 100, you know that the total of the remaining scores is 110 ($210 - 100$) and that their mean is 55 $\left(\frac{110}{2}\right)$.

ONE ITEM, ONE VOTE

Means are democratic. Every item counts the same as every other, even if there are repeats. For example, the mean of 10, 10, 10, and 50 is $\frac{(10 + 10 + 10 + 50)}{4}$, *not* $\frac{(10 + 50)}{4}$ or $\frac{(10 + 50)}{2}$.

Suppose a student takes two tests and scores an 80 on one and a 50 on the other. The mean score on his tests is $\frac{(80 + 50)}{2}$, or 65. Now, suppose he takes a third test and scores another 50. Does the mean stay the same? No. The new mean is $\frac{(80 + 50 + 50)}{3}$, or 60.

Every item is always counted equally with every other. *This is true even if the item is 0.* For example, the mean of 4, 0, 0, and 0 is $\frac{(4 + 0 + 0 + 0)}{4}$, or 1. It is *not* 4.

THE BEHAVIOR OF MEANS

You should know automatically what happens to the mean in certain situations. Suppose you have taken three tests and earned a mean score of 80. Now you take a fourth test:

1. If the mean score *goes up* as a result, then you know that your score on the fourth test was greater than 80.

2. If the mean score *stays the same*, then your fourth score was exactly 80.

3. If the mean score *goes down*, then your fourth score was less than 80.

MEANS: ADVANCED PRINCIPLES

Difficult mean problems are often difficult only because some of the information is missing. Here's an example.

PROBLEM:

A group of 10 students has a mean test score of 80 on the test. If 4 of the students have a mean score is 65, what is the mean for the remaining 6 students?

SOLUTION:

The first thing you must do on mean problems is find the total. If 10 students have a mean score of 80, their total score is 800 (because 10 × 80 = 800). If 4 students have a mean score of 65, their total score is 260 (because 4 × 65 = 260). To find the total score of the remaining 6 students, subtract 260 from 800. The result is 540. To find the mean score of the remaining 6 students, divide 540 by 6. The answer is 90.

WHAT IS A MEDIAN?

The median of a group of numbers is the number that is exactly in the middle of the group when the group is arranged from smallest to largest, as on a number line. For example, in the group 3,6,6,6,6,7,8,9,10,10,11, the median is 7. Five numbers come before 7 in the group, and 5 come after.

It's easy to remember what median means. On a highway, the median is the strip of grass than runs right down the middle. In a group of numbers, the median is the number that is sitting right in the middle of the group. It's the number sitting on the median strip.

WHAT IS A MODE?

The mode of a group of numbers is the number in the group that appears most often. In the group 3,4,4,5,7,7,8,8,8,9,10, the mode is 8, because it appears three times while no other number in the group appears more than twice.

It is easy to remember what mode means. One meaning of mode is "current fashion." Apple pie à la mode is apple pie with ice cream on it, which at one time was a new and fashionable dessert idea. The mode in a group of numbers is the most "fashionable" number—the one you see most often.

EXPONENTS AND RADICALS

EXPONENTS ARE A KIND OF SHORTHAND

Many numbers are the product of the same factor multiplied over and over again. For example, $32 = 2 \times 2 \times 2 \times 2 \times 2$. Another way to write this would be $32 = 2^5$, or "thirty-two equals two to the fifth power." The little number, or *exponent*, denotes the number of times that 2 is to be used as a factor. In the same way, $10^3 = 10 \times 10 \times 10$, or 1,000, or "ten to the third power," or "ten cubed." In this example, the 10 is called the *base* and the 3 is called the *exponent*. (You won't need to know these terms on the SAT, but you will need to know them to follow our explanations.)

MULTIPLYING NUMBERS WITH EXPONENTS

When you multiply two numbers with the same base, you simply add the exponents. For example, $2^3 \times 2^5 = 2^{3+5} = 2^8$.

> **WARNING!** Don't get careless with this rule; it applies to multiplication, not to addition. $2^3 + 2^5$ does not equal 2^8.

DIVIDING NUMBERS WITH EXPONENTS

When you divide two numbers with the same base, you simply subtract the exponents. For example, $\dfrac{2^5}{2^3} = 2^{5-3} = 2^2$.

> **WARNING!** Don't get careless with this rule; it applies to division, not to subtraction. $2^5 - 2^3$ does not equal 2^2.

RAISING A POWER TO A POWER

When you raise a power to a power, you multiply the exponents. For example, $(2^3)^4 = 2^{3 \times 4} = 2^{12}$.

> **WARNING!** Parentheses are very important with exponents, because you must remember to distribute powers to everything within them. For example: $(3x)^2 = 9x^2$, not $3x^2$. Many students carelessly forget that they must also square the 3. Similarly, $\left(\dfrac{3}{2}\right)^2 = \dfrac{3^2}{2^2} = \dfrac{9}{4}$, not $\dfrac{9}{2}$.

CALCULATOR EXPONENTS

You can easily compute simple exponents on your calculator. To find 2^{10}, for example, simply use your calculator to multiply $2 \times 2 \times 2 \times 2 \times 2 \times 2 \times 2 \times 2 \times 2 \times 2$. Just be careful to count correctly. This may be especially useful if you are asked to compare exponents.

THE PECULIAR BEHAVIOR OF EXPONENTS

Raising a number to a power can have quite peculiar and unexpected results, depending on what sort of number you start out with. Here are some examples:

1. If you square or cube a number greater than 1, it becomes *larger*. For example, $2^3 = 8$.

2. If you square or cube a fraction, it becomes *smaller*. For example $\left(\dfrac{1}{2}\right)^3 = \dfrac{1}{8}$.

3. A negative number raised to an even power becomes *positive*. For example, $(-2)^2 = 4$.

4. A negative number raised to an odd power remains *negative*. For example, $(-2)^3 = -8$.

You should also have a feel for relative sizes of exponential numbers without calculating them. For example 2^{10} is much larger than 10^2. ($2^{10} = 1,024$; $10^2 = 100$.) To take another example, 2^5 is twice as large as 2^4, even though 5 only seems a bit larger than 4. You always do simple exponents using a calculator. See above.

RADICALS

The sign $\sqrt{}$ indicates the square root of a number. For example, $\sqrt{25} = 5$.

> **Important note: When you are asked for $\sqrt{x}$, or the square root of any number, you are being asked for a positive root only. Although 5^2 and $(-5)^2$ both equal 25, only 5 is a square root of 25.**

The sign $\sqrt[3]{}$ indicates the cube root of a number. Thus, $\sqrt[3]{8} = 2$, since $2^3 = 8$.

THE ONLY RULES YOU NEED TO KNOW

Here are the only rules regarding radicals that you need to know for the SAT:

1. $\sqrt{x}\sqrt{y} = \sqrt{xy}$. For example, $\sqrt{3}\sqrt{3} = \sqrt{9} = 3$.

2. $\sqrt{\dfrac{x}{y}} = \dfrac{\sqrt{x}}{\sqrt{y}}$. For example, $\sqrt{\dfrac{5}{4}} = \dfrac{\sqrt{5}}{\sqrt{4}} = \dfrac{\sqrt{5}}{2}$.

Note that rule 1 works in reverse: $\sqrt{50} = \sqrt{25} \times \sqrt{2} = 5\sqrt{2}$. This is really a kind of factoring. You are using rule 1 to factor a large, clumsy radical into numbers that are easier to work with.

BEWARE OF COMMON SENSE

Don't make careless mistakes. Remember that the square root of a positive fraction less than 1 is *larger* than the fraction. For example, $\sqrt{\dfrac{1}{4}} = \dfrac{1}{2}$, and $\dfrac{1}{2} > \dfrac{1}{4}$.

ARITHMETIC SUMMARY

1. There are only six arithmetic operations: addition, subtraction, multiplication, division, raising to a power, and finding a square root or a cube root.

2. These operations must be performed in the proper order, beginning with operations inside parentheses.

3. The associative law states that when you are adding or multiplying a series of numbers, you can group or regroup the numbers any way you like.

4. The distributive law is one of the most important principles on the SAT. You must be absolutely certain that you know it:

   $$a(b + c) = ab + ac$$
   $$a(b - c) = ab - ac$$

   This law is so important that you must *always* apply it *whenever* you have a chance. If a problem gives you information in "factored form"—$a(b + c)$—then you should multiply through or *distribute* the first variable before you do anything else. If you are given information that has already been distributed—$ab + ac$—then you should factor out the common term, putting the information back in factored form. Very often, simply doing this will enable you to spot Jim's answer.

5. A fraction is just another way of expressing division.

6. You must know how to add, subtract, multiply, and divide fractions. You must also know how to raise them to a power and find their roots.

7. In any problem involving large or confusing fractions, try to reduce the fractions first. For example, you should never multiply two fractions before looking to see if you can reduce either or both.

8. The most common source of mistakes on word problems involving fractions is misreading. Read fraction word problems carefully!

9. A decimal is just another way of expressing a fraction.

10. Use a calculator to add, subtract, multiply, and divide decimals.

11. If you get confused about decimals, remember dollars and cents.

12. A ratio is a fraction. If you can do it to a fraction, you can do it to a ratio.

13. Use the ratio box to solve ratio questions.

14. A percentage is just a convenient way of expressing a fraction whose denominator is 100.

15. To convert a percentage to a fraction, simply put the percentage over a denominator of 100 and reduce.

16. To convert a fraction to a percentage, simply divide the numerator by the denominator and move the decimal point in the result two places to the right.

17. To convert a percentage to a decimal, simply move the decimal point two places to the left. To convert a decimal to a percentage, simply move the decimal point two places to the right.

18. In problems requiring you to determine the effect of series of percentage increases or reductions, remember that each successive increase or reduction is performed on the result of the previous one.

19. To find the mean of several values, add up the values and divide the total by the number of values.

20. The key to solving any problem involving a mean is to find the *total* of the items before you do anything else.

21. In finding the mean, every item counts the same as every other, even if there are repeats.

22. The median is the number that has an equal number of numbers above and below it.

23. The mode is the number that appears most often in a group of numbers.

24. Exponents are a kind of shorthand for expressing numbers that are the product of the same factor multiplied over and over again.

25. When you multiply two numbers with the same base you simply add the exponents. (This rule applies to multiplication, *not* to addition.)

26 When you divide two numbers with the same base, you simply subtract the exponents. (This rule applies to division, *not* to subtraction.)

27. When you raise a power to a power, you multiply the exponents.

28. A positive number greater than 1 raised to a power greater than 1 becomes *larger*. A positive fraction less than 1 raised to an exponent greater than 1 becomes *smaller*. A negative number raised to an even power becomes *positive*. A negative number raised to an odd power remains *negative*.

29. When you are asked for $\sqrt{x}$ or the square root of any number, you are being asked for a *positive* root only.

30. Here are the only rules regarding radicals that you need to know for the SAT:

1. $\sqrt{x}\sqrt{y} = \sqrt{xy}$

2. $\sqrt{\dfrac{x}{y}} = \dfrac{\sqrt{x}}{\sqrt{y}}$

Chapter 11
Algebra

ALGEBRA: CRACKING THE SYSTEM

About a third of the math problems on your SAT will involve algebra. Some students are terrified of algebra. Fortunately, we have several techniques that should enable you to solve the most frightening-looking algebra problems—even word problems.

This chapter is divided into three main sections:

1. Working Backward

2. Plugging In

3. Basic Princeton Review Algebra

Princeton Review algebra is our name for the kind of algebra you need to do well on the SAT. It isn't the same as the algebra you were taught in math class. Why did we bother to create our own kind of algebra? *Because math-class algebra takes too much time on the SAT.* If you want big score gains, you're going to have to forget about your algebra class and learn the techniques that work on the SAT. Math-class algebra is slower and riskier than Princeton Review algebra. On the SAT, do it our way instead.

Your biggest scoring gains will come from the next two sections: "Working Backward" and "Plugging In." These are two simple but extremely powerful techniques that work on multiple-choice questions. You won't need to know much algebra in order to use them, but you'll have to stay on your toes.

The third section of this chapter is a summary of basic Princeton Review algebra. It's a bit dull by comparison with the rest of the chapter, but you should read it carefully, even if you already feel comfortable with algebra. You should think of our summary as a sort of guide to the small handful of algebraic concepts that you'll need to answer problems that can't be solved by working backward or plugging in. If you find that you are confused by some of the concepts, you should go back to your old algebra textbook or to a teacher for a fuller explanation.

WORKING BACKWARD

Algebra uses letters to stand for numbers, but no one else does. You don't go to the grocery store to buy x eggs or y bottles of milk. Most people think in terms of numbers, not letters that stand for numbers.

You should do the same thing on the SAT as much as possible. On many SAT algebra problems, even very difficult ones, you will be able to find Jim's answer without using any algebra at all. You will do this by working backward from the answer choices instead of trying to solve the problem using math-class algebra.

Working backward is a technique for solving word problems whose answer choices are all numbers. Many so-called algebra problems on the SAT can be solved simply and quickly by using this powerful technique.

In algebra class at school, you solve word problems by using equations. Then, if you're careful, you check your solution by plugging in your answer to see if it works. But why not avoid equations entirely by simply checking the five solutions ETS offers on the multiple-choice questions? One of these has to be correct. You don't have to do any algebra, you will seldom have to try more than three choices, and you will never have to try all five.

Here's an example:

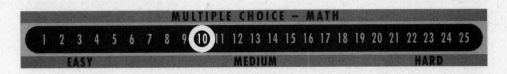

10 The units digit of a 2-digit number is 3 times the tens digit. If the digits are reversed, the resulting number is 36 more than the original number. What is the original number?

(A) 26
(B) 31
(C) 36
(D) 62
(E) 93

HERE'S HOW TO CRACK IT

If ETS didn't give you any answer choices on this problem, finding the solution would take a very, very long time. After all, there are 90 two-digit numbers. But ETS has limited your decision to five choices—they've already gotten rid of 85 possible answers! Eliminating four more ought to be easy.

What you want to do is look at each answer choice to see if it fulfills the *conditions* stated in the problem. If it doesn't, you can use POE to get rid of it.

Doing that on this problem is a piece of cake. You simply take the stated conditions *one at a time* and try them out against the answer choices.

The first condition stated in the problem is that the units (or ones) digit of the number you are looking for is three times the tens digit. Now you look at the choices:

(A) Is 6 three times 2? Yes. A possibility.
(B) Is 1 three times 3? No. Eliminate.
(C) Is 6 three times 3? No. Eliminate.
(D) Is 2 three times 6? No. Eliminate.
(E) Is 3 three times 9? No. Eliminate.

Jim's answer is A. You found it without even testing the other conditions stated in the problem. Mark your answer and move on.

Never mark your answer until you have either tested all the conditions or eliminated all but one of the choices. In this problem, if there had been another choice whose units digit was three times its tens digit, you would have had to move on to the next condition.

Here's another example:

11 A woman made 5 payments on a loan with each payment being twice the amount of the preceding one. If the total of all 5 payments was $465, how much was the first payment?

(A) $5
(B) $15
(C) $31
(D) $93
(E) $155

HERE'S HOW TO CRACK IT

To solve this problem in math class, you'd have to set up and solve an equation like this:

$$p + 2p + 4p + 8p + 16p = 465$$

Forget it! That's too much work. Why not just try out the answers?

Numeric answer choices on the SAT are always given in order of size. Thus, when you are working backward on a problem like this, you should always start out with the number in the middle—choice C. If that number turns out to be too big, you can try a lower number next; if it's too small, you can try a higher one. That way you'll save time.

Let's look at what happens when you try choice C: If the payments double each month, the woman will pay 31 + 62 + 124 + 248 + 496—you can stop right there. You don't have to add up these numbers to see clearly that the total is going to be much more than 465; the fifth number alone is more than that. You need to eliminate this choice and try again with a smaller number.

Two of the choices are smaller. Which one should you try? Why not A, the *smaller* of the two? It will be easier and faster to work with. If it works, you'll pick it; if it doesn't, you'll eliminate it and pick B.

Here's what you get when you try choice A: 5 + 10 + 20 + 40 + 80. You don't have to add up these numbers to see clearly that they aren't going to come anywhere near totaling 465. Jim's answer must be B. (It is.)

WORKING BACKWARD: ADVANCED PRINCIPLES

Working backward is the same on difficult problems as it is on easy and medium ones. You just have to watch your step and make certain you don't make any careless mistakes or fall for Joe Bloggs attractors. Here's one of our examples:

18 Out of a total of 154 games played, a ball team won 54 more games than it lost. If there were no ties, how many games did the team win?

(A) 94
(B) 98
(C) 100
(D) 102
(E) 104

HERE'S HOW TO CRACK IT

What's the Joe Bloggs attractor here? It is choice C. Be careful!

To solve the problem all you have to do is work backward. You've eliminated choice C already, so start with D. If the team won 102 games, how many games did it lose? It lost 52 (154 − 102 = 52). Is 102 (wins) 54 greater than 52 (losses)? No. 102 − 52 = 50. You need more wins to make the problem come out right. That means that Jim's answer must be E. (It is.)

Here's another example we created:

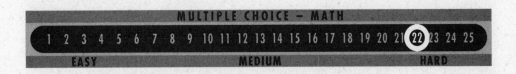

22 Committee A has 18 members and Committee B has 3 members. How many members from Committee A must switch to Committee B so that Committee A will have twice as many members as Committee B?

(A) 4
(B) 6
(C) 7
(D) 9
(E) 14

HERE'S HOW TO CRACK IT

This problem represents one of the most difficult principles tested in the SAT math section. Only a tiny percentage of students get it right. But if you work backward, you won't have any trouble.

This problem is about two committees, so the first thing you should do is quickly draw a picture in your test booklet to keep you from getting confused, like this:

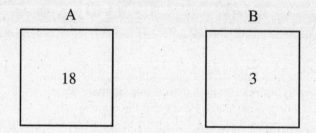

Now work backward, starting with answer choice C. If you move 7 members out of Committee A, there will be 11 members left in A and 10 members in B. Is 11 twice as many as 10? No, eliminate.

As you work through the choices, keep track of them, like this:

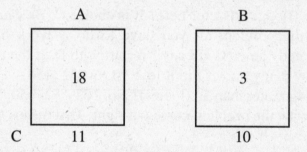

Choice C didn't work. To make the answer come out right, you need more members in Committee A and fewer in Committee B. In other words, you need to try a smaller number. Try the smallest one, choice A. Moving 4 members from Committee A will leave 14 in A and 7 in B. Is 14 twice as many as 7? Yes, of course. This is Jim's answer.

> **Don't worry if you can't tell whether you should next try a smaller or larger number. If you get confused, just try all the choices until you find the answer. And keep track of the ones you've eliminated by crossing them out in your test booklet. You'll end up with Jim's answer.**

PLUGGING IN

Working backward enables you to find Jim's answer on problems where all the answer choices are numbers. What about problems whose answer choices contain letters? On these problems, you will usually be able to find Jim's answer by plugging in. Plugging in is similar to working backward. And, like working backward, it has very little to do with the algebra you learned in math class.

Plugging in is easy. It has three steps:

1. Pick numbers for the letters in the problem.

2. Using your numbers, find an answer to the problem.

3. Plug your numbers into the answer choices to see which choice equals the answer you found in step 2.

BASIC PLUGGING IN

Plugging in is simple to understand. Here's an example:

3   Kim was k years of age 2 years ago. In terms of k, how old will Kim be 2 years from now?

(A) $k + 4$

(B) $k + 2$

(C) $2k$

(D) k

(E) $\dfrac{k}{2}$

HERE'S HOW TO CRACK IT

First, pick a number for k. Pick something easy to work with, like 10. In your test booklet, write *10* directly above the letter k in the problem, so you won't forget.

If $k = 10$, then Kim was 10 years old 2 years ago. That means she's 12 right now. The problem has asked you to find out how old Kim will be in 2 years. She will be 14. Using your number for k, the answer is A. Write a nice big 14 in your test booklet *and circle it.* Jim's answer will be the choice that, when you plug in 10 for k, equals 14.

Now it's time to plug in. (Don't worry about phrases like "in terms of k"; they're for students who solve these problems the math-class way. You don't need to pay attention.)

Plugging in 5 for k in answer choice A, you get $5 + 4$, or 9. This is the number you are looking for, so this must be Jim's answer. (It is.) Go ahead and try the other choices just to make sure you're right, and to practice plugging in.

> **Don't try to solve problems like this by writing equations and "solving for x" or "solving for y." Plugging in is faster, easier, and less likely to produce errors.**

Here's another example:

17 The sum of two positive consecutive integers is x. In terms of x, what is the value of the smaller of these two integers?

    (A) $\dfrac{x}{2} - 1$

    (B) $\dfrac{x-1}{2}$

    (C) $\dfrac{x}{2}$

    (D) $\dfrac{x+1}{2}$

    (E) $\dfrac{x}{2} + 1$

HERE'S HOW TO CRACK IT

If we pick 2 and 3 for our two positive consecutive integers, then $x = 5$. Write 2, 3, and $x = 5$ in your test booklet.

The smaller of our two integers is 2. Circle it; we are looking for the choice that equals 2 when we plug in 5. Let's try each choice:

(A) Plugging in 5 gives us $\dfrac{5}{2} - 1$. You shouldn't have to work that out to see that it doesn't equal 2. Eliminate.

(B) Plugging in 5 gives us $\dfrac{4}{2}$, or 2. This is Jim's answer.

Check all of your choices just to be sure.

WHICH NUMBERS?

Although you can plug in any number, you can make your life much easier by plugging in "good" numbers—numbers that are simple to work with or that make the problem easier to manipulate. Picking a small number like 2 will usually make finding the answer easier. If the problem asks for a percentage, plug in 10 or 100. If the problem has to do with minutes, try 60. If you plug in wisely, you can sometimes eliminate computation altogether.

You should avoid plugging in 0 and 1; they are special cases and using them may allow you to eliminate only one or two choices at a time. You should also avoid plugging in any number that appears in the question or in any of the answer choices.

(Plugging in 0 and 1 is useful, though, on inequalities and quant comp, as we'll explain in the next section. Later on, we'll tell you about even more situations in which you should plug in 0 and 1.)

Many times you'll find that there is an advantage to picking a particular number, even a very large one, because it makes solving the problem easier.

Here's an example:

17 If 100 equally priced tickets cost a total of *d* dollars, 5 of these tickets cost how many dollars?

(A) $\dfrac{d}{20}$

(B) $\dfrac{d}{5}$

(C) 5d

(D) $\dfrac{5}{d}$

(E) $\dfrac{20}{d}$

HERE'S HOW TO CRACK IT

Should you plug in 2 for *d*? You could, but plugging in 100 would make the problem easier. After all, if 100 tickets cost a total of $100, then each ticket costs $1. Write *d* = 100 in your test booklet.

If each ticket costs a dollar, then 5 tickets cost $5. Write a "5" in your test booklet and circle it. You are looking for the answer choice that works out to 5 when you plug in 100 for d. Let's try each choice:

(A) $\dfrac{100}{20} = 5$

This is Jim's answer.

Here's another example:

25 A watch loses x minutes every y hours. At this rate, how many hours will the watch lose in one week?

(A) $7xy$

(B) $\dfrac{7y}{x}$

(C) $\dfrac{x}{7y}$

(D) $\dfrac{14y}{5x}$

(E) $\dfrac{14x}{5y}$

HERE'S HOW TO CRACK IT

This is an extremely difficult problem for students who try to solve it the math-class way. You'll be able to find the answer easily, though, if you plug in carefully.

What should you plug in? As always, you can plug in anything, but if you select wisely you'll make things easier on yourself. There are three units of time in this problem: minutes, hours, and weeks. If we plug in 60 for x, we can get it down to two, because 60 minutes equal an hour. Write $x = 60$ in your test booklet.

We can also make things easier for ourselves by plugging in 24 for y. There are 24 hours in a day. What we are saying so far is that the watch loses 60 minutes every 24 hours. In other words, it loses an hour a day. Write $y = 24$ in your test booklet.

At this rate, how many hours will the watch lose in a week? It will lose 7, obviously, because there are 7 days in a week. Write 7 in your test booklet and circle it. We are looking for the answer choice that equals 7 when we plug in 60 for x and 24 for y.

Now let's check each choice:

(A) $7xy = (7)(60)(24)$. You don't have to use your calculator to see that it doesn't equal 7! Eliminate.

(B) $7\dfrac{y}{x} = \dfrac{(7)(24)}{(60)} = \dfrac{168}{60} = 2.8$. Eliminate.

(C) $\dfrac{x}{7y} = \dfrac{(60)}{(7)(24)} = \dfrac{60}{128} = 0.46875$. Eliminate.

(D) $\dfrac{14y}{5x} = \dfrac{(14)(24)}{(5)(60)} = \dfrac{336}{300} = 1.12$. Eliminate.

(E) $\dfrac{14x}{5y} = \dfrac{(14)(60)}{(5)(24)} = \dfrac{840}{120} = 7$. This is Jim's answer.

INEQUALITIES

Plugging in works on problems containing inequalities, but you will have to be careful and follow some different rules. Plugging in *one* number is often not enough; to find Jim's answer you may have to plug in several. For example, on one problem you might have to plug in two or three of the following numbers: -1, 0, 1, $\dfrac{1}{2}$, and $-\dfrac{1}{2}$.

The five numbers just mentioned all have special properties. Negatives, fractions, 0, and 1 all behave in peculiar ways when, for example, they are squared. Don't forget about them!

Sometimes you can avoid plugging in altogether by simplifying. Here's an example:

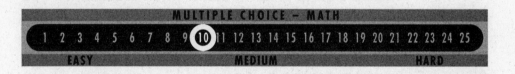

10   If $-3x + 6 \geq 18$, which of the following is true?

    (A) $x \leq -4$
    (B) $x \leq 6$
    (C) $x \geq -4$
    (D) $x \geq -6$
    (E) $x = 2$

HERE'S HOW TO CRACK IT

The inequality in the problem can be simplified quite a bit. Do it:

$$-3x + 6 \geq 18$$
$$-3x \geq 12$$
$$-x \geq 4$$

We're close to one of the answer choices, but not quite there yet. Multiply through by -1 to make x positive. (Remember to change the direction of the inequality sign!)

$$x \leq -4$$

So choice A is Jim's answer.

"IT CANNOT BE DETERMINED"

A couple of times on every SAT, choice E on an algebra problem will be "It cannot be determined from the information given." You have already learned in chapter 8, that this choice is almost *never* Jim's answer in the difficult part of either math section (with the exception of quantitative comparisons). But in the easy and medium parts of the test, "It cannot be determined" is Jim's answer about half the time. If you get stumped on one of these questions, therefore, choice E is a very good guess. But you'd probably like to be right on these problems more than half the time. If you plug in carefully, you can be right all the time.

On an ordinary algebra problem based on an equation, all you need to do is find one answer that works. That's why you plug in. But on a problem in which "It cannot be determined" is one of the choices, you have to be certain that your answer is *always* correct. If it isn't, then a definite answer "cannot be determined," even though the example you chose may have worked.

To see why this is true, look at this simple example.

If $x^2 = 4$, then $x = ?$

(A) 2
(B) It cannot be determined from the
 information given.

Suppose you try to solve this little problem by working backward from the answer choices. You plug in 2 for x and find that, indeed, $2^2 = 4$. But choice B is "cannot be determined." Are you certain that 2 is the only number that works in the equation $x^2 = 4$?

If you are, you shouldn't be, because –2 also works. The correct answer to this question, therefore, is B, even though working backward and plugging in initially made it appear as though the correct choice was A.

Here's another example:

15 If $x > 0$, which of the following is greatest?

(A) $\dfrac{1}{x}$

(B) $\sqrt{x}$

(C) x

(D) x^2

(E) It cannot be determined from the information given.

HERE'S HOW TO CRACK IT

First, plug in a number that satisfies the condition ($x > 0$) stated in the problem. How about 2? If $x = 2$, we come up with the following values for the first four answer choices:

(A) $\dfrac{1}{2}$

(B) 1.4

(C) 2

(D) 4

The greatest number here is 4. Does that mean choice D is correct?

Not necessarily. Because "cannot be determined" is one of the choices, we have to be certain that x^2 will *always* be the greatest, no matter what we plug in for x.

What should we plug in next? One of the numbers with special properties. The problem says that $x > 0$, but it doesn't say that x has to be an integer. Let's try a fraction. Plugging in $\frac{1}{2}$ for x, we come up with the following:

(A) 2

(B) $\frac{1}{1.4}$

(C) $\frac{1}{2}$

(D) $\frac{1}{4}$

Choice A is now the greatest. That means that neither choice D nor choice A can *always* be correct. Therefore, Jim's answer has to be E.

JOE BLOGGS ALERT!

On this problem, where you are asked to find the *greatest* number, Joe Bloggs is irresistibly attracted to choice D, x^2. Any number squared must be pretty large, right? Wrong! Joe forgets about *fractions*, which get *smaller* when they are squared. Don't be fooled!

We said earlier that on easy and medium problems where it is offered as a choice, "cannot be determined" is Jim's answer about half the time. But that also means that "cannot be determined" is *wrong* about half the time. Don't assume that it's necessarily your best choice just because it's offered. Here's an example:

MULTIPLE CHOICE – MATH

1 2 3 4 5 6 7 8 9 10 11 12 13 14 15 **16** 17 18 19 20 21 22 23 24 25

EASY   MEDIUM   HARD

16 A certain number n is multiplied by 10. If a number that is 7 less than n is also multiplied by 10, how much greater is the first product than the second?

(A) 7
(B) 10
(C) 17
(D) 70
(E) It cannot be determined from the information given.

HERE'S HOW TO CRACK IT

First, plug in an easy number. How about 10? Write $n = 10$ in your test booklet. $10 \times 10 = 100$. This is the first product. Write it in your test booklet, too.

To obtain the second product, multiply $10(10 - 7)$, or 10×3, which equals 30. What is the difference of the two products? It is 70, which is choice D.

Should you select choice D as your answer? Not yet. You have to be certain that the difference between the two products will *always* be 70, no matter what you plug in for n.

Before you do, you should cross out choices A, B, and C in your test booklet. If D can be right at least *some* of the time, then A, B, and C can't be right *all* the time, so you can eliminate all of them. You've narrowed your choices down to D and E. If you guess right now, you'll have a fifty-fifty chance of being correct.

Your job now is to try to find a case in which the difference is *not* 70. To do this, check one of the numbers with special properties that we mentioned earlier. How about 0? If $n = 0$, $n \times 10 = 0$. The number 7 less than 0 is -7. $10 \times -7 = -70$, which is 70 less than n. Once again, D works out.

It seems fairly certain now that D is Jim's answer. (It is.)

OTHER SPECIAL CASES

Sometimes SAT algebra problems will require you to determine certain *characteristics* of a number or numbers. Is x odd or even? Is it small or large? Is it positive or negative?

On questions like this, you will probably have to plug in more than one number, just as you do on problems containing inequalities and "cannot be determined." Sometimes ETS's wording will tip you off. If the problem states only that $x > 0$, you know for certain that x is positive but you *don't* know that x is an integer. See what happens when you plug in a fraction.

Here are some other tip-offs you should be aware of:

If the problem asked for this	and you plugged in this	also try this, just to be sure
an integer	3	1, 0, or –1
a fraction	$\frac{1}{4}$	$-\frac{1}{4}$
two even numbers	2, 4	2, –2
a number	an integer	a fraction
a number	an even number	an odd number
a number	a small number	a huge number
a multiple of 7	7	7,000 or –7
consecutive numbers	odd, even	even, odd
$x^2 = 4$	2	–2
$xy > 0$	(2, 4)	(–2, –4)
$x = 2y$	(4, 2)	(–4, –2) or (0, 0)

ODDS OR EVENS

Here's an example of a problem involving odds and evens.

MULTIPLE CHOICE – MATH

1 2 3 4 5 6 7 8 9 10 11 (12) 13 14 15 16 17 18 19 20 21 22 23 24 25

EASY   MEDIUM   HARD

12   If x is an odd integer and y is an even integer, which of the following could be an even integer?

(A) $x + y$

(B) $x - y$

(C) $\frac{x}{2} + y$

(D) $x + \frac{y}{2}$

(E) $\frac{x}{y} + \frac{x}{2}$

HERE'S HOW TO CRACK IT

Because of the word *could*, all you have to do to solve this problem is find a single instance in which one of the choices is an even integer. The easiest way to do this is to plug in simple choices for x and y and see what happens.

The easiest odd number to deal with is 1; the easiest even is 2. Plugging in these values for x and y, we discover the following:

(A) $x + y = 1 + 2 = 3$ (not even)

(B) $x - y = 1 - 2 = -1$ (not even)

(C) $\dfrac{x}{2} + y = \dfrac{1}{2} + 2 = 2\dfrac{1}{2}$ (not even)

(D) $x + \dfrac{y}{2} = 1 + \dfrac{2}{2} = 1 + 1 = 2$ (even—this is Jim's answer)

(E) We don't even need to check E. All we had to do was find one instance in which the choice *could* be even, and we found it in D.

PLUGGING IN: ADVANCED PRINCIPLES

As you have just learned, you should plug in whenever you don't know what a number is. But you can also plug in when you have numbers that are too big, too ugly, or too inconvenient to work with. On such problems you can often find Jim's answer simply by using numbers that aren't as ugly as the ones ETS has given you. Here's an example:

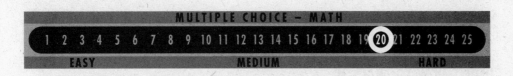

20 On the last day of a one-week sale, customers numbered 149 through 201 were waited on. How many customers were waited on that day?

(A) 51
(B) 52
(C) 53
(D) 152
(E) 153

HERE'S HOW TO CRACK IT

This is a number 20—a difficult question. Finding Jim's answer *has* to be harder than simply subtracting 149 from 201 to get 52, which means that choice B *has* to be wrong. Cross it out. (You can also immediately eliminate D and E, which are much, much too big.)

One way to find the answer would be to count this out by hand. But to count from 149 to 201 is an awful lot of counting. You can achieve the same result by using simpler numbers instead.

It doesn't matter which numbers you use. How about 7 and 11? The difference between 7 and 11 is 4. But if you count out the numbers on your hand—7, 8, 9, 10, 11—you see that there are 5 numbers. In other words, if the store had served customers 7 through 11, the number of customers would have been 1 greater than the difference of 7 and 11. Jim's answer, therefore, will be 1 greater than the difference of 149 and 201. Jim's answer, in other words, is C.

Here's another example:

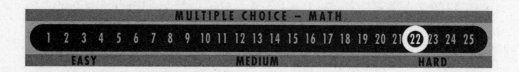

22    $2^{23} - 2^{22} =$

    (A) 2^1

    (B) $2^{\frac{23}{22}}$

    (C) 2^{22}

    (D) 2^{23}

    (E) 2^{45}

HERE'S HOW TO CRACK IT

These are big, ugly, inconvenient exponents. No wonder this item is a number 22. But you'll be able to solve it if you plug in easier numbers.

Instead of 2^{23}, let's use 2^4. And instead of 2^{22}, let's use 2^3. Now we can rewrite the problem: $2^4 - 2^3 = 16 - 8 = 8 = 2^3$.

Our answer is the second of the two numbers we started with. Jim's answer, therefore, must be the second number *he* started with, or 2^{23}, which is choice C. (If you don't believe this always works, try it with 2^2 and 2^3, and with 2^3 and 2^4, or any other similar pair of numbers. By the way, choices A and B are Joe Bloggs attractors.)

BASIC PRINCETON REVIEW ALGEBRA

Working backward and plugging in will be huge helps to you on the math SAT. But they won't be enough to answer every algebra problem. On some problems, you'll have to know a few basic principles of

Princeton Review algebra. If the explanations we give you leave you still confused, you should dig out your old algebra textbook or check with your math teacher.

UNIMPORTANT TERMINOLOGY

Here are some words that you won't need to know on the SAT but that you will need to know to follow the rest of this chapter. After you finish reading the chapter, you can forget about them.

> **Term:** If an equation is like a sentence, then a term is the equivalent of a word in that sentence. For example, $9x^2$ is a term in the equation $9x^2 + 3x = 5y$.
>
> **Coefficient:** In the same equation, the coefficient of the term $9x^2$ is 9 and the coefficient of $3x$ is 3.
>
> **Expression:** An expression is a combination of terms and mathematical operations. For example, $9x^2 + 3x$ is an expression. If an equation is like a sentence, then an expression is like a phrase or clause.
>
> **Binomial:** A binomial is an expression that contains two terms. For instance, $12x + 4$ is binomial.
>
> **Trinomial:** A trinomial is an expression that contains three terms. For example, $2x^2 + 12x + 4$ is a trinomial.
>
> **Polynomial:** A polynomial is any expression containing two or more terms. Binomials and trinomials are both polynomials.

SIMPLIFYING EXPRESSIONS

If a problem contains an expression that can be factored, you should factor it immediately. For example, if you come upon a problem containing the expression $2x + 2y$, you should factor it immediately to produce the expression $2(x + y)$.

If a problem contains an expression that is already factored, you should multiply it out according to the distributive law to return it to its original unfactored state. For example, if you come upon a problem containing the expression $2(x + y)$, you should *un*factor it by multiplying through to produce the expression $2x + 2y$.

Here are five worked examples:

1. $4x + 24 = 4(x) + 4(6) = 4(x + 6)$

2. $\dfrac{10x - 60}{2} = \dfrac{10(x) - 10(6)}{2} = \dfrac{10(x - 6)}{2}$
$= 5(x - 6) = 5x - 30$

3. $\dfrac{x + y}{y} = \dfrac{x}{y} + \dfrac{y}{y} = \dfrac{x}{y} + 1$

4. $2(x + y) + 3(x + y) = (2 + 3)(x + y) = 5(x + y)$

5. $p(r + s) + q(r + s) = (p + q)(r + s)$

MULTIPLYING POLYNOMIALS

Multiplying polynomials is easy. Just be sure that every term in the first polynomial gets multiplied by every term in the second.

$$(x + 2)(x + 4) = (x + 2)(x + 4)$$
$$= (x \times x) + (x \times 4) + (2 \times x) + (2 \times 4)$$
$$= x^2 + 4x + 2x + 8$$
$$= x^2 + 6x + 8$$

ETS'S FAVORITE QUADRATIC EXPRESSIONS

ETS has two favorite quadratic expressions. They appear over and over again on the SAT. You should train yourself to recognize them instantly in *both factored and unfactored form*. Here they are:

$$x^2 - y^2 = (x + y)(x - y)$$
$$x^2 + 2xy + y^2 = (x + y)^2$$

Here's an example:

Factor the following expression:

$$\frac{3x^2 - 3}{x - 1}$$

HERE'S HOW TO CRACK IT

First, simply factor out a 3 from the expression in the numerator: $3x^2 - 3 = 3(x^2 - 1)$. Now, because we told you to be on the lookout for it, you should realize instantly that $x^2 - 1 = (x + 1)(x - 1)$, which means that $3(x^2 - 1) = 3(x + 1)(x - 1)$. Doing this gives you the following:

$$\frac{3(x + 1)(x - 1)}{(x - 1)}$$

Since $(x - 1)$ is a common factor in the numerator and the denominator, you can cancel it from both. The final factored form of the original expression is simply $3(x + 1)$.

Here are a few more worked examples:

1. $x^2 - y^2 + 2y(y + x) = x^2 - y^2 + 2y^2 + 2yx$

    $= x^2 + y^2 + 2yx$

    $= (x + y)^2$

2. $(45)^2 + 2(45)(55) + (55)^2 = (45 + 55)^2$

    $= 100^2$

    $= 10{,}000$

3. $0.84^2 - 0.83^2 = (0.84 + 0.83)(0.84 - 0.83)$

    $= (1.67)(0.01)$

    $= 0.0167$

COMBINE SIMILAR TERMS FIRST

In manipulating long, complicated algebraic expressions, combine all similar terms before doing anything else. In other words, if one of the terms is $5x$ and another is $-3x$, simply combine them into $2x$. Then you won't have as many terms to work with. Here's a worked example:

$$(3x^2 + 3x + 4) + (2 - x) - (6 + 2x) =$$

$$3x^2 + 3x + 4 + 2 - x - 6 - 2x =$$

$$3x^2 + (3x - x - 2x) + (4 + 2 - 6) =$$

$$3x^2$$

EVALUATING EXPRESSIONS

Sometimes ETS will give you the value of one of the letters in an algebraic expression and ask you to find the value of the entire expression. All you have to do is plug in the given value and see what you come up with.

Here is an example:

PROBLEM:

If $2x = -1$, then $(2x - 3)^2 = ?$

SOLUTION:

Don't solve for x; simply plug in -1 for $2x$, like this:

$$(2x - 3)^2 = (-1 - 3)^2$$
$$= (-4)^2$$
$$= 16$$

SOLVING EQUATIONS

In algebra class you learned to solve equations by "solving for x" or "solving for y." In doing this you isolate x or y on one side of the equal sign and put everything else on the other side. This is a long, laborious process with many steps and many opportunities for mistakes.

On the SAT, you usually won't have time to solve equations this way. You've already learned how to work backward and plug in. On problems where these techniques don't work, you should still hesitate before using math-class algebra. Instead, you should learn to find *direct solutions*. To demonstrate what we mean, we'll show you the same problem solved two different ways.

PROBLEM:

If $2x = 5$ and $3y = 6$, then $6xy = ?$

MATH-CLASS SOLUTION:

Your teacher would tell you to:

1. find x
2. find y
3. multiply 6 times x times y

Using this procedure, you find that $x = \dfrac{5}{2}$ and $y = 2$. Therefore,

$6xy = (6)\left(\dfrac{5}{2}\right)(2)$, or 30.

PRINCETON REVIEW SOLUTION:

You notice that $6xy$ equals $(2x)(3y)$. Therefore, $6xy$ equals 5×6, or 30.

ANALYSIS

Finding direct solutions will save you time. ETS never expects you to perform long, complicated calculations on the SAT. You should always stop and think for a moment before beginning such a process. Look for a trick—a shortcut to the answer.

Here's another example:

If a, b, c, and d are integers and $ab = 12$,
$bc = 20$, $cd = 30$, and $ad = 18$, then $abcd = ?$

HERE'S HOW TO CRACK IT

If you try to solve this the math-class way, you'll end up fiddling forever with the equations, trying to find individual values for a, b, c, and d. Once again, you may get the correct answer, but you'll spend an eternity doing it.

This problem is much simpler if you look for a direct solution. The first thing to notice is that you have been given a lot of information you don't need. For example, the problem would have been much simpler to answer if you had been given only *two* equations: $ab = 12$ and $cd = 30$. You should know that $(ab)(cd) = abcd$, which means that $abcd = (12)(30)$, which means that the answer is 360.

> *Never let yourself get bogged down looking for a direct solution. But you should always ask yourself if there is a simple way to find the answer. If you train yourself to think in terms of shortcuts, you won't waste a lot of time.*

SOLVING INEQUALITIES

In an equation, one side equals the other. In an inequality, one side *does not* equal the other. The following symbols are used in inequalities:

$\neq$ is not equal to
$>$ is greater than
$<$ is less than
$\geq$ is greater than or equal to
$\leq$ is less than or equal to

Solving inequalities is pretty much like solving equations. You can collect similar terms, and you can simplify by doing the same thing to both sides. *All you have to remember is that if you multiply or divide both sides of an inequality by a negative number, the direction of the inequality symbol changes.* For example, here's a simple inequality:

$x > y$

Now, just as you can with an equation, you can multiply both sides of this inequality by the same number. But if the number you multiply by is negative, you have to change the direction of the symbol in the result. For example, if we multiply both sides of the inequality above by -2, we end up with the following:

$-2x < -2y$

SOLVING SIMULTANEOUS EQUATIONS

Sometimes on the SAT you will be asked to find the value of an expression based on two given equations. To find Jim's answer on such problems, simply add or subtract the two equations. Here's an example:

If $4x + y = 14$ and $3x + 2y = 13$, then $x - y = ?$

HERE'S HOW TO CRACK IT

You've been given two equations here. But instead of being asked to solve for a variable (x or y), you've been asked to solve for an expression ($x - y$). *Why? Because there must be a direct solution.*

In math class, you're taught to multiply one equation by one number and then subtract equations to find the second variable. Or you're taught to solve one equation for one variable in terms of the other and to substitute that value into the second equation to solve for the other variable, and, having found the other variable, to plug it back into the equation to find the value of the first variable.

Whew! Forget it. Fortunately, we have a better way. Just add or subtract the two equations; either addition or subtraction will produce an easy answer. Adding the two equations produces this:

$$\begin{array}{r} 4x + y = 14 \\ +3x + 2y = 13 \\ \hline 7x + 3y = 27 \end{array}$$

This doesn't get us anywhere. So try subtracting:

$$\begin{array}{r} 4x + y = 14 \\ -3x + 2y = 13 \\ \hline x - y = 1 \end{array}$$

The value of ($x - y$) is precisely what you are looking for, so this must be Jim's answer.

> *Never solve simultaneous equations on the SAT the way you are taught to do them in school (by multiplying one equation by one coefficient, the other equation by the other coefficient, and then adding or subtracting). We have rarely seen an SAT on which simultaneous equations had to be solved this way. Simply add or subtract the two equations as they are written.*

SOLVING QUADRATIC EQUATIONS

To solve quadratic equations, remember everything you've learned so far: look for direct solutions and either factor or unfactor when possible. Here's an example:

If $(x + 3)^2 = (x - 3)^2$, then $x = ?$

HERE'S HOW TO CRACK IT

Since both sides of the equation have been factored, you should *un*factor them by multiplying them out:

Left: $(x + 3)(x + 3) = x^2 + 6x + 9$
Right: $(x - 3)(x - 3) = x^2 - 6x + 9$
Therefore: $x^2 + 6x + 9 = x^2 - 6x + 9$

Now you can simplify by eliminating like terms from both sides of the new equations, leaving you with

$$6x = -6x$$
$$x = -x$$
$$x = 0$$

Here's another example:

If $x^2 - 4 = (18)(14)$, then x could be ?

HERE'S HOW TO CRACK IT

You should recognize instantly that $x^2 - 4$ is one of ETS's two favorite quadratic expressions in unfactored form and that it can easily be factored. Do so.

$x^2 - 4 = (x + 2)(x - 2)$
Therefore: $(x + 2)(x - 2) = (18)(14)$

Notice that each side of the equation consists of two terms multiplied by each other. Set the corresponding parts equal to each other and see what you get.

$(x + 2) = 18$
$(x - 2) = 14$

Both equations work if x is 16.

SOLVING QUADRATIC EQUATIONS SET TO ZERO

If $ab = 0$, what do you know about a and b? You know that at least one of them has to equal 0. You can use this fact in solving some quadratic equations. Here's an example:

> What are all the values of x for which
> $x(x - 3) = 0$?

HERE'S HOW TO CRACK IT

Because the product of x and $(x - 3)$ is 0, you know that x or $(x - 3)$— or both of them—has to equal 0. To solve the problem, simply ask yourself what x would have to be to make either expression equal 0. The answer is obvious: x could be either 0 or 3.

FUNCTIONS

When you learned about functions in algebra class, you probably talked about "f of x," or $f(x)$.

The SAT is different. It tests functions, but in a peculiar way. Instead of using $f(x)$, it uses funny symbols to stand for operations. If you understand functions, just remember them when you see the funny symbols. If you don't understand functions, just follow what we tell you.

In a function problem, an arithmetic operation is defined and then you are asked to perform it on a number, a pair of numbers, or an ordered pair of numbers. All you have to do is keep your wits about you, use your booklet as scratch paper, and do as you are told. A function is like a set of instructions: follow it and you'll find Jim's answer.

Here's an example:

18 If $x \# y = \dfrac{1}{x - y}$, what is the value $\dfrac{1}{2} \# \dfrac{1}{3}$?

(A) 6

(B) $\dfrac{6}{5}$

(C) $\dfrac{1}{6}$

(D) −1

(E) −6

HERE'S HOW TO CRACK IT

First of all, let's give operation # a name; let's call it Bloggs. (You can call all functions Bloggs. It will help you keep track of what you're doing.)

Finding Jim's answer is just a matter of careful plugging in. What you need to do is to find the value of the following very intimidating complex fraction:

$$\frac{1}{2} \# \frac{1}{3} = \cfrac{1}{\cfrac{1}{2} - \cfrac{1}{3}}$$

$$= \cfrac{1}{\cfrac{3}{6} - \cfrac{2}{6}}$$

$$= \cfrac{1}{\cfrac{1}{6}}$$

$$= 6$$

Jim's answer, therefore, is choice A.

> There are usually three function problems on every SAT. One of the three will be extremely difficult. If you're not trying to score in the 700s, you should probably skip it. On the others, work very, very carefully and don't make careless mistakes.

WORD PROBLEMS I

Most word problems can be solved quickly by working backward or plugging in. But there will be a few algebra word problems on your SAT that will be more complicated. You'll still be able to answer them, but you should save them for last.

In solving a word problem that can't be done by working backward or plugging in, you should simply translate the problem into an equation. As we said earlier, equations are a kind of shorthand. You will be able to set up equations easily if you train yourself to notice words that are longhand versions of arithmetic symbols. Here are some words and their equivalent symbols:

WORD	SYMBOL
is	=
of, times, product	×
what (or any unknown value)	any letter (x, k, b)
more, sum	+
less, difference	−
ratio, quotient	÷

Here are two examples:

Words: 14 is 5 more than x
Equation: $14 = x + 5$
Words: If $\frac{1}{8}$ of a number is 3, what is $\frac{1}{3}$ of the same number?
Equation: $\frac{1}{8} n = 3$, $k = \frac{1}{3} n$

WORD PROBLEMS II

In solving word problems, you should be familiar with the following formulas:

1. distance = (rate)(time). (This is the most frequently tested formula on the SAT. It can appear in several forms, including time = $\frac{\text{distance}}{\text{rate}}$.)

2. total price = (number of items)(cost per item)

3. sale price = (original price) − (%discount)(original price)

ALGEBRA SUMMARY

1. Math-class algebra takes too much time on the SAT. Do it our way instead.

2. In working backward on an SAT algebra word problem, you put numeric choices into the problem until you find one that works.

3. Plugging in is the technique for multiple-choice problems whose answer choices contain letters. It has three steps:

    A. Pick numbers for the letters in the problem.

    B. Using your numbers, find an answer to the problem.

    C. Plug your numbers into the answer choices to see which choice equals the answer you found in step B.

4. When you plug in, use "good" numbers—ones that are simple to work with and make the problem easier to manipulate.

5. Plugging in works on problems containing inequalities, but you will have to be careful and follow some different rules. Plugging in *one* number is often not enough; to find Jim's answer you may have to plug in several numbers, including ones with special properties.

6. You should plug in whenever you don't know what a number is, but you can also plug in when you have numbers that are too big, too ugly, or too inconvenient to work with.

7. If a problem contains an expression that can be factored, you should factor it immediately. If it contains an expression that already has been factored, you should unfactor it.

8. ETS has two favorite quadratic expressions. Be sure you know them cold in both factored and unfactored form:

$$x^2 - y^2 = (x + y)(x - y)$$
$$x^2 + 2xy + y^2 = (x + y)^2$$

9. Don't "solve for x" or "solve for y" unless you absolutely have to. (Don't worry; your math teacher won't find out.) Instead, look for direct solutions to SAT problems. ETS never uses problems that require time-consuming computations or endless fiddling with big numbers. There's always a trick—if you can spot it.

10. In solving simultaneous equations, simply add or subtract the equations.

11. Learn to recognize SAT function problems. They're the ones with the funny symbols.

12. If you come across a word problem you can't beat by working backward or plugging in, simply translate the problem into an equation and solve it.

Chapter 12
Geometry

SAT GEOMETRY PROBLEMS: CRACKING THE SYSTEM

About a third of the math problems on your SAT will involve geometry. Fortunately, you won't need much specific knowledge of geometry to solve them. You won't have to prove any theorems and you won't need to know many terms. You'll have to use a few formulas, but they will be printed on the first page of each math section in your test booklet.

In this chapter we will teach you

1. the fundamental facts you *must* know to solve SAT geometry problems;

2. how to find Jim's answers and avoid careless mistakes by guesstimating;

3. how to find Jim's answers by plugging in;

4. the advanced principles that will help you on harder problems.

BASIC PRINCIPLES: FUNDAMENTALS OF SAT GEOMETRY

The SAT doesn't cover any really difficult geometry, but you will have to have a thorough knowledge of several fundamental rules. You will use these fundamentals in applying the techniques that we will teach you later in the chapter. You don't need to linger over these rules if you have already mastered them. But be sure you understand them *completely* before you move on. Some of these rules will be provided to you in the instructions on your SAT, but you should know them cold before you go to the test center. Consulting the instructions as you work is a waste of time. (On the other hand, if the Pythagorean theorem suddenly vaporizes from your brain while you are taking the test, don't hesitate to peek back at the instructions.)

For the sake of simplicity, we have divided SAT geometry into four basic topics:

1. degrees and angles
2. triangles
3. circles
4. rectangles and squares

DEGREES AND ANGLES

1. A CIRCLE CONTAINS 360 DEGREES

In ancient times, it was believed that the sun revolved around the earth and that it required 360 days to do so. Every day, it was thought, the sun moved $\frac{1}{360}$ of the total distance it had to travel around the earth.

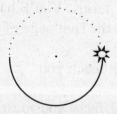

We know today that the earth revolves around the sun, not the other way around, and that it takes 365 days to do so. When the conventions of geometry were created, though, the older idea was incorporated. Every circle, therefore, is said to contain 360 degrees. Each degree is $\frac{1}{360}$ of the total distance around the outside of the circle. It doesn't matter whether the circle is large or small; it still has exactly 360 degrees.

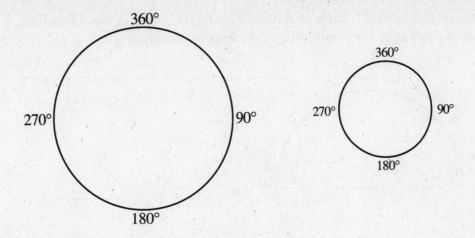

2. WHEN YOU THINK ABOUT ANGLES, REMEMBER CIRCLES

An angle is formed when two line segments extend from a common point. If you think of the point as the center of a circle, the *measure of the angle* is the number of degrees enclosed by the lines when they pass through the edge of the circle. Once again, the size of the circle doesn't matter; neither does the length of the lines.

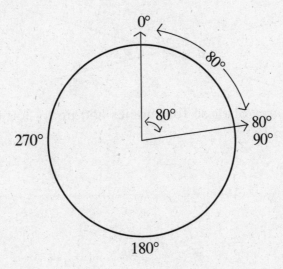

3. A LINE IS A 180-DEGREE ANGLE

You probably don't think of a line as an angle, but it is one. Think of it as a *flat* angle. The following drawings should help:

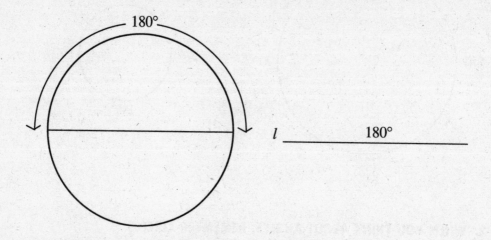

4. WHEN TWO LINES INTERSECT, FOUR ANGLES ARE FORMED

The following diagram should make this clear. The four angles are indicated by letters.

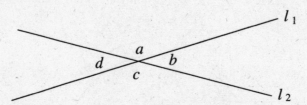

The measures of these four angles add up to 360 degrees. (Remember the circle.)

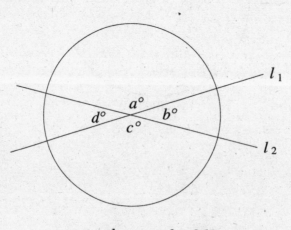

$$a + b + c + d = 360$$

If two lines are perpendicular to each other, each of the four angles formed will be 90 degrees. A 90-degree angle is called a *right angle*.

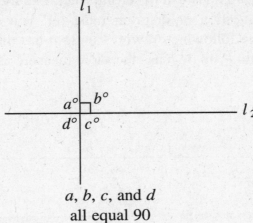

a, b, c, and d
all equal 90

The little box at the intersection of the two lines is the symbol for a right angle. If the lines are not perpendicular to each other, then none of the angles will be right angles, but angles opposite each other will have the same measures. Such angles are called *vertical angles*. They are like mirror images, or like the blades and handles of a pair of scissors. In the following diagram, angles a and c are equal; so are angles b and d. The total of all four angles is still 360 degrees.

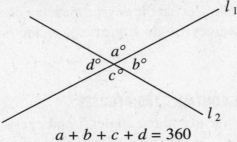

$a + b + c + d = 360$

It doesn't matter how many lines you intersect through a single point. The total measure of all the angles formed will still be 360 degrees.

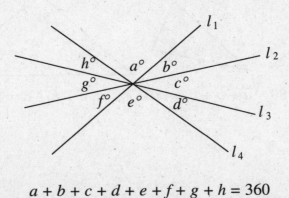

$a + b + c + d + e + f + g + h = 360$

5. WHEN TWO PARALLEL LINES ARE CUT BY A THIRD LINE, ANGLES THAT *LOOK* EQUAL *ARE* EQUAL

Parallel lines are lines that never intersect, like the lines on notebook paper. The question or diagram must tell you that two lines are parallel. In the following drawing, angle *a* has the same measure as angles *c*, *e*, and *h*; angle *b* has the same measure as angles *d*, *f*, and *g*.

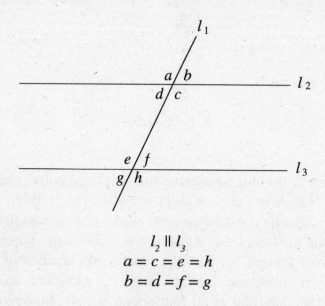

$$l_2 \parallel l_3$$
$$a = c = e = h$$
$$b = d = f = g$$

You should be able to see that the degree measure of angles *a*, *b*, *c*, and *d* add up to 360 degrees. So do angles *e*, *f*, *g*, and *h*.

TRIANGLES

1. EVERY TRIANGLE CONTAINS 180 DEGREES

The word *triangle* means "three angles," and every triangle contains three interior angles. The measures of these three angles *always* add up to *exactly* 180 degrees. You don't need to know why this is true or how to prove it. You just need to know it. And we mean *know* it.

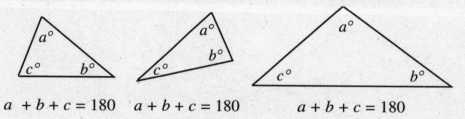

$$a + b + c = 180 \quad a + b + c = 180 \qquad a + b + c = 180$$

2. AN *EQUILATERAL* TRIANGLE IS ONE IN WHICH ALL THREE SIDES ARE EQUAL IN LENGTH

Because the angles opposite equal sides are also equal, all three angles in an equilateral triangle are equal, too. (Their measures are always 60 degrees each.)

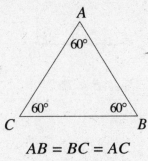

$$AB = BC = AC$$

3. AN *ISOSCELES* TRIANGLE IS ONE IN WHICH TWO OF THE SIDES ARE EQUAL IN LENGTH

The sides opposite those equal angles are also equal in length, because, as we just mentioned, angles opposite equal sides are also equal.

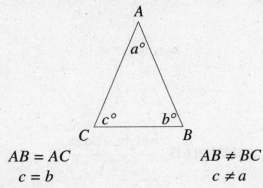

$$AB = AC$$
$$c = b$$

$$AB \neq BC$$
$$c \neq a$$

4. A *RIGHT TRIANGLE* IS A TRIANGLE IN WHICH ONE OF THE ANGLES IS A RIGHT ANGLE (90 DEGREES)

The longest side of a right triangle is called the hypotenuse.

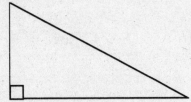

Some isosceles triangles are also right triangles.

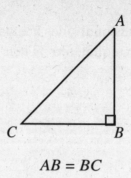

$$AB = BC$$

5. THE PERIMETER OF A TRIANGLE IS THE SUM OF THE LENGTHS OF ITS SIDES

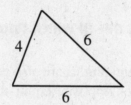

perimeter = 16

6. THE AREA OF A TRIANGLE IS: $\dfrac{\text{height} \times \text{base}}{2}$

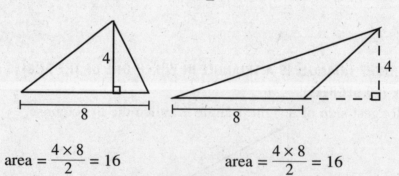

area = $\dfrac{4 \times 8}{2}$ = 16   area = $\dfrac{4 \times 8}{2}$ = 16

CIRCLES

1. THE CIRCUMFERENCE OF A CIRCLE IS $2\pi R$ OR πD, WHERE R IS THE RADIUS OF THE CIRCLE AND D IS THE DIAMETER

You'll be given this information in your test booklet, but you should know it cold before you take the test.

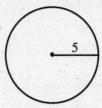 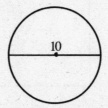

circumference = $2 \times \pi \times 5 = 10\pi$ circumference = 10π

In math class you probably learned that $\pi = 3.14$ (or even 3.14159). On the SAT, $\pi = 3^+$ (a little more than 3) is a good enough approximation. Even with a calculator, using $\pi = 3$ will give you all the information you need to solve even complicated SAT multiple-choice geometry questions.

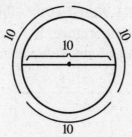

circumference = about 30

2. THE AREA OF A CIRCLE IS πR^2, WHERE R IS THE RADIUS OF THE CIRCLE

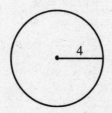

area = $\pi 4^2 = 16\pi$

RECTANGLES AND SQUARES

1. THE PERIMETER OF A RECTANGLE IS THE SUM OF THE LENGTHS OF ITS SIDES

Just add them up.

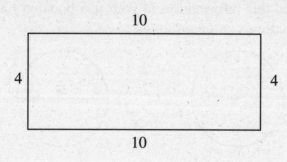

perimeter = 10 + 4 + 10 + 4 = 28

2. THE AREA OF A RECTANGLE IS LENGTH × WIDTH

The area of the preceding rectangle, therefore, is 10 × 4, or 40.

3. A SQUARE IS A RECTANGLE WHOSE FOUR SIDES ARE ALL EQUAL IN LENGTH

The perimeter of a square, therefore, is four times the length of any side. The area is the length of any side squared.

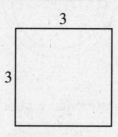

perimeter = 12
area = 9

BASIC PRINCIPLES: GUESSTIMATING

On many SAT geometry problems, you will be presented with a drawing in which some information is given and you will be asked to find some of the information that is missing. In most such problems, Jim expects you to apply some formula or perform some calculation, often an algebraic one. But you'll almost always be better off if you look at the drawing and make a rough estimate of Jim's answer (based on the given information) before you try to work it out. We call this "guesstimating." It will often enable you to find Jim's answer without working the problem out at all.

Guesstimating is extremely helpful on SAT geometry problems. At the very least, it will enable you to avoid careless mistakes. It will allow you to eliminate *immediately* answer choices that could not possibly be Jim's answer. It will always save you time and points.

For these reasons, we have to declare a general rule: *If an SAT geometry problem has a drawing in it, you must never, never, never leave it blank.*

THE BASIC GUESSTIMATING TOOLS

The basic principles just outlined (such as the number of degrees in a triangle and the fact that $\pi \approx 3$) will be enormously helpful to you in guesstimating on the SAT. You should also know the approximate values of several common square roots. Be sure to memorize them before moving on. Knowing them cold will help you solve problems and save time even if your calculator has a square root function.

Square Roots
$\sqrt{1} = 1$
$\sqrt{2} \approx 1.4$
$\sqrt{3} \approx 1.7$
$\sqrt{4} = 2$

You will also find it very helpful if you have a good sense of how large certain common angles are. Study the following examples.

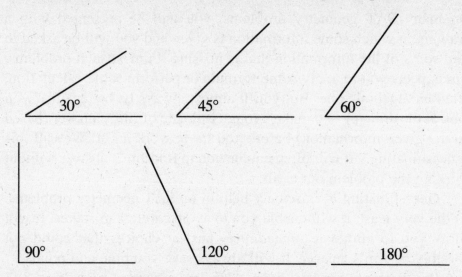

To get a little practice using the material you've memorized to guesstimate, do the following drill.

DRILL 1

Guesstimate the following values. Use simple values for $\sqrt{2}$, $\sqrt{3}$, and π rather than using your calculator to figure out each value.

1. $\sqrt{2} - 1 =$
2. $3\sqrt{\pi} =$
3. $2\sqrt{2} =$
4. $\sqrt{\dfrac{3}{4}}$
5. $\sqrt{18}$

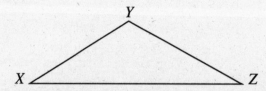

6. In the figure above, given $XY = 16$, estimate all angles and the lengths of other sides.

HOW TALL IS THE CEILING?

If your father stood next to a wall in your living room and asked you how tall the ceiling was, what would you do? Would you get out your trigonometry textbook and try to triangulate using the shadow cast by your father? Of course not. You'd look at your father and think something like this: "Dad's about 6 feet tall. The ceiling's a couple of feet higher than he is. It must be about 8 feet tall."

Your guesstimation wouldn't be exact, but it would be close. If your mother later claimed that the ceiling in the living room was 15 feet high, you'd be able to tell her with confidence that she was mistaken.

You'll be able to do the same thing on the SAT. Every geometry figure on your test will be drawn exactly to scale unless there is a note in that problem *telling you otherwise*. That means that you can trust the proportions in the drawing. If line segment *A* has a length of 2 and line segment *B* is exactly half as long, then the length of line segment *B* is 1. All such problems are ideal for guesstimating.

Look at the following example:

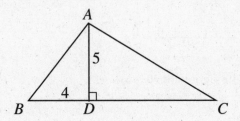

10 If the area of △*ABC* in the figure above is 30, then the length of *DC* is

(A) 2 (B) 4 (C) 6 (D) 8 (E) 12

HERE'S HOW TO CRACK IT

In guesstimation problems like this, it's usually a good idea to start at the edges and work your way in. When an SAT problem has numeric choices, as this one does, they are always given in increasing or decreasing order of size. Choices at either extreme will be the easiest to dispute and hence the easiest to eliminate if they are wrong.

Look at the drawing. Line *DC* is obviously a good bit longer than line *BD*. Since *BD* = 4, we know for certain that *DC* has to be greater than 4. That means we can eliminate choices A and B. Just cross them out so you won't waste time thinking about them again. They couldn't possibly be correct.

Now look at *DC* again. Is it 3 times as long as *BD*? No way. That means choice E can be eliminated as well.

We've narrowed it down to choice C or D. Does *DC* look like it's twice as long as *BD*, or like it's one and a half times as long? That's all you have to decide.

(Jim's answer is D. Notice that you found it without having to use the area of the triangle, which was given in the problem.)

Here's another example:

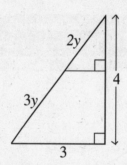

13 In the figure above, *y* =

(A) 1
(B) 2
(C) 3
(D) 4
(E) 5

HERE'S HOW TO CRACK IT

You can use any of a number of guesstimating approaches in solving this problem. Here's one of them:

The hypotenuse of the little triangle is 2y. That means that y equals half the length of the hypotenuse. Is half the length of the small hypotenuse larger or smaller than 3 (the base of the triangle)? Smaller, obviously. Therefore, you can eliminate choices C, D, and E, all of which are *larger*.

You now know that y has to be either 1 or 2. You can probably see that it has to be 1. (Jim's answer, therefore, is A. Don't get careless on this problem and select choice E after figuring out that 5y has to equal 5.)

Here's one final example. It's a good bit harder than the others, but you still shouldn't have trouble with it.

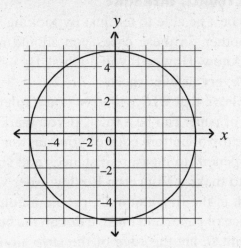

19 What is the circumference of the circle in the figure above?

(A) 5π

(B) 10π

(C) $\dfrac{25}{2}\pi$

(D) 20π

(E) 25π

HERE'S HOW TO CRACK IT

Let's say you've forgotten the formula for circumference and don't have the time to look it up. What do you do? Just count "squares." If you count units along the rim of the circle, you get about 7 for a quarter of the way around the circle. That means that the entire circumference is approximately 28. Now look at the choices:

(A) 5π is about 15. Could this be Jim's answer? No. Eliminate.

(B) 10π is about 30. A good possibility.

(C) $\frac{25}{2}$ is 12.5. Therefore, $\frac{25}{2}\pi$ is about 37.5. Could this be Jim's answer? It doesn't seem likely; it's a good bit more than 28.

(D) 20π is about 60. That's way off. Eliminate.

(E) 25π is about 75. That's even farther off. Eliminate. (Jim's answer is choice B. This problem didn't turn out to be very hard after all, did it?)

WHEN YOU CAN'T EYEBALL, MEASURE

Sometimes you won't be able to tell just by looking whether one line is longer than another. In these cases you should actually *measure* what you need to know. How will you do this? By using the *ruler* that ETS provides on every answer sheet.

You don't believe that ETS will give you a ruler on your answer sheet? Any piece of paper can be a ruler, if you mark off distances on it. You can use the top or bottom edge of your answer sheet (or of your finger or of your pencil) to measure distances and solve problems.

Here's how to make a Princeton Review ruler with your answer sheet. Take a look at the first example, problem number 10, on page 239. Take any piece of paper and make a dot on the bottom edge. Now put the dot on point *B*, lay the edge of the strip along *BD*, and mark another dot on the edge of the paper beside point *D*. Here's what it should look like:

What's the length of the space between the dots? It's exactly 4, of course—the same as the length of *BD* in the diagram. You now have a ruler. You can use it to measure the length of *DC*, which is what the problem asks you for.

> *You can make your ruler as precise as you need to. By placing the ruler against side AD and noting the difference between its length and the length of BD, you'll be able to mark off your ruler in units of 1.*

You can even use your Princeton Review ruler to measure the circumference of a circle or the length of a curved line. Just carefully turn the paper around the curved distance you want to measure, mark off the distance on your ruler with your pencil, and then compare the ruler with some known distance in the problem.

Here's how it works. Look at the last example, problem number 19, on page 241. Take any piece of paper, turn it around the circle, mark off the distance, and measure it on the grid in the problem. You'll come up with a length of about 30, just as you did by eyeballing.

IMPORTANT NOTE

You'll have to make a new ruler for each problem on which you need to measure something. ETS figures are drawn to scale (unless they're labeled otherwise), but they aren't all drawn to the *same* scale. A ruler that measures 4 on one diagram won't measure 4 on another. Also, don't forget to erase your markings after you've finished each problem, so that they don't throw off ETS's grading machines.

YOU CAN ALSO MEASURE ANGLES

ETS is also kind enough to give you a protractor. Where? On any of the three square corners of your answer sheet. The square corner of a sheet of paper is a perfect 90-degree angle, like this:

90°

If you fold the paper on the diagonal, taking care not to leave a crease, you end up with a perfect 45-degree angle, like this:

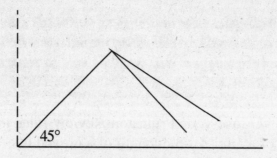

45°

With a tool like this, you'll be able to measure almost any angle with a fair degree of accuracy. Actually, if you practice eyeballing angles, you may never need to consult the corner of your answer sheet. If you spend an hour or so teaching yourself to guesstimate the size of angles just by looking at them, you'll improve your SAT score. In fact, you should be able to answer at least one question on your SAT without doing anything except eyeballing or measuring.

Here's an example:

MULTIPLE CHOICE — MATH

1 2 3 4 5 ⑥ 7 8 9 10 11 12 13 14 15 16 17 18 19 20 21 22 23 24 25

EASY   MEDIUM   HARD

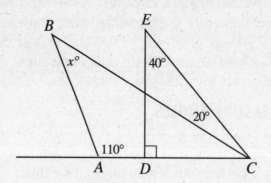

6   In the figure above, x =

(A) 15
(B) 20
(C) 30
(D) 40
(E) 50

HERE'S HOW TO CRACK IT

By using your page-corner protractor you should be able to see that *x* is a little bit less than 45. (You should also be able to tell this just by eyeballing.) Therefore, you can definitely eliminate answer choices A, B, and E. Your best choice is D. (It is also Jim's answer.)

> *Using rulers and protractors will keep you from making careless computational errors on SAT geometry problems. Because measuring the figures enables you to skip the arithmetic, it also enables you to avoid all the traps that Jim has laid for Joe Bloggs.*

WHAT IF A DIAGRAM IS NOT DRAWN TO SCALE?

Don't worry if a diagram is *not* drawn to scale. In many cases you will simply be able to *redraw* the diagram in your test booklet and then measure. Sometimes Jim uses a nonscale drawing because his answer would be obvious even to Joe Bloggs in a scale drawing.

Let's look at an example. Imagine a problem in which you are given a drawing like the following one and asked to determine which is bigger, line segment *AB* or line segment *BC*.

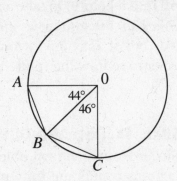

Note: Figure not drawn to scale.

HERE'S HOW TO CRACK IT

This figure is not drawn to scale, so simply measuring the segments won't help. In addition, Jim has drawn the figure so that the segments seem to be the same length. What should you do? *Redraw the figure in your test booklet exaggerating the difference in the given information.* In this case, you are given the measures of two angles. One angle is a little larger than the other, but both seem to be about the same size in the drawing. All you have to do is redraw the figure exaggerating this difference. Since one angle is bigger than the other, you should make it *much* bigger. Your drawing should look something like this:

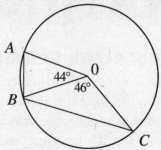

Now you shouldn't have any trouble seeing that line segment *BC* has to be bigger than line segment *AB*. Jim used a nonscale drawing because his answer would have been obvious if he had not.

Sometimes you will find it helpful to take a nonscale drawing and *redraw it to scale.* This can be somewhat time-consuming if the problem is complicated, but it may give you a shortcut to Jim's answer. Just use your ruler to redraw the figure based on the information given you.

WHEN YOU CAN'T MEASURE, SKETCH, AND GUESSTIMATE

You will sometimes encounter geometry problems that have no diagrams, or that have diagrams containing only partial information. In these cases, you should use the given information to *sketch* a complete diagram and then use your drawing as a basis for guesstimating. *You must not hesitate to fill your test booklet with sketches and scratch work: this is precisely what you are supposed to do.* Finding Jim's answer will be much harder, if not impossible, if you don't take full advantage of the materials ETS gives you.

Here's an example:

18 All faces of a cube with a 4-meter edge are covered with striped paper. If the cube is then cut into cubes with 1-meter edges, how many of the 1-meter cubes have striped paper on exactly one face?

(A) 24
(B) 36
(C) 48
(D) 60
(E) 72

HERE'S HOW TO CRACK IT

This problem doesn't have a diagram. It would be much easier to solve if it did. What should you do? Draw a diagram, of course! Just sketch the cube quickly in your test booklet and mark it off into 1-meter cubes as described. Your sketch should look like this:

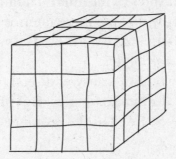

You should be able to see that there are four cubes on each side of the big cube that will have striped paper on only one face. Since a cube has six sides, this means that Jim's answer is choice A.

BASIC PRINCIPLES: PLUGGING IN

As you learned in chapter 11, plugging in is one of the most helpful techniques for solving SAT algebra problems. It is also very useful on geometry problems. On some problems, you will be able to plug in guesstimated values for missing information and then use the results either to find Jim's answer directly or to eliminate answers that could not possibly be correct.

Here's an example:

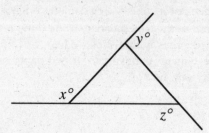

18 In the figure above, $x + y + z =$

(A) 90
(B) 180
(C) 270
(D) 360
(E) 450

HERE'S HOW TO CRACK IT

We don't know the measures of the interior angles of the triangle in the drawing, but we do know that the three interior angles of *any* triangle add up to 180, and 180 divided by 3 is 60. Now, simply plug in 60 for the value of each *interior* angle.

This doesn't give you Jim's answer directly; the problem does not ask you for the sum of the interior angles. But plugging in does enable you to find Jim's answer. Look at the redrawn figure:

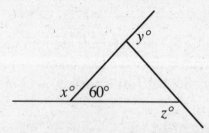

If the marked interior angle is 60, what must x be? Remember that every line is a 180-degree angle. That means that the measure of x must be $180 - 60$, or 120. You can now do the same thing for the other two angles. Using this method you find that x, y, and z each equal 120. That means that $x + y + z = 360$. Jim's answer, therefore, is choice D.

ALTERNATE SOLUTION

It is possible to solve this problem by guesstimating. Angle x looks like it's about, oh, 135 degrees; angle y looks like about 100 degrees; angle z looks like about 120. (Don't spend a lot of time eyeballing; you don't have to be very precise.) What does that add up to? 355. Not bad!

Guesstimating like this won't always give you exactly Jim's answer, but it will usually enable you to eliminate at least three of the four incorrect choices. Other kinds of geometry problems also lend themselves to plugging in.

Here's an example:

25 The length of rectangle S is 20 percent longer than the length of rectangle R, and the width of rectangle S is 20 percent shorter than the width of rectangle R. The area of rectangle S is

(A) 20% greater than the area of rectangle R
(B) 4% greater than the area of rectangle R
(C) equal to the area of rectangle R
(D) 4% less than the area of rectangle R
(E) 20% less than the area of rectangle R

HERE'S HOW TO CRACK IT

This is a very hard problem. You should recognize first of all that choices A, C, and E are Joe Bloggs attractors and should be eliminated. Even if you don't see this, though, you'll be able to find Jim's answer by sketching and plugging in.

In plugging in, always use numbers that are easy to work with. Twenty percent equals one fifth; the easiest number to work with, therefore, is 5. Let's say that the length of rectangle R is 5; that means that the length of rectangle S, which is 20 percent longer, must be 6. You can use 5 again in figuring widths. If the width of rectangle R is 5, then the width of rectangle S, which is shorter, must be 4. You should come up with two sketches that look like this:

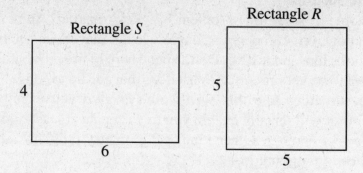

Rectangle S

Rectangle R

4

6

5

5

R turns out to be a square, but that's all right; squares are rectangles, too. The area of rectangle S is 24; the area of R is 25. The area of S, which is what the problem asks for, is thus a little bit less than the area of R. In fact, it is 4 percent less, although you don't need to figure it out exactly. Jim's answer is choice D.

THE PYTHAGOREAN THEOREM

The Pythagorean theorem states that in a right triangle (a triangle with one interior angle that is exactly 90 degrees), the square of the hypotenuse equals the sum of the squares of the other two sides. As we told you earlier, the hypotenuse is the *longest* side of a right triangle; it's the side that doesn't touch the right angle. The square of the hypotenuse is its length squared. Applying the Pythagorean formula to the following drawing, we find that $c^2 = a^2 + b^2$.

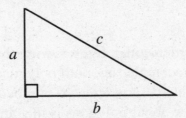

Jim makes fairly frequent use of math problems that require you to know the Pythagorean formula. Fortunately, he is extremely predictable in how he does so. If you memorize the formula and the proportions of a few common triangles, you will have a big advantage on these problems.

The most common Pythagorean triangle on the SAT has sides measuring 3, 4, and 5 or multiples of those numbers, as in the following two examples:

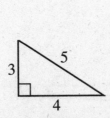
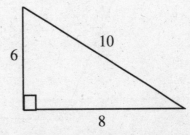

> *You should also be on the lookout for problems in which the application of the Pythagorean theorem is not obvious. For example, every rectangle contains two right triangles. That means that if you know the length and width of the rectangle, you also know the length of the diagonal, which is the hypotenuse of both triangles.*

Here's an example:

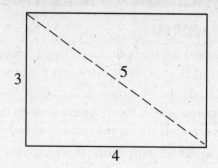

POLYGONS

Polygons are two-dimensional figures with three or more straight sides. Triangles and rectangles are both polygons. So are figures with five, six, seven, eight, or any greater number of sides. The most important fact to know about polygons is that any one of them can be *divided into triangles*. This means that you can always determine the sum of the measures of the interior angles of any polygon.

For example, the sum of the interior angles of any four-sided polygon (called a "quadrilateral") is 360 degrees. Why? Because any quadrilateral can be divided into two triangles, and a triangle contains 180 degrees. Look at the following example:

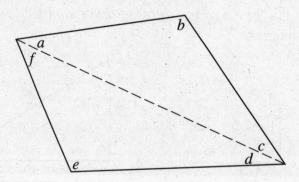

In this polygon, $a + b + c = 180$; so does $d + e + f$. That means that the sum of the interior angles of the quadrilateral must be 360 ($a + b + c + d + e + f$).

A *parallelogram* is a quadrilateral whose opposite sides are parallel. In the following parallelogram, side *AB* is parallel to side *DC*, and *AD* is parallel to *BC*. Because a parallelogram can also be thought of as a pair of parallel lines intersected by another pair of parallel lines, *Fred's theorem applies to it:* interior angles that *look* equal *are* equal. In the drawing, therefore, the interior angle at point *A* is equal to the one at point *C*, and the one at point *B* is equal to the one at point *D*.

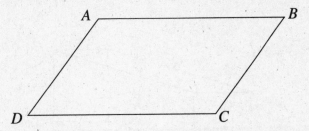

ANGLE/SIDE RELATIONSHIPS OF TRIANGLES

The *longest* side of any triangle is opposite the *largest* interior angle; the *shortest* side is opposite the *smallest* angle. In the following triangle, side *A* is longer than side *B*, which is longer than side *C*, because angle *a* is larger than angle *b*, which is larger than angle *c*.

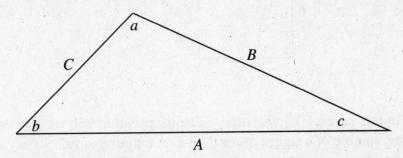

The same rule applies to isosceles and equilateral triangles. An isosceles triangle, remember, is one in which two of the sides are equal in length; therefore, the angles opposite those sides are also equal. In an equilateral triangle, all three sides are equal; so are all three angles.

VOLUME

Jim will occasionally ask a question that will require you to calculate the volume of a rectangular solid (a box or a cube) on the SAT. The formula for the volume of a rectangular solid is *length × width × height*. Since length, width, and height are equal in a cube, the volume of a cube can be calculated simply by *cubing* (where do you think they get the name?) the length of any of the sides.

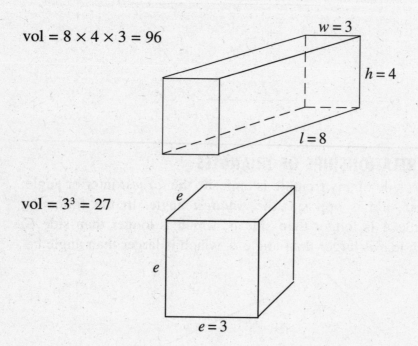

$\text{vol} = 8 \times 4 \times 3 = 96$

$w = 3$

$h = 4$

$l = 8$

$\text{vol} = 3^3 = 27$

e

e

$e = 3$

(In rare cases, ETS will ask you a question that will require you to find the volume of a figure other than a rectangular solid. In any such case, the formula will either be provided with the question or will appear in the instructions.)

CARTESIAN GRIDS

If you've ever looked for a particular city on a map in an atlas, you're probably familiar with the idea behind Cartesian grids. You look up Philadelphia in the atlas's index and discover that it is located at D5 on the map of Pennsylvania. On the map itself you find letters of the alphabet running along the top of the page and numbers running down one side. You move your finger straight down from the D at the top of the page until it is at the level of the 5 along the side, and there you are: in Philadelphia.

Cartesian grids work the same way. The standard grid is shaped like a cross. The horizontal line is called the *X-axis;* the vertical line is the *Y-axis.* The four areas formed by the intersection of the axes are called *quadrants.* The location of any quadrant can be described with a pair of numbers (*x, y*), just the way you would on a map: (0,0) are the coordinates of the intersection of the two axes (also called the "origin"); (1,2) are the coordinates of the point one space to the right and two spaces up; (–1,5) are the coordinates of the point one space to the left and five spaces up; (–4,–2) are the coordinates of the point four spaces to the left and two spaces down. All these points are located on the following diagram:

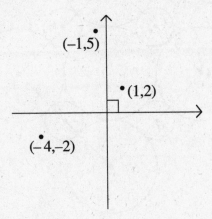

ADVANCED SKETCHING AND GUESSTIMATION

Some extremely difficult SAT geometry problems can be solved quickly and easily through sketching and guesstimation, but you will have to stay on your toes if you want to crack them. The way to do this is always to ask yourself three questions:

1. What information have I been given?

2. What information have I been asked to find?

3. What is the relation between them?

Here's an example. It was the second hardest problem on the SAT in which it appeared:

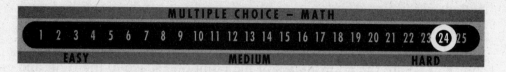

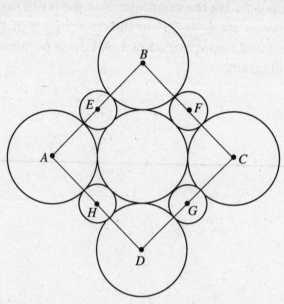

24 Four circles of radius 2 with centers A, B, C, and D are arranged symmetrically around another circle of radius 2, and four smaller equal circles with centers E, F, G, and H each touch three of the larger circles as shown in the figure above. What is the radius of one of the small circles?

(A) $\sqrt{2} - 2$
(B) $\sqrt{2} - 1$
(C) $2\sqrt{2} - 2$
(D) 1
(E) $3\sqrt{2} - 1$

HERE'S HOW TO CRACK IT
First answer the three questions:

1. I have been given the radius of a large circle.

2. I have been asked for the radius of a small circle.

3. Both are distances and both, therefore, can be measured.

What at first appeared to be an extremely difficult geometry problem now reveals itself to be a simple matter of measurement. Mark off the distance of one large-circle radius along the edge of your answer sheet. This equals 2. Now align your ruler on a small-circle radius. The small-circle radius is smaller, obviously. How much smaller? You can probably see that it is a little bit less than half as long. That means that the answer to the question is "a little bit less than 1."

Now turn to the answer choices and solve them one at a time:

(A) $\sqrt{2}$, as you know, equals 1.4, so $\sqrt{2} - 2 = -0.6$. A distance cannot be negative. Eliminate.

(B) $\sqrt{2} - 1 = 0.4$. This is less than 1, but a lot less. A possibility.

(C) $2\sqrt{2} - 2 = 0.8$. This is a little bit less than 1. An excellent possibility.

(D) $1 = 1$. One can't be less than 1. Eliminate.

(E) $3\sqrt{2} - 1 = 3.2$. Eliminate.

You're right. Jim's answer is C. You must be a genius!

SUMMARY

1. Degrees and angles:

   A. A circle contains 360 degrees.

   B. When you think about angles, remember circles.

   C. A line is a 180-degree angle.

   D. When two lines intersect, four angles are formed; the sum of their measures is 360 degrees.

   E. Fred's theorem: When two parallel lines are cut by a third line, angles that *look* equal *are* equal.

2. Triangles:

   A. Every triangle contains 180 degrees.

   B. An equilateral triangle is one in which all three sides are equal in length, and all three angles are equal in measure (60 degrees).

   C. An isosceles triangle is one in which two of the sides are equal in length, and the two angles opposite the equal sides are equal in measure.

   D. A right triangle is one in which one of the angles is a right angle (90 degrees).

   E. The perimeter of a triangle is the sum of the lengths of its sides.

   F. The area of a triangle is: $\dfrac{\text{height} \times \text{base}}{2}$

3. Circles:

   A. The circumference of a circle is $2\pi r$ or πd, where r is the radius of the circle and d is the diameter.

   B. The area of a circle is πr^2, where r is the radius of the circle.

4. Rectangles and squares:

   A. The perimeter of a rectangle is the sum of the lengths of its sides.

   B. The area of a rectangle is length × width.

   C. A square is a rectangle whose four sides are all equal in length.

5. When you encounter a geometry problem on the SAT, *guesstimate* the answer before trying to work it out.

6. You must never skip an SAT problem that has a drawing with it.

7. You must know the following values:

$$\pi = 3$$

$$\sqrt{2} = 1.4$$

$$\sqrt{3} = 1.7$$

8. You must also be familiar with the size of certain common angles.

9. Most SAT geometry diagrams are drawn to scale. Use your eyes before you use your pencil. Try to eliminate impossible answers.

10. When your eyes aren't enough, use the edges and corners of your answer sheet as rulers and protractors.

11. When a diagram is not drawn to scale, redraw it.

12. When no diagram is provided, make your own; when a provided diagram is incomplete, complete it.

13. When information is missing from a diagram, guesstimate and plug in.

14. The Pythagorean theorem states that in a right triangle the square of the hypotenuse equals the sum of the squares of the other two sides.

15. Any polygon can be divided into triangles.

16. The *longest* side of any triangle is opposite the *largest* interior angle; the *shortest* side is opposite the *smallest* angle.

17. The volume of a rectangular solid is length × width × height. The formulas to compute the volume of other three-dimensional figures are supplied in the instructions.

18. You must know how to locate points on a Cartesian grid.

19. Some extremely difficult SAT geometry problems can be solved quickly and easily through sketching and guesstimation, but you will have to stay on your toes. The way to do this is always to ask yourself three questions:

What information have I been given?

What information have I been asked to find?

What is the relationship between them?

Chapter 13

Quantitative Comparisons

QUANTITATIVE COMPARISONS: CRACKING THE SYSTEM

One scored math section on your SAT will contain a group of fifteen quantitative comparisons, or quant comps. The quant comps will start easy and become difficult. The first third will be easy, the middle third will be medium, and the final third will be difficult.

WHAT IS A QUANTITATIVE COMPARISON?

Here are the instructions for and three examples of quant comps as they will appear on your SAT.

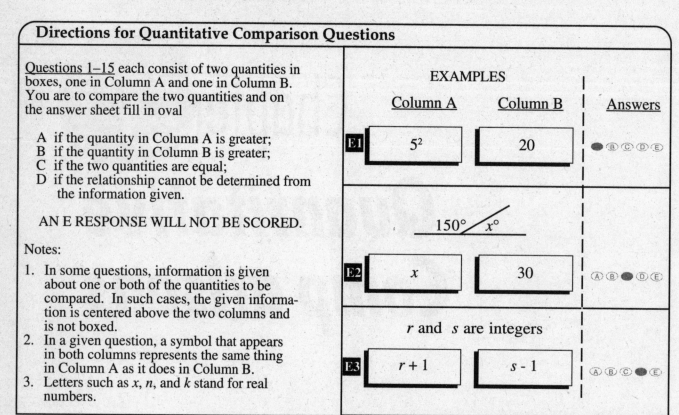

Jim's answer to the first example is A, because the quantity in Column A (25) is greater than the quantity in Column B (20). Jim's answer to the second example is C. You know that $x + 150 = 180$; $180 - 150$, therefore, must equal 30, and the two quantities are the same. Jim's answer to the third example is D. Since you can't tell what r or s is, you can't determine whether one quantity is greater than the other.

Be sure that you know these instructions cold before you take the SAT. If you have to look them up each time you answer a question, you'll be wasting time and robbing yourself of points.

To start our explanation, let's look at a very simple quant comp example:

Column A	Column B
$2 + 2$	2×2

Your task, remember, is to determine the relationship between the quantity in Column A and the quantity in Column B. The quantity in Column A is 4; so is the quantity in Column B. Will this always be true? Yes, $2 + 2$ will always equal 4, and so will 2×2. Therefore, the correct answer is C, "the two quantities are equal."

Suppose we rewrite the problem as follows:

$$3 + 2 \qquad\qquad 2 \times 2$$

The quantity in Column A now equals 5, while the quantity in Column B still equals 4. Because $3 + 2$ will always equal 5, and 5 will always be greater than 4, the correct answer now is A, "the quantity in Column A is greater."

Let's rewrite the problem one more time:

$$x + 2 \qquad\qquad 2 - x$$

What's the answer now? Suppose that x equals 5. In that case, the quantity in Column A would be greater than the quantity in Column B. But x can be *any* number; suppose it's 0. In that case, the two quantities would be equal. Now suppose that x equals -2. In that case the quantity in Column B would be greater than the quantity in Column A.

In other words, depending on which numbers we plug in for x, we can make choice A, B, *or* C seem to be the correct answer. That means that *none* of these answers is *always* correct. Jim's answer has to be D, "the relationship cannot be determined from the information given."

THE INFORMATION GIVEN

Many quant comps contain given information that you are supposed to use in solving the problem. This information is placed *between* the two columns. Here's an example:

Column A	Column B

During a 100-day period last year, it rained on exactly 40 days.

1 Percent of days when it did not rain — 40%

HERE'S HOW TO CRACK IT

The statement centered between the columns is the given. You are supposed to use it in solving the problem.

You shouldn't have any trouble with this one. Since it rained on 40 percent of the days, 60 percent must have been dry. The quantity in Column A is thus greater than the quantity in Column B, and Jim's answer is A.

QUANT COMPS ARE QUICK BUT TRICKY

Most students are able to answer quant comps very quickly. Answering quant comps usually takes much less time than answering regular math questions or grid-ins. Because of this, many students breathe a sigh of relief when they come to the quant comp section.

But this apparent ease is deceptive. Quant comps go quickly because certain answers tend to *seem* correct immediately. Because of this, Joe Bloggs loves quant comps. When he looks at a question, he doesn't have to think very long before an "obvious" answer choice jumps off the page.

THIS IS BAD NEWS FOR JOE, BUT GOOD NEWS FOR YOU

Since certain answer choices on quant comps have a strong tendency to *seem* correct to Joe Bloggs, he quickly finds himself in the same predicament he is in on the rest of the SAT:

1. On easy questions the answers that seem right to him really are right, so he earns points.

2. On medium questions his hunches are sometimes right and sometimes wrong, so he just about breaks even.

3. On difficult questions the answers that seem right to him are always wrong, so he loses points.

This is unlucky for Joe, but very lucky for you. Quant comps are the easiest math questions to crack because the Joe Bloggs attractors are easy to spot—if you know what to look for and if you are careful. You can use POE, the process of elimination, to eliminate obviously incorrect choices, improve your guessing odds, and zero in on Jim's answer.

MATHEMATICAL CONTENT

In terms of mathematical content, most quant comps will seem familiar to you. You'll find arithmetic problems, algebra problems, and geometry problems. You will be able to solve most of these problems by using the techniques we have already taught you.

SOLVING QUANT COMPS: BASIC PRINCIPLES

Not all quant comps can be solved simply by using the techniques we have already taught you. Quant comps are a unique problem type, and there are a number of special rules and techniques that apply only to them.

Even on quant comps that can be solved simply by using techniques you already know, there are still some unique features that you need to be familiar with. For instance, some regular techniques must be modified slightly for quant comps. We'll start with some basic principles and then move on to some more advanced ones.

QUANT COMPUTATION

Many quant comps can be solved without any sort of computation. Look at the following example:

13 Area of a circle with diameter 12   Surface area of a sphere with diameter 12

HERE'S HOW TO CRACK IT

Do you remember the formula for the surface area of a sphere? No? Good! You don't need it.

Just use your common sense to picture what you're being asked to compare: the area of a circle—say, a paper plate—and the surface area of a sphere—say, a beach ball with the same diameter as the plate. Which is bigger? It's obvious: the surface of the beach ball. (Imagine trying to cover the beach ball completely with the paper plate. It can't be done!) Jim's answer is B.

NUMBERS ONLY

If a quant comp problem contains nothing but numbers, choice D *cannot* be Jim's answer.

In a quant comp that has no variables, it will always be possible to obtain a definite solution. For example, the quantity $2 + 2$ can only have one value: 4. The quantity $2 + x$, on the other hand, can have an infinite number of values, depending on what you plug in for x.

When you see a quant comp that contains only numbers, therefore, you can eliminate choice D right off the bat. This tilts the odds in your favor, of course, which means that even if you can't get any farther, you should guess among the remaining choices.

Here's an example:

| 2 | $10 - (8 - 6 - 4)$ | $10 - 8 - (6 - 4)$ |

HERE'S HOW TO CRACK IT

This problem contains nothing but numbers. Therefore, it *must* have a solution, and choice D can be eliminated.

(Jim's answer is A. Because you know you are always to perform *first* any operations enclosed in parentheses, you can see that the quantity in Column A equals 12, while the quantity in Column B equals 0.)

EQUATIONS

In the same way that you add or subtract on both sides of an equation, you can add or subtract on both sides of a quant comp. (Just don't multiply or divide on both sides.)

Here's an example:

| 1 | $\dfrac{1}{4} + \dfrac{1}{2} + \dfrac{1}{13}$ | $\dfrac{1}{13} + \dfrac{1}{2} + \dfrac{1}{3}$ |

HERE'S HOW TO CRACK IT

Before doing anything else, you should notice that this quant comp contains nothing but numbers and that choice D, therefore, cannot possibly be Jim's answer.

Your next impulse may be to find a common denominator for all those fractions. Don't you dare! You can solve this problem in a second by eliminating common terms from both sides.

The quantities in Column A and Column B both include $\frac{1}{2}$ and $\frac{1}{13}$.

That means you *subtract both fractions from both sides*. Doing so leaves you with the following:

$$\frac{1}{4} \qquad \frac{1}{3}$$

It should be obvious to you now that Jim's answer has to be B, because $\frac{1}{3}$ is bigger than $\frac{1}{4}$. (Don't make the common careless error of thinking that $\frac{1}{4}$ is bigger than $\frac{1}{3}$ because 4 is bigger than 3!—see comparing fractions on page 169.)

SOLVING QUANT COMPS: MEDIUM AND DIFFICULT QUESTIONS

ATTACKING HUNCHES

On medium and difficult quant comps, you should *attack* your hunches. Joe Bloggs's hunches begin to let him down after the easy questions. Jim's answers, which seemed right to him on the easy questions, now begin to seem wrong. By the time Joe gets to the hard questions, his hunches are invariably leading him to incorrect choices.

What does this mean for you? It means that on medium and difficult questions, you should be extremely suspicious of choices that *seem* to be obvious or correct. In fact, you should attack these very choices. For example, when it is obvious that one column *could* be greater than the other, you should attack that column and try to find a case where the *other* column could be greater.

Here's an example:

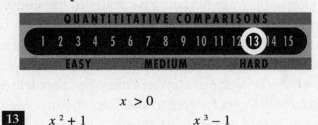

$$x > 0$$

| 13 | $x^2 + 1$ | | $x^3 - 1$ |

HERE'S HOW TO CRACK IT

It is easy to think of a value for x that would make the quantity in Column B greater than the quantity in Column A. How about 4? You know that $4^3 - 1$ equals 63, and $4^2 + 1$ equals 17. Because 63 is greater than 17, the correct answer *could* be B.

But would Column B *always* have to be greater than Column A? This is what you have to find out. (Before you do, notice that you have already eliminated choices A and C as possibilities: C is out because if one quantity is even *sometimes* greater than the other, the two quantities cannot *always* be equal; A is out because if Column B is even *sometimes* greater than Column A, then Column A cannot *always* be greater than Column B.)

The easiest number greater than 0 to plug in is 1. Doing so produces a value of 2 for Column A and a value of 0 for Column B. In other words, when you plug in 1, the value in Column A is greater—just the opposite of what happened when you plugged in 4. Since you have now found a case in which Column A *could* be greater than Column B, you can also eliminate choice B as a possibility. The only choice left is D—Jim's answer.

PLUGGING IN

When you plug in on quant comps, remember the numbers with special properties: negatives, fractions, 0, and 1.

In ordinary algebra problems on the SAT, you don't have to be very careful about which numbers you plug in. Since you're only looking for numbers that make the equations work, you can just pick numbers that are easy to work with. This is what we taught you in chapter 10.

Quant comps, though, are a little different. On these questions you are looking for answers that *always* work. A single exception, therefore, is enough to make an answer choice wrong. The key to finding Jim's answer on hard questions is being certain that you've taken into account all possible exceptions. This is why Joe Bloggs has trouble on medium and difficult quant comps.

This is a hard fact for many students to keep in mind. In plugging in on quant comps, they are attracted naturally to the numbers we use most often: positive whole numbers. But there are many other numbers, and Jim loves to write quant comp problems that depend on the special qualities of these numbers. In fact, many difficult quant comps are difficult *only because* these numbers must be considered in finding a solution, and Joe Bloggs forgets to consider them.

Because this is true, you should always ask yourself the following question on quant comp plug-ins:

Would my answer be different if I plugged in a negative number, a fraction, 0, or 1?

To find out whether it would, you should plug in one of each until you have found a definite answer.

Here's an example:

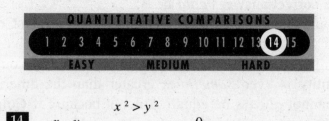

$$x^2 > y^2$$

14     $x - y$ 0

HERE'S HOW TO CRACK IT

When Joe Bloggs solves this problem, he plugs in easy positive integers—say, 3 for x and 2 for y. Because $3 - 2 = 1$, and 1 is greater than 0, he selects A as his answer. What happens? He loses points.

This is a number 26—a very hard question. If finding the answer were as easy as plugging in 3 and 2, Joe Bloggs would get this question right and it would be in the easy third. There must be something Joe has forgotten.

Indeed there is. Joe has forgotten the special cases. If you want to find Jim's answer, you're going to have to remember them.

First, try plugging in negative numbers instead of positive ones: -3 for x and -2 for y. $(-3)^2$ is 9; $(-2)^2$ is 4. Because 9 is greater than 4, you've fulfilled the requirement in the given.

Now look at Column A. What is $x - y$ now? It is -1. Is -1 greater than 0? No, it's less than 0.

Before plugging in negatives, you had already proved that Jim's answer couldn't be B or C. (Do you see why?) Now you've proved that it also can't be A. This means that it must be D. (It is.)

SKETCHING AND GUESSTIMATING

You must also be very careful about sketching and guesstimating on medium and difficult quant comp geometry problems.

Ordinary guesstimating can occasionally be misleading on these problems for the same reason that ordinary plugging in can be misleading on quant comp algebra. Because a single exception is enough to disqualify an answer choice, you must be certain that you have considered all the possibilities. Approximate answers are usually good enough on ordinary geometry problems, but they are very often *wrong* on geometry quant comps.

Here's an example:

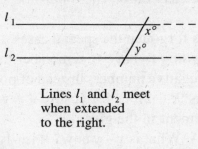

Lines l_1 and l_2 meet
when extended
to the right.

11 $x + y$ 180

HERE'S HOW TO CRACK IT

By simply eyeballing and guesstimating (or using your Princeton Review protractor) you would decide that $x + y$ equals *about* 180 degrees. Is Jim's answer therefore C?

No! You know from the given that the two lines are *not* parallel, even though they look it. So $x + y$ can only be a *little bit less* than 180. Jim's answer, therefore, must be B. (It is.)

On problems like this, it will help you to redraw the figure in exaggerated form. The given says that the two lines meet somewhere to the right. Redraw the figure so that they meet *immediately*, something like this:

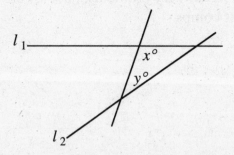

Now the difference between $x + y$ and 180 is very easy to see.

> *Always note the order of difficulty on quant comps. On medium and difficult questions, you should be extremely suspicious of answer choices that seem correct immediately, or that have misleading diagrams, or that you arrive at quickly and without much thought (unless you arrive at them by using our techniques!).*

PACING AND DIFFICULTY

Quant comps and grid-ins will be in the same section of your SAT. (We'll tell you all you need to know about grid-ins in the next chapter.) Because the hardest quant comps are much harder than the easiest grid-ins, you should not waste time on the hardest quant comps until you have answered the easiest grid-ins. Here's what you should do:

1. Do the first ten quant comps (there are fifteen all together).

2. Do the first few grid-ins (there are 10 all together).

3. If you have time left, do the remaining quant comps, then the remaining grid-ins.

4. When you can answer no more, check or double-check your work.

By following this strategy you will be sure to finish all the easy and medium questions in the section before time expires.

QUANTITATIVE COMPARISONS SUMMARY

1. Quant comps, unlike all other SAT questions, offer only four answer choices: A, B, C, and D. These four choices are always the same. On every quant comp, you will be given two quantities or values and asked to select

   Choice A if you think the first quantity is *always* greater than the second.

   Choice B if you think the second quantity is *always* greater than the first.

   Choice C if you think the two quantities are *always* equal.

   Choice D if you think that it cannot be determined whether one quantity will *always* be greater than or equal to the other.

2. Many quant comps contain given information that you are supposed to use in solving the problem. This information is placed *between* the two columns.

3. Quant comps are ideal for POE because the Joe Bloggs attractors are easy to spot—*if you know what to look for and if you are careful.*

4. Many quant comps can be solved using the arithmetic, algebraic, and geometric techniques that you have already learned.

5. Many quant comps can be solved without any sort of computation.

6. If a problem contains nothing but numbers, choice D *cannot* be Jim's answer.

7. You can add and subtract from both Column A and Column B as if they were two sides of an equation.

8. If a quant comp can be simplified, simplify it.

9. If you have to do a lengthy or laborious calculation to find your answer, then you've probably missed the trick.

10. On medium and difficult quant comps, *attack* your hunches.

11. When you plug in on quant comps, remember the numbers with special properties: negatives, fractions, 0, and 1.

12. You must also be very careful about sketching and guesstimating on medium and difficult quant comp geometry problems.

13. Always note the number on quant comps. On medium and difficult questions, you should be extremely suspicious of answer choices that *seem* correct immediately, or that you arrive at quickly and without much thought (unless you arrive at them by using our techniques!).

Chapter 14
Grid-ins

GRID-INS: CRACKING THE SYSTEM

One of the math sections on your SAT will contain a group of ten problems that will not be multiple-choice. ETS calls these problems Student Produced Responses. We call them grid-ins, because you have to mark your answers on a complicated grid printed on your answer sheet.

Despite their daunting format, grid-ins are really just like other math questions on the SAT, and the same techniques that you have learned will still apply. You will still be able to plug-in, you will still be able to call on Joe Bloggs, and you will often be able to use your calculator. The only major difference is that instead of using POE to pluck Jim's answer from a group of choices you'll have to arrive at it yourself. But you will do that by using methods that you have already learned. In fact, many grid-ins are simply regular SAT multiple-choice math problems with the answer choices lopped off.

It is true that you will need to be extra careful on grid-ins. The complexity of the grid format increases the likelihood of careless errors. It is vitally important that you understand this format before you take your test. In particular, you will need to memorize ETS's sometimes arbitrary-sounding rules about which kinds of answers count and which kinds don't.

WHAT IS A GRID-IN?

Grid-ins are just like many other SAT math questions, except that you have to arrive at your answer from scratch, rather than choosing it from among four or five possibilities. The most complicated part is how to enter your answers on your answer sheet.

Because of the way the grid is arranged, certain types of regular SAT math questions cannot be used as grid questions. For example, there can be no algebraic variables (letters) in the answers to grid questions (although there can be variables in the questions), because the grid can accommodate only numbers, including fractions and decimals. This is a good thing for you. Manipulating numbers is easier than manipulating variables.

Because of the limitations of the format, therefore, quite a few of the questions will be arithmetic questions. (Algebra questions will be used, but there won't be any variables in the answers.) On five or six of the ten grid-ins on your test, your calculator should be extremely helpful. As always when using the calculator, be sure to set your problem up in your test booklet before punching in a lot of numbers.

Grid-ins are scored somewhat differently from multiple-choice questions on the SAT. On multiple-choice questions, you lose a fraction of a raw-score point for every incorrect answer. This deducted fraction is commonly referred to as a "guessing penalty." We explained earlier in the book why there is really no guessing penalty on SAT multiple-choice questions. For different reasons, there is no guessing penalty for grid-ins, either. Why? Because nothing is deducted for an incorrect answer on a grid-in. An incorrect answer on one of these questions is no worse for your score than a question left blank. And, by the same token, a blank is just as costly as an error. Therefore you should be very aggressive in answering these questions. Don't leave a question blank just because you're worried that the answer you've found may not be correct. ETS's scoring computers treat incorrect answers and blanks exactly the same. If you have arrived at an answer, you have a shot at earning points, and if you have a shot at earning points, you should take it.

That doesn't mean you should guess blindly. Your chance of helping your score with a blind guess on a grid-in is very, very small. You would be better off spending your time working on problems that you know you can answer or checking your work on problems you have already finished.

THE INSTRUCTIONS

Here are the instructions for grid questions as they will appear on your SAT:

Directions for Student-Produced Response Questions

Each of the remaining 10 questions (16-25) requires you to solve the problem and enter your answer by marking the ovals in the special grid, as shown in the example below.

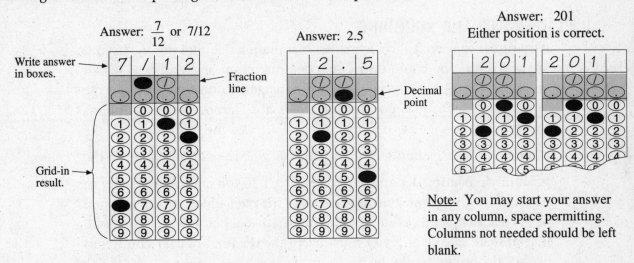

- Mark no more than one oval in any column.

- Because the answer sheet will be machine-scored, **you will receive credit only if the ovals are filled in correctly.**

- Although not required, it is suggested that you write your answer in the boxes at the top of the columns to help you fill in the ovals accurately.

- Some problems may have more than one correct answer. In such cases, grid only one answer.

- No question has a negative answer.

- **Mixed numbers** such as $2\frac{1}{2}$ must be gridded as 2.5 or 5/2. (If [2 1 / 2] is gridded, it will be interpreted as $\frac{21}{2}$, not $2\frac{1}{2}$.)

- <u>Decimal Accuracy:</u> If you obtain a decimal answer, **enter the most accurate value the grid will accommodate.** For example, if you obtain an answer such as 0.6666 . . ., you should record the result as .666 or .667. **Less accurate values such as .66 or .67 are not acceptable.**

Acceptable ways to grid $\frac{2}{3}$ = .6666 . . .

WHAT THE INSTRUCTIONS MEAN

Of all the instructions on the SAT, these are the most important to understand thoroughly before you take the test. Pity the unprepared student who takes the SAT cold and spends ten minutes of potential point-scoring time reading and puzzling over how to grid in answers. There are just a few really important points, but you need to know them.

PLACE VALUE AND ROUNDING

Any of the four boxes in the grid can contain a decimal point. If your answer is 40, you could throw in a decimal point and grid it as 40. or as 40.0. But obviously you are not expected to do this. Where the position of a decimal point does make a difference is in problems where the number of decimal places affects the precision of the answer. ETS's example is $\frac{2}{3}$, a fraction whose decimal value is the infinitely repeating decimal 0.6666666. . . . If you enter this answer in decimal form, you must not put a zero in the ones place, on the left side of the decimal point (even though your math teacher may ask you to do that in math class), and you must carry the decimal out far enough to use all the boxes available.

ETS permits you to round up a repeating decimal, as long as you do it in the way that ETS wants you to do it; our advice is not to round up. Simply transfer as many decimal places from your calculator display to the grid as will fit into the grid. Rounding is an extra step, and extra steps take extra time and increase the likelihood of careless errors.

Notice also that ETS doesn't care where you begin to grid as long as it doesn't affect the precision of your answer, and as long as you can fit your entire answer into the grid. In gridding the number 40, for example, you can use the first two columns, the middle two columns, or the last two columns and still have your answer counted as correct by the scoring machine. It makes the most sense to begin with the first column—the one on the far left—on every answer. But don't fret over which method to use. Just pick one and move on to the next question.

MIXED FRACTIONS

As the instructions tell you, ETS's scoring machines do not recognize mixed fractions. To the machines, $2\frac{1}{2}$ is $\frac{21}{2}$. If your answer is a mixed fraction, you must convert it to a different form before gridding it. If you have to do this, be careful in converting your answer so that you don't inadvertently change its value in addition to changing its form.

FILLING IN THE BOXES

You should always fill in the number boxes at the top of each grid before darkening the ovals to grid in your answer. Your written answers won't affect the scoring of your test; if you write the correct answer in the boxes and grid the wrong one in the ovals, you will lose points and you won't be able to appeal to ETS. But writing in the answer first will make you less likely to make an error when you grid in. Having the number written there will also make it easier for you to check your work later, if you have time.

DON'T WORRY

The vast majority of grid-in answers will not be hard or tricky to enter in the grid. Most problems whose answers are confusing to grid in will not survive the statistical checks that ETS uses in trying out new test questions. Jim won't try to trick you by purposely writing questions that are confusing to grid in. Just pay attention to these guidelines and watch out for careless errors.

GRIDDING IN: A TEST DRIVE

To get a feel for this format, let's work through two examples. As you will see, grid-in problems are just regular SAT math problems. The gridding, however, can be a little tricky.

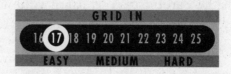

17 If $a + 2 = 6$ and $b + 3 = 21$, what is the value of $\frac{b}{a}$?

HERE'S HOW TO CRACK IT

You need to solve the first equation for a and the second equation for b. Start with the first equation, and solve for a. By subtracting 2 from both sides of the equation, you should see that $a = 4$.

Now move to the second equation, and solve for b. By subtracting 3 from both sides of the second equation you should see that $b = 18$.

The question asked you to find the value of $\frac{b}{a}$. That's easy. The value of b is 18, and the value of a is *4*. Therefore, the value of $\frac{b}{a}$ is $\frac{18}{4}$.

That's an ugly looking fraction. How in the world do you grid it in? Here are five acceptable ways to do it (the two on the far left are highly recommended to avoid confusion):

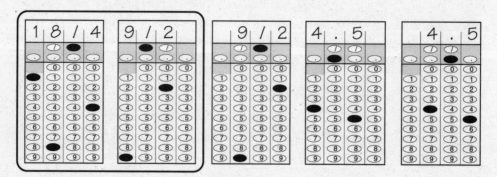

ANALYSIS

The first acceptable way is simply to grid in $\frac{18}{4}$. There are exactly enough spaces in the grid to do it.

In the second and third acceptable ways, we reduced $\frac{18}{4}$ to $\frac{9}{2}$ before gridding it in. That's fine, too. Though it doesn't matter which box in the grid you begin with, as long as you can fit your answer in, we strongly recommend you get in the habit of always beginning at the far left box. The consistency will help you avoid careless mistakes. If you can't fit your answer in, you'll know you've made a mistake somewhere. Jim's answer will always fit.

In the fourth and fifth acceptable ways, we have used our calculator to convert $\frac{18}{4}$ to a decimal, by dividing 18 by 4. There is no reason to do this. In fact, there are a couple of good reasons not to (it's time-consuming and you might make a careless error). But if you do do it, your answer will still count. ETS's scoring computers recognize each correct answer in a variety of forms. On some problems, they even recognize more than one answer.

What is the best way to grid in the answer to this question? The best way is simply to grid in $\frac{18}{4}$. It's not a pretty answer, and your math teacher wouldn't like it, but arriving at it takes fewer steps than arriving at the others. You shouldn't waste time reducing $\frac{18}{4}$ to a prettier fraction or converting it to a decimal. Spend that time on another problem instead. The fewer steps you follow, the less likely you will be to make a careless mistake.

Here's another example. This one is quite a bit harder. If you get lost in the problem, skip to the end and look at three different acceptable ways in which the answer can be gridded.

23 Forty percent of the members of the sixth-grade class wore white socks. Twenty percent wore black socks. If 25% of the remaining students wore gray socks, what percentage of the sixth-grade class wore socks that were not white, black, or gray? (Disregard the % when gridding your answer.)

HERE'S HOW TO CRACK IT

The problem doesn't tell you how many students are in the class, so you can plug in any number you like. This is a percentage problem, so the easiest number to plug in is 100. Forty percent of 100 is 40; that means 40 students wore white socks. Twenty percent of 100 is 20. That means that 20 students wore black socks.

Your next piece of information says that 25 percent of the *remaining* students wore gray socks. How many students remain? Forty, because 60 students wore either white or black socks, and 100 − 60 = 40. Therefore, 25 percent of these 40—10 students—wore gray socks.

How many students are left? Thirty. This is Jim's answer. Here are three acceptable ways to grid in this result (with the preferred way highlighted on the far left):

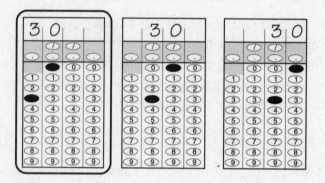

ORDER OF DIFFICULTY

Like all other questions on the math SAT, grid problems are arranged in order of increasing difficulty. In each group of ten, the first third are medium, the second third are medium-difficult, and the final third are very difficult. As always, the order of difficulty will be your guide to how much faith you can place in your hunches.

Guessing is highly unlikely to help you on grid questions. For that reason, you must not waste time on questions that are too hard for you to solve. Only students shooting for 700 or above should consider attempting all ten grid questions.

Quant comps and grid-ins appear in the same section of the SAT. In the chapter on quant comps, we told you to do the first ten quant comps, then the first few grid-ins, then the last five quant comps, then the remaining grid-ins. If you follow that pacing strategy, you won't miss any easy points. For most students, that's an important key to scoring higher on the SAT. If you run out of steam on grid-ins and still have time, go back and work on the hardest quant comps. Use Joe Bloggs and POE to eliminate incorrect choices on the quant comps, and then guess. Guessing on hard grid-ins is unlikely to get you anywhere, while intelligent guessing on hard quant comps may earn you unexpected points.

You should also use any extra time on the grid-in group to check your work on the rest of the section. You could check the entire section in the time it would take you to come up with (probably incorrect) answers on the three hardest grid-ins. *Most students will catch at least three errors when they check their sections.* If you don't check your work, you are probably throwing points away.

If you have checked every other question twice and have done all you can with the quant comps and still have time left over, scan the hardest grid-ins for one or two that seem especially susceptible to Princeton Review techniques. Here's an example:

24 Grow-up potting soil is made from only peat moss and compost in a ratio of 3 pounds of peat moss to 5 pounds of compost. If a bag of Grow-up potting soil contains 12 pounds of potting soil, how many pounds of peat moss does it contain?

HERE'S HOW TO CRACK IT

To solve this difficult problem, set up a ratio box (the ratio box is explained in detail on page 175).

	Peat moss	Compost	Whole
Ratio (parts)	3	5	8
Multiply By			
Actual Number			12 (lbs)

What do you multiply by 8 to get 12? If you don't know, divide 12 by 8 on your calculator. The answer is 1.5. Write 1.5 in each of the boxes on the multiply-by row of your ratio box, like this:

	Peat moss	Compost	Whole
Ratio (parts)	3	5	8
Multiply By	1.5	1.5	1.5
Actual Number			12 (lbs)

The problem asks you how many pounds of peat moss are in a bag. To find out, multiply the numbers in the peat moss column. That is, multiply 3×1.5, yielding 4.5. Jim's answer is 4.5.

	Peat moss	Compost	Whole
Ratio (parts)	3	5	8
Multiply By	1.5	1.5	1.5
Actual Number	4.5 (lbs)	7.5 (lbs)	12 (lbs)

Grid it in like this:

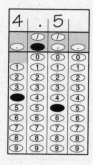

JOE BLOGGS AND GRID QUESTIONS

On grid questions, you obviously can't use the Joe Bloggs principle to eliminate tempting but incorrect answer choices, since you aren't offered choices to choose from. But you can—and must—use your knowledge of Joe Bloggs to double-check your work and keep yourself from making careless mistakes or falling into dumb traps.

The basic idea still holds: easy questions have easy answers, and hard questions have hard answers. On hard questions, you must be extremely suspicious of answers that come to you easily or through simple calculations.

Unfortunately, your knowledge of Joe Bloggs alone will never lead you all the way to Jim's answers, the way it sometimes does on multiple-choice questions. In order to earn points on grid questions, you're going to have to be able to find the real answers, and you're going to have to be extremely careful when you enter your answers on your answer sheet. But Joe Bloggs may help you find the correct path to Jim's answer. On a hard problem, you may be torn between two different approaches, one easy and one hard. Which should you pursue? The harder one. Joe will take the easy path and, as always on hard questions, it will lead him to the wrong answer.

RANGE OF ANSWERS

Some grid-in problems will have many possible correct answers. It won't matter which correct answer you choose, as long as the one you choose really is correct. Here's an example:

20 What is one possible value for x for which $\frac{1}{4} < x < \frac{1}{3}$?

HERE'S HOW TO CRACK IT

Joe Bloggs has trouble imagining how *anything* could squeeze between $\frac{1}{4}$ and $\frac{1}{3}$, but you know there are lots and lots of numbers in there. Any one of them will satisfy Jim.

The numbers in this problem are both fractions, but your answer doesn't have to be. The easiest approach is to forget about math-class solutions and head straight for your calculator (or your mental calculator). Convert $\frac{1}{4}$ to a decimal by dividing 1 by 4, yielding .25. Now convert $\frac{1}{3}$ to a decimal by dividing 1 by 3, yielding .33333. All you need to answer the question is any number that falls between those two. How about .26? Or .3? Or .331? Your answer merely has to be bigger than .25 and smaller than .33333. Pick one, grid it in, and move on.

Don't lose points to carelessness. Practice by gridding the following numbers in the sample grids below. Answers can be found on page 362.

1. 1.5

2. 5.60

3. 81

4. $\frac{1}{3}$

5. $\frac{8}{11}$

6. 0.33333

7. $4\frac{2}{5}$

8. x, such that $6 < x < 7$

GRID-INS SUMMARY

1. One of the math sections on your SAT will contain a group of ten problems that will not be multiple-choice. ETS calls these problems Student Produced Responses. We call them grid-ins, because you have to mark your answers on a complicated grid printed on your answer sheet.

2. Despite their daunting format, grid-ins are really just like other math questions on the SAT, and many of the same techniques that you have learned will still apply.

3. The complexity of the grid format increases the likelihood of careless errors. Know the instructions, and check your work carefully.

4. On five or six of the ten grid-ins on your test, your calculator should be extremely helpful.

5. There is no guessing penalty for grid-ins, so you should be aggressive, but blind guessing is highly unlikely to improve your score.

6. When you grid repeating decimals, you must make your answer as accurate as the space will allow by filling in all the spaces.

7. There is no need to round numbers even though it is permitted.

8. ETS's scoring machines do not recognize mixed fractions. Convert them to a different form before gridding.

9. You should always fill in the number boxes at the top of each grid before darkening the ovals to grid in your answer.

10. While you *can* technically begin gridding anywhere in the empy boxes, you will cut down on careless errors if you are consistant with your starting point. Try beginning always at the far left.

11. The vast majority of grid-in answers will not be hard or tricky to enter in the grid.

12. ETS's scoring computers recognize each correct answer in a variety of forms. On some problems, they even recognize more than one answer.

13. Like all other questions on the math SAT, grid problems are arranged in order of increasing difficulty. In each group of ten, the first third are medium, the second third are medium-difficult, and the final third are very difficult.

14. On grid-ins as on all other SAT questions, easy questions have easy answers, and hard questions have hard answers. On hard grid-ins, you must be extremely suspicious of answers that come to you easily or through simple calculations.

PART 4

Taking the SAT

TICK, TICK, TICK . . .

The SAT is a week away. What should you do?

First of all, you should practice the techniques we have taught you by using real SATs. If you don't own any real SATs, go buy a copy of *10 SATs* at your local bookstore. If you can't find one, ask your guidance counselor for *Taking the SAT-I: Reasoning–Test* or *A Guide to the New SAT*. You should also take and score the diagnostic test at the back of this book. *The practice tests in most other SAT preparation books won't help you; they aren't enough like real SATs*. If you have more than a week, you can order a copy directly from the College Board. Here's the address:

> College Board Publications
> Box 886
> New York, NY 10101

You can also order by phone. The number is 800/323-7155. Visa and MasterCard are accepted.

A GOOD SCHOOL PROJECT

If your school's guidance office doesn't have a complete collection of released SATs, putting one together might make a good project for your student council. More than fifty real SATs have been made public since New York's Truth-in-Testing Law went into effect in 1980. Tracking all of them down will take some work, but studying real SATs is one of the best ways to improve SAT scores. The College Board has published collections of real tests called *4 SATs*, *5 SATs*, *6 SATs*, and *10 SATs*. Only recent editions of *5 SATs* and *10 SATs* are still available from the College Board. You might look for them in your own school library or in the libraries of other schools. In addition, other tests have been released through ETS's Question and Answer Service. Extra copies of these can sometimes be ordered from the College Board. Here are the address and phone number of the board's headquarters:

> The College Board
> 45 Columbus Avenue
> New York, NY 10023-6917
> (212) 713-8000

GETTING PSYCHED

The SAT is a big deal, but you don't want to let it scare you. Sometimes students get so nervous about doing well that they freeze up on the test and murder their scores. The best thing to do is to think of the SAT as a game. It's a game you can get good at, and beating the test can be fun. When you go into the test center, just think about all those poor slobs who don't know how to eyeball geometry diagrams.

The best way to keep from getting nervous is to build confidence in yourself and in your ability to remember and use our techniques. When you take practice tests, time yourself exactly as you will be timed on the real SAT. Develop a sense of how long 30 minutes is and how much time you can afford to spend on cracking difficult problems. If you know ahead of time what to expect, you won't be as nervous.

Of course, taking a real SAT is much more nerve-racking than taking a practice test. Prepare yourself ahead of time for the fact that 30 minutes will seem to go by a lot faster on a real SAT than it did on your practice tests.

It's all right to be nervous; the point of being prepared is to keep from panicking.

SHOULD YOU SLEEP FOR THIRTY-SIX HOURS?

Some guidance counselors tell their students to get a lot of sleep the night before the SAT. This probably isn't a good idea. If you aren't used to sleeping twelve hours a night, doing so will just make you groggy for the test. The same goes for going out and drinking a lot of beer: people with hangovers are not good test takers.

A much better idea is to get up early each morning for the entire week before the test and do your homework before school. This will get your brain accustomed to functioning at that hour of the morning. You want to be sharp at test time.

Before you go to sleep the night before the test, spend an hour or so reviewing the Hit Parade. This will make the list fresh in your mind in the morning. You might also practice estimating some angles and looking for direct solutions on real SAT math problems. You don't want to exhaust yourself, but it will help to brush up.

FURTHERMORE

Here are a few pointers for test day and beyond:

1. You are supposed to take identification to your test center. ETS's definition of acceptable ID is "any official document bearing the candidate's name and photograph, or name and description (driver's license, school ID, or current passport)."

    If you find yourself at the test center with *unacceptable* ID (one with name and signature only) you *should* be admitted anyway. According to the ETS rule book, you should be asked to fill out an identification verification form and then be allowed to take the test. If you really do turn out to be yourself, your scores will count.

    If you arrive without any identification at all, a literal-minded supervisor could turn you away. You can keep this from happening by quickly writing out a brief description of yourself and signing it. Your description probably won't count as "accept-able" ID, but it is ID and should allow you to take the test. You might also ask permission to call home and have someone drop off your driver's license or other acceptable ID while you're taking the test. That way you can have everything cleared up before you leave.

2. The only outside materials you are allowed to use on the test are No. 2 pencils (take four or five them, all sharp), a wristwatch (an absolute necessity), and a calculator. Digital watches are best, but if it has a beeper, make sure you turn it off. Proctors should confiscate pocket dictionaries, word lists, portable computers, and the like. Proctors have occasionally also confiscated stop-watches and travel clocks. Technically, you should be permitted to use these, but you can never tell with some proctors. Take a watch and avoid the hassles.

3. Some proctors allow students to bring food into the test room; others don't. Take a soda and a candy bar with you and see what happens. If you don't flaunt them, they probably won't be confis-cated. Save them until you're about halfway through the test. Remember that it takes about ten minutes for sugar to work its way to your tired brain. If the proctor yells at you, surrender them cheerfully and continue with the test.

4. You are going to be sitting in the same place for more than three hours, so make sure your desk isn't broken or unusually uncomfortable. If you are left-handed, ask for a left-handed desk. (The center may not have one, but it won't hurt to ask.) If the sun is in your eyes, ask to move. If the room is too dark, ask someone to turn on the lights. Don't hesitate to speak up. Some proctors just don't know what they're doing.

5. *Before* you start the test, make sure your booklet is complete. You can quickly turn through all the pages without reading them. Booklets sometimes contain printing errors that make some pages impossible to read. Last year more than ten thousand students had to retake the SAT because of a printing error in their booklets. This would not have happened had the students checked their booklets. Find out ahead of time and demand a new booklet if yours is defective. Also, check your answer sheet to make sure it isn't flawed.

6. You should get a five-minute break after the first hour of the test. Ask for it if your proctor doesn't give it to you. You should be allowed to go to the bathroom at this time. You should also be allowed to take a one-minute break at your desk at the end of the second hour. The breaks are a very good idea. They let you clear your head. Insist on them.

7. ETS allows you to cancel your SAT scores. Unfortunately, you can't cancel only your math or verbal score—it's all or nothing. You can cancel scores at the test center by asking your proctor for a "Cancellation Request Form." If you decide to cancel later on, you can do so by sending a telegram to ETS. You must do this before the fifth business day following the test.

   We recommend that you *not* cancel your scores unless you know you made so many errors, or left out so many questions, that your score will be unacceptably low. Don't cancel your scores because you have a bad feeling—students frequently have an exaggerated sense of how many mistakes they made, and it's possible you did much better than you realize.

8. Make sure you darken all your responses before the test is over. At the same time, erase any extraneous marks on the answer sheet. **A stray mark in the margin of your answer sheet can result in correct responses being marked wrong.**

9. Don't assume that your test was scored correctly. Send away for ETS's Question and Answer Service. It costs money, but it's worth it. You'll get back copies of your answer sheet, a test booklet, and an answer key. Check your answers against the key and complain if you think you've been misscored. (Don't throw away the test booklet you receive from the Question and Answer Service. If you're planning to take the SAT again, save it for practice. If you're not, give it to your guidance counselor or school library.)

10. You deserve to take your SAT under good conditions. If you feel that your test was not administered properly (the high school band was practicing outside the window, your proctor hovered over your shoulder during the test) call us immediately at 1-800-333-0369 and we'll tell you what you can do about it.

PART **5**

Vocabulary

THE VERBAL SAT IS A VOCABULARY TEST

Despite ETS's talk about "reasoning ability," half of the verbal SAT is a vocabulary test. If you don't know the words on the test, you won't earn a good score. It's as simple as that.

The Princeton Review's techniques for beating the verbal SAT are intended to help you get the maximum possible mileage out of the words you do know. The bigger your vocabulary is, the more our techniques will help. But if your vocabulary is small, not even The Princeton Review will be able to do much about your score.

For this reason, it is extremely important that you get to work on your vocabulary immediately. Even if you have procrastinated until just a few days before the test, you can still improve your chances by studying this chapter in the time remaining.

DON'T MEMORIZE THE DICTIONARY

Some students try to prepare for the SAT by sitting down with the dictionary and *reading* it. They start with the first word, *a,* and plow along—their eyelids growing heavy—until they get to, say, *agamogenesis* (a word that never has been, and never will be, tested on the SAT), and then they quit.

Some other students try to prepare for the SAT by learning only the very *hardest* words in the dictionary—words like *endogenous* and *endoblast.* Most of the popular SAT coaching books concentrate on words like this. The SAT is a test of how smart you are, right? And smart people know a lot of big words, right?

Forget it.

Only a tiny percentage of all the words in the English language are ever tested on the SAT. In fact, many of the same ones are tested over and over again. Virtually all of these are words you've heard before, even if you aren't sure what they mean.

There would never be a word as hard as *agamogenesis* on the SAT. Why? Because almost nobody has ever heard of it before. The SAT is a test for high school juniors and seniors. If it tested really hard words, every kid in the country would get blown away.

WHAT KIND OF WORDS DOES THE SAT TEST?

Generally speaking, the SAT tests the kind of words that an educated adult—your English teacher, for example—would know without having to look up. It tests the sort of words that you encounter in your daily reading, from a novel in English class to the daily newspaper.

We can even be a bit more specific than that. For nearly five years, we have used a computer to analyze the actual words tested on every SAT administered in the United States. Using the results of this analysis, we have compiled a vocabulary list that we call the Hit Parade. It contains the words that come up again and again on the SAT. Your SAT vocabulary-building program should begin with them.

THE HIT PARADE

Well, here it is: the infamous, new and revised 1994 Princeton Review Hit Parade. Don't panic. Learning these words won't be as tedious as you think. You don't have to devour the whole list at once. Study a word in the car, in the shower, during television commercials, during dinner. Make a tape of the words and listen to it while you're jogging.

To beat the SAT you need more than a good vocabulary, but a good vocabulary is a great place to start. By learning the Hit Parade you'll be starting out in the right direction; learn this list, and you'll be learning words that you'll use long after the SAT is over.

These are the most commonly tested words on the SAT. We've included short definitions to make it easier for you to learn. These definitions aren't always exactly like the ones you'll find in the dictionary; they're the definitions of the words as they are tested on the SAT.

Please keep in mind that these are not the *only* words you need to know for the SAT.

Some SATs are absolutely loaded with Hit Parade words; others don't contain as many. One of the most important things the Hit Parade will teach you is the *level* of the vocabulary on the test. Once you get a feel for this level, you'll be able to spot other possible SAT words in your reading. If you want to learn more, get a copy of our vocabulary builders, *Word Smart* and *Word Smart II*. Good luck!

LEARN THE WORDS IN GROUPS

Don't learn words in isolation. Instead, learn groups of related words at the same time. This way even when you don't remember the exact meaning of a word, you may remember what group it is from.

WAR

• The Strong Warrior •

POTENT

powerful; mighty

*The **potent** blow knocked him off his feet.*

ROBUST

having strength or vigorous health

*People who swim in the winter are very **robust**.*

HARDY

bold; brave; robust

*He was a **hardy** soul; strong, brave, and sturdy.*

INSURMOUNTABLE

not able to be climbed or overcome

*John's problem with alcohol seemed **insurmountable**, but he eventually got over it.*

IMMUNE

marked by protection; exemption; not susceptible to

*I am **immune** to his feeble charms.*

VEHEMENT

deeply felt; impassioned

*He **vehemently** opposed military action in the Middle East.*

• The Dangerous Enemy •

INFAMOUS

famous for something bad

> *He is **infamous** for hanging people by their toenails.*

NOTORIOUS

well known for evil; infamous

> *Marie Antoinette was **notorious** for her extravagant parties and costumes.*

PUGNACIOUS

inclined to fight, quarrelsome

> *The pit bull is **pugnacious,** to say the least.*

BELLIGERENT

warlike; hostile

> *The **belligerent** child was removed from class.*

VIRULENT

extremely poisonous; virus-like

> *Television violence is a **virulent** force in our culture.*

FORMIDABLE

causing fear, dread, or apprehension

> *Hulk Hogan is a truly **formidable** opponent.*

RUTHLESS

having no mercy

> *The **ruthless** general killed the children first.*

CALLOUS

having no sympathy for others

*Experience with tragedy had rendered him **callous.***

UNYIELDING

inflexible

*He remained **unyielding** to my entreaties for mercy.*

MISANTHROPE

one who hates people

*The **misanthrope** sought to isolate himself from man-kind.*

INSIDIOUS

gradually harmful

*Procrastination is an **insidious** habit.*

JINGOIST

an extreme patriot

*The **jingoist** wanted to establish a belligerent foreign policy.*

• The Weak Enemy •

VULNERABLE

open to injury or attack

*I am most **vulnerable** to attack after having consumed vast quantities of my grandmother's chocolate cake.*

SUSCEPTIBLE

vulnerable; prone to

*Riding a motorcycle without a helmet makes you **susceptible** to a head injury.*

GULLIBLE

easily fooled

*The **gullible** children followed the clown down the road to doom.*

OBLIVIOUS

lacking mindful attention

*He was **oblivious** to the insults.*

SUBMISSIVE

tending to give in to authority; servile

*He **submissively** nodded his head and did what he was told.*

INNOCUOUS

producing no injury or effect

*It was an **innocuous** remark; no one bothered to respond.*

MERCENARY

one who serves in an army for money

*The French **mercenary** was hired by the Spanish army.*

• Cheerleaders •

ALLY

a friend or fellow participant in a common cause

*Our **allies** agreed to support the air strike.*

BIASED

a prejudice; a preference

*I am **biased** against prejudiced people.*

PARTISAN

exhibiting allegiance to a cause

*Their **partisan** feelings led them to donate large amounts of money to the politician's campaign.*

• Mediators •

IMPARTIAL

unbiased; treating all equally

*Thank goodness the referee was **impartial,** because the crowd certainly wasn't.*

NEUTRAL

not aligned with a cause; not taking a side

*I am **neutral** in this matter, so don't ask me to take sides.*

INDIFFERENT

not caring for one thing or another; unbiased

*His **indifference** to the fans' yells made him a hero to the visiting team.*

• Avoiding the War •

APPEASE

to make quiet; calm

*Mom **appeased** my little brother with a cupcake—a small price to pay for peace.*

MOLLIFY

to ease a bad temper

*My friends **mollified** me after my parents refused to let me go to the party.*

RELINQUISH

to give up

*I **relinquished** my fishing license at the request of the game warden.*

PACIFIST

a person who promotes peace and harmony

*My friend Darren is a **pacifist;** he has organized several nonviolent demonstrations on his campus.*

EVADE

to avoid or move away from

*He **evaded** her question deftly and moved on to other subjects*

RECANT

to withdraw or regret a former belief or opinion

*Okay, okay, I **recant** my belief that you're an idiot.*

PARRY

to evade a blow; dodge; deflect

*She **parried** by turning the question back to him.*

EXTRICATE

to release or free from entanglement; to disengage

*I **extricated** myself from the sticky situation.*

• Ready for Battle •

MALICE

ill will; intent to cause harm

*His **malice** was understandable; she was the one who had run over his dog that dark, stormy night.*

REPREHENSIBLE

deserving of disapproval

*Kicking dogs is a **reprehensible** pastime.*

REVULSION

strong pulling or drawing away

*The teacher's ugly green trousers inspired **revulsion** among his students.*

NEFARIOUS

extremely wicked

> *The **nefarious** cheerleader stole the other team's pom-poms.*

DEFIANT

daring; bold; resistant to authority

> *The teen was **defiant** toward his parents.*

OBSTINATE

stubborn; unyielding; firm in position

> *He is **obstinate**—I refuse to give in to him!*

RESENTMENT

persistent ill will at something seen as wrong

> *I **resented** having to read aloud when I had just had my tooth pulled.*

VINDICTIVE

wanting to get revenge

> *Tommy felt **vindictive** toward the teacher who spanked him.*

VENDETTA

a prolonged feud of bitter hostility

> *The gangsters' **vendetta** led to many deaths.*

VENGEANCE

punishment inflicted in retaliation

> *He delivered the blows with a **vengeance**.*

ENMITY

hatred or ill will

*The **enmity** between the two countries led to a war.*

AVERSION

a strong dislike; strongly opposed to

*I have an **aversion** to chocolate-covered bugs.*

PROVOKE

to anger, arouse, bring to action

*He **provoked** his sister by pulling on her pigtails.*

INSTIGATE

to urge forward

*Herbie **instigated** a revolution against the evil math teacher.*

• The War •

VILIFY

to make abusive statements

*My parents **vilify** people they don't like.*

OBLITERATE

to completely destroy

*We **obliterated** our enemies with stink bombs and bad cheese.*

STYMIE

to block an effort; to create difficulties

*My efforts to create an adequate theme were **stymied** by my lack of interest in the project.*

MORTIFY

to humiliate severely

*I was **mortified** by her insult.*

SUBJUGATE

to bring under control; conquer; subdue

*In order to perform well, you must **subjugate** your fear of speaking in public.*

SUPPRESS

to stop by putting an end to activities

***Suppress** the rebel activity!*

RAZE

to tear down; demolish

*They **razed** the enemy's hideout.*

ROUT

to force or drive out; a disastrous defeat

*Let's **rout** the enemy, darn it.*

USURP

seize without legal fight

*He **usurped** the crown, the throne, the queen, and the royal dog.*

SUPPLANT

to replace by force

*The old regime was **supplanted** by an ultraviolent faction of the opposing party.*

PLUNDER

to take something by force

***Plundering** is how armies historically supported themselves when making war in foreign lands.*

PILLAGE

to loot or plunder

*The rioters **pillaged** the town, breaking many windows.*

EXPLOIT

a heroic feat

*His **exploits** are now famous.*

RETALIATE

to take revenge

*She **retaliated** by putting gum in her brother's hair.*

• Not So Obvious War •

MANIPULATE

to manage deceitfully for personal advantage

*Sure, I **manipulated** my parents to get the car keys, but it worked, didn't it?*

COVERT

secret; concealed

> *People were surprised to hear about the **covert** selling of arms for hostages.*

UNDERMINE

to weaken by wearing away gradually and unnoticeably

> *His persistent declarations of affection would **undermine** anyone's resolve.*

SUBVERT

to cause the covert ruin of something; to corrupt

> *The Princeton Review is out to **subvert** ETS.*

DUPLICITY

deliberate deceptiveness in behavior or speech

> *The **duplicitous** girl told him that the pizza with laxatives on it was good to eat.*

SURREPTITIOUS

secret and stealthy; furtive

> *He **surreptitiously** passed me a note; the teacher didn't even notice.*

• After the War •

UPSHOT

the final result

> *The **upshot** of the war was the redistribution of land.*

SERENE

calm; tranquil

*Her **serenity** is something to be desired and emulated.*

• Making Up •

RECONCILE

to restore to friendship or harmony

*Let's **reconcile** our differences.*

THE GOOD, THE BAD, AND THE UGLY

• The Distinguished •

RENOWN

fame

> *Many people attended the **renowned** author's funeral.*

PROMINENT

important; standing out

> *His most **prominent** feature is not his nose.*

PRESTIGE

high regard in other people's eyes

> *The **prestige** attached to this job is imaginary.*

• Goody Two Shoes •

VIRTUE

moral excellence; goodness

> *His many **virtues** include honesty, humility, and generosity.*

MODEST

humble; shy; limited in size, amount, or aim

> *Strangely, she forgot **"modesty"** in the long list of her best character traits.*

HUMBLE (ADJ)/HUMILITY (N)

not proud or haughty

*His **humility**, in light of his achievements, is amazing.*

PRUDENT

careful; having foresight

*She went about the purchase of a new car slowly and **prudently**.*

INTEGRITY

having moral character, honesty

*The judge's **integrity** was questioned when it was discovered that he had a multitude of outstanding parking violations.*

PROPRIETY

keeping standards of proper behavior; appropriate

*Our notions of **propriety** are quite different from those of our grandparents, if you know what I mean.*

SCRUPULOUS

having strict moral standards

*Her **scrupulous** attention to detail can be quite irritating.*

METICULOUS

marked by extreme attention to detail, careful

*He is a good proofreader because he is **meticulous** by nature.*

SYCOPHANT

one who sucks up to others

*His **sycophantic** tactics were the only thing that kept him from failing the course entirely.*

• In God We Trust •

PIOUS (ADJ)/PIETY (N)

deeply religious

*The **pious** woman prayed every day.*

THEOLOGY

the study of God and His relation to the world

*St. Augustine was a great **theologian**.*

REVERE

to regard with awe

*Martina's athletic record is one to be **revered**.*

VENERATE

revere

***Venerate** your mother—she's the only one you have.*

• Lust for Life •

VITALITY

great physical or mental strength

*Exercise increases your **vitality**.*

VITAL

essential to continued worth or well-being

*The microfilm is **vital** to the survival of the Resistance.*

VIVID

sharp; intense; producing strong or clear impression on the senses

She has a vivid imagination.

JOVIAL

joyous; happy; full of good fellowship

He's a jovial chap.

VIGOR

vitality; energy

The parakeet had been full of life and vigor the previous day.

ZEAL

eagerness in pursuit of something; fervor; passion

Since science was her favorite subject, she did her science homework with much zeal.

VIABLE

capable of living, developing, or functioning

Her casserole was not a viable alternative for nourishment.

SALUTARY

favorable to or promoting health

Fruits and vegetables have salutary effects.

• Making It Better •

THERAPEUTIC

of or relating to treatment; medicinal

*He finds writing in his journal every night **therapeutic**.*

RESOLUTION

firmness in having reached a decision or in determination

*Like most people, when presented with temptation, her **resolutions** were promptly forgotten.*

RECTIFY

to set right; remedy

*Corporal punishment will not **rectify** his behavioral problem, no matter what Dr. Spock says.*

STABILIZE

to make stable, steadfast, or firm

*Her heartbeat was **stabilized** as soon as EMS treated her.*

FACILITATE

to make easier; to help

*She **facilitated** my transition to city life.*

REDRESS

to set right; correct; remedy

*I am seeking **redress** for my grievances.*

• Lazy Bum •

SLOTH

a lazy person

*While the work piled up, the **sloth** managed to sneak a nap in the supply room.*

INDOLENT

lazy

*Darcy's **indolence** was seen as charming by those wishing to gain his favor.*

LISTLESS

characterized by lack of inclination or energy to do anything

*Beth was often **listless** and wan in the worst stages of her illness.*

SLUGGISH

lazy

*The heat made us all feel **sluggish** and grouchy.*

STUPOR

a state of extreme apathy or of mental and physical inactivity

*The movie left us in a **stupor**.*

DORMANT

asleep; inactive

*The seeds are **dormant** until spring arrives.*

APATHY

lack of interest; lack of feeling

*The financial aid office was **apathetic** to my request for more money.*

NEGLIGENCE

carelessness

*Upon the death of our favorite maple tree, the incompetent tree surgeon was sued for **negligence**.*

SOPORIFIC

sleep-inducing; boring

*The dean's speech was **soporific**.*

• Rejection •

CONDEMN

to criticize; pronounce guilty

*Socrates was **condemned** for corrupting the youth.*

DENOUNCE

to criticize publicly

*Some U.S. citizens **denounced** our nation's prolonged involvement in the Vietnam War.*

SPURN

to reject strongly

*The **spurned** lover angrily ripped up all his photos of her and sat dejectedly staring out of the balcony window.*

REFUTE

to disprove

*I'll **refute** your false claims, you villain.*

SCORN

extreme dislike involving anger and disgust

*The young man's shallow and insincere words were met with **scorn.***

REPROACH

to find fault with; scold

*Cassidy's mother **reproached** him for his continued truancy.*

REPUDIATE

to reject with strong disapproval

*The lawyer **repudiated** the defendant's claim that he had not committed the theft.*

REPROOF (N)/REPROVE (V)

to disapprove of; a criticism

*I received a stinging **reproof** from my parents after I stayed out too late.*

REBUFF

to refuse sharply

*She was soundly **rebuffed** when she attempted to get a job with the FBI.*

NEGATE

to deny the truth value of; to invalidate

*Grace moved quickly to **negate** his alibi with eyewitnesses who contradicted him.*

UPBRAID

to find fault with; blame

*My boss **upbraided** me for my mistake.*

CENSURE

harsh criticism

*His slanted reporting drew **censure** from the editorial staff.*

• How Important? •

RELEVANT

related, significant to the matter at hand

*Leave out anything that is not **relevant** to your paper's thesis.*

TRIVIAL

unimportant

*Buying a new aardvark is **trivial** when compared with paying your rent on time.*

EXTRANEOUS

not essential; having no relevance

*The **extraneous** information in the sentence so increased its length that no one bothered to finish reading it, although it was very good and the person who wrote it tried very hard to make it entertaining, and the weather was so nice outside.*

SUPERFLUOUS

unnecessary; excessive; extra

*After bathing in scented water, using scented powder, scented moisturizer, scented hairspray, and scented deodorant, her perfume was **superfluous.***

FULL OF IT OR LACK OF IT (HMMM?)

• Hot Air Club •

POMPOUS

showy parade of importance

*The school had a reputation for snobbishness, acknowledged by students in referring to their own graduation ceremony as "**Pompous** and Circumstance."*

PRETENTIOUS

characterized by the assumption of dignity and importance

*Maxwell's restaurant typically attracted **pretentious** snobs who wanted to be seen at the hottest spot in town.*

PRESUMPTUOUS

overstepping due bounds of propriety or courtesy

*It was **presumptuous** of him to think that he could eat all the food I had in the refrigerator.*

SUPERCILIOUS

thinking a lot of oneself and little of others; haughty; patronizing; condescending

*The **supercilious** party guest frequently made others feel inadequate by hogging conversations and making sarcastic remarks when others tried to speak.*

SCARCITY

insufficient supply; rarity

*Money is a **scarcity**.*

MEAGER

deficient in quality of quantity; scanty

> *The **meager** nature of his salary did not negatively affect his generosity.*

THREADBARE

worn out; meager

> *Grandma patched the elbows of my **threadbare** sweater.*

PAUCITY

an insufficient amount; dearth

> *The committee turned down the proposal to renovate the building due to a **paucity** of funds.*

INSOLVENT

unable to pay debts; bankrupt; impoverished

> *When his business went bankrupt, Mr. Bailey became **insolvent**.*

THRIFTY

practicing economy

> *A person who saves his money rather than spend it on foolish things is a **thrifty** person.*

MISER

one who hoards his wealth

> *My brother was a **miser** until he met Ella; now he's nearly broke.*

CLOSEFISTED

stingy

> *He is so **closefisted** that he wouldn't buy water if his foot was on fire.*

PARSIMONIOUS

stingy; frugal

> *Mr. Stingy **parsimoniously** declined to buy the Girl Scouts' cookies.*

• Full of Stuff Other Than Air •

MASSIVE

bulky; heavy; large

> *The **massive** gorilla raised its hand and squashed the unsuspecting fly.*

ABUNDANT

great quantity

> *The millionaire used his **abundant** wealth to assist needy charities.*

RIFE

abundant

> *George's apartment is **rife** with cockroaches, yet he refuses to call an exterminator.*

SUBSTANTIAL

considerable in quantity; consisting of or relating to substance; important

> *Unsurprisingly, a **substantial** number of rocks were flung at the stoning.*

REPLETE

abundantly supplied or filled

> *Margaret's letter was **replete** with the latest gossip.*

VOLUMINOUS

large quantity (of writing), to fill many volumes

*The author's **voluminous** works filled her library book-shelves.*

SURFEIT

an excessive amount; overindulgence of eating and drinking

*There was a **surfeit** of people buying tickets for the TV raffle.*

PRODIGIOUS

extraordinary in size or amount

*There was a **prodigious** mound of books at the book-burning party.*

• Wealth and Its Use •

PROSPERITY

state of being financially successful

*Dreams of **prosperity** are all that kept him at his dead-end job.*

PRODIGAL

extravagant; wasteful

*Your **prodigal** son will waste all your hard-earned money.*

SPENDTHRIFT

one who spends wastefully

*The **spendthrift** spent all of the money on bubble gum, so there was none left to buy milk for the baby.*

• The Bold and the Beautiful •

AESTHETIC

dealing with the beautiful

> The Brady Bunch *living room is not* **aesthetically** *pleasing to the sophisticated audience of today.*

REFINED

improved or perfected by pruning or polishing

> *Eliza's crude manners and speech were* **refined** *through careful teaching and much practice.*

LUXURIANT

characterized by abundant growth; rich; lush

> *Rapunzel's hair was so* **luxuriant** *she was known throughout the land.*

LAVISH

expended or produced in abundance

> *The* **lavish** *banquet had over fifty courses and a giant ice sculpture of a camel for a centerpiece.*

• Lacking Substance •

INSIPID

not interesting; boring; silly

*The documentary on the praying mantis proved to be so **insipid** that I lost interest.*

SUPERFICIAL

on the surface; shallow

*The **superficial** nature of her comments testified to her lack of understanding and compassion.*

• STINGINESS—HARD TIMES OR NOT •

• Small Minds •

PROVINCIAL

unsophisticated; narrow-minded

*Belle wants much more than this **provincial** life, so she's moving in with that cultured rich guy that lives across town.*

PAROCHIAL

very narrow in scope; narrow-minded

*Theresa's **parochial** outlook kept her from appreciating all that the city had to offer.*

OBTUSE

not sharp; dull; blockheaded

*She continued to speak, although her comments were **obtuse** and boring.*

• Small Mouths •

BREVITY

conciseness; shortness of duration

*Due to our lack of time and interest, **brevity** is much appreciated.*

UNDERSTATED

avoiding obvious emphasis or embellishment

*The **understated** decor of the living room clashed harshly with the garish display of wealth in the dining room.*

TERSE

brief; neatly concise in language

*His manner was **terse** and reserved; he said no more than was necessary.*

TACITURN

quiet; saying little

*He was so **taciturn** that people thought he was asleep.*

CURT

terse; marked by rude shortness

*Gillian's **curt** manner of speaking led some to believe she was from New York.*

LACONIC

concise; to the point of seeming rude

*Her **laconic** comments resulted in everyone becoming offended and leaving abruptly.*

• Big Minds •

PHENOMENON

an observable fact or event

*Mark fell off the chair, demonstrating the everyday **phenomenon** of gravity.*

PARADIGM

example; pattern; model; archetype

*Messy Gertrude uses a scarecrow as her fashion **paradigm.***

THEORIZE

to form a theory; to speculate

*The Buddha **theorized** about the meaning of life.*

SPECULATION

the act of thinking, pondering, or reflecting on something

*There was much **speculation** regarding the possible actions of the president after the plane was hijacked.*

ESOTERIC

understood by only a select few

*The eight-fold Buddha path—whatever that is—is an **esoteric** subject.*

OBSCURE

not clear; not noticeable; not important

*Cricket mating behavior is an **obscure** topic.*

UNTENABLE

not able to be defended

*The idea of racial supremacy is an **untenable** position, though there still are those who argue its validity.*

• Big Mouths •

ARTICULATE

speaking well or clearly

*The famous football player was **articulate** and culturally literate, to the surprise of much of the audience.*

VERBOSE (ADJ) / VERBOSITY (N)

wordy; having too many words

> *"And so, to sum up, finally, I say to you all—the young, the old, the middle-aged, the not-so-middle-aged, men, women and children alike, students and teachers and anyone else I may have forgotten—if you want to keep your audience's attention, if you want to keep them interested, if you want to leave them begging for more, avoid* **verbosity,** *whatever the cost."*

RHETORICAL

concerned with the art of speaking or writing effectively

> *Her* **rhetorical** *skill greatly aided her progress in law school.*

VOCIFEROUS

crying out noisily; loud

> *His* **vociferous** *complaints rose up over the noise of the crowd.*

GARRULOUS

talkative or chatty

> *While some people become taciturn when they drink, he becomes quite* **garrulous.**

EXHORTATION

an act or instance of appealing urgently

> *The hostage* **exhorted** *the police to give the robber the money.*

TIRADE

a long, harsh speech, often abusive

*His **tirade** against her behavior left her crying in the corner.*

DIATRIBE

bitter and abusive speech or writing

*His **diatribe** on the evils of the demon liquor fell on deaf ears.*

• Change •

VARIABLE

changeable; not constant

*The **variable** nature of the climate made it impossible to pack for their vacation.*

CONTRACT

to reduce in size

*When apples sit around long enough they shrivel and **contract** to about half their original size.*

TRANSITION

change

*Rather than say he had been fired, he preferred to say he was in a career **transition.***

TRANSIENT

passing in and out of existence; fleeting; short-lived

*At best, his attraction to her might be called **transient;** he never hangs around for long.*

MUTABLE

capable of being changed in form, quality, or nature

*Known as the Man of a Thousand Faces, his appearance was more **mutable** than the weather of an Iowa spring.*

VOLATILE

(1) subject to constant change; (2) easily evaporated

*They ducked under their desks quickly, not trusting the **volatile** nature of the chemicals the professor was using.*

SPORADIC

occurring occasionally; infrequent

*Earthquakes and phone calls from my brother can be classified as **sporadic** occurrences.*

MOBILE

can be moved

*He called the beat-up car his **mobile** office.*

REACTIONARY

favoring a former and usually outmoded political or social order

*His **reactionary** statements regarding feminism brought laughter and scorn from the women in the audience.*

CAPRICIOUS

led by whim or fancy; erratic

*Most of these sentences were composed by a **capricious** person.*

ERRATIC

inconsistent; irregular

*The fly buzzed about his head, causing him to wave his arms **erratically**.*

• Fresh •

UNIQUE

rare; uncommon

> *Mr. Rogers believes we are all **unique** whether we are fancy on the outside or the inside.*

NOVICE

a person who is new at something; inexperienced

> *I'm a **novice** at this, but I'm eager to learn.*

NOVEL

new

> *What a **novel** idea—using a cliché to illustrate our point!*

INNOVATIVE

characterized by a new idea, method, or novelty

> *Ten years ago, the fax machine was an **innovative** device.*

• It Ain't Gonna Happen •

TENTATIVE

uncertain; hesitant

> *Tomorrow's meeting is **tentative;** it might be canceled.*

PRECLUDE

to make impossible; to exclude

> *His ill-conceived plan **precluded** all of the things that might have made it possible for him to reach his ultimate goal.*

• Permanence •

SUSTAIN

support; nourish; maintain

*Oxygen **sustains** life.*

PREDILECTION

inclination toward something; bias

*I heard Hillary has a **predilection** for saxophone music.*

DOGMATIC

stubbornly opinionated

*The **dogmatic** teacher alienated everyone with his rules and regulations.*

UNIMPEACHABLE

beyond doubt; not to be attacked or discredited

*She maintains that her character is **unimpeachable**, but boy, do I have a story for you.*

• Stale •

UNIFORM

constant; without variety

*The marching band was **uniform** in its movement.*

MONOTONOUS

unvarying in tone; extremely repetitive

*Tim's **monotonous** life was exactly the same, week after week, day after day, hour after boring, empty hour.*

MUNDANE

everyday; ordinary

> *While she thought her comments were sparkling with insight, we found them quite **mundane**.*

TRITE

stale; overused; hackneyed

> *"Have a nice day" is a **trite** sentiment.*

CONVENTIONAL

based on custom; traditional; mundane

> ***Conventional** fashion rules dictate a man must never wear black shoes and white socks with a red suit, Santa Claus excepted.*

FACT, FICTION, FORECAST

• Nothing but the Truth •

INFALLIBLE

incapable of making a mistake

*Mr. Perfect thought he was **infallible**.*

IRREFUTABLE

not able to be disproved

*Descartes said it was **irrefutable** that he existed some-where, because if the question was being asked, someone had to be doing the asking, right?*

VALID

being true or confirmed

*After much research and double-checking, it was agreed that the contract was **valid**.*

VERIFIABLE

able to be proven or authenticated

*There are many stories floating around about Edgar Allan Poe's sordid personal life, but none are **verifiable**.*

• Doubting Thomas •

SKEPTICAL

doubting (not gullible)

*The **skeptical** children refused the candy, threw rocks at the clown, and ran home to their parents.*

IMPLAUSIBLE

not having truth or credibility

> I find it highly **implausible** that you saw Elvis at the 7-Eleven.

EQUIVOCAL

open to interpretation; uncertain

> His **equivocal** remarks did nothing to quell their fears.

• Birds and the Bees •

FERTILE

capable of producing vegetation or offspring; lush and abundant

> **Fertile** Myrtle was mother of seventeen children.

FRUITFUL

yielding or producing fruit or results

> Her efforts proved **fruitful** in the end.

FECUND

creative and/or intellectually productive; fruitful

> Walt Disney's **fecundity** gave us a colorful array of cartoon characters.

PROLIFIC

marked by abundant inventiveness or productivity

> She is a **prolific** writer, as this 1,000-page book, fourth in a series of twelve, demonstrates.

• Phonies •

EMBELLISH

decorate; to enhance by adding ornamental details

*The writer **embellished** her meager tale of woe until it could be used as a movie of the week.*

HYPERBOLE

obvious exaggeration

*Elliot has a gift for **hyperbole**, to put it nicely.*

SPURIOUS

not genuine, authentic, or true

*The hair-growth company made **spurious** claims about their product.*

APOCRYPHAL

of doubtful origin or authenticity; fictitious

*Despite the evidence, the judge allowed the **apocryphal** document to be entered as "exhibit A."*

HYPOCRISY

saying one thing and doing another

*The **hypocrisy** of the organization caused many members to band together and branch out on their own.*

• Grim Reaper •

MOROSE

gloomy; sullen

*The rainy afternoon following the funeral had a particularly **morose** air about it.*

BARREN

unproductive; infertile

*At three o'clock in the morning, her brain was **barren** of ideas.*

OMINOUS

foreboding or foreshadowing evil

*You'd think that all the **ominous** music would have caused those meddling kids to turn back rather than proceed deeper into the forest; what were they thinking?*

HOW TO MEMORIZE NEW WORDS

Different people have different ways of memorizing new words. Some people find it easier to remember things if they write them down. Others find it helps to say them aloud. Many people say they can remember new things better if they review them right before they go to sleep. You should do what works best for you. Here are two methods that many Princeton Review students have found to be effective.

FLASH CARDS

You can make your own flash cards out of 3-by-5-inch index cards. Write the word on one side and the definition on the other. Then quiz yourself on the words, or practice with a friend. You can even carry a few cards around with you every day and work on them in spare moments—when you're riding the bus, for example.

One of the most important keys to memorizing new words is to start far enough in advance of the test so that you only have to learn a few each day. You'll be less likely to become confused if you tackle the Hit Parade one small chunk at a time—say, five words a day, starting with the first words on the list. You'll probably know a lot of the words already; there's no need to memorize those. Just be certain that you know each definition cold.

THE IMAGE APPROACH

The image approach involves letting each new word suggest a wild image to you, and then using that image to help you remember the word. For example, the word *enfranchise* means "to give the right to vote." (Women didn't become *enfranchised* in the United States until 1920, when the Nineteenth Amendment to the Constitution guaranteed them the right to vote in state and federal elections.) *Franchise* might suggest to you a McDonald's franchise—and you could remember the new word by imagining people lined up to vote in a McDonald's. The weirder the image the better. To give another example, the word *slake* means "to satisfy thirst." You might remember that by picturing yourself drinking an entire *lake* on a hot summer day.

JUST KNOWING THEY'RE THERE

You should also be sure that you can recognize a Hit Parade word whenever you see one, even if you can't remember what it means. Doing this is easier than you probably think. If you put any effort at all into memorizing the definitions, you'll remember the words themselves when you see them.

Why is this important? Because Hit Parade words make very good guesses when you're stumped on difficult verbal questions.

OTHER WORDS

As important as Hit Parade words are, they aren't the only words on the SAT. As you go about learning the Hit Parade, you should also try to incorporate other new words into your vocabulary. The Hit Parade will help you determine what *kinds* of words you should be learning— good solid words that are fairly difficult but not impossible.

One very good source of SAT words is the "Week in Review" section of the Sunday *New York Times*. If you live in an area where you can get the *Times* on Sunday, it's probably worth the effort to buy it and read it. (You'll learn something about the world as well.) Other well-written general publications are also good sources of SAT words.

WHAT DO THEY MEAN?

Before you can memorize the definition of a word you come across in your reading, you have to find out what it means. You'll need a dictionary for that. Pam uses two dictionaries in writing the SAT: the *American Heritage Dictionary* and the *Webster's New Collegiate Dictionary*. You should own a copy of one or the other. (You'll use it in college, too—it will be a good investment.)

When you come across a new word, write it down, look it up, and remember it. You may want to start a special notebook for new words—your own SAT minidictionary. Keep in mind that most words have more than one definition. The dictionary will list these in order of their frequency, from the most common usage to the most obscure. ETS will sometimes trip you up by testing the third or fourth definition of a familiar-sounding word. For example, the word *pedestrian* turns up repeatedly on the SAT. When ETS uses it, though, it never uses it to mean a person on foot—the definition of pedestrian you're probably familiar with. It uses it to mean "common; ordinary; banal"—a secondary definition. Very often, when you see *easy* words on *hard* SAT questions, ETS is testing a second, third, or fourth definition that you may not be familiar with.

ROOTS

Most of the words in the English language were borrowed from other languages at some point in our history. Many of the words you use every day contain bits and pieces of ancient Greek and Latin words that meant something similar. These bits and pieces are called "roots." The dictionary describes each word's roots by giving its *etymology*—a minihistory of where it came from. For example, the *American Heritage Dictionary* gives the following etymology for *apathy*, the sixteenth word on the Hit Parade: "Greek *apatheia*, for *apathés*, without feeling: *A*-(without) + *pathos*, feeling." Similar-sounding words, like *pathos*, *pathetic*, *sympathy*, and *empathy*, are all related and all have to do with feeling.

Many people say the best way to prepare for the SAT is simply to learn a lot of roots. Students who know a lot of roots, they say, will be able to "translate" any unfamiliar words they encounter on the test. There is some truth in this; the more you know about etymology, the easier it will be to build your vocabulary. But roots can also mislead you. The hardest words on the SAT are often words that *seem* to contain a familiar root, but actually do not. For example, *audacity*, a hard word sometimes tested on the SAT, means "boldness or daring." It has nothing to do with sound, even though it seems to contain the root *aud-* from a Latin word meaning "to hear" (as in *audio*, *audiovisual*, or *auditorium*).

Still, learning about roots can be very helpful—if you do it properly. You should think of roots not as a code that will enable you to decipher unknown words on the SAT, but as a tool for learning new words and making associations between them. For example, *eloquent*, *colloquial*, and *circumlocution* all contain the Latin root *loqu/loc*, which means to "speak." Knowing the root and recognizing it in these words will make it easier for you to memorize all of them. You should think of roots as a tool for helping you organize your thoughts as you build your vocabulary.

The worst thing you can do is try to memorize roots all by themselves, apart from words they appear in. In the first place, it can't be done. In the second place, it won't help.

HIT PARADE OF ROOTS

Just as the Hit Parade is a list of the most frequently tested words on the SAT in order of their frequency, the Hit Parade of Roots is a list of the roots that show up most often in SAT vocabulary words. You may find it useful in helping you organize your vocabulary study. Don't try to memorize these roots. In approaching the Hit Parade of Roots, you should focus on the *words*, using the roots simply as reminders to help you learn or remember the meanings. When you take the SAT, you may be able to prod your memory about the meaning of a particular word by thinking of the related words that you associate with it.

The roots on the Hit Parade of Roots are presented in order of their importance on the SAT. The roots at the top of the list appear more often than the roots at the bottom. Each root is followed by a number of real SAT words that contain it. (What should you do every time you don't know the meaning of a word on the Hit Parade of Roots? Look it up!) Note that roots often have several different forms. Be on the lookout for all of them.

CAP/CIP/CEIPT/CEPT/CEIV/CEIT (take)

capture	exceptionable
intercept	susceptible
receptive	deception
recipient	conception
incipient	receive
perceptive	conceit
percipient	accept
anticipate	emancipate
except	precept
exceptional	

GEN (birth, race, kind)

generous	homogeneous
generate	heterogeneous
degenerate	genealogy
regenerate	indigenous
genuine	congenital
congenial	gender
ingenious	engender
ingenuous	genre
ingenue	progeny

DIC/DICT/DIT (tell, say, word)

predicament	malediction
condition	benediction
dictate	extradite
dictator	verdict
abdicate	indict
predict	diction
contradict	dictum
addict	

SPEC/SPIC/SPIT (look, see)

perspective	spectrum
aspect	specimen
spectator	introspection
spectacle	respite
suspect	conspicuous
speculation	circumspect
suspicious	perspicacious
auspicious	

SUPER/SUR (above)

surpass	superstition
superficial	superimpose
summit	supersede
superlative	superfluous
supernova	
supercilious	

TENT/TENS/TEND/TENU (stretch, thin)

tension	contention
extend	distend
tendency	tenuous
tendon	attenuate
tent	portent

TEND (stretch, thin)

tentative	tendentious
contend	

TRANS (across)

transfer	transitory
transaction	transient
transparent	transmutation
transgress	transcendent
transport	intransigent
transform	traduce
transition	

DOC/DUC/DAC (teach, lead)

conduct	document
reduce	docile
seduce	didactic
conducive	indoctrinate
inductee	traduce
doctrine	induce

CO/CON/COM (with, together)

company	contrition
collaborate	commensurate
conjugal	conclave
congeal	conciliate
congenial	comply
convivial	congruent
coalesce	

VERS/VERT (turn)

controversy	aversion
convert	extrovert
revert	introvert
subvert	inadvertent
inversions	versatile
divert	adversity
diverse	

LOC/LOG/LOQU (word, speech)

eloquent	colloquial
logic	eulogy
apology	loquacious
circumlocution	

LOC/LOG/LOQ (word, speech)

dialogue	monologue
prologue	neologism
epilogue	philology

SEN (feel, sense)

sensitive	consent
sensation	dissent
sentiment	assent
sensory	consensus
sensual	sentry
resent	sentinel

DE (away, down, off)

denounce	delineate
debility	deface
defraud	devoid
decry	defile
deplete	desecrate
defame	derogatory

NOM/NOUN/NOWN/NAM/NYM (name, order, rule)

name	astronomy
anonymous	ignominy
antonym	renown
nominate	misnomer
economy	nomenclature

CLA/CLO/CLU (shut, close)

closet	exclusive
claustrophobia	preclude
enclose	recluse
disclose	seclude
include	cloister
conclude	

VO/VOC/VOK/VOW (call)

voice	convoke
vocal	vociferous
provocative	irrevocable
advocate	evocative
equivocate	revoke
vocation	

MAL (bad)

malicious	malodorous
malady	malefactor
dismal	malevolent
malfunction	malediction
malign	maladroit
malcontent	

FRA/FRAC/FRAG (break)

fracture	refraction
fraction	refractory
fragment	infraction
fragmentary	infringe
fragile	fractious
frail	

OB (against)

objective	obstinate
obsolete	obliterate
oblique	oblivious
obscure	obsequious
obstruct	obfuscate

SUB (under)

submissive	subordinate
subsidiary	sublime
subjugation	subtle
subliminal	subversion
subdue	subterfuge

AB (from, away)

abandon	abstain
abhor	absolve
abnormal	abstemious
abstract	abstruse
abdicate	abrogate

GRESS/GRAD (step)

progress	degrade
regress	downgrade
retrogress	aggressor
retrograde	digress
gradual	transgress

SEC/SEQU (follow)

second	execute
sequel	subsequent
sequence	prosecute
consequence	obsequious
inconsequential	

PRO (much, for, a lot)

prolific	prodigal
profuse	protracted
propitious	proclivity
prodigious	propensity
profligate	prodigy

QUE/QUIS (ask, seek)

inquire	querulous
question	acquire
request	acquisitive
quest	acquisition
query	exquisite

SACR/SANCT/SECR (sacred)

sacred	sacrosanct
sacrifice	consecrate
sanctuary	desecrate
sanctify	execrable
sanction	sacrament

SCRIB/SCRIP (write)

scribble	proscribe
describe	ascribe
script	inscribe
postscript	circumscribe
prescribe	

PATHY/PAS/PAT (feeling)

apathy	compassion
sympathy	compatible
empathy	dispassionate
antipathy	impassive
passionate	

DIS/DIF (not)

dissonance	dispassionate
discrepancy	disparate

DIS/DIF (not)

disdain	diffident
dissuade	disparage
dismay	

CIRCU (around)

circumference	circuitous
circulation	circumscribe
circumstance	circumvent
circumnavigate	circumlocutory

PART 6

Answer Key to Drills

CHAPTER 5
DRILL 1
(*page 53*)

✗ 1. financial
monetary
economic

✓ 2. hurt   disappear
ravaged   end
damaged   vanish

✓ 3. boring   liveliness
unexciting   excitement
lifeless   style

DRILL 2
(*page 54*)

1. Pam's answer is C. Choices A, B, E, and possibly D are all Joe Bloggs attractors, because they remind him of "critics," "book," "brilliant," and "author."

2. Pam's answer is B. Each of the other answer choices contains *one* word that makes sense in the sentence. Be careful!

3. Pam's answer is B. Many hard words here.

DRILL 3
(*page 59*)

GROUP A
1. interrupted
2. force..lacking
3. inevitable..mitigates

GROUP B
1. detect..overlook
2. postulate..explore
3. paradigm

GROUP C
1. vague..traditions
2. represent..diversity
3. certitudes..elusive

GROUP D
1. increased..inadequate
2. gullible..distant
3. parsimony..chary of

CHAPTER 6

DRILL 1

(*page 70*)

An architect designs a building.

A warden is in charge of a prison.

Legible means clear writing.

Aquatic pertains to water.

Callous is without sensitivity.

A philanthropist is very generous.

DRILL 2

(*page 74*)

4. Solar pertains to the sun.
5. Glue is by its nature sticky.
6. X
7. "Thanks" is what you say when you are grateful.
8. A morsel is a quantity of food.
9. Equine means horselike.
10. X
11. To preach is to engage in exhortation.
12. X
13. An alias is a false identity.

DRILL 3

(page 83)

Here's the proper difficulty ranking of each group of words. A number 1 is easiest; a number 5 is hardest.

GROUP A
1. striped:lines
2. scribble:penmanship
3. urban:city
4. preamble:statute
5. banality:bore

GROUP B
1. trees:forest
2. mural:painting
3. finale:opera
4. taste:connoisseur
5. mendicant:beggar

GROUP C
1. word:sentence
2. mirror:reflection
3. reflex:involuntary
4. garrulous:speaker
5. arson:conflagration

GROUP D
1. fins:aquatic
2. novel:literature
3. loyal:devotion
4. threadbare:clothing
5. insurrectionist:docile

Group D was a tough call. Review these rearranged groups to get a feel for the progression of difficulty on the SAT.

CHAPTER 7

DRILL 1

(page 116)

Here are the same sentences and phrases again, with disputable words in italics:

(A) leads politicians to place *complete* reliance upon the results of opinion polls

(B) Baker's ideas had *no* influence on the outcome.

(C) Foreign languages should *never* be studied.

(D) *All* financial resources should be directed toward improving the work environment.

(E) the belief that nature is inscrutable and *cannot* be described

DRILL 2

(page 117)

Here are the same sentences and phrases again, with hard-to-dispute words in italics:

(A)   New research *may* lead to improvements in manufacturing technology.

(B)   *Not all* workers respond the same way to instruction.

(C)   Improved weather was *but one of the many* factors that led to the record crop.

(D)   *Most* scientists believe that continued progress is possible.

(E)   Everyone *cannot* expect to be happy *all* the time.

DRILL 3

(page 127)

Here are the six sentences in the reading passage that contain trigger words:

First Paragraph: "There is more than one kind of innovation at work in the region, of course, *but* I have chosen to focus on three related patterns of family behavior."

Third Paragraph: "They continue to migrate *but* on a reduced scale, often modifying their schedules of migration to allow children to finish the school year."

Fourth Paragraph: "The greatest amount of change from pattern I, *however,* is found in pattern III families, who no longer migrate at all."

"They not only work full time *but* may, in addition, return to school."

"*Although* these women are in the minority among residents of the region, they serve as role models for others, causing ripples of change to spread in their communities."

Fifth Paragraph: "*But* some of the women decided to stay at their jobs after the family's distress was over."

CHAPTER 10

DRILL 1

(page 163)

1. 109
2. 38
3. -3
4. 10
5. 15

DRILL 2
(page 165)
1. $(6 \times 57) + (6 \times 18)$
2. $51(52 + 53 + 54)$
3. $ab + ac - ad$
4. $x(y - z)$
5. $c(ab + xy)$

DRILL 3
(page 171)

1. 3

2. $\dfrac{31}{5}$

3. $-1\dfrac{4}{15}$ or $-\dfrac{19}{15}$

4. $\dfrac{1}{15}$

5. $\dfrac{6}{7}$

6. $\dfrac{2}{25}$

7. $\dfrac{4}{9}$

DRILL 4
(page 173)
1. .37
2. 1457.7
3. 186
4. −2.89

DRILL 5
(page 182)

	Fraction	Decimal	Percent
1.	$\dfrac{1}{2}$	0.5	50
2.	$\dfrac{3}{1}$	3.0	300
3.	$\dfrac{1}{200}$	0.005	0.5
4.	$\dfrac{1}{3}$	0.3333	$33\dfrac{1}{3}$

CHAPTER 12

DRILL 1

(*page 238*)

1. 0.4
2. a little bit more than 5 or a little bit less than 6
3. 2.8
4. a little bit more than 0.85
5. A little bit more than 4
6. x = about 30°
   y = about 125°
   z = about 25°
   yz is about 16
   xz is about 30 (a little *less* than 32!)

(None of these angle measurements is exact, but remember, you don't have to be exact when you guesstimate. Even a very rough guesstimation will enable you to eliminate one or two answer choices.)

CHAPTER 14

DRILL 1

(*page 288*)

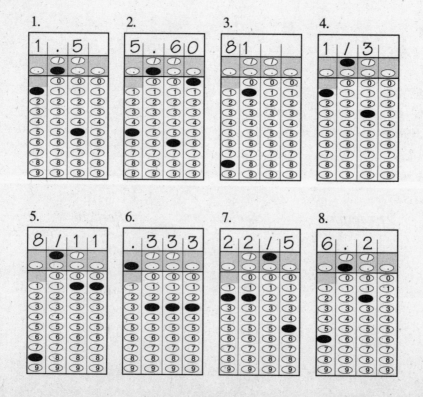

PART 7

The Princeton Review Diagnostic Test

The best way to learn our techniques for cracking the SAT is to practice them. The following diagnostic test will give you a chance to do that.

The diagnostic test was designed to be as much like a real SAT as possible. It contains three verbal sections, three math sections, and an experimental section (two of the sections only last for 15 minutes). Our questions test the same concepts that are tested on real SATs.

Since one of the sections in this test is experimental, none of the questions in it count toward your final score. The actual SAT will have an experimental section—verbal *or* math—that ETS now euphemistically terms an "equating section."

Some of the questions in the experimental section may have two answers or possibly no answers at all. Questions in this section may all be very easy or may all be incredibly tough. Furthermore, questions in this section may not be arranged in order of difficulty. If a section on your SAT seems bizarre, don't lose faith. Finish the section and start fresh on the next one. The weird section was probably experimental.

It is extremely difficult for most students to tell if a section is experimental, so you'll have to treat all of the sections like real sections.

When you take the diagnostic test, you should try to take it under conditions that are as much like real testing conditions as possible. Take it in a room where you won't be disturbed, and have someone else time you. (It's too easy if you time yourself.) You can give yourself a brief break halfway through, but don't stop for longer than five minutes or so. To put yourself in the proper frame of mind, you might take it on a Saturday morning.

After taking our test, you'll have a very good idea of what taking the real SAT will be like. In fact, we've found that students' scores on Princeton Review's diagnostic tests correspond very closely to the scores they earn on real SATs.

The answers to the questions and a scoring guide can be found on pages 411, 413, and 414. The answer sheet is at the back of the book.

If you have any questions about the diagnostic test, the SAT, ETS, or The Princeton Review, give us a call, toll-free, at 1-800-995-5585.

The following sample test was written by the authors and is not an actual SAT. The directions and format were used by permission of Educational Testing Service. This permission does not constitute review or endorsement by Educational Testing Service or the College Board of this publication as a whole or of any sample questions or testing information it may contain.

The Princeton Review Diagnostic Test

Time—30 Minutes 25 Questions	In this section solve each problem, using any available space on the page for scratchwork. Then decide which is the best of the choices given and fill in the corresponding oval on the answer sheet.

Notes:

(1)   The use of a calculator is permitted. All numbers used are real numbers.

(2)   Figures that accompany problems in this test are intended to provide information useful in solving the problems. They are drawn as accurately as possible EXCEPT when it is stated in a specific problem that the figure is not drawn to scale. All figures lie in a plane unless otherwise indicated.

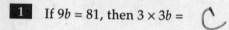

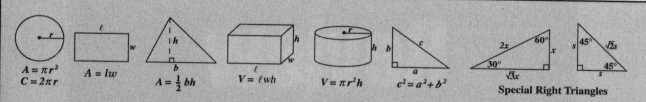

$A = \pi r^2$
$C = 2\pi r$

$A = lw$

$A = \frac{1}{2}bh$

$V = lwh$

$V = \pi r^2 h$

$c^2 = a^2 + b^2$

Special Right Triangles

The number of degrees of arc in a circle is 360.
The measure in degrees of a straight angle is 180.
The sum of the measures in degrees of the angles of a triangle is 180.

1   If $9b = 81$, then $3 \times 3b =$

(A)   9
(B)   27
(C)   81
(D)   243
(E)   729

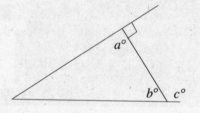

2   In the figure above, what is the sum of $a + b + c$?

(A)   180
(B)   240
(C)   270
(D)   360
(E)   It cannot be determined from the information given.

GO ON TO THE NEXT PAGE

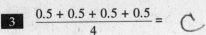 

3 $\dfrac{0.5 + 0.5 + 0.5 + 0.5}{4} =$ C

(A) 0.05
(B) 0.125
(C) 0.5
(D) 1
(E) 2.0

A   B   C   D

Note: Figure not drawn to scale.

5 If $AB > CD$, which of the following must be true?   X

I. $AB > BC$
II. $AC > BD$
III. $AC > CD$

(A) I only
(B) II only
(C) III only
(D) II and III only
(E) I, II, and III

4 Steve ran a 12-mile race at an average speed of 8 miles per hour. If Adam ran the same race at an average speed of 6 miles per hour, how many minutes longer than Steve did Adam take to complete the race?

(A) 9
(B) 12
(C) 16
(D) 24
(E) 30

6 If 3 more than x is 2 more than y, what is x in terms of y?

(A) $y - 5$
(B) $y - 1$
(C) $y + 1$
(D) $y + 5$
(E) $y + 6$

C

$3 + x = 2 + y$

$1 + x = y$

GO ON TO THE NEXT PAGE →

7 $\dfrac{4^2}{2^3} + \dfrac{2^3}{4^2} =$

(A) $\dfrac{5}{2}$

(B) 2

(C) 1

(D) $\dfrac{1}{2}$

(E) $\dfrac{1}{4}$

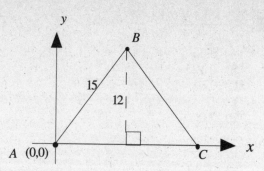

9 In the figure above, side AB of triangle ABC contains which of the following points?

(A) $(3, 2)$
(B) $(3, 5)$
(C) $(4, 6)$
(D) $(4, 10)$
(E) $(6, 8)$

8 If 8 and 12 each divide K without a remainder, what is the value of K?

(A) 16
(B) 24
(C) 48
(D) 96
(E) It cannot be determined from the information given.

10 What is the diameter of a circle with circumference 5?

(A) $\dfrac{5}{\pi}$

(B) $\dfrac{10}{\pi}$

(C) 5

(D) 5π

(E) 10π

GO ON TO THE NEXT PAGE →

11 Carol subscribed to four publications that cost $12.90, $16.00, $18.00, and $21.90 per year, respectively. If she made an initial down payment of one half of the total amount, and paid the rest in 4 equal monthly payments, how much was each of the 4 monthly payments?

(A) $8.60
(B) $9.20
(C) $9.45
(D) $17.20
(E) $34.40

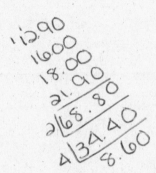

MERCHANDISE SALES		
Type	Amount of Sales	Percent of Total Sales
Shoes	$12,000	15%
Coats	$20,000	25%
Shirts	$x	40%
Pants	$y	20%

12 According to the table above, what were the sales, in dollars, of shirts and pants combined?

(A) $32,000
(B) $48,000
(C) $60,000
(D) $68,000
(E) $80,000

13 For all integers $n \neq 1$, let $< n > = \dfrac{n+1}{n-1}$. Which of the following has the greatest value?

(A) $< 0 >$
(B) $< 2 >$
(C) $< 3 >$
(D) $< 4 >$
(E) $< 5 >$

14 If the product of $(1 + 2)$, $(2 + 3)$, and $(3 + 4)$ is equal to one half the sum of 20 and x, then $x =$

(A) 10
(B) 85
(C) 105
(D) 190
(E) 1,210

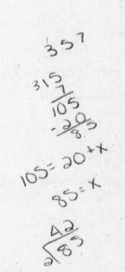

GO ON TO THE NEXT PAGE

15 If $\dfrac{2+x}{5+x} = \dfrac{2}{5} + \dfrac{2}{5}$, then $x =$

(A) $\dfrac{2}{5}$

(B) 1

(C) 2

(D) 5

(E) 10

17 A survey of Town X found a mean of 3.2 persons per household and a mean of 1.2 televisions per household. If 48,000 people live in Town X, how many televisions are in Town X?

(A) 15,000
(B) 16,000
(C) 18,000
(D) 40,000
(E) 57,600

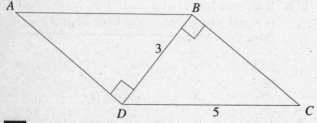

16 In parallelogram $ABCD$ above, $BD = 3$ and $CD = 5$. What is the area of $ABCD$?

(A) 12
(B) 15
(C) 18
(D) 20
(E) It cannot be determined from the information given.

18 How many numbers from 1 to 200 inclusive are equal to the cube of an integer?

(A) one
(B) two
(C) three
(D) four
(E) five

GO ON TO THE NEXT PAGE

Note: Figure not drawn to scale.

19 If the perimeter of rectangle $ABCD$ is equal to p, and $x = \frac{2}{3}y$, what is the value of y in terms of p?

(A) $\dfrac{p}{10}$

(B) $\dfrac{3p}{10}$

(C) $\dfrac{p}{3}$

(D) $\dfrac{2p}{5}$

(E) $\dfrac{3p}{5}$

20 A basketball team had a ratio of wins to losses of 3:1. After winning six games in a row, the team's ratio of wins to losses was 5:1. How many games had the team won <u>before</u> it won the six games?

(A) 3
(B) 6
(C) 9
(D) 15
(E) 24

21 A college student bought 11 books for Fall classes. If the cost of his anatomy textbook was three times the mean cost of the other 10 books, then the cost of the anatomy textbook was what fraction of the total amount he paid for the 11 books?

(A) $\dfrac{2}{13}$

(B) $\dfrac{3}{13}$

(C) $\dfrac{3}{11}$

(D) $\dfrac{3}{10}$

(E) $\dfrac{3}{4}$

22 In rectangle $PQRS$ above, what is the sum of $a + b$ in terms of x?

(A) $90 + x$
(B) $180 - x$
(C) $180 + x$
(D) $270 - x$
(E) $360 - x$

GO ON TO THE NEXT PAGE

23 What is the area of square *ABCD*?

(A) 25
(B) $18\sqrt{2}$
(C) 26
(D) $25 + \sqrt{2}$
(E) 36

24 If 0.1 % of *m* is equal to 10 % of *n*, then *m* is what percent of 10*n*?

(A) $\dfrac{1}{1000}\%$

(B) 10%

(C) 100%

(D) 1,000%

(E) 10,000%

25 If $n \neq 0$, which of the following could be true?

  I. $2n < n^2$
  II. $2n < n$
  III. $n^2 < -n$

(A) None
(B) I only
(C) I and II only
(D) I and III only
(E) I, II, and III

IF YOU FINISH BEFORE TIME IS CALLED, YOU MAY CHECK YOUR WORK ON THIS SECTION ONLY. DO NOT TURN TO ANY OTHER SECTION IN THE TEST. STOP

374

GO ON TO THE NEXT PAGE

Time-30 Minutes— For each question in this section, select the best answer among the choices given
35 Questions and fill in the corresponding oval on the answer sheet.

Each sentence below has one or two blanks,
each blank indicating that something has been
omitted. Beneath the sentence are five words
or set of words labeled A through E. Choose
the word or set of words that, when inserted in
the sentence, best fits the meaning of the
sentence as a whole.

Example:

Medieval kingdoms did not become
constitutional republics overnight; on the
contrary, the change was ----.

(A) unpopular
(B) unexpected
(C) advantageous
(D) sufficient
(E) gradual

1 Since the island soil has been barren for so
many years, the natives must now ---- much
of their food.

(A) deliver
(B) import
(C) produce
(D) develop
(E) utilize

2 Because Jenkins neither ---- nor defends
either management or the striking workers,
both sides admire his journalistic ----.

(A) criticizes. .acumen
(B) attacks. .neutrality
(C) confronts. .aptitude
(D) dismisses. .flair
(E) promotes. .integrity

3 Some anthropologists claim that a few apes
have been taught a rudimentary sign
language, but skeptics argue that the apes
are only ---- their trainers.

(A) imitating
(B) condoning
(C) instructing
(D) acknowledging
(E) belaboring

4 It is ironic that the ---- insights of the great
thinkers are voiced so often that they have
become mere ----.

(A) original. .clichés
(B) banal. .beliefs
(C) dubious. .habits
(D) philosophical. .questions
(E) abstract. .ideas

5 The most frustrating periods of any diet are
the inevitable ----, when weight loss ----
if not stops.

(A) moods. .accelerates
(B) feasts. .halts
(C) holidays. .contracts
(D) plateaus. .slows
(E) meals. .ceases

6 Since the author's unflattering references to
her friends were so ----, she was surprised
that her ---- were recognized.

(A) laudatory. .styles
(B) obvious. .anecdotes
(C) oblique. .allusions
(D) critical. .eulogies
(E) apparent. .motives

7 Mark was intent on maintaining his status
as first in his class; because even the
smallest mistakes infuriated him, he
reviewed all his papers ---- before
submitting them to his teacher.

(A) explicitly
(B) perfunctorily
(C) honestly
(D) mechanically
(E) assiduously

8 Since many disadvantaged individuals view
their situations as ---- as well as intolerable,
their attitudes are best described as ----.

(A) squalid. .obscure
(B) unpleasant. .bellicose
(C) acute. . sanguine
(D) immutable. .resigned
(E) political. .perplexed

9 The subtleties of this novel are evident not
so much in the character ---- as they are in
its profoundly ---- plot structure.

(A) assessment. .eclectic
(B) development. .trite
(C) portrayal. .aesthetic
(D) delineation. .intricate
(E) illustration. .superficial

GO ON TO THE NEXT PAGE

Each question below consists of a related pair of words or phrases, followed by five pairs of words or phrases labeled A through E. Select the pair that best expresses a relationship similar to that expressed in the original pair.

Example:

CRUMB : BREAD::

(A) ounce: unit
(B) splinter: wood
(C) water: bucket
(D) twine: rope
(E) cream: butter

10 SHIP : OCEAN ::

(A) fish : gill
(B) plane : air
(C) child : bath
(D) camel : water
(E) car : passengers

11 BOTANY : PLANTS ::

(A) agriculture : herbs
(B) astronomy : stars
(C) philosophy : books
(D) anthropology : religion
(E) forestry : evergreens

12 CENSUS : POPULATION ::

(A) catalog : pictures
(B) inventory : supplies
(C) detonation : explosion
(D) dictionary : words
(E) election : tally

13 CONSTELLATION : STARS ::

(A) earth : moon
(B) center : circle
(C) archipelago : islands
(D) rain : water
(E) maverick : herd

14 REFINE : OIL ::

(A) winnow : wheat
(B) harness : energy
(C) mine : coal
(D) mold : plastic
(E) conserve : resource

15 PERSPICACIOUS : INSIGHT ::

(A) zealous : mobility
(B) audacious : hearing
(C) delicious : taste
(D) avaricious : generosity
(E) amiable : friendliness

GO ON TO THE NEXT PAGE

The passage below is followed by questions based on its content. Answer the questions on the basis of what is stated or implied in the passage and in any introductory material that may be provided.

Questions 16–21 are based on the following passage.

The following passage is an excerpt from a book by novelist Gregor von Rezzori.

Skushno is a Russian word that is difficult to translate. It means more than dreary boredom: a spiritual void that sucks you in like a vague but
Line intensely urgent longing. When I was thirteen, at
(5) a phase that educators used to call the awkward age, my parents were at their wits' end. We lived in the Bukovina, today an almost astronomically remote province in southeastern Europe. The story I am telling seems as distant—not only in
(10) space but also in time—as if I'd merely dreamed it. Yet it begins as a very ordinary story.
I had been expelled by a *consilium abeundi*—an advisory board with authority to expel unworthy students—from the schools of the then Kingdom
(15) of Rumania, whose subjects we had become upon the collapse of the Austro-Hungarian Empire after the first great war. An attempt to harmonize the imbalances in my character by means of strict discipline at a boarding school in Styria (my
(20) people still regarded Austria as our cultural homeland) nearly led to the same ignominious end, and only my pseudo-voluntary departure from the institution in the nick of time prevented my final ostracism from the privileged ranks of
(25) those for whom the path to higher education was open. Again in the jargon of those assigned the responsible task of raising children to become "useful members of society," I was a "virtually hopeless case." My parents, blind to how the
(30) contradictions within me had grown out of the highly charged difference between their own natures, agreed with the schoolmasters; the mix of neurotic sensitivity and a tendency to violence, alert perception and inability to learn, tender
(35) need for support and lack of adjustability, would only develop into something criminal.

One of the trivial aphorisms my generation owes to Wilhelm Busch's *Pious Helene* is the homily "Once your reputation's done / You can
(40) live a life of fun." But this optimistic notion results more from wishful thinking than from practical experience. In my case, had anyone asked me about my state of mind, I would have sighed and answered, "*Skushno!*" Even though
(45) rebellious thoughts occasionally surged within me, I dragged myself, or rather I let myself be dragged, listlessly through my bleak existence in the snail's pace of days. Nor was I ever free of a sense of guilt, for my feeling guilty was not
(50) entirely foisted upon me by others; there were deep reasons I could not explain to myself; had I been able to do so, my life would have been much easier.

16 It can be inferred from the passage that the author's parents were

(A) frustrated by the author's inability to do well in school
(B) oblivious to the author's poor academic performance
(C) wealthy, making them insensitive to the needs of the poor
(D) schoolmasters who believed in the strict disciplining of youth
(E) living in Russia while their son lived in Bukovina

17 Lines 17–25 are used by the author to demonstrate that

(A) the author was an unstable and dangerous person
(B) the schools that the author attended were too difficult
(C) the tactics being used to make the author a more stable person were failing
(D) the author was not accepted well by his classmates
(E) the author's academic career was nearing an end

GO ON TO THE NEXT PAGE →

18 The word *ignominious* in line 21 means

(A) dangerous
(B) pitiless
(C) unappreciated
(D) disgraceful
(E) honorable

19 In line 23, the word *ostracism* most likely means

(A) praise
(B) abuse
(C) appreciation
(D) departure
(E) banishment

20 The passage as a whole suggests that the author felt

(A) happy because he was separated from his parents
(B) upset because he was unable to maintain good friends
(C) melancholy and unsettled in his environment
(D) suicidal and desperate because of his living in Russia
(E) harmonic and hopeful because he'd soon be out of school

21 The passage indicates that the author regarded the aphorism mentioned in the last paragraph with

(A) relief because it showed him that he would eventually feel better
(B) despair because the author did not believe it was true
(C) contempt because he saw it working for others
(D) bemusement because of his immunity from it
(E) sorrow because his faith in it nearly killed him

GO ON TO THE NEXT PAGE

Questions 22–30 are based on the following passage.

Fear of communism swept through the United States in the years following the Russian Revolution of 1917. Several states passed espionage acts that restricted political discussion, and radicals of all descriptions were rounded up in so-called Red Raids conducted by the attorney general's office. Some were convicted and imprisoned; others were deported. This was the background of a trial in Chicago involving twenty men charged under Illinois's espionage statute with advocating the violent overthrow of the government. The charge rested on the fact that all the defendants were members of the newly formed Communist Labor party.

The accused in the case were represented by Clarence Darrow, one of the foremost defense attorneys in the country. Throughout his career, Darrow had defended the poor and the despised against exploitation and prejudice. He defended the rights of labor unions, for example, at a time when many sought to outlaw the strike, and he was resolute in defending constitutional freedoms. The following are excerpts from Darrow's summation to the jury.

Members of the Jury . . . If you want to convict these twenty men, then do it. I ask no consideration on behalf of any one of them. They
Line are no better than any other twenty men or
(5) women; they are no better than the millions down through the ages who have been prosecuted and convicted in cases like this. And if it is necessary for my clients to show that America is like all the rest, if it is necessary that my clients shall go to
(10) prison to show it, then let them go. They can afford it if you members of the jury can; make no mistake about that . . .

The State says my clients "dare to criticize the Constitution." Yet this police officer (who the
(15) State says is a fine, right-living person) twice violated the federal Constitution while a prosecuting attorney was standing by. They entered Mr. Owen's home without a search warrant. They overhauled his papers. They found
(20) a flag, a red one, which he had the same right to have in his house that you have to keep a green one, or a yellow one, or any other color, and the officer impudently rolled it up and put another flag on the wall, nailed it there. By what right was
(25) that done? What about this kind of patriotism that violates the Constitution? Has it come to pass in this country that officers of the law can trample on constitutional rights and then excuse it in a court of justice? . . .
(30) Most of what has been presented to this jury to stir up feeling in your souls has not the slightest bearing on proving conspiracy in this case. Take Mr. Lloyd's speech in Milwaukee. It had nothing to do with conspiracy.
(35) Whether that speech was a joke or was serious, I will not attempt to discuss. But I will say that if it was serious it was as mild as a summer's shower compared with many of the statements of those who are responsible for working conditions
(40) in this country. We have heard from people in high places that those individuals who express sympathy with labor should be stood up against a wall and shot. We have heard people of position declare that individuals who criticize the actions
(45) of those who are getting rich should be put in a cement ship with leaden sails and sent out to sea. Every violent appeal that could be conceived by the brain has been used by the powerful and the strong. I repeat, Mr. Lloyd's speech was gentle in
(50) comparison . . . .

My clients are condemned because they say in their platform that, while they vote, they believe the ballot is secondary to education and organization. Counsel suggests that those who get
(55) something they did not vote for are sinners, but I suspect you the jury know full well that my clients are right. Most of you have an eight-hour day. Did you get it by any vote you ever cast? No.
(60) It came about because workers laid down their tools and said we will no longer work until we get an eight-hour day. That is how they got the twelve-hour day, the ten-hour day, and the eight-hour day—not by voting but by laying down their
(65) tools. Then when it was over and the victory won . . . then the politicians, in order to get the labor vote, passed legislation creating an eight-hour day. That is how things changed; victory preceded law . . . .
(70) You have been told that if you acquit these defendants you will be despised because you will endorse everything they believe. But I am not here to defend my clients' opinions. I am here to defend their right to express their opinions. I ask
(75) you, then, to decide this case upon the facts as you have heard them, in light of the law as you understand it, in light of the history of our country, whose institutions you and I are bound to protect.

GO ON TO THE NEXT PAGE

22 Clarence Darrow's statement that "They can afford it if you members of the jury can" is most probably meant to imply that

(A) the defendants will not be harmed if convicted
(B) if the jurors convict the defendants, they will be harshly criticized
(C) the defendants do not care whether they are convicted
(D) everyone involved in the trial will be affected financially by whatever the jury decides
(E) if the defendants are found guilty, everyone's rights will be threatened

23 Lines 12–27 suggest that the case against Owen would have been dismissed if the judge had interpreted the constitution in which of the following ways?

(A) Defendants must have their rights read to them when they are arrested.
(B) Giving false testimony in court is a crime.
(C) Evidence gained by illegal means is not admissible in court.
(D) No one can be tried twice for the same crime.
(E) Defendants cannot be forced to give incriminating evidence against themselves.

24 Darrow's defense in lines 28–47 relies mainly on persuading the jury that

(A) the prosecution is using a double standard
(B) the evidence used by the prosecution is unreliable
(C) the defendants' views are similar to those of the jury
(D) labor unions are guaranteed the right to hold a strike
(E) a federal court is a more appropriate place to try the defendants than is a state court

25 Lines 28–47 indicate that the prosecution attempted to characterize Mr. Lloyd's speech as

(A) bitter sarcasm
(B) deceptive propaganda
(C) valid criticism
(D) a frightening threat
(E) a bad joke

26 What does Clarence Darrow accuse "people in high places" (lines 38–39) of doing?

(A) Trying to kill Communist party members
(B) Advocating violence against labor sympathizers
(C) Lying to the jury
(D) Encouraging the use of harsh punishment against criminals
(E) Making foolish and insulting suggestions

27 The word *counsel* in line 51 refers to

(A) expert psychologists
(B) the prosecution
(C) an assembly
(D) a recommendation
(E) an expert

28 Lines 66–68 imply that the prosecution had told the jury that finding for the innocence of the defendants would be similar to

(A) denying the validity of the Constitution
(B) permitting workers to go on strike
(C) promoting passive resistance
(D) limiting freedom of expression
(E) promoting communism

29 In line 74, the word *bound* most nearly means

(A) intellectually committed
(B) personally determined
(C) morally compelled
(D) violently coerced
(E) inevitably destined

30 Darrow's defense hinges on the ability of the jurors to

(A) understand complicated legal terms and procedures
(B) sympathize with union organizers
(C) comprehend the beliefs of the Communist Labor party
(D) separate the defendants' rights from their views
(E) act in the interest of the national economy

IF YOU FINISH BEFORE TIME IS CALLED, YOU MAY CHECK YOUR WORK ON THIS SECTION ONLY. DO NOT TURN TO ANY OTHER SECTION IN THE TEST. **STOP**

Time—30 Minutes	In this section solve each problem, using any available space on the page for scratchwork. Then decide which is the best of the choices given and fill in the corresponding oval on the answer sheet.
25 Questions	

Notes:

(1)   The use of a calculator is permitted. All numbers used are real numbers.

(2)   Figures that accompany problems in this test are intended to provide information useful in solving the problems. They are drawn as accurately as possible EXCEPT when it is stated in a specific problem that the figure is not drawn to scale. All figures lie in a plane unless otherwise indicated.

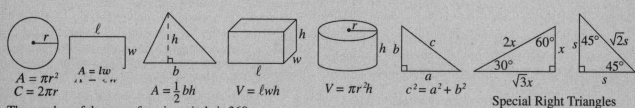

$A = \pi r^2$
$C = 2\pi r$

$A = lw$

$A = \frac{1}{2} bh$

$V = lwh$

$V = \pi r^2 h$

$c^2 = a^2 + b^2$

Special Right Triangles

The number of degrees of arc in a circle is 360.
The measure in degrees of a straight angle is 180.
The sum of the measures in degrees of the angles of a triangle is 180.

Directions for Quantitative Comparison Questions

<u>Questions 1–15</u> each consist of two quantities in boxes, one in Column A and one in Column B. You are to compare the two quantities and on the answer sheet fill in oval

A   if the quantity in Column A is greater;
B   if the quantity in Column B is greater;
C   if the two quantities are equal;
D   if the relationship cannot be determined from the information given.

AN E RESPONSE WILL NOT BE SCORED.

Notes:

1.   In some questions, information is given about one or both of the quantities to be compared. In such cases, the given information is centered above the two columns and is not boxed.
2.   In a given question, a symbol that appears in both columns represents the same thing in Column A as it does in Column B.
3.   Letters such as x, n, and k stand for real numbers.

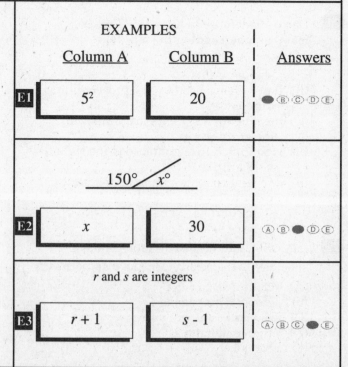

EXAMPLES

Column A	Column B	Answers
E1 5^2	20	● Ⓑ Ⓒ Ⓓ Ⓔ

150° $x°$

| E2 x | 30 | Ⓐ Ⓑ ● Ⓓ Ⓔ |

r and s are integers

| E3 $r + 1$ | $s - 1$ | Ⓐ Ⓑ Ⓒ ● Ⓔ |

GO ON TO THE NEXT PAGE

	Column A	**Column B**
1	$\dfrac{3}{7}$	$\dfrac{1}{2}$

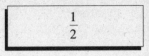

$AB = 8$

	Column A	**Column B**
2	The radius of the circle	4

$7a > 4b$

	Column A	**Column B**
3	a	b

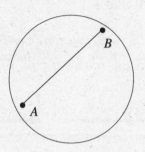

	Column A	**Column B**
4	$x + y$	90

Column A   **Column B**

The novelty clock above has hands that move at the correct speed, but counter-clockwise. The clock tells the correct time every 6 hours (at 6:00 and 12:00).

	Column A	**Column B**
5	3 hours, 15 minutes	Amount of time that has passed since 12:00

$9^n - 8^n = 1^n$

	Column A	**Column B**
6	1	n

A rectangle of area 4 has two sides of length r and s, where r and s are integers.

	Column A	**Column B**
7	$\dfrac{r}{2}$	$2s$

GO ON TO THE NEXT PAGE

SUMMARY DIRECTIONS FOR QUANTITATIVE COMPARISON QUESTIONS

<u>Answer:</u> A if the quantity in Column A is greater;
B if the quantity in Column B is greater;
C if the two quantities are equal;
D if the relationship cannot be determined from the information given.

AN E RESPONSE WILL NOT BE SCORED.

| <u>Column A</u> | <u>Column B</u> | <u>Column A</u> | <u>Column B</u> |

In a group of 28 children, there are 6 more girls than boys.

x, y, and **z** are positive.
$x + y + z = 10$ and $x = y$

8 | Two times the number of girls | Three times the number of boys

11 | x | 5

9 | $\dfrac{\frac{3}{2}}{\left(\frac{3}{2}\right)^2}$ | $\dfrac{2}{3}$

12 | $\sqrt{3} + \sqrt{4}$ | $\sqrt{3} \times \sqrt{4}$

The area of the square is 25. Points A, B, C, and D are on the square.

13 | The number of distinct prime factors of 30 | The number of distinct prime factors of 60

14 | x^2 | $(x + 1)^2$

10 | Perimeter of the rectangle ABCD | 20

15 | The percent increase from 99 to 100 | The percent decrease from 100 to 99

GO ON TO THE NEXT PAGE

Directions for Student-Produced Response Questions

Each of the remaining 10 questions (16–25) requires you to solve the problem and enter your answer by marking the ovals in the special grid, as shown in the example below.

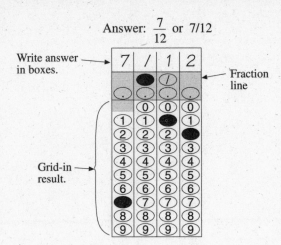

Answer: $\frac{7}{12}$ or 7/12

Write answer in boxes.

Fraction line

Grid-in result.

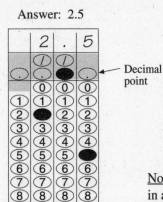

Answer: 2.5

Decimal point

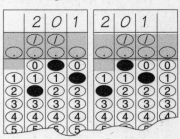

Answer: 201
Either position is correct.

<u>Note:</u> You may start your answer in any column, space permitting. Columns not needed should be left blank.

- Mark no more than one oval in any column.

- Because the answer sheet will be machine-scored, **you will receive credit only if the ovals are filled in correctly.**

- Although not required, it is suggested that you write your answer in the boxes at the top of the columns to help you fill in the ovals accurately.

- Some problems may have more than one correct answer. In such cases, grid only one answer.

- No question has a negative answer.

- **Mixed numbers** such as $2\frac{1}{2}$ must be gridded as 2.5 or 5/2. (If ⟨2 1 / 2⟩ is gridded, it will be interpreted as $\frac{21}{2}$, not $2\frac{1}{2}$.)

- <u>Decimal Accuracy:</u> If you obtain a decimal answer, **enter the most accurate value the grid will accommodate.** For example, if you obtain an answer such as 0.6666 . . ., you should record the result as .666 or .667. **Less accurate values such as .66 or .67 are not acceptable.**

Acceptable ways to grid $\frac{2}{3}$ = .6666 . . .

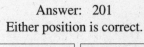

---

16 If $\dfrac{x + 2x + 3x}{2} = 6$, then $x =$

17 There are 24 fish in an aquarium. If $\frac{1}{8}$ of them are tetras and $\frac{2}{3}$ of the remaining fish are guppies, how many guppies are in the aquarium?

GO ON TO THE NEXT PAGE →

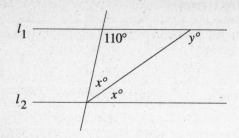

18   If l_1 is parallel to l_2 in the figure above, what is the value of y?

19   The daily newspaper always follows a particular format. Each even-numbered page contains 6 articles and each odd-numbered page contains 7 articles. If today's paper has 36 pages, how many articles does it contain?

20   When n is divided by 5, the remainder is 4.
When n is divided by 4, the remainder is 3.
If $0 < n < 100$, what is one possible value of n?

21   If $x^2 = 16$ and $y^2 = 4$, what is the greatest possible value of $(x - y)^2$?

GO ON TO THE NEXT PAGE

22 Segment *AB* is perpendicular to segment *BD*. Segment *AB* and segment *CD* bisect each other at point *x*. If *AB* = 8 and *CD* = 10, what is the length of *BD*?

24 At a certain high school, 30 students study French, 40 study Spanish, and 25 study neither. If there are 80 students in the school, how many study both French and Spanish?

23 At a music store, the price of a CD is three times the price of a cassette tape. If 40 CDs were sold for a total of $480, and the combined sales of CDs and cassette tapes totaled $600, how many cassette tapes were sold?

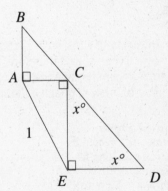

25 In the figure above, if *AE* = 1, what is the sum of the area of △*ABC* and the area of △*CDE*?

Time–30 Minutes— For each question in this section, select the best answer from among the choices
given 35 Questions fill in the corresponding oval on the answer sheet.

Each sentence below has one or two blanks,
each blank indicating that something has been
omitted. Beneath the sentence are five words
or set of words labeled A through E. Choose
the word or set of words that, when inserted in
the sentence, best fits the meaning of the
sentence as a whole.

Example:

Medieval kingdoms did not become
constitutional republics overnight; on the
contrary, the change was ----.

(A) unpopular
(B) unexpected
(C) advantageous
(D) sufficient
(E) gradual

Ⓐ Ⓑ Ⓒ Ⓓ ●

1 If it is true that morality cannot exist without
religion, then does not the erosion of religion
herald the ---- of morality?

(A) regulation
(B) basis
(C) belief
(D) collapse
(E) value

2 Certain animal behaviors, such as mating
rituals, seem to be ----, and therefore ---- external
factors such as climate changes, food supply, or
the presence of other animals of the same
species.

(A) learned..immune to
(B) innate..unaffected by
(C) intricate..belong to
(D) specific..confused with
(E) memorized..controlled by

3 Shaken by two decades of virtual anarchy, the
majority of people were ready to buy ---- at any
price.

(A) order
(B) emancipation
(C) hope
(D) liberty
(E) enfranchisement

4 As a person who combines care with ----, Marisa
completed her duties with ---- as well as zeal.

(A) levity..resignation
(B) geniality..ardor
(C) vitality..willingness
(D) empathy..rigor
(E) enthusiasm..meticulousness

5 Her shrewd campaign managers were
responsible for the fact that her political slogans
were actually forgotten clichés revived and ----
with new meaning.

(A) fathomed
(B) instilled
(C) foreclosed
(D) instigated
(E) foreshadowed

6 The former general led his civilian life as he had
his military life, with simplicity and ---- dignity.

(A) benevolent
(B) informal
(C) austere
(D) aggressive
(E) succinct

7 Although bound to impose the law, a judge is
free to use his discretion to ---- the anachronistic
barbarity of some criminal penalties.

(A) mitigate
(B) understand
(C) condone
(D) provoke
(E) enforce

8 Henry viewed Melissa to be ----; she seemed to
be against any position regardless of its merits.

(A) heretical
(B) disobedient
(C) contrary
(D) inattentive
(E) harried

9 Dr. Schwartz's lecture on art, while detailed and
scholarly, focused ---- on the premodern; some
students may have appreciated his specialized
knowledge, but those with more ---- interests
may have been disappointed.

(A) literally..medieval
(B) completely..pedantic
(C) expansively..technical
(D) voluminously..creative
(E) exclusively..comprehensive

10 Only when one actually visits the ancient ruins
of marvelous bygone civilizations does one
truly appreciate the sad ---- of human greatness.

(A) perspicacity
(B) magnitude
(C) artistry
(D) transience
(E) quiescence

GO ON TO THE NEXT PAGE ➡

Each question below consists of a related pair of words or phrases, followed by five pairs of words or phrases labeled A through E. Select the pair that best expresses a relationship similar to that expressed in the original pair.

Example:

CRUMB : BREAD ::

(A) ounce: unit
(B) splinter: wood
(C) water: bucket
(D) twine: rope
(E) cream: butter

Ⓐ ● Ⓒ Ⓓ Ⓔ

11 CAKE : DESSERT ::

(A) coach : football
(B) lawyer : jury
(C) poet : writing
(D) actor : troupe
(E) pediatrician : doctor

12 WEIGHTLIFTER : STRENGTH ::

(A) goalie : skill
(B) dancer : speed
(C) marathoner : endurance
(D) hiker : agility
(E) fisherman : luck

13 BREEZE : HURRICANE ::

(A) water : pebble
(B) gulf : coast
(C) eye : cyclone
(D) sun : cloud
(E) hill : mountain

14 IMMORTAL : DEATH ::

(A) anonymous : fame
(B) hopeless : situation
(C) vital : life
(D) indisputable : agreement
(E) daily : year

15 TAPESTRY : THREAD ::

(A) pizza : pie
(B) mosaic : tiles
(C) ruler : divisions
(D) computer : switch
(E) car : engine

16 LUBRICANT : FRICTION ::

(A) motor : electricity
(B) speed : drag
(C) insulation : heat
(D) adhesive : connection
(E) muffler : noise

17 PARODY : IMITATION ::

(A) stanza : verse
(B) limerick : poem
(C) novel : book
(D) portrait : painting
(E) riddle : puzzle

18 COMET : TAIL ::

(A) traffic : lane
(B) missile : trajectory
(C) vessel : wake
(D) engine : fuel
(E) wave : crest

19 NEOLOGISM : LANGUAGE ::

(A) rhetoric : oratory
(B) syllogism : grammar
(C) innovation : technology
(D) iconography : art
(E) epistemology : philosophy

20 ADDENDUM : BOOK ::

(A) signature : letter
(B) vote : constitution
(C) codicil : will
(D) heading : folder
(E) stipulation : contract

21 PENCHANT : INCLINED ::

(A) loathing : contemptuous
(B) abhorrence : delighted
(C) burgeoning : barren
(D) loss : incessant
(E) decision : predictable

22 VAGRANT : DOMICILE ::

(A) pagan : morals
(B) despot : leadership
(C) arsonist : fire
(D) exile : country
(E) telephone : ear

23 MERITORIOUS : PRAISE ::

(A) captious : criticism
(B) kind : admiration
(C) questionable : response
(D) reprehensible : censure
(E) incredible : ecstasy

GO ON TO THE NEXT PAGE ➡

The passages below is followed by questions based on its content. Answer the questions on the basis of what is stated or implied in the passage and in any introductory material that may be provided.

Questions 24–35 are based on the following passage.

The following passage is from a book written by a zoologist and published in 1986.

The domestic cat is a contradiction. No other animal has developed such an intimate relationship with humanity, while at the same time demanding
Line and getting such independent movement and action.
(5) The cat manages to remain a tame animal because of the sequence of its upbringing. By living both with other cats (its mother and littermates) and with humans (the family that has adopted it) during its infancy and kittenhood, it becomes attached to and
(10) considers that it belongs to both species. It is like a child that grows up in a foreign country and as a consequence becomes bilingual. The young cat becomes bimental. It may be a cat physically but mentally it is both feline and human. Once it is fully
(15) adult, however, most of its responses are feline ones, and it has only one major reaction to its human owners. It treats them as pseudoparents. The reason is that they took over from the real mother at a sensitive stage of the kitten's development and went
(20) on giving it milk, solid food, and comfort as it grew up.

This is rather different from the kind of bond that develops between human and dog. The dog sees its human owners as pseudoparents, as does the cat.
(25) On that score the process of attachment is similar. But the dog has an additional link. Canine society is group-organized; feline society is not. Dogs live in packs with tightly controlled status relationships among the individuals. There are top dogs, middle
(30) dogs, and bottom dogs and under natural circumstances they move around together, keeping tabs on one another the whole time. So the adult pet dog sees its human family both as pseudoparents and as the dominant members of the pack, hence its
(35) renowned reputation for obedience and its celebrated capacity for loyalty. Cats do have a complex social organization, but they never hunt in packs. In the wild, most of their day is spent in solitary stalking. Going for a walk with a human,
(40) therefore, has no appeal for them. And as for "coming to heel" and learning to "sit" and "stay," they are simply not interested. Such maneuvers have no meaning for them.

So the moment a cat manages to persuade a
(45) human being to open a door (that most hated of human inventions), it is off and away without a backward glance. As it crosses the threshold, the cat becomes transformed. The kitten-of-human brain is
(50) switched off and the wildcat brain is clicked on. The dog, in such a situation, may look back to see if its human packmate is following to join in the fun of exploring, but not the cat. The cat's mind has floated off into another, totally feline world, where strange
(55) bipedal* primates have no place.

Because of this difference between domestic cats and domestic dogs, cat-lovers tend to be rather different from dog-lovers. As a rule cat-lovers have a stronger personality bias toward working alone,
(60) independent of the larger group. Artists like cats; soldiers like dogs. The much-lauded "group loyalty" phenomenon is alien to both cats and cat-lovers. If you are a company person, a member of the gang, or a person picked for the squad, the chances are that at
(65) home there is no cat curled up in front of the fire. The ambitious Yuppie, the aspiring politician, the professional athlete, these are not typical cat-owners. It is hard to picture football players with cats in their laps—much easier to envisage them taking their
(70) dogs for walks.

Those who have studied cat-owners and dog-owners as two distinct groups report that there is also a gender bias. The majority of cat-lovers are female. This bias is not surprising in view of the
(75) division of labor evident in the development of human societies. Prehistoric males became specialized as group-hunters, while the females concentrated on food-gathering and childbearing. This difference contributed to a human male "pack
(80) mentality" that is far less marked in females. Wolves, the wild ancestors of domestic dogs, also became pack-hunters, so the modern dog has much more in common with the human male than with the human female.

(85) The argument will always go on—feline self-sufficiency and individualism *versus* canine camaraderie and good-fellowship. But it is important to stress that in making a valid point I have caricatured the two positions. In reality there
(90) are many people who enjoy equally the company of both cats and dogs. And all of us, or nearly all of us, have both feline and canine elements in our personalities. We have moods when we want to be alone and thoughtful, and other times when we
(95) wish to be in the center of a crowded, noisy room.

*bipedal: having two feet

GO ON TO THE NEXT PAGE

24 The primary purpose of the passage is to

(A) show the enmity that exists between cats and dogs
(B) advocate dogs as making better pets than cats
(C) distinguish the different characteristics of dogs and cats
(D) show the inferiority of dogs because of their dependent nature
(E) emphasize the role that human society plays in the personalities of domestic pets

25 According to the passage, the domestic cat can be described as

(A) a biped because it possesses the characteristics of animals with two feet
(B) a pseudopet because it can't really be tamed and will always retain its wild habits
(C) a contradiction because although it lives comfortably with humans, it refuses to be dominated by them
(D) a soldier because it is militant about preserving its independence
(E) a ruler because although it plays the part of a pet, it really dominates humans

26 In line 17 the word *pseudoparents* means

(A) part-time parents that are only partially involved with their young
(B) individuals who act as parents of adults
(C) parents that neglect their young
(D) parents that have both the characteristics of humans and their pets
(E) adopted parents that aren't related to their young

27 The author suggests that an important difference between dogs and cats is that, unlike dogs, cats

(A) do not regard their owners as the leader of their social group
(B) obey mainly because of their obedient nature
(C) have a more creative nature
(D) do not have complex social organizations
(E) are not skilled hunters

28 It can be inferred from the passage that the social structure of dogs is

(A) flexible
(B) abstract
(C) hierarchical
(D) male dominated
(E) somewhat exclusive

29 Lines 39–43 are used to stress

(A) the laziness of cats that keeps them from being pack animals
(B) the ignorance of dogs, which makes them more obedient pets
(C) the antipathy that cats feel for humans
(D) a difference between cats and dogs that emphasizes the independent nature of cats
(E) the stubborn and complacent disposition of cats

30 In line 60, *much-lauded* means

(A) vehemently argued
(B) overly discussed
(C) unnecessarily complicated
(D) typically controversial
(E) commonly praised

31 The "ambitious Yuppie" mentioned in line 65 is an example of a person

(A) that is power hungry
(B) that craves virtue
(C) that is a stereotypical pet owner
(D) that has a weak personality
(E) that seeks group-oriented status

32 Paragraph 6 indicates that human females

(A) are more like dogs than cats
(B) developed independent roles that didn't require group behavior
(C) had to gather food because they were not strong enough to hunt
(D) are not good owners for the modern dog
(E) were negatively affected by the division of labor of human societies

GO ON TO THE NEXT PAGE

33 The author uses lines 84–88 to

(A) show that the argument stated in the passage is ultimately futile

(B) disclaim glaring contradictions that are stated in the passage

(C) qualify the generalizations used to make the author's point

(D) ensure that the reader doesn't underestimate the crux of the passage

(E) highlight a difference between individualism and dependency

34 The last four sentences in the passage (lines 86–94) provide

(A) an example of the argument that has been made earlier

(B) a summary of the points made earlier

(C) a reason for the statements made earlier

(D) a modification of the position taken earlier

(E) a rebuttal to opposing views referred to earlier

35 The passage as a whole does all of the following EXCEPT

(A) use a statistic

(B) make parenthetic statements

(C) use a simile

(D) restate an argument

(E) make a generalization

IF YOU FINISH BEFORE TIME IS CALLED, YOU MAY CHECK YOUR WORK ON THIS SECTION ONLY. DO NOT TURN TO ANY OTHER SECTION IN THE TEST. **STOP**

Time—30 Minutes
25 Questions

In this section solve each problem, using any available space on the page for scratchwork. Then decide which is the best of the choices given and fill in the corresponding oval on the answer sheet.

Notes:

(1) The use of a calculator is permitted. All numbers used are real numbers.

(2) Figures that accompany problems in this test are intended to provide information useful in solving the problems. They are drawn as accurately as possible EXCEPT when it is stated in a specific problem that the figure is not drawn to scale. All figures lie in a plane unless otherwise indicated.

Reference Information

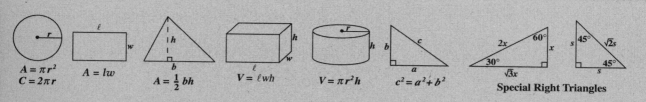

$A = \pi r^2$
$C = 2\pi r$

$A = lw$

$A = \frac{1}{2}bh$

$V = lwh$

$V = \pi r^2 h$

$c^2 = a^2 + b^2$

Special Right Triangles

The number of degrees of arc in a circle is 360.
The measure in degrees of a straight angle is 180.
The sum of the measures in degrees of the angles of a triangle is 180.

1   If $2 + a = 2 - a$, then $a =$

(A) –1
(B)   0
(C)   1
(D)   2
(E)   4

2   In which of the following patterns is the number of horizontal lines three times the number of vertical lines?

(A)   (B)   (C)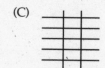

(D) 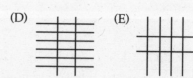   (E)

GO ON TO THE NEXT PAGE ⟩

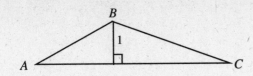

3 If $AC = 4$, what is the area of $\triangle ABC$ above?

(A) $\dfrac{1}{2}$

(B) 2

(C) $\sqrt{7}$

(D) 4

(E) 8

5 If $x + y = z$ and $x = y$, then all of the following are true EXCEPT

(A) $2x + 2y = 2z$

(B) $x - y = 0$

(C) $x - z = y - z$

(D) $x = \dfrac{z}{2}$

(E) $z - y = 2x$

4 If $\dfrac{4}{5}$ of $\dfrac{3}{4} = \dfrac{2}{5}$ of $\dfrac{x}{4}$, then $x =$

(A) 12

(B) 6

(C) 3

(D) $\dfrac{3}{2}$

(E) 1

Note: Figure not drawn to scale.

6 In the figure above, $AC \parallel ED$. If the length of $BD = 3$, what is the length of BE?

(A) 3
(B) 4
(C) 5
(D) $3\sqrt{3}$
(E) It cannot be determined from the information given.

GO ON TO THE NEXT PAGE

7 $\dfrac{900}{10} + \dfrac{90}{100} + \dfrac{9}{1000} =$

(A) 90.09
(B) 90.099
(C) 90.909
(D) 99.09
(E) 999

9 In the figure above, the perimeter of square A is $\dfrac{2}{3}$ the perimeter of square B, and the perimeter of square B is $\dfrac{2}{3}$ the perimeter of square C. If the area of square A is 16, what is the area of square C?

(A) 24
(B) 36
(C) 64
(D) 72
(E) 81

8 Fifteen percent of the coins in a piggy bank are nickels and 5% are dimes. If there are 220 coins in the bank, how many are <u>not</u> nickels or dimes?

(A)   80
(B) 176
(C) 180
(D) 187
(E) 200

10 A bakery uses a special flour mixture that contains corn, wheat, and rye in the ratio of 3:5:2. If a bag of the mixture contains 5 pounds of rye, how many pounds of wheat does it contain?

(A)   2
(B)   5
(C)   7.5
(D) 10
(E) 12.5

GO ON TO THE NEXT PAGE

11 If $a^2b = 12^2$, and b is an odd integer, then a could be divisible by all of the following EXCEPT

(A) 3
(B) 4
(C) 6
(D) 9
(E) 12

13 If l_1 is parallel to l_2 in the figure above, what is the value of x?

(A) 20
(B) 50
(C) 70
(D) 80
(E) 90

12 A coin was flipped 20 times and came up heads 10 times and tails 10 times. If the first and last flips were both heads, what is the greatest number of consecutive heads that could have occurred?

(A) 1
(B) 2
(C) 8
(D) 9
(E) 10

14 Which of the following must be true?

  I. The sum of two consecutive integers is odd.
  II. The sum of three consecutive integers is even.
  III. The sum of three consecutive integers is a multiple of 3.

(A) I only
(B) II only
(C) I and II only
(D) I and III only
(E) I, II, and III

GO ON TO THE NEXT PAGE

15 Which of the following is equal to .064?

(A) $\left(\dfrac{1}{80}\right)^2$

(B) $\left(\dfrac{8}{100}\right)^2$

(C) $\left(\dfrac{1}{8}\right)^2$

(D) $\left(\dfrac{2}{5}\right)^3$

(E) $\left(\dfrac{8}{10}\right)^3$

16 If the average (arithmetic mean) of four distinct positive integers is 11, what is the greatest possible value of any one of the integers?

(A) 35
(B) 38
(C) 40
(D) 41
(E) 44

For $x = 0$, $x = 1$, and $x = 2$,
Set A = $\{x,\ x + 3,\ 3x,\ x^2\}$.

17 What is the mode of Set A?

(A) 0
(B) 1
(C) 2
(D) 2.5
(E) 3

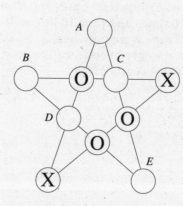

18 If the figure above is filled in so that each row of four circles contains two circles marked with an X and two circles marked with an O, which circle must be marked with an X?

(A) A
(B) B
(C) C
(D) D
(E) E

GO ON TO THE NEXT PAGE

19 If c is positive, what percent of $3c$ is 9?

(A) $\dfrac{c}{100}\%$

(B) $\dfrac{c}{3}\%$

(C) $\dfrac{9}{c}\%$

(D) 3%

(E) $\dfrac{300}{c}\%$

21 S is the set of all positive numbers n such that
$n < 100$ and $\sqrt{n}$ is an integer. What is the median value of the members of set S?

(A) 5

(B) 5.5

(C) 25

(D) 50

(E) 99

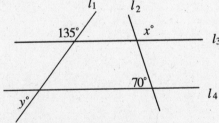

Note: Figure not drawn to scale.

20 If four lines intersect as shown in the figure above, $x + y =$

(A) 65
(B) 110
(C) 155
(D) 205
(E) It cannot be determined from the information given.

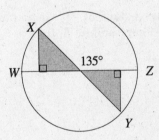

22 If segment WZ and segment XY are diameters with lengths of 12, what is the area of the shaded region?

(A) 36
(B) 30
(C) 18
(D) 12
(E) 9

GO ON TO THE NEXT PAGE

23 At the beginning of 1992, the population of Rockville was 204,000 and the population of Springfield was 216,000. If the population of each city increased by exactly 20% in 1992, how many more people lived in Springfield than in Rockville at the end of 1992?

(A) 9,600
(B) 10,000
(C) 12,000
(D) 14,400
(E) 20,000

25 A researcher found that a certain student's score on each of a series of tests could be predicted using the formula

$$P = \frac{310T + (LT)^2}{100}$$

where P is the number of points scored on the test, T is the number of hours spent studying, L is the number of hours of sleep the night before the test, and where $P \leq 100$. If, before a particular test, this student spent no more than 10 hours studying, what is the least number of hours of sleep she should get if she wants to score at least 80 points?

(A) 6
(B) 7
(C) $\sqrt{56}$
(D) 8
(E) $\sqrt{69}$

24 Line A has a slope of $-\frac{3}{2}$. If points $(-2, 6)$ and $(m, -9)$ are on line A, then $m =$

(A) 3
(B) 4
(C) 6
(D) 8
(E) 12

IF YOU FINISH BEFORE TIME IS CALLED, YOU MAY CHECK YOUR WORK ON THIS SECTION ONLY. DO NOT TURN TO ANY OTHER SECTION IN THE TEST. **STOP**

Time-15 Minutes — 13 Questions   For each question in this section, select the best answer from the choices given and fill in the corresponding oval on the answer sheet.

The two passages below are followed by questions based on their content and on the relationship between the two passages. Answer the questions on the basis of what is <u>stated</u> or <u>implied</u> in the passage and in any introductory material that may be provided.

Questions 1–13 are based on the following passages.

In passage 1, the author presents his view of the early years of the silent film industry. In passage 2, the author draws on her experiences as a mime to generalize about her art. (A mime is a performer who, without speaking, entertains through gesture, facial expression, and movement.)

Passage 1

Talk to those people who first saw films when they were silent, and they will tell you the experience was magic. The silent film had
Line extraordinary powers to draw members of an
(5) audience into the story, and an equally potent capacity to make their imaginations work. It required the audience to become engaged—to supply voices and sound effects. The audience was the final, creative contributor to the process
(10) of making a film.

The finest films of the silent era depended on two elements that we can seldom provide today— a large and receptive audience and a well-orchestrated score. For the audience, the fusion of
(15) picture and live music added up to more than the sum of the respective parts.

The one word that sums up the attitude of the silent filmmakers is *enthusiasm*, conveyed most strongly before formulas took shape and when
(20) there was more room for experimentation. This enthusiastic uncertainty often resulted in such accidental discoveries as new camera or editing techniques. Some films experimented with players; the 1915 film *Regeneration*, for example,
(25) by using real gangsters and streetwalkers, provided startling local color. Other films, particularly those of Thomas Ince, provided tragic endings as often as films by other companies supplied happy ones.

(30) Unfortunately, the vast majority of silent films survive today in inferior prints that no longer reflect the care that the original technicians put into them. The modern versions of silent films may appear jerky and flickery, but the vast
(35) picture palaces did not attract four to six thousand people a night by giving them eyestrain. A silent film depended on its visuals;

as soon as you degrade those, you lose elements that go far beyond the image on the surface. The
(40) acting in silents was often very subtle, very restrained, despite legends to the contrary.

Passage 2

Mime opens up a new world to the beholder, but it does so insidiously, not by purposely injecting points of interest in the manner of a tour
(45) guide. Audiences are not unlike visitors to a foreign land who discover that the modes, manners, and thoughts of its inhabitants are not meaningless oddities, but are sensible in context.

I remember once when an audience seemed
(50) perplexed at what I was doing. At first, I tried to gain a more immediate response by using slight exaggerations. I soon realized that these actions had nothing to do with the audience's understanding of the character. What I had
(55) believed to be a failure of the audience to respond in the manner I expected was, in fact, only their concentration on what I was doing; they were enjoying a gradual awakening—a slow transference of their understanding from their
(60) own time and place to one that appeared so unexpectedly before their eyes. This was evidenced by their growing response to succeeding numbers.

Mime is an elusive art, as its expression is
(65) entirely dependent on the ability of the performer to imagine a character and to re-create that character for each performance. As a mime, I am a physical medium, the instrument upon which the figures of my imagination play their dance of life.
(70) The individuals in my audience also have responsibilities—they must be alert collaborators. They cannot sit back, mindlessly complacent, and wait to have their emotions titillated by mesmeric

GO ON TO THE NEXT PAGE ➡

musical sounds or visual rhythms or acrobatic
(75) feats, or by words that tell them what to think.
Mime is an art that, paradoxically, appeals both
to those who respond instinctively to
entertainment and to those whose appreciation is
more analytical and complex. Between these
(80) extremes lie those audiences conditioned to resist
any collaboration with what is played before
them; and these the mime must seduce despite
themselves. There is only one way to attack those
reluctant minds—take them unaware! They will
(85) be delighted at an unexpected pleasure.

1 Lines 14–16 of passage 1 indicate that

(A) music was the most important element
of silent films
(B) silent films rely on a combination of
music and image in affecting an
audience
(C) the importance of music in silent film
has been overestimated
(D) live music compensated for the poor
quality of silent film images
(E) no film can succeed without a receptive
audience

2 The "formulas" mentioned in line 19 of the
passage most probably refer to

(A) movie theaters
(B) use of real characters
(C) standardized film techniques
(D) the fusion of disparate elements
(E) contemporary events

3 The author uses the phrase *enthusiastic
uncertainty* in line 21 to suggest that the
filmmakers were

(A) excited to be experimenting in an
undefined area
(B) delighted at the opportunity to study
new acting formulas
(C) optimistic in spite of the obstacles that
faced them
(D) eager to challenge existing conventions
(E) eager to please but unsure of what the
public wanted

4 The author uses the phrase *but the . . .
eyestrain* (lines 33–35) in order to

(A) indicate his disgust with the incompetence of early film technicians
(B) suggest that audiences today perceive
silent films incorrectly
(C) convey his regret about the decline of
the old picture palaces
(D) highlight the pitfalls of the silent movie
era
(E) argue for the superiority of modern
film technology over that of silent
movies

5 The word *legends* in line 39 most nearly
means

(A) arguments
(B) symbolism
(C) propaganda
(D) movie stars
(E) misconceptions

6 The last sentence of passage 1 implies that

(A) the stars of silent movies have been
criticized for overacting
(B) many silent film actors became legends
in their own time
(C) silent film techniques should be studied
by filmmakers today
(D) visual effects defined the silent film
(E) many silent films that exist today are of
poor quality

7 The word *restrained* (line 39) most nearly
means

(A) sincere
(B) dramatic
(C) understated
(D) inexpressive
(E) consistent

GO ON TO THE NEXT PAGE

8 The author mentions the incident in lines 47–59 in order to imply that

(A) the audience's lack of response was a positive sign and reflected their captivated interest in the performance

(B) she was forced to resort to stereotypes in order to reach an audience that was otherwise unattainable

(C) exaggeration is an essential part of mime because it allows the forums used to be fully expressed

(D) her audience, though not initially appearing knowledgeable, had a good understanding of the subtlety of mime

(E) although vocalization is not necessary in mime, it is sometimes helpful for slower audiences

9 Lines 47–59 indicate that the author of passage 2 and the silent filmmakers of passage 1 were similar because

(A) neither used many props

(B) both conveyed universal truths by using sophisticated technology

(C) for both, trial and error was a part of the learning process

(D) both used visual effects and dialogue

(E) both had a loyal following

10 The sentence *As a . . . life* (lines 63–65) suggests that the author of passage 2 feels mimes

(A) cannot control the way audiences interpret their characters

(B) must suspend their own identities in order to successfully portray their characters

(C) have to resist outside attempts to define their acting style

(D) should focus on important events in the lives of specific characters

(E) know the limitations of performances that do not incorporate either music or speech

11 Which of the following pieces of information makes mime and silent film seem less similar?

(A) Vaudeville and theatrical presentations were also popular forms of entertainment during the silent film era.

(B) Silent films presented both fictional drama and factual information.

(C) Silent film sometimes relied on captions to convey dialogue to the audience.

(D) Musicians working in movie theaters were usually employed for long periods of time.

(E) Many of the characters in silent films gained wide popularity among movie-goers.

12 Passages 1 and 2 are similar in that both are mainly concerned with

(A) the use of special effects

(B) differences among dramatic styles

(C) the visual aspects of performance

(D) the suspension of disbelief in audiences

(E) nostalgia for a bygone era

13 Which of the following is an element that figures in the success of the dramatic arts described in both passages?

(A) A successful combination of different dramatic styles

(B) The exaggeration of certain aspects of a character

(C) The incorporation of current events in the narrative

(D) High audience attendance

(E) The active participation of the audience

IF YOU FINISH BEFORE TIME IS CALLED, YOU MAY CHECK YOUR WORK ON THIS SECTION ONLY. DO NOT TURN TO ANY OTHER SECTION IN THE TEST. STOP

Time—15 Minutes
10 Questions

In this section solve each problem, using any available space on the page for scratchwork. Then decide which is the best of the choices given and fill in the corresponding oval on the answer sheet.

Notes:

(1)   The use of a calculator is permitted. All numbers used are real numbers.

(2)   Figures that accompany problems in this test are intended to provide information useful in solving the problems. They are drawn as accurately as possible EXCEPT when it is stated in a specific problem that the figure is not drawn to scale. All figures lie in a plane unless otherwise indicated.

Reference Information

$A = \pi r^2$
$C = 2\pi r$

$A = lw$

$A = \frac{1}{2} bh$

$V = \ell wh$

$V = \pi r^2 h$

$c^2 = a^2 + b^2$

Special Right Triangles

The number of degrees of arc in a circle is 360.
The measure in degrees of a straight angle is 180.
The sum of the measures in degrees of the angles of a triangle is 180.

Price of Buttons in Store X	
Color	Price
Black	$2 per 5 buttons
Blue	$2 per 6 buttons
Brown	$3 per 8 buttons
Orange	$4 per 12 buttons
Red	$4 per 7 buttons

1   In Store X, which color button costs the most per individual unit?

(A) Black
(B) Blue
(C) Brown
(D) Orange
(E) Red

2   Which of the following numbers can be written in the form $6K + 1$, where K is a positive integer?

(A) 70
(B) 71
(C) 72
(D) 73
(E) 74

GO ON TO THE NEXT PAGE

3 $\left(\dfrac{4}{5} \times 3\right)\left(\dfrac{3}{4} \times 5\right)\left(\dfrac{5}{3} \times 4\right) =$

(A) 1
(B) 3
(C) 6
(D) 20
(E) 60

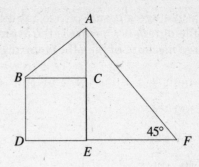

5 If the area of square $BCED = 25$, and the area of $\triangle ABC = 10$, what is the length of EF?

(A) 7
(B) 8
(C) 9
(D) 10
(E) 14

4 For which of the following values of x is $\dfrac{x^2}{x^3}$ the LEAST?

(A) 1
(B) –1
(C) –2
(D) –3
(E) –4

6 The Wilsons drove 450 miles in each direction to Grandmother's house and back again. If their car gets 25 miles per gallon and their cost for gasoline was $1.25 per gallon for the trip to Grandmother's but $1.50 per gallon for the return trip, how much <u>more</u> money did they spend for gasoline returning from Grandmother's than they spent going to Grandmother's?

(A) $2.25
(B) $4.50
(C) $6.25
(D) $9.00
(E) $27.00

GO ON TO THE NEXT PAGE

7 If the average measure of two angles in a parallelogram is $y°$, what is the average degree measure of the other two angles?

(A) $180 - y$

(B) $180 - \dfrac{y}{2}$

(C) $360 - 2y$

(D) $360 - y$

(E) y

9 On a map, 1 centimeter represents 6 kilometers. A square on the map with a perimeter of 16 centimeters represents a region with what <u>area</u>?

(A) 64 km²
(B) 96 km²
(C) 256 km²
(D) 576 km²
(E) 8,216 km²

8 A swimming pool with a capacity of 36,000 gallons originally contained 9,000 gallons of water. At 10:00 A.M. water begins to flow in at a constant rate. If the pool is exactly three fourths full at 1:00 P.M. on the same day and the water continues to flow in at the same rate, what is the earliest time the pool will be completely full?

(A) 1:40 P.M.
(B) 2:00 P.M.
(C) 2:30 P.M.
(D) 3:00 P.M.
(E) 3:30 P.M.

10 If $4 < a < 7 < b < 9$, then which of the following best defines $\dfrac{a}{b}$?

(A) $\dfrac{4}{9} < \dfrac{a}{b} < 1$

(B) $\dfrac{4}{9} < \dfrac{a}{b} < \dfrac{7}{9}$

(C) $\dfrac{4}{7} < \dfrac{a}{b} < \dfrac{7}{9}$

(D) $\dfrac{4}{7} < \dfrac{a}{b} < 1$

(E) $\dfrac{4}{7} < \dfrac{a}{b} < \dfrac{9}{7}$

IF YOU FINISH BEFORE TIME IS CALLED, YOU MAY CHECK YOUR WORK ON THIS SECTION ONLY. DO NOT TURN TO ANY OTHER SECTION IN THE TEST. **STOP**

408

DIAGNOSTIC TEST ANSWERS

Section 1	Section 2	Section 3	Section 4	Section 5	Section 6	Section 7
1. C	1. B	1. B	1. D	1. B	1. B	1. E
2. C	2. B	2. A	2. B	2. D	2. C	2. D
3. C	3. A	3. D	3. A	3. B	3. A	3. E
4. E	4. A	4. C	4. E	4. B	4. B	4. B
5. D	5. D	5. B	5. B	5. E	5. E	5. C
6. B	6. C	6. C	6. C	6. A	6. A	6. B
7. A	7. E	7. D	7. A	7. C	7. C	7. A
8. E	8. D	8. A	8. C	8. B	8. A	8. C
9. E	9. D	9. C	9. E	9. E	9. C	9. D
10. A	10. B	10. B	10. D	10. E	10. B	10. A
11. A	11. B	11. B	11. E	11. D	11. C	
12. B	12. B	12. A	12. C	12. D	12. C	
13. B	13. C	13. C	13. E	13. C	13. E	
14. D	14. A	14. D	14. A	14. D		
15. E	15. E	15. A	15. B	15. D		
16. A	16. A	16. 2	16. E	16. B		
17. C	17. C	17. 14	17. B	17. A		
18. E	18. D	18. 145	18. C	18. E		
19. B	19. E	19. 234	19. C	19. E		
20. C	20. C	20. 19, 39,	20. C	20. C		
21. B	21. B	59, 79,	21. A	21. C		
22. A	22. E	or 99	22. D	22. C		
23. C	23. C	21. 36	23. D	23. D		
24. D	24. A	22. 3	24. C	24. D		
25. E	25. D	23. 30	25. C	25. B		
	26. B	24. 15	26. E			
	27. B	25. 1/2 or	27. A			
	28. E	.5	28. C			
	29. C		29. D			
	30. D		30. E			
			31. E			
			32. B			
			33. C			
			34. D			
			35. C			

You will find a detailed explanation for each question beginning on page 417.

HOW TO SCORE YOUR DIAGNOSTIC TEST
VERBAL

After you have checked your answers to the diagnostic test against the key, you can calculate your score. For the three verbal sections (sections 2, 4, and 6), tally up the number of correct answers and the number of incorrect answers. Enter these numbers on the worksheet on the opposite page. Multiply the number of incorrect answers by 1/4 and subtract the result from the number of correct answers. Put this number in box A. Then round the numbers to the nearest whole number and place it in box B.

MATHEMATICS

Figuring your math score is a little trickier, because some of the questions have five answer choices, some have four, and some have none. In sections 1 and 7, count the number of correct answers and incorrect answers. Enter these numbers on the worksheet. Multiply the number of incorrect answers by 1/4 and subtract this from the number of correct answers. Put the result in box C.

Count the number of correct and incorrect answers in section 3, questions 1–15. (E choices count as blanks). Enter these on the worksheet. Multiply the number of incorrect answers by 1/3 and subtract this from the number of correct answers in section 3. Put the result in box D.

Count up the number of correct answers in section 3, questions 16–25. Put the result in box E. There is no penalty for incorrect Grid-in questions.

Note: Section 5 is experimental and should not be scored.

Add up the numbers in boxes C, D, and E, and write the result in box F.

Round F to the nearest whole number, and place the result in box G.

WORKSHEET FOR CALCULATING YOUR SCORE

VERBAL

	Correct	Incorrect	
A. Sections 2, 4, and 6	_____	– (1/4 × _____) =	[ ] A
B. Total rounded verbal raw score			[ ] B

MATHEMATICS

	Correct	Incorrect	
C. Sections 1 and 7	_____	– (1/4 × _____) =	[ ] C
D. Section 3 (Questions 1–15)	_____	– (1/3 × _____) =	[ ] D
E. Section 3 (Questions 16–25)	_____	=	[ ] E
F. Total unrounded math raw score (C + D + E)			[ ] F
G. Total rounded math raw score			[ ] G

Use the table on the next page to convert your raw score to scaled scores. For example, a raw score verbal score of 39 corresponds to verbal scaled score of 450; a math raw score of 24 corresponds to a math scaled score of 430.

Scores on the SAT range from 200 to 800.

SCORE CONVERSION TABLE

Raw Score	Verbal Scaled Score	Math Scaled Score	Raw Score	Verbal Scaled Scored	Math Scaled Score
78	800		36	430	540
77	750		35	430	530
76	740		34	420	520
75	730		33	410	510
74	710		32	400	500
73	700		31	400	490
72	690		30	390	480
71	680		29	380	470
70	680		28	380	460
69	670		27	370	450
68	660		26	370	450
67	650		25	360	440
66	640		24	350	430
65	630		23	350	420
64	620		22	340	410
63	610		21	330	400
62	600		20	320	390
61	590		19	310	390
60	590	800	18	300	380
59	580	770	17	300	370
58	570	760	16	290	360
57	570	750	15	280	350
56	560	740	14	270	340
55	550	730	13	270	340
54	550	720	12	260	330
53	540	710	11	250	320
52	530	700	10	240	310
51	530	690	9	230	300
50	520	670	8	220	300
49	510	660	7	210	290
48	510	650	6	210	280
47	500	640	5	200	270
46	490	630	4	200	270
45	490	620	3	200	260
44	480	610	2	200	250
43	480	600	1	200	250
42	470	590	0	200	240
41	470	580	−1	200	230
40	460	570	−2	200	230
39	450	560	−3	200	220
38	450	550	−4	200	210
37	440	550	−5 and below	200	200

PART 8

Answers and Explanations to the Diagnostic Test

What follows is a detailed explanation for each question in our diagnostic test. Although you will naturally be more curious about the questions you got wrong, don't forget to read the explanations for the questions you left blank. In fact, you should even read the explanation for the questions you got right! Our explanations present the safest, most direct solution to each question. Even though you may have gotten a question right does not mean you analyzed it in the most efficient way.

SECTION 1

1   If $9b = 81$, then $3 \times 3b =$

(A)   9
(B)   27
(C)   81
(D) 243
(E) 729

1.   Jim's answer is C.
The key point to make here is that you should not have solved for b. We're looking for $3 \times 3b$, which equals $9b$, which we are told equals 81. If you solved first for b, which equals 9, you didn't see the point of the question. If you answered A you solved for b and forgot what the question was asking.

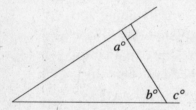

2   In the figure above, what is the sum of $a + b + c$?

(A) 180
(B) 240
(C) 270
(D) 360
(E)   It cannot be determined from the information given.

2.   Jim's answer is C.
The number of degrees in a line is 180. Therefore, $b + c = 180$. And since $a + 90 = 180$, $a = 90$. So $a + b + c = 270$.

3 $\dfrac{0.5 + 0.5 + 0.5 + 0.5}{4} =$

(A) 0.05
(B) 0.125
(C) 0.5
(D) 1
(E) 2.0

3. Jim's answer is C.
Here again, as with question 1, the "slow" way to solve the question would be to do the arithmetic. The numerator sums to 2, divided by 4, which equals $\frac{1}{2}$ or 0.5. The point of the question was to see if you noticed that four equivalent decimals on top divided by 4 would be the decimal itself. Like $\dfrac{4(0.5)}{4} = 0.5$

4 Steve ran a 12-mile race at an average speed of 8 miles per hour. If Adam ran the same race at an average speed of 6 miles per hour, how many minutes longer than Steve did Adam take to complete the race?

(A) 9
(B) 12
(C) 16
(D) 24
(E) 30

4. Jim's answer is E.
Steve runs 12 miles at 8 miles per hour. Using the formula distance = rate × time, you get
$12 = 8 \times t$, or $t = 1\frac{1}{2}$ hours. (Use your calculator if you're not sure.) Similarly, Adam, running at 6 miles per hour, would take 2 hours to complete the course ($12 = 6 \times t$; $t = 2$). Adam takes half an hour, or 30 minutes, longer.

5. Jim's answer is D.
You should have noticed several things about

```
|____|____|____|
A    B    C    D
```

Note: Figure not drawn to scale.

5 If $AB > CD$, which of the following must be true?

   I. $AB > BC$
  II. $AC > BD$
 III. $AC > CD$

(A) I only
(B) II only
(C) III only
(D) II and III only
(E) I, II, and III

this question. First, that the figure was not drawn to scale. So a good first step would be to redraw the figure to comply with the condition ($AB > CD$). Second, the question asks for which of the following *must* be true. *Must* is an important word—which of the following *could* be true would change your analysis completely. So, redrawing the figure, you'd get something like this:

```
|_____|____|____|
A        B    C    D
```

In this figure, AB is clearly larger than CD. Since plugging in numbers makes the distance more concrete, you might have made $AB = 3$, for example, and $CD = 2$. Since you don't know what BD is, however, you'd have to leave it alone. Now, let's check the conditions. <u>Option I:</u> Well, this could be true, but it doesn't have to be. So Option I is false. This allows us to eliminate choices A and E. <u>Option II:</u> Since we let $AB = 3$ and $CD = 2$, then $AC = 3 + BC$ while $BD = BC + 2$. No matter what BC is, $AC > BD$. Option II is true. This allows us to eliminate choice C, which does not include Option II. We still need to check Option III. <u>Option III:</u> Since $AB > CD$, and $AC > AB$, then $AC > CD$. Option III is true; therefore, D is the answer.

6 If 3 more than x is 2 more than y, what is x in terms of y?

(A) $y - 5$
(B) $y - 1$
(C) $y + 1$
(D) $y + 5$
(E) $y + 6$

6. Jim's answer is B.
The best way to have solved this problem would be to have plugged in numbers. You know this by the letters in the answers. Let x equal 10, for example. Then since 3 more than 10(13) is 2 more than 11, y equals 11. We're looking for the choice that gives us $x =$ 10. Choice B, $y - 1$, equals $11 - 1$, or 10. If you answered A, C, or D, you screwed up the algebraic manipulation. Plug in numbers! (The algebraic solution was to solve the equation $3 + x = 2 + y$. True, a simple equation, but just the kind to trip you up under time pressure.)

7 $\dfrac{4^2}{2^3} + \dfrac{2^3}{4^2} =$

(A) $\dfrac{5}{2}$

(B) 2

(C) 1

(D) $\dfrac{1}{2}$

(E) $\dfrac{1}{4}$

7. Jim's answer is A.
$$\frac{4^2}{2^3} + \frac{2^3}{4^2} = \frac{16}{8} + \frac{8}{16} = \frac{2}{1} + \frac{1}{2} = 2\frac{1}{2}, \text{ or } \frac{5}{2}$$

8 If 8 and 12 each divide K without a remainder, what is the value of K?

(A) 16
(B) 24
(C) 48
(D) 96
(E) It cannot be determined from the information given.

8. Jim's answer is E.
The best way to solve questions like this is to try choices rather than to reason it out algebraically. Now, trying our choices, B works, but so do C and D. If you chose A, you should review remainders. If you chose B, C, or D, you jumped at an answer too quickly. Remember, this question is already edging into medium territory, so you have to be on your toes.

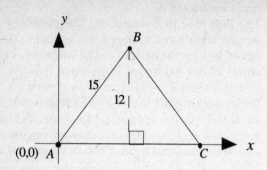

9 In the figure above, side *AB* of triangle *ABC* contains which of the following points?

(A) (3, 2)
(B) (3, 5)
(C) (4, 6)
(D) (4, 10)
(E) (6, 8)

9. Jim's answer is E.

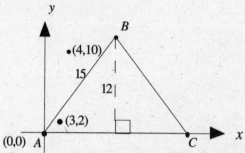

The first step in solving this problem is to plot points. By doing this you can eliminate choice A and D. To solve this question mathematically, you must figure out the ratio between the *x* and the *y* values on the line *AB*. To do this, you must find the *x* value of *B* (the *y* value is 12). Using the left "half" of triangle *ABC*, we can calculate *x* with the Pythagorean theorem: $x^2 + 12^2 = 15^2$. Using a calculator, we get $x = 9$. So the ratio of *x* to *y* is 9 to 12, or 3 to 4. The only point that maintains the ratio is (6,8).

10 What is the diameter of a circle with circumference 5?

(A) $\frac{5}{\pi}$

(B) $\frac{10}{\pi}$

(C) 5

(D) 5π

(E) 10π

10. Jim's answer is A.
Since formulas are given at the beginning of this section, if you got this question wrong you misread the formula for the circumference of a circle. Using the formula $C = \pi d$, we get $5 = \pi d$, or $\frac{5}{\pi} = d$. If you picked D, you thought the question was asking for the circumference and not diameter.

11 Carol subscribed to four publications that cost $12.90, $16.00, $18.00, and $21.90 per year, respectively. If she made an initial down payment of one half of the total amount, and paid the rest in 4 equal monthly payments, how much was each of the 4 monthly payments?

(A) $8.60
(B) $9.20
(C) $9.45
(D) $17.20
(E) $34.40

11. Jim's answer is A.
The first step is to use your calculator to compute the sum of the subscriptions: $68.80. The down payment was half that amount, leaving $34.40 to be paid in 4 installments of $8.60 each. If you answered choices D or E, you misread the question.

MERCHANDISE SALES		
Type	Amount of Sales	Percent of Total Sales
Shoes	$12,000	15%
Coats	$20,000	25%
Shirts	$x	40%
Pants	$y	20%

12 According to the table above, what were the sales, in dollars, of shirts and pants combined?

(A) $32,000
(B) $48,000
(C) $60,000
(D) $68,000
(E) $80,000

12. Jim's answer is B.
We're solving for shirts and pants, which constitute 60% of total sales. Since shoes ($12,000) account for 15%, shirts and pants would be four times that amount, or $48,000. Another solution would be to use any other convenient ratio. For example,

$$\frac{\text{coats}}{\text{shirts and pants}} = \frac{25\% \text{ sales}}{60\% \text{ sales}} = \frac{\$20,000}{\$?},$$

solving for "?". A less direct solution would be to solve for the total sales ($80,000), and then to take 60% of that amount (60% of $80,000 equals $48,000).

QUESTIONS	EXPLANATIONS

13 For all integers $n \neq 1$, let $<n> = \dfrac{n+1}{n-1}$.

Which of the following has the greatest value?

(A) $<0>$
(B) $<2>$
(C) $<3>$
(D) $<4>$
(E) $<5>$

13. Jim's answer is B.

You can tell by the question number that you have to be careful on this question. If you selected choice E, you grabbed impulsively at the Joe Bloggs answer. On this question, the safest way—as usual—is to try choices rather than to reason algebraically. Plugging in the choices for n, we'd get the following work:

(A) $<0> = \dfrac{0+1}{0-1} = \dfrac{1}{-1} = -1$

(B) $<2> = \dfrac{2+1}{2-1} = \dfrac{3}{1} = 3$

(C) $<3> = \dfrac{3+1}{3-1} = \dfrac{4}{2} = 2$

(D) $<4> = \dfrac{4+1}{4-1} = \dfrac{5}{3} = 1\dfrac{2}{3}$

(E) $<5> = \dfrac{5+1}{5-1} = \dfrac{6}{4} = \dfrac{3}{2} = 1\dfrac{1}{2}$

By inspection, choice (B) is the answer.

14 If the product of $(1 + 2)$, $(2 + 3)$, and $(3 + 4)$ is equal to one half the sum of 20 and x, then $x =$

(A) 10
(B) 85
(C) 105
(D) 190
(E) 1,210

14. Jim's answer is D.

If you got this question wrong, you either misread it or forgot the correct order of operations. Remember to do parentheses first. Translating the information to an equation, we'd get the following:

$(1 + 2)(2 + 3)(3 + 4) = \dfrac{1}{2}(20 + x)$

$(3)(5)(7) = \dfrac{1}{2}(20 + x)$

$105 = \dfrac{1}{2}(20 + x)$

$210 = 20 + x$

$190 = x$

15 If $\dfrac{2+x}{5+x} = \dfrac{2}{5} + \dfrac{2}{5}$, then $x =$

(A) $\dfrac{2}{5}$

(B) 1

(C) 2

(D) 5

(E) 10

15. Jim's answer is E.

If you selected choice A, you fell for a Joe Bloggs trap. This question is well into medium territory—check out the difficulty meter. Anyway, simplifying the equation, we get the following:

$$\frac{2+x}{5+x} = \frac{2}{5} + \frac{2}{5}$$
$$\frac{2+x}{5+x} = \frac{4}{5}$$

At this point, the fast solution would be to backsolve by checking each of the choices until you found the answer. Using answer choice E,

$$\frac{2+x}{5+x} = \frac{4}{5}$$
$$\frac{2+(10)}{5+(10)} = \frac{4}{5}$$
$$\frac{12}{15} = \frac{4}{5}$$

The slow solution would be to cross-multiply the ratios:

$$(2 + x)(5) = (5 + x)(4)$$
$$10 + 5x = 20 + 4x$$
$$5x = 10 + 4x$$
$$x = 10$$

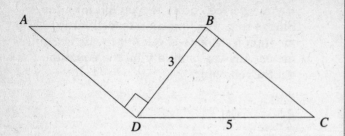

16 In parallelogram *ABCD* above, *BD* = 3 and *CD* = 5. What is the area of *ABCD*?

(A) 12
(B) 15
(C) 18
(D) 20
(E) It cannot be determined from the information given.

16. Jim's answer is A.
If you tried to compute the area of this parallelogram by trying first to calculate the base and height, you missed the point of this question. Jim wanted you to notice that the two triangles were identical. Using the Pythagorean theorem, you can compute the length of *AD* (= *BC*):

$$BC^2 + 3^2 = 5^2$$
$$BC^2 = 9 = 25$$
$$BC^2 = 16$$
$$BC = 4$$

(That's right, both triangles are 3-4-5—Jim's favorite!) Looking at either triangle from the side, you'd see a base of 3 and a height of 4. Using the area formula for triangles, you'd get:

$$A = \frac{1}{2} bh$$
$$A = \frac{1}{2} (3)(4)$$
$$A = 6$$

Since the parallelogram consists of two triangles, its area is 12. (By the way, if you had estimated the area of the parallelogram, the base is 5 and the height is less than 3.) The area must be less than 15, and only one answer choice is less than 15: the answer!

17 A survey of Town X found an average of 3.2 persons per household and an average of 1.2 televisions per household. If 48,000 people live in Town X, how many televisions are in Town X?

(A) 15,000
(B) 16,000
(C) 18,000
(D) 40,000
(E) 57,600

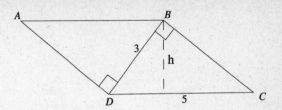

17. Jim's answer is C.
This is an excellent time to turn on your calculator. Since 48,000 people live in Town X, and each household has 3.2 people, we can determine the number of households:

$$48{,}000 \div 3.2 = 15{,}000$$

And since each household has 1.2 televisions, we can now determine the number of televisions:

$$15{,}000 \times 1.2 = 18{,}000$$

18 How many numbers from 1 to 200 inclusive are equal to the cube of an integer?

(A) one
(B) two
(C) three
(D) four
(E) five

18. Jim's answer is E.
Once again, the way <u>not</u> to solve an SAT question is to reason algebraically when you can check each of the choices. In other words, you don't want to set up some kind of equation like this:

$$1 \le n^3 \le 200$$

Instead, use your calculator to start cubing integers and stop just before you exceed 200.

Integer	Cube	
1	1	
2	8	
3	27	} 5 integers
4	64	
5	125	
6	216	

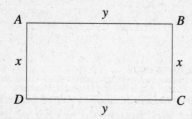

Note: Figure not drawn to scale.

19 If the perimeter of rectangle *ABCD* is equal to *p*, and $x = \frac{2}{3}y$, what is the value of *y* in terms of *p*?

(A) $\dfrac{p}{10}$

(B) $\dfrac{3p}{10}$

(C) $\dfrac{p}{3}$

(D) $\dfrac{2p}{5}$

(E) $\dfrac{3p}{5}$

19. Jim's answer is B.
A Princeton Review student, noticing the algebraic answer choices, would immediately plug in numbers to solve the problem. Since the values we choose for *x* and *y* must satisfy the equation, let's let *x* equal 2 and *y* equal 3. The perimeter *p* would then equal 2 + 2 + 3 + 3, or 10. Plugging 10 into *p* in each of the choices, we'd get B as the answer. By way of comparison, the slow, algebraic solution would look like this:

$$x + x + y + y = p \quad x = \frac{2}{3}y$$

$$\frac{2}{3}y + \frac{2}{3}y + y + y = p$$

$$\frac{2}{3}y + \frac{2}{3}y + \frac{3}{3}y + \frac{3}{3}y = p$$

$$\frac{10}{3}y = p$$

$$p = \frac{3}{10}p$$

Although some of you might have answered this question right by using algebra, doing so might have caused you to make a mistake without realizing it. Trust us, plugging in is always the safer method for this type of problem. The Joe Bloggs choice, by the way, was C.

20 A basketball team had a ratio of wins to losses of 3:1. After winning six games in a row, the team's ratio of wins to losses was 5:1. How many games had the team won <u>before</u> it won the six games?

(A) 3
(B) 6
(C) 9
(D) 15
(E) 24

20. Jim's answer is C.
And yet again, the slow way to solve word problems like this would be to set up equations. Letting w and l represent the number of wins and losses respectively, the slow method of setting up equations would yield the following:

$$\frac{w}{l} = \frac{3}{1}$$
$$\frac{w+6}{l} = \frac{5}{1}$$

Let's see how Princeton Review students approach this question. Using backsolving, we start in the middle—choice C—and see if it works:

		Before		After	
	Wins	Losses		Wins	Losses
(A)	3				
(B)	6				
(C)	9	3 (3:1)		15	3 (5:1)
(D)	15				
(E)	24				

Bingo! We found the answer on the first try! If C didn't work, we'd move up or down depending on whether the result was too small or too big.

21 A college student bought 11 books for fall classes. If the cost of his anatomy textbook was three times the average cost of the other 10 books, then the cost of the anatomy textbook was what fraction of the total amount he paid for the 11 books?

(A) $\frac{2}{13}$

(B) $\frac{3}{13}$

(C) $\frac{3}{11}$

(D) $\frac{3}{10}$

(E) $\frac{3}{4}$

21. Jim's answer is B.
The first thing to notice is that choices D and E are probably too simple to be correct on an otherwise simple-looking question. Since we aren't given the cost of any book, we can plug in our own values. Let's say that the average cost of the textbooks, excluding the anatomy textbook, is $10. We can make all the books cost $10 to make the problem easier. The anatomy textbook, then, would cost $30. The total cost of our textbooks would then be $130 (one $30 textbook plus ten $10 textbooks). The anatomy textbook contributes $\frac{\$30}{\$130}$, or $\frac{3}{13}$ of this amount.

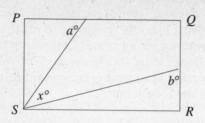

22. In rectangle *PQRS* above, what is the sum of
$a + b$ in terms of x?

(A) $90 + x$
(B) $180 - x$
(C) $180 + x$
(D) $270 - x$
(E) $360 - x$

22. Jim's answer is A.
For those students who chose to notice the
variables in the answer choices, this
question was easily solved using plugging
in. It was easiest to plug in for a and b first,
and then to solve for x. Let $a=50$ and $b=70$.
Now the two triangles are right triangles
since they are formed from the corners of
rectangle PQRS, so you can determine the
measure of the third angle in each triangle.

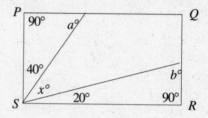

Since $\angle S = 90° = 40° + 20° + x°$

$\qquad x° = 30!$

Having computed the value of x, you can
now move to the answer choices. $a + b = 50
+ 70 = 120$, so you are looking for the
answer choice that equals 120°. Circle 120 in
your margin. Choice A is $90 + x = 90 + 30 =
120$. If you forgot to plug in, you could
have guesstimated. a, b, and x look to be
roughly 60, 70, and 40, respectively. Thus $a
+ b$ would be roughly 130. Clearly we can
eliminate C, D, and E. If this is all you could
do, don't sweat it. 50–50 on a hard problem
is not bad at all!
By the way, Jim wanted you to set up some
geometric equations. Here is one of the
many ways you could have chosen to
complete the problem if you forgot about
the above.
The sum of the angles in the quadrilateral in
between the triangles is 360°. Thus,

$$\angle Q + (180 - a) + (180 - b) = 360$$
$$\text{or } 90 + 180 + 180 - (a + b) = 360 - x$$
$$450 - (a + b) = 360 - x$$
$$- (a + b) = -x - 90$$
$$a + b = 90 + x.$$

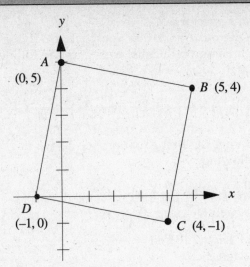

23 What is the area of square *ABCD*?

(A) 25

(B) $18\sqrt{2}$

(C) 26

(D) $25 + \sqrt{2}$

(E) 36

23. Jim's answer is C.

First a little error avoidance: since 5 is one of the numbers we see, 5^2, or 25 is not going to be the answer. Next, let's estimate the area before we try to solve directly. The length of the square's side is a little more than 5, so the area is going to be a little more than 5^2 or 25. Choice E is too large, so before solving the problem, we've eliminated choices A and E. If we couldn't calculate the area exactly, we could guess among the remaining choices. To determine the area, let's begin by assigning the variable *s* to indicate the length of the square's side. The area is given by the formula:

$A = s^2$

Now, using the Pythagorean theorem, we can determine s^2 directly:

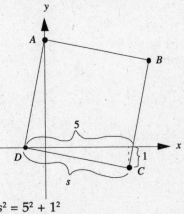

$s^2 = 5^2 + 1^2$

$s^2 = 25 + 1$

$s^2 = 26$

QUESTIONS	EXPLANATIONS

24 If 0.1% percent of m is equal to 10% of n, then m is what percent of $10n$?

(A) $\frac{1}{1000}$%

(B) 10%

(C) 100%

(D) 1,000%

(E) 10,000%

24. Jim's answer is D.

Using our translation approach to solving percentage problems, we set up the following equations:

If $\left(\frac{0.1}{100}\right)\left(\frac{m}{1}\right) = \left(\frac{10}{100}\right)\left(\frac{n}{1}\right)$, then $\left(\frac{m}{1}\right) = \left(\frac{x}{100}\right)\left(\frac{10n}{1}\right)$

Solving the first equation, we derive the following:

$$\left(\frac{0.1}{100}\right)\left(\frac{m}{1}\right) = \left(\frac{10}{100}\right)\left(\frac{n}{1}\right)$$
$$100\left(\frac{0.1}{100}\right)\left(\frac{m}{1}\right) = 100\left(\frac{10}{100}\right)\left(\frac{n}{1}\right)$$
$$(0.1)(m) = (10)(n)$$
$$m = 100n$$

Then, substituting this value of m into the second equation, we solve for x:

$$\left(\frac{m}{1}\right) = \left(\frac{x}{100}\right)\left(\frac{10n}{1}\right)$$
$$\left(\frac{100n}{1}\right) = \left(\frac{x}{100}\right)\left(\frac{10n}{1}\right)$$

$$10,000n = (x)(10n)$$

$$\frac{10,000n}{10n} = x$$

$$1,000 = x$$

25 If $n \neq 0$, which of the following could be true?

  I. $2n < n^2$
 II. $2n < n$
III. $n^2 < -n$

(A) None
(B) I only
(C) I and II only
(D) I and III only
(E) I, II, and III

25. Jim's answer is E.

Again, the variables in the answers should indicate to you that plugging in is going to be your best approach. This is a COULD question, so you will want to try several different plug ins to attempt to make I, II, and III true.

The exponents might have tipped you off that a negative fraction would be a good choice. Plugging in $-\frac{1}{2}$ for n we find:

I. $2n = 2(-\frac{1}{2}) = -1 < n^2 = (-\frac{1}{2})^2 = \frac{1}{4}$. TRUE

II. $2n = 2(-\frac{1}{2}) = -1 < n = -\frac{1}{2}$. TRUE

III. $n^2 = (-\frac{1}{2})^2 = \frac{1}{4} < -n = -(-\frac{1}{2}) = \frac{1}{2}$. TRUE

Thus, I, II, and III COULD be true and E is the answer.

SECTION 2

1 Since the island soil has been barren for so many years, the natives must now ---- much of their food.

(A) deliver
(B) import
(C) produce
(D) develop
(E) utilize

1. Pam's answer is B.
The doctor in this sentence is the phrase *barren for so many years*, provides answer B. The other choices miss what the sentence is getting at.

2 Because Jenkins neither ---- nor defends either management or the striking workers, both sides admire his journalistic ----.

(A) criticizes. .acumen
(B) attacks. .neutrality
(C) confronts. .aptitude
(D) dismisses. .flair
(E) promotes. .integrity

2. Pam's answer is B.
The first blank is some negative word like attacks. Eliminate choice E. Because Jenkins neither attacks nor defends either side (the doctor), he is *impartial* or *objective*. Choice B is the answer. If you chose A, keep in mind that an easy question such as this would not have such a difficult answer (*acumen*).

3 Some anthropologists claim that a few apes have been taught a rudimentary sign language, but skeptics argue that the apes are only ---- their trainers.

(A) imitating
(B) condoning
(C) instructing
(D) acknowledging
(E) belaboring

3. Pam's answer is A.
The doctor is *been taught*, which skeptics doubt. So the skeptics must be arguing that the apes are *fooling* their trainers. Choice A works perfectly. Again, if you chose B, *condoning* is too difficult an answer for such an easy question.

4 It is ironic that the ---- insights of the great thinkers are voiced so often that they have become mere ----.

(A) original. .clichés
(B) banal. .beliefs
(C) dubious. .habits
(D) philosophical. .questions
(E) abstract. .ideas

4. Pam's answer is A.
Greater thinkers must have *deep* insights; at any rate the first blank is a positive word. The doctor here is *voiced so often*. Things that are voiced often can be called *repetitions*, or some related negative word. The only choice that has a positive word followed by a negative word is A. Once again, choice B would be too difficult for aggression in medium territory.

QUESTIONS	EXPLANATIONS

5 The most frustrating periods of any diet are the inevitable ----, when weight loss ---- if not stops.

(A) moods. .accelerates
(B) feasts. .halts
(C) holidays. .contracts
(D) plateaus. .slows
(E) meals. .ceases

5. Pam's answer is D.
The two blanks are both negative. The only choice that contains two negative words is D. Remember, a word like *plateaus*, while not negative by definition, has negative connotations in this case through its association with dieting.

6 Since the author's unflattering references to her friends were so ----, she was surprised that her ---- were recognized.

(A) laudatory. .styles
(B) obvious. .anecdotes
(C) oblique. .allusions
(D) critical. .eulogies
(E) apparent. .motives

6. Pam's answer is C.
We're in medium, approaching difficult, territory. The first blank should be a negative, or at best neutral, word. Since the doctor is *surprised* and *recognized*, the first blank must be a word like *unrecognized*. The second blank should be a word that means *unflattering references*. Working first with the second blank, we can quickly eliminate A and E. Turning now to the first blank, *obvious* doesn't fit the doctor since we're looking for a word that means unrecognizable. Eliminate B. Ditto for *critical*, so eliminate D. The answer is C, even if we aren't sure what either word means!

7 Mark was intent on maintaining his status as first in his class; because even the smallest mistakes infuriated him, he reviewed all his papers ---- before submitting them to his teacher.

(A) explicitly
(B) perfunctorily
(C) honestly
(D) mechanically
(E) assiduously

7. Pam's answer is E.
Because Mark hates mistakes, he will review his papers *carefully*. We can eliminate choices C and D immediately. If you weren't sure what A, B, or E meant, you had to guess. Give yourself a pat on the back if you guessed A or B rather than leave the question blank. Even though you got the question wrong, you did the right thing. And in the long run, that's how your score goes up.

8 Since many disadvantaged individuals view their situations as ---- as well as intolerable, their attitudes are best described as ----.

(A) squalid. .obscure
(B) unpleasant. .bellicose
(C) acute. .sanguine
(D) immutable. .resigned
(E) political. .perplexed

8. Pam's answer is D.
The first and second blanks are negative, possibly neutral, words. What's more, you should notice that they are saying similar things. Choice E is the only bad guess; choices A, B, and C are all good guesses. Again, guessing one of these choices would have been better than leaving the question blank.

QUESTIONS	EXPLANATIONS

9 The subtleties of this novel are evident not so much in the character ---- as they are in its profoundly ---- plot structure.

(A) assessment. .eclectic
(B) development. .trite
(C) portrayal. .aesthetic
(D) delineation. .intricate
(E) illustration. .superficial

9. Pam's answer is D.
The doctor in this question is *subtleties*. If you weren't sure what this word meant, the sentence probably gave you a lot of trouble. Choices B and E are the only bad guesses; this question is too hard to have such easy answers. Choices A and C are good guesses, but D is the answer.

10 SHIP : OCEAN ::

(A) fish : gill
(B) plane : air
(C) child : bath
(D) camel : water
(E) car : passengers

10. Pam's answer is B.
A ship travels in the ocean just as a *plane* travels in the *air*.

11 BOTANY : PLANTS ::

(A) agriculture : herbs
(B) astronomy : stars
(C) philosophy : books
(D) anthropology : religion
(E) forestry : evergreens

11. Pam's answer is B.
Botany is the study of plants; *astronomy* is the study of *stars*.

12 CENSUS : POPULATION ::

(A) catalog : pictures
(B) inventory : supplies
(C) detonation : explosion
(D) dictionary : words
(E) election : tally

12. Pam's answer is B.
A census counts the population; an *inventory* counts the *supplies*. Choice E was close, but it doesn't quite work.

13 CONSTELLATION : STARS ::

(A) earth : moon
(B) center : circle
(C) archipelago : islands
(D) rain : water
(E) maverick : herd

13. Pam's answer is C.
A constellation is a group of stars. You could quickly eliminate A, B, and D. Now, let's say you didn't know what an archipelago is. Could it mean a group of islands? Sure, Hawaii is a group of islands; maybe that's what an archipelago is. Looking at E, if you weren't sure what a maverick is, could it mean a group or herd? That doesn't makes sense, does it? Still,
E is a good guess on a hard question like this, so we're proud of you if you guessed it rather than leave the question blank.

14 REFINE : OIL ::

(A) winnow : wheat
(B) harness : energy
(C) mine : coal
(D) mold : plastic
(E) conserve : resource

14. Pam's answer is A.
If you weren't sure how to make a sentence with *refine* and *oil* we hope you noticed that choices B, C, and E were Joe Bloggs traps, and that D was too easy. To refine oil is to purify it just as to winnow wheat is to purify it.

15 PERSPICACIOUS : INSIGHT ::

(A) zealous : mobility
(B) audacious : hearing
(C) delicious : taste
(D) avaricious : generosity
(E) amiable : friendliness

15. Pam's answer is E.
If you aren't sure what *perspicacious* means, you can't make a sentence. Looking over the choices, C is way too easy. If you know the definitions of *zealous* and *audacious*, you know choices A and B are unrelated. If you didn't know their meanings, A and B are good guesses, as is D.

The passage below is followed by questions based on its content. Answer the questions on the basis of what is <u>stated</u> or <u>implied</u> in the passage and in any introductory material that may be provided.

Questions 16-21 are based on the following passage.

The following passage is an excerpt from a book by novelist Gregor von Rezzori.

Skushno is a Russian word that is difficult to translate. It means more than dreary boredom: a spiritual void that sucks you in like a vague but
Line intensely urgent longing. When I was thirteen, at a
(5) phase that educators used to call the awkward age, my parents were at their wits' end. We lived in the Bukovina, today an almost astronomically remote province in southeastern Europe. The story I am telling seems as distant—not only in space but also
(10) in time—as if I'd merely dreamed it. Yet it begins as a very ordinary story.

I had been expelled by a *consilium abeundi*—an advisory board with authority to expel unworthy students—from the schools of the then Kingdom of
(15) Rumania, whose subjects we had become upon the collapse of the Austro-Hungarian Empire after the first great war. An attempt to harmonize the imbalances in my character by means of strict discipline at a boarding school in Styria (my people
(20) still regarded Austria as our cultural homeland) nearly led to the same ignominious end, and only my pseudo-voluntary departure from the institution in the nick of time prevented my final ostracism from the privileged ranks of those for whom the
(25) path to higher education was open. Again in the jargon of those assigned the responsible task of raising children to become "useful members of society," I was a "virtually hopeless case." My parents, blind to how the contradictions within me
(30) had grown out of the highly charged difference between their own natures, agreed with the schoolmasters; the mix of neurotic sensitivity and a tendency to violence, alert perception and inability to learn, tender need for support and lack of
(35) adjustability, would only develop into something criminal.

One of the trivial aphorisms my generation owes to Wilhelm Busch's *Pious Helene* is the homily "Once your reputation's done / You can live a life of
(40) fun." But this optimistic notion results more from wishful thinking than from practical experience. In my case, had anyone asked me about my state of mind, I would have sighed and answered, "*Skushno!*" Even though rebellious thoughts
(45) occasionally surged within me, I dragged myself, or rather I let myself be dragged, listlessly through my bleak existence in the snail's pace of days. Nor was I ever free of a sense of guilt, for my feeling guilty was not entirely foisted upon me by others; there
(50) were deep reasons I could not explain to myself; had I been able to do so, my life would have been much easier.

When answering critical reading questions, it is important to do the general questions first, the vocabulary-in-context second (these are the questions that ask you for the meaning of a word; they are the fastest of the critical reading questions), and the explicit questions last. We have rearranged the questions in these explanations to show you how a Princeton Review student should look at the test.

16 It can be inferred from the passage that the author's parents were

(A) frustrated by the author's inability to do well in school
(B) oblivious to the author's poor academic performance
(C) wealthy, making them insensitive to the needs of the poor
(D) schoolmasters who believed in the strict disciplining of youth
(E) living in Russia while their son lived in Bukovina

16. Pam's answer is A.
Although the passage never states it directly, you can infer that answer choice A is correct. The author states in the passage (lines 28–36) that his parents were at their wits' end. Is this just because they were having nervous breakdowns? No, it relates somehow to the main idea.

The main idea of the passage is that the author suffered from *skushno*, and some of his suffering affected his life in very real ways. Doing poorly in many different schools is what put his parents at their wits' end. The author tells us about his parents' trauma just before he launches into an explanation of how many schools he went through when he was depressed. It's all connected, and his parents were frustrated by his failures.

In answer choice B, Pam wants you to think that the boy's poor performance and problems stem from neglectful parents—an assumption that is incorrect given the passage. The parents must know about the author's poor performance, because he's been expelled from numerous schools.

Answer choice C has nothing to do with the passage. You may assume that the author's parents have money because they send him to boarding school, but you can't infer anything about what they might think of the poor.

Answer choice D overlaps several things that are mentioned in the passage but are not connected. There are schoolmasters mentioned in the text, and there is strict discipline. The schoolmasters who disciplined the students must have believed it to some extent, but you have no way of knowing what the author's parents did as a profession.

Answer choice E is factually incorrect. The first paragraph states that the author's family lived together in Bukovina.

2

17 Lines 17–25 are used by the author to demonstrate that

(A) the author was an unstable and dangerous person
(B) the schools that the author attended were too difficult
(C) the tactics being used to make the author a more stable person were failing
(D) the author was not accepted well by his classmates
(E) the author's academic career was nearing an end

17. Pam's answer is C.

The lines mentioned show that the author has been sent to boarding schools in order to "harmonize" (line 17) imbalances in his character. The author is demonstrating in these lines his inability to be harmonized by any school. He is continuing to be depressed and unsuccessful and eventually leaves school before being kicked out forever. We can assume that whatever they are doing in boarding school to make him perform well enough to not get kicked out isn't working.

Answer choice A is bad. Pam puts the word *unstable* there to distract you from thinking about the question. The word reminds you of the passage as a whole so it is more attractive. You already know that the author is unstable, but you don't know if he's dangerous.

Answer B is another trap of Pam's. You might infer from this section of the passage that the schools were too hard. Or you might also infer that the author was intelligent enough to do well, but he had no motivation, or that he was just too depressed to do the work necessary to do well.

More important, the question asks you why the author wrote what the question refers to. What is he trying to show you, the reader?

Anything that the author is going to demonstrate is going to be connected to the main idea. This passage as a whole is not about the difficulty of boarding schools; it is about a depressed and unsettled person.

Answer choice D is the same trap as B is. There is no evidence stated or implied that demonstrates how unpopular the author was.

Answer choice E is another assumption. Pam is getting you to anticipate what will probably happen to the author given what he's told you, however, is that what the author is trying to demonstrate: how he is done with school. Again, what is the main idea of the passage and how does the section the question refers to relate to it?

QUESTIONS	EXPLANATIONS

18 The word *ignominious* in line 21 means

    (A) dangerous
    (B) pitiless
    (C) unappreciated
    (D) disgraceful
    (E) honorable

18. Pam's answer is D.
Questions 18 and 19 are line reference vocabulary questions and can be done fairly quickly. All you need to do is understand how the word is used in the context of the sentence to figure out what it means. In line 21 *ignominious* means disgraceful, or answer choice D. In the context of the sentence the word is used to show that the author avoided something bad "in the nick of time" by leaving the boarding school. The ignominious end that the author is referring to is expulsion from yet another school. Because he avoided this "ignominious" end and prevented his "final ostracism from the privileged ranks. .." answer choice E is obviously out. He is not saving himself from anything good. B and C don't really make sense if you plug them into the sentence in place of ignominious. Pam is just using words that remind you of the tone of the passage as a whole. The author's situation may be pitiful and he may feel unappreciated, but these words don't work in the sentence. Finally, with answer choice A, the only dangerous thing about the sentence would be if it caused you to pick A as the correct answer.

19 In line 23, the word *ostracism* most likely means

    (A) praise
    (B) abuse
    (C) appreciation
    (D) departure
    (E) banishment

19. Pam's answer is E.
Conveniently it refers to the same sentence as question 18, so you've already done half of the work. Privileged rank is a sign or level of status. If the author is saving himself from something final in regard to this rank, we first want to determine if it's something good or something bad. Because of question 19 we know that he's saving himself from something bad. The author has been expelled from many schools and his "pseudo-voluntary" departure (line 22) is saving him from a final form of the same fate. Expulsion is most like a banishment, so E is the correct answer. Answer choices A and C are first and foremost positive words. You can cross those off right away. You can't really be abused by ". ..ranks of those for whom the path to higher education was open" (lines 24–25). And departure (answer choice D) isn't strong enough to be Pam's choice here. D is a close second and Pam will trick a number of people, because the answer choice makes sense in the sentence. However, departure is a neutral word and banishment is negative; therefore, banishment is the better choice.

20 The passage as a whole suggests that the author felt

(A) happy because he was separated from his parents
(B) upset because he was unable to maintain good friends
(C) melancholy and unsettled in his environment
(D) suicidal and desperate because of his living in Russia
(E) harmonic and hopeful because he'd soon be out of school

20. Pam's answer is C.

Question 20 is the first and only general question for this passage. C is the correct answer for several reasons.

The first two sentences introduce the idea of *Skushno* and its melancholic nature, so there's a good chance that the author is not going to be happy. The first two sentences of the second paragraph show you that the passage is written in the first person (you know, the author says "I felt" and "I did" etc.), so you can connect the *Skushno* with the author.

The second paragraph's first two sentences also tell you that the author has been expelled from numerous schools and has "imbalances in his character" (line 18). You also know that the author left school to avoid an "ignominious end" (line 21). These facts point to an unhappy situation.

The first two sentences of the last paragraph indicate that the author doesn't really cheer up much. The optimistic aphorism mentioned is labeled "wishful thinking" by the author and therefore doesn't indicate a change in his feelings.

The last two sentences reinforce how the author is stuck in his depressed emotional state.

Answer choices A and E are obviously wrong because there is not anything really "happy" or "harmonic" mentioned by the author.

Answer choices B and D are too narrow in their scope. The author has more problems than just maintaining good friends, and he is not upset because he is living in Russia. Moreover, *suicidal* and *desperate* are too strong for Pam. Remember, Pam wouldn't pick a passage in which the author was suicidal.

Questions 18 and 19 are line reference vocabulary questions and can be done fairly quickly. All you need to do is understand how the word is used in the context of the sentence to figure out what it means.

21 The passage indicates that the author regarded the aphorism mentioned in the last paragraph with

(A) relief because it showed him that he would eventually feel better
(B) despair because the author did not believe it was true
(C) contempt because he saw it working for others
(D) bemusement because of his immunity from it
(E) sorrow because his faith in it nearly killed him

21. Pam's answer is B.

"The passage indicates . . . ," means that 21 is a specific question about something stated directly in the passage. Here ETS gives you where in the text whatever they want you to find is located (last paragraph). Pam isn't always that generous.

For these questions you need to locate what the question is referring to (in this case an aphorism), read it, think for a second, and eliminate bad answer choices.

By reading the first two sentences of the last paragraph again, plus one more sentence, you can see that the author didn't regard the aphorism too highly. Moreover, the author states that "this optimistic notion results more from wishful thinking than from practical experience " (line 41).

Answer choice B is the best answer. The author didn't believe the aphorism, and he regarded it with *Skushno!* (line 43).

We know the author got no relief from the aphorism, nor did it amuse him at all. A and D are therefore out of the question.

In answer choice E the first half is acceptable. It's feasible that the author felt sorrow when thinking of the aphorism. But we know that the author never had "faith" in it that almost "killed" him. This choice is too strong and downright silly.

Inference questions should be done last. They take up the most time and require you to think more about what you read rather than hunt for information in the passage. An inference is an assumption that is valid given what is stated or implied in the passage.

Questions 22–30 are based on the following passage.

Fear of communism swept through the United States in the years following the Russian Revolution of 1917. Several states passed espionage acts that restricted political discussion, and radicals of all descriptions were rounded up in so-called Red Raids conducted by the attorney general's office. Some were convicted and imprisoned; others were deported. This was the background of a trial in Chicago involving twenty men charged under Illinois's espionage statute with advocating the violent overthrow of the government. The charge rested on the fact that all the defendants were members of the newly formed Communist Labor party.

The accused in the case were represented by Clarence Darrow, one of the foremost defense attorneys in the country. Throughout his career, Darrow had defended the poor and the despised against exploitation and prejudice. He defended the rights of labor unions, for example, at a time when many sought to outlaw the strike, and he was resolute in defending constitutional freedoms. The following are excerpts from Darrow's summation to the jury.

Members of the Jury . . . If you want to convict these twenty men, then do it. I ask no consideration on behalf of any one of them. They are no better
Line than any other twenty men or women; they are no
(5) better than the millions down through the ages who have been prosecuted and convicted in cases like this. And if it is necessary for my clients to show that America is like all the rest, if it is necessary that my clients shall go to prison to show it, then let
(10) them go. They can afford it if you members of the jury can; make no mistake about that . . .

The State says my clients "dare to criticize the Constitution." Yet this police officer (who the State says is a fine, right-living person) twice violated the
(15) federal Constitution while a prosecuting attorney was standing by. They entered Mr. Owen's home without a search warrant. They overhauled his papers. They found a flag, a red one, which he had the same right to have in his house that you have to
(20) keep a green one, or a yellow one, or any other color, and the officer impudently rolled it up and put another flag on the wall, nailed it there. By what right was that done? What about this kind of patriotism that violates the Constitution? Has it
(25) come to pass in this country that officers of the law can trample on constitutional rights and then excuse it in a court of justice? . . .

Most of what has been presented to this jury to stir up feeling in your souls has not the slightest
(30) bearing on proving conspiracy in this case. Take Mr. Lloyd's speech in Milwaukee. It had nothing to do with conspiracy.

Whether that speech was a joke or was serious, I will not attempt to discuss. But I will say that if it
(35) was serious it was as mild as a summer's shower compared with many of the statements of those who are responsible for working conditions in this country. We have heard from people in high places that those individuals who express sympathy with
(40) labor should be stood up against a wall and shot. We have heard people of position declare that individuals who criticize the actions of those who

are getting rich should be put in a cement ship with leaden sails and sent out to sea. Every violent appeal
(45) that could be conceived by the brain has been used by the powerful and the strong. I repeat, Mr. Lloyd's speech was gentle in comparison. . . .

My clients are condemned because they say in their platform that, while they vote, they believe the
(50) ballot is secondary to education and organization. Counsel suggests that those who get something they did not vote for are sinners, but I suspect you the jury know full well that my clients are right. Most of you have an eight-hour day. Did you get it by any
(55) vote you ever cast? No. It came about because workers laid down their tools and said we will no longer work until we get an eight-hour day. That is how they got the twelve-hour day, the ten-hour day,
(60) and the eight-hour day—not by voting but by laying down their tools. Then when it was over and the victory won . . . then the politicians, in order to get the labor vote, passed legislation creating an eight-hour day. That is how things changed; victory
(65) preceded law. . . .

You have been told that if you acquit these defendants you will be despised because you will endorse everything they believe. But I am not here to defend my clients' opinions. I am here to defend
(70) their right to express their opinions. I ask you, then, to decide this case upon the facts as you have heard them, in light of the law as you understand it, in light of the history of our country, whose institutions you and I are bound to protect.

22 Clarence Darrow's statement that "They can afford it if you members of the jury can" is most probably meant to imply that

(A) the defendants will not be harmed if convicted
(B) if the jurors convict the defendants, they will be harshly criticized
(C) the defendants do not care whether they are convicted
(D) everyone involved in the trial will be affected financially by whatever the jury decides
(E) if the defendants are found guilty, everyone's rights will be threatened

23 Lines 12–27 suggest that the case against Owen would have been dismissed if the judge had interpreted the constitution in which of the following ways?

(A) Defendants must have their rights read to them when they are arrested.
(B) Giving false testimony in court is a crime.
(C) Evidence gained by illegal means is not admissible in court.
(D) No one can be tried twice for the same crime.
(E) Defendants cannot be forced to give incriminating evidence against themselves.

22. Pam's answer is E.

For this question you need to locate the statement in the text and read "around" it. This means read the sentence before it, the sentence it's in, and the sentence after it to determine what it implies. Remember, for implications and inferences, think about how what's being said relates to the main idea.

The statement is in line 10, and it follows a comment by Darrow in which he tells the jury that if they want America to be like any other place where people are persecuted for their beliefs, they should let the accused go to prison. Darrow is implying that letting his clients go to prison would imperil that in America which makes it special. (Remember, Pam loves America and everything it stands for. She wants to put passages in the SAT that stress the freedoms that Americans are blessed with.)

23. Pam's answer is C.

In the lines referred to in queston 23, Darrow is stressing an inconsistency or contradiction on the part of the prosecution: that it is okay to disregard constitutional rights in order to prosecute someone for violating the Constitution.

Answer choice C is therefore correct. Darrow stresses that the evidence against Owen was obtained by violating his constitutional rights; therefore, if the judge had interpreted the Constitution like answer choice C suggests, then Owen's trial would have been dismissed.

24 Darrow's defense in lines 28–47 relies mainly on persuading the jury that

(A) the prosecution is using a double standard.
(B) the evidence used by the prosecution is unreliable.
(C) the defendants' views are similar to those of the jury.
(D) labor unions are guaranteed the right to hold a strike.
(E) a federal court is a more appropriate place to try the defendants than is a state court.

24. Pam's answer is A.
Answer choice A is correct here because Darrow believes that the prosecution is using a double standard. You can use the information you gained from answering the previous question in answering this one.

The lines referred to in the question cite more examples of how Darrow is showing that the prosecution is guilty of exactly what they are accusing the defendants of. In this case the accused are said to have used violent words, and Darrow is giving examples of violent threats that have been aimed at the defendants.

25 Lines 28–47 indicate that the prosecution attempted to characterize Mr. Lloyd's speech as

(A) bitter sarcasm
(B) deceptive propaganda
(C) valid criticism
(D) a frightening threat
(E) a bad joke

25. Pam's answer is D.
For this question, line 32 indicates that Lloyd's speech was accused of being a "conspiracy," and line 47 says that it was gentle in comparison to the violent epithets of anti-Communists; therefore, answer choice D is correct. The violent or harsh part of the speech is why it is frightening, and the conspiratorial nature is what makes it a threat.

26 What does Clarence Darrow accuse "people in high places" (lines 38–39) of doing?

(A) Trying to kill Communist party members
(B) Advocating violence against labor sympathizers
(C) Lying to the jury
(D) Encouraging the use of harsh punishment against criminals
(E) Making foolish and insulting suggestions

26. Pam's answer is B.
In lines 38 and 39 Clarence Darrow speaks of people in high places advocating that labor sympathizers "should be stood up against a wall and shot" (line 40). This matches answer choice B exactly.

27 The word *counsel* in line 51 refers to

(A) expert psychologists
(B) the prosecution
(C) an assembly
(D) a recommendation
(E) an expert

27. Pam's answer is B.
This is a line reference vocabulary question, so it will take you less time than other questions. *Counsel* in line 51 refers to answer choice B, the prosecution. Because Darrow is arguing in this passage, you can assume he is arguing against someone. By reading the sentence before and after the sentence with *counsel* in it, you can see that Darrow is refuting a point made by *counsel*. Counsel is whom Darrow is arguing against. In a court battle you have two sides: the defense, which is Darrow; and the prosecution, which is the counsel.

28 Lines 66–68 imply that the prosecution had told the jury that finding for the innocence of the defendants would be similar to

(A) denying the validity of the Constitution
(B) permitting workers to go on strike
(C) promoting passive resistance
(D) limiting freedom of expression
(E) promoting communism

28. Pam's answer is E.
The statement "you will be despised because you will endorse everything they believe" links the jurors with Communists and makes E the best answer choice.

Be careful of Pam's trap here. Notice she is asking what the prosecution implies, not what Darrow, the defense implies. Darrow is restating what the prosecution already told the jury. Pam will often shift whose statement has implications. This will usually happen when a passage has someone quoting another person's quote. Just read the questions carefully so you know whose speech Pam is referring to.

QUESTIONS	EXPLANATIONS

29 In line 74, the word *bound* most nearly means

(A) intellectually committed
(B) personally determined
(C) morally compelled
(D) violently coerced
(E) inevitably destined

29. Pam's answer is C.
In line 74 *bound* means morally compelled. By reading the last paragraph , you see that Darrow's argument is hinged on the jury's commitment to uphold the law despite how they feel personally about communism. Therefore, *bound* must mean something very compelling, something beyond an intellectual commitment and stopping short of inevitability. *Bound* means tied to something, and in this case Darrow is saying that the jury is tied to upholding the law by a moral obligation.

30 Darrow's defense hinges on the ability of the jurors to

(A) understand complicated legal terms and procedures
(B) sympathize with union organizers
(C) comprehend the beliefs of the Communist Labor party
(D) separate the defendants' rights from their views
(E) act in the interest of the national economy

30. Pam's answer is D.
This is the only real general question in the bunch. It asks you to determine what Darrow is trying to get the jury to do through implication and examples. You know from your 2-2-2-F reading of the passage that the accused are said to be a threat to the Constitution (line 12) and the country. Darrow's summation also points to an inconsistency in the prosecution (paragraph 2) to highlight constitutionality as the issue, not communism. All of Darrow's testimony, which you can get a good feel for in 2-2-2-F reading, relies on getting away from what the defendants believe and focuses on their rights under the Constitution to have this belief.

SECTION 3

SUMMARY DIRECTIONS FOR QUANTITATIVE COMPARISON QUESTIONS

Answer: A if the quantity in Column A is greater;
B if the quantity in Column B is greater;
C if the two quantities are equal;
D if the relationship cannot be determined from the information given.

AN E RESPONSE WILL NOT BE SCORED.

Column A	Column B

1 | $\dfrac{3}{7}$ | $\dfrac{1}{2}$

1. Jim's answer is B.
   This is a simple arithmetic problem. Using a calculator, we could convert each fraction to a decimal. If we wanted to operate with fractions, we could find a common denominator to simplify the comparison.

   $$\dfrac{3}{7} \qquad \dfrac{1}{2}$$
   $$\dfrac{6}{14} \qquad \dfrac{7}{14}$$

   Notice choice (D) is out because both sides have only numbers.

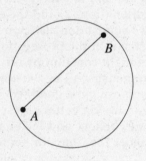

$AB = 8$

2 | The radius of the circle | 4

2. Jim's answer is A.
   Since AB is 8, the diameter of the circle must be more than 8. If the diameter is more than 8, the radius must be more than 4.

$7a > 4b$

3 | a | b

3. Jim's answer is D.
   If we divide both sides of the inequality by 7, we'd get the following:
   $7a > 4b$
   $a > \dfrac{4b}{7}$

   Now, just because a is greater than $\dfrac{4}{7}b$ does not mean it's greater than b. We can't tell. You could plug in a few numbers for a and b and you'll find that the answer varies.

Column A   Column B

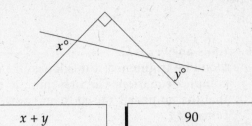

4 | $x + y$ | | 90 |

4. Jim's answer is C.
    Although we don't know what x and y are, we can use their vertical angles within the triangle:

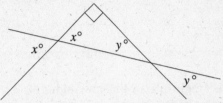

And since $x + y + 90 = 180$, $x + y = 90$. Plug-in.

The novelty clock above has hands that move at the correct speed, but counterclockwise. The clock tells the correct time every 6 hours (at 6:00 and 12:00).

5 | 3 hours, 15 minutes | | Amount of time that has passed since 12:00 |

5. Jim's answer is B.
    This is a little confusing, but not that difficult if we're careful. Moving backward from 12:00, 11:00 would be 1 hour, 10:00 would be 2 hours, 9:00 would be 3 hours, and 8:00 would be 4 hours. 8:15 is 3 hours and 45 minutes.

Column A   **Column B**

$$9^n - 8^n = 1^n$$

6 | 1 | | n |

6. Jim's answer is C.
Don't be frightened if this looks like some complex equation. The first thing to notice is that the number 1 raised to any power remains 1:
$9^n - 8^n = 1^n$
$9^1 - 8^1 = 1$
The only value of n that satisfies this equation is 1.

A rectangle of area 4 has two sides of length r and s, where r and s are integers.

7 | $\dfrac{r}{2}$ | | $2s$ |

7. Jim's answer is D.
The Joe Bloggs response to this question is B, so the answer should be A, C, or D. Joe Bloggs thinks $2s$ must be greater than $\frac{r}{2}$.
Now, let's use the formula for the area of a rectangle:
$A = rs$
$4 = rs$
Let's let $r = 1$ and $s = 4$. Now let's compare the quantities:

$$\frac{r}{2} \qquad 2s$$
$$\frac{1}{2} \qquad 2(4)$$

Clearly, Column B is larger than Column A. So the answer can't be A or C. Since Joe thinks the answer is B, the answer should be D. (If you let $r = 4$ and $s = 1$, the two quantities could be equal.)

In a group of 28 children, there are 6 more girls than boys.

8 | Two times the number of girls | | Three times the number of boys |

8. Jim's answer is A.
The Joe Bloggs response is B which is, of course, incorrect. The condition tells us that there are 6 more girls than boys in a group of 28 children. Either solving this equation or fiddling with it, we determine that there are 17 girls and 11 boys. So two times the number of girls (34) is greater than three times the number of boys (33).

<u>Column A</u>   <u>Column B</u>

9

$$\frac{\frac{3}{2}}{\left(\frac{3}{2}\right)^2}$$

$$\frac{2}{3}$$

9. Jim's answer is C.
First, cross out D because the problem contains only numbers. If you got this question wrong, you were careless in manipulating the fractions:

$\dfrac{\frac{3}{2}}{\left(\frac{3}{2}\right)^2}$ $\dfrac{2}{3}$

$\dfrac{3}{2}\left(\dfrac{2}{3}\right)^2$ $\dfrac{2}{3}$

$\dfrac{3}{2}\left(\dfrac{2}{3}\right)\left(\dfrac{2}{3}\right)$ $\dfrac{2}{3}$

$\dfrac{2}{3}$ $\dfrac{2}{3}$

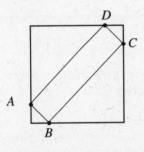

The area of the square is 25. Points A, B, C, and D are on the square.

10   Perimeter of the rectangle *ABCD*   20

10. Jim's answer is B.
If the area of the square is 25, the length of each side is 5. The perimeter of the square, then, is 20. If the perimeter of the square is 20, the perimeter of the inscribed rectangle must be less than 20.

x, y, and z are positive.
$x + y + z = 10$ and $x = y$

11 x 5

11. Jim's answer is B.
Solving the two equations for x, we get the following:
$x + y + z = 10$ and $x = y$
$x + x + z = 10$
$2x + z = 10$
$2x = 10 - z$
$x = 5 - \dfrac{z}{2}$

If x equals $\dfrac{z}{2}$ less 5, where z is positive, x must be less than 5.

3

Column A	Column B

12 | $\sqrt{3} + \sqrt{4}$ | $\sqrt{3} \times \sqrt{4}$ |

12. Jim's answer is A.
The Joe Bloggs response here is B. This problem should give you little trouble on your calculator. Again, (D) should have been eliminated because there are only numbers.

13 | The number of distinct prime factors of 30 | The number of distinct prime factors of 60 |

13. Jim's answer is C.
The Joe Bloggs response here, of course, is B. Let's determine the prime factors of 30 and 60:

$$30 = 2 \times 15 \qquad 60 = 2 \times 30$$
$$ = 2 \times 3 \times 5 \qquad = 2 \times 2 \times 15$$
$$ = 2 \times 2 \times 3 \times 5$$

Now, 30 has three distinct prime factors (2, 3, 5) and so does 60!

14 | x^2 | $(x + 1)^2$ |

14. Jim's answer is D.
The classic Joe Bloggs response here, of course, is B. The answer must be A, C, or D. Now, if we let x equal, say, 2, we get the following quantities:

x^2	$(x + 1)^2$
2^2	$(2 + 1)^2$
4	9

Since Column B is greater, the answer cannot be A or C. Only one choice remains: D. (If you had to prove this to yourself, try negative numbers.)

15 | The percent increase from 99 to 100 | The percent decrease from 100 to 99 |

15. Jim's answer is A.
The answer here requires your understanding of percentage changes, which is always based on the "starting" amount:

$$\frac{100 - 99}{99} \qquad \frac{100 - 99}{100}$$
$$\frac{1}{99} \qquad \frac{1}{100}$$

QUESTIONS	EXPLANATIONS

16 If $\dfrac{x + 2x + 3x}{2} = 6$, then $x =$

16. Jim's answer is 2.

$$\frac{x + 2x + 3x}{2} = 6$$

$$\frac{6x}{2} = 6$$

Grid it like this:

Remember that the first grid in question returns the difficulty meter to easy.

17 There are 24 fish in an aquarium. If $\dfrac{1}{8}$ of them are tetras and $\dfrac{2}{3}$ of the remaining fish are guppies, how many guppies are in the aquarium?

17. Jim's answer is 14.

Of the 24 fish, $\dfrac{1}{8}$ are tetras. Of the remaining 21 fish, $\dfrac{2}{3}$ are guppies.

Two thirds of 21 is 14.

Grid in like this:

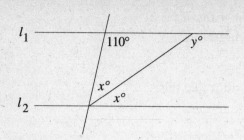

18 If l_1 is parallel to l_2 in the figure above, what is the value of y?

18. Jim's answer is 145.

Since the two lines are parallel, then $110 + 2x = 180$. Solving this equation for x, we get $x = 35$. Looking at the triangle, the missing angle (m) can be found by solving the equation $110 + x + m = 180$. Since $x = 35$, $m = 35$. Since $m + y = 180$ and $m = 35$, $y = 145$. Grid it like this:

```
1 4 5
```

19 The daily newspaper always follows a particular format. Each even-numbered page contains 6 articles and each odd-numbered page contains 7 articles. If todays paper has 36 pages, how many articles does it contain?

19. Jim's answer is 234.

Since every even-numbered page has 6 articles and every odd-numbered page has 7, there are 13 articles every two pages. A 36-page paper, then, would contain 18 such paired pages, or $18 \times 13 = 234$ articles. Grid in like this:

```
2 3 4
```

20 When n is divided by 5, the remainder is 4. When n is divided by 4, the remainder is 3. If $0 < n < 100$, what is one possible value of n?

20. Jim's answer is 19, 39, 59, 79 or 99.

The simplest way to solve this question would be to find values of n that satisfy the first condition, and then to check which of those also satisfy the second condition. So, let's find some numbers that leave a remainder of 4 when divided by 5:

9, 14, 19, 24, 29, . . .

That should be enough. Now, let's check which of these leaves a remainder of 3 when divided by 4.

$$9 \div 4 = 2 \text{ R } 1$$
$$14 \div 4 = 3 \text{ R } 2$$
$$19 \div 4 = 4 \text{ R } 3$$

Bingo. 19 is one acceptable response. Grid it like this:

21 If $x^2 = 16$ and $y^2 = 4$, what is the greatest possible value of $(x - y)^2$?

21. Jim's answer is 36.

If $x^2 = 16$, then $x = \pm 4$. If $y^2 = 4$, then $y = \pm 2$. To maximize $(x - y)^2$, we need to maximize the difference:

$$(4 - 2)^2 = 2^3 = 4$$
$$[4 - (-2)]^2 = 6^2 = 36$$
$$[(-4) - 2]^2 = (-6)^2 = 36$$
$$[(-4) - (-2)]^2 = (-2)^2 = 4$$

Thus, the maximum value of the expression is 36.

Grid it like this:

22 Segment *AB* is perpendicular to segment *BD*. Segment *AB* and segment *CD* bisect each other at point *x*. If *AB* = 8 and *CD* = 10, what is the length of *BD*?

22. Jim's answer is 3.
The first step is to draw a diagram, which requires some thought:

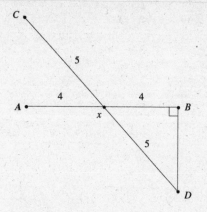

Using the Pythagorean theorem, we can calculate *BD*.

$(BD)^2 + (4)^2 = (5)^2$
$(BD)^2 + 16 = 25$
$(BD)^2 = 9$
$BD = 3$
Grid it like this:

23 At a music store, the price of a CD is three times the price of a cassette tape. If 40 CDs were sold for a total of $480, and the combined sales of CDs and cassette tapes totaled $600, how many cassette tapes were sold?

23. Jim's answer is 30.
Let's proceed step by step, starting with the easiest equations to solve. If 40 CDs equal $480, each one equals $12. Since this is three times the cost of a cassette tape, each cassette tape costs $4. Since $600 equals the CDs ($480) and the cassette tapes, the total cassette tape sales were $120. At $4 a cassette tape, 30 cassette tapes were sold.
Grid it like this:

24 At a certain high school, 30 students study French, 40 study Spanish, and 25 study neither. If there are 80 students in the school, how many study both French and Spanish?

24. Jim's answer is 15.
To solve this question, you must draw a Venn diagram. First draw a circle for the 30 students who study French.

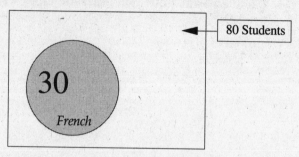

Then draw a circle that overlap the first circle for the students studying Spanish.

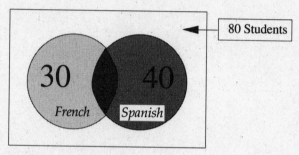

Since 25 students study neither, the overlap region must have 15 students.

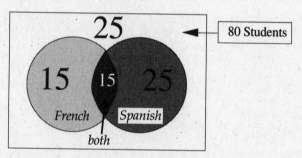

If you had no idea how to approach this question you should have been spending your time checking your work on the rest on the selection. Grid it like this:

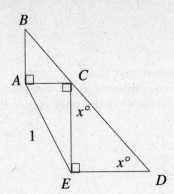

In the figure above, if $AE = 1$, what is the sum of the area of $\triangle ABC$ and the area of $\triangle CDE$?

25. Jim's answer is .5.

First, let's set up equations for the areas of the two triangles:

$(\frac{1}{2})(AC)(AB) + (\frac{1}{2})(CE)(ED)$

Since both triangles are isosceles, $AC = AB$ and $CE = ED$. Thus, the previous equation becomes

$(\frac{1}{2})(AC)^2 + \frac{1}{2}(CE)^2$

$\frac{1}{2}[(AC)^2 + (CE)^2]$

Now, using the Pythagorean theorem, we know that

$(AC)^2 + (CE)^2 = 1$

So the required areas are $\frac{1}{2}(1) = \frac{1}{2}$

Grid it like this:

SECTION 4

1 If it is true that morality cannot exist without religion, then does not the erosion of religion herald the ---- of morality?

(A) regulation
(B) basis
(C) belief
(D) collapse
(E) value

1. Pam's answer is D.
We're looking for a word along the lines of *erosion*; *collapse* is the only choice that fits.

2 Certain animal behaviors, such as mating rituals, seem to be ----, and therefore ---- external factors such as climate changes, food supply, or the presence of other animals of the same species.

(A) learned. .immune to
(B) innate. .unaffected by
(C) intricate. .belong to
(D) specific. .confused with
(E) memorized. .controlled by

2. Pam's answer is B.
The doctor here is *external factors*. If animal behaviors are *innate*, they would be relatively *unaffected by* external factors.

3 Shaken by two decades of virtual anarchy, the majority of people were ready to buy ---- at any price.

(A) order
(B) emancipation
(C) hope
(D) liberty
(E) enfranchisement

3. Pam's answer is A.
To answer this question, it helps to know what anarchy means. But even if we aren't sure what it means, we know that the majority have been "shaken" for two decades. So they'd be willing to buy peace. Choice C and D are saying the same thing, and miss the doctor. Choice E is way too difficult for an easy question. Anarchy, by the way, means lack of order.

4 As a person who combines care with ----, Marisa completed her duties with ---- as well as zeal.

(A) levity. .resignation
(B) geniality. .ardor
(C) vitality. .willingness
(D) empathy. .rigor
(E) enthusiasm. .meticulousness

4. Pam's answer is E.
The doctor here is *care* and *zeal*. Even if you don't know what zeal means, the second blank must reflect Marisa's being careful. D and E are the only choices that indicate her careful completion of duties. *Zeal* means enthusiasm, which locks in E as the answer. If you chose A or B, remember that this is not yet a difficult question that calls for difficult answers.

5 Her shrewd campaign managers were responsible for the fact that her political slogans were actually forgotten clichés revived and ---- with new meaning.

    (A) fathomed
    (B) instilled
    (C) foreclosed
    (D) instigated
    (E) foreshadowed

5. Pam's answer is B.
We know that her slogans were "forgotten clichés." Now, even if you aren't sure what a cliché is, you know that it has been "revived." The blank must be a positive word and something along the lines of *given*. Choice C is negative; choice E misses the doctor. Choice D makes absolutely no sense, and for a medium question is probably too difficult to be the answer anyway. Choice A is way off base.

6 The former general led his civilian life as he had his military life, with simplicity and ---- dignity.

    (A) benevolent
    (B) informal
    (C) austere
    (D) aggressive
    (E) succinct

6. Pam's answer is C.
We know the general's civilian life is simple, dignified, and military-like. The only blank that fits is C. Choices B and D miss the doctor. Choices A and E, if you weren't sure what they mean, are good guesses but wrong.

7 Although bound to impose the law, a judge is free to use his discretion to ---- the anachronistic barbarity of some criminal penalties.

    (A) mitigate
    (B) understand
    (C) condone
    (D) provoke
    (E) enforce

7. Pam's answer is A.
The doctor is *barbarity of some criminal penalties*. We're looking for a word that means avoid or lessen. Choices B and D miss the point completely. If you know what *condone* means, it also misses the point; if not, it's not a bad guess. Choice E is a Joe Bloggs trap that contradicts the doctor.

8 Henry viewed Melissa to be ----; she seemed to be against any position regardless of its merits.

    (A) heretical
    (B) disobedient
    (C) contrary
    (D) inattentive
    (E) harried

8. Pam's answer is C.
Melissa is "against any position regardless of its merits," so we know her to be argumentative. Choices B and D are way off base; choices A and E are too, though you may not know what they mean.

9 Dr. Schwartz's lecture on art, while detailed and scholarly, focused ---- on the pre modern; some students may have appreciated his specialized knowledge, but those with more ---- interests may have been disappointed.

    (A) literally. .medieval
    (B) completely. .pedantic
    (C) expansively. .technical
    (D) voluminously. .creative
    (E) exclusively. .comprehensive

9. Pam's answer is E.
The second blank is easier to attack. We know that Dr. Schwartz's lecture "focused . . . on the premodern." Who would this disappoint? Those who wanted either a more general lecture, or one on a different topic. Choice E is the only on that fits.

10 Only when one actually visits the ancient ruins of marvelous bygone civilizations does one truly appreciate the sad ---- of human greatness.

    (A) perspicacity
    (B) magnitude
    (C) artistry
    (D) transience
    (E) quiescence

10. Pam's answer is D.
You have to get the doctor on this one. Choices B and C are too easy to be correct on this very difficult question, and miss the doctor (*sad, bygone*). Choices A and E are excellent, though incorrect, guesses.

11 CAKE : DESSERT ::

    (A) coach : football
    (B) lawyer : jury
    (C) poet : writing
    (D) actor : troupe
    (E) pediatrician : doctor

11. Pam's answer is E.
A cake is a kind of dessert just as a pediatrician is a kind of doctor.

12 WEIGHTLIFTER : STRENGTH ::

    (A) goalie : skill
    (B) dancer : speed
    (C) marathoner : endurance
    (D) hiker : agility
    (E) fisherman : luck

12. Pam's answer is C.
A good weightlifter needs strength just as a good marathoner needs endurance.

13 BREEZE : HURRICANE ::

    (A) water : pebble
    (B) gulf : coast
    (C) eye : cyclone
    (D) sun : cloud
    (E) hill : mountain

13. Pam's answer is E.
A hurricane is a larger version of a breeze just as a mountain is a larger version of a hill.

14 IMMORTAL : DEATH ::

(A) anonymous : fame
(B) hopeless : situation
(C) vital : life
(D) indisputable : agreement
(E) daily : year

14. Pam's answer is A.
Immortal means without death just as anonymous means without fame.

15 TAPESTRY : THREAD ::

(A) pizza : pie
(B) mosaic : tiles
(C) ruler : divisions
(D) computer : switch
(E) car : engine

15. Pam's answer is B.
A tapestry is made up of threads just as a mosaic is made up of tiles. If you weren't sure what tapestry means, you'd have to work backward from the choices. For example, a car is powered by an engine, yet nothing is powered by thread. The other choices can be likewise eliminated.

16 LUBRICANT : FRICTION ::

(A) motor : electricity
(B) speed : drag
(C) insulation : heat
(D) adhesive : connection
(E) muffler : noise

16. Pam's answer is E.
A lubricant reduces friction just as a muffler reduces noise. If you weren't sure what lubricant means, you could have worked backward from the choices. For example, a motor runs on electricity, yet nothing runs on friction.

17 PARODY : IMITATION ::

(A) stanza : verse
(B) limerick : poem
(C) novel : book
(D) portrait : painting
(E) riddle : puzzle

17. Pam's answer is B.
A parody is a humorous imitation just as a limerick is a humorous poem. If you chose C, D, or E, your sentence may not have been specific enough.

18 COMET : TAIL ::

(A) traffic : lane
(B) missile : trajectory
(C) vessel : wake
(D) engine : fuel
(E) wave : crest

18. Pam's answer is C.
A comet is followed by a tail just as a vessel is followed by a wake. If you chose A or B, your sentence may not have been specific enough. We hope you also noticed that on a difficult question like this, all the wrong choices are too easy.

19 NEOLOGISM : LANGUAGE ::

(A) rhetoric : oratory
(B) syllogism : grammar
(C) innovation : technology
(D) iconography : art
(E) epistemology : philosophy

19. Pam's answer is C.
This is a tough question. Remember that Joe Bloggs is attracted to choices that remind him of the stem words, so B is a trap. Choices A, D, and E are good guesses that are wrong. By working backward, you could have answered this question. An *innovation* is a new development in *technology* while it is possible to have a new development in *language*: a *neologism*.

20 ADDENDUM : BOOK ::

(A) signature : letter
(B) vote : constitution
(C) codicil : will
(D) heading : folder
(E) stipulation : contract

20. Pam's answer is C.
Choices A and D are Joe Bloggs traps; choice B is unrelated. Choice E, though wrong, is a good guess. An *addendum* is an addition to a *book* just as a *codicil* is an addition to a *will*.

21 PENCHANT : INCLINED ::

(A) loathing : contemptuous
(B) abhorrence : delighted
(C) burgeoning : barren
(D) loss : incessant
(E) decision : predictable

21. Pam's answer is A.
Choices D and E are too easy and are also unrelated. A *penchant* means being very *inclined* just as a *loathing* means being very *contemptuous*.

22 VAGRANT : DOMICILE ::

(A) pagan : morals
(B) despot : leadership
(C) arsonist : fire
(D) exile : country
(E) telephone : ear

22. Pam's answer is D.
Working backwards was quite helpful here if you could not make a sentence with the stem words. An *exile* is a person without a *country*, and a *vagrant* is a person without a *domicile*. Answer choice A traps anyone who defines *pagan* incorrectly. Pagan and morals really have no relationship by definition.

23 MERITORIOUS : PRAISE ::

(A) captious : criticism
(B) kind : admiration
(C) questionable : response
(D) reprehensible : censure
(E) incredible : ecstasy

23. Pam's answer is D.
Joe Bloggs would pick B, so that could not be the answer. Choice C has no relationship, and E is too easy considering A and D have hard words. *Meritorious* means deserving of *praise*, and *reprehensible* means deserving of *censure*.

Questions 24-35 are based on the following passage.

The following passage is from a book written by a zoologist and published in 1986.

Line
(5)

The domestic cat is a contradiction. No other animal has developed such an intimate relationship with humanity, while at the same time demanding and getting such independent movement and action.

The cat manages to remain a tame animal because of the sequence of its upbringing. By living both with other cats (its mother and littermates) and with humans (the family that has adopted it) during its infancy and kittenhood, it becomes attached to and considers that it belongs to both species. It is like a child that grows up in a foreign country and as a consequence becomes bilingual. The young cat becomes bimental. It may be a cat physically but mentally it is both feline and human. Once it is fully adult, however, most of its responses are feline ones, and it has only one major reaction to its human owners. It treats them as pseudoparents. The reason is that they took over from the real mother at a sensitive stage of the kitten's development and went on giving it milk, solid food, and comfort as it grew up.

This is rather different from the kind of bond that develops between human and dog. The dog sees its human owners as pseudoparents, as does the cat. On that score the process of attachment is similar. But the dog has an additional link. Canine society is group-organized; feline society is not. Dogs live in packs with tightly controlled status relationships among the individuals. There are top dogs, middle dogs, and bottom dogs and under natural circumstances they move around together, keeping tabs on one another the whole time. So the adult pet dog sees its human family both as pseudoparents and as the dominant members of the pack, hence its renowned reputation for obedience and its celebrated capacity for loyalty. Cats do have a complex social organization, but they never hunt in packs. In the wild, most of their day is spent in solitary stalking. Going for a walk with a human, therefore, has no appeal for them. And as for "coming to heel" and learning to "sit" and "stay," they are simply not interested. Such maneuvers have no meaning for them.

So the moment a cat manages to persuade a human being to open a door (that most hated of human inventions), it is off and away without a backward glance. As it crosses the threshold, the cat becomes transformed. The kitten-of-human brain is switched off and the wildcat brain is clicked on. The dog, in such a situation, may look back to see if its

(10)

(15)

(20)

(25)

(30)

(35)

(40)

(45)

human packmate is following to join in the fun of exploring, but not the cat. The cat's mind has floated off into another, totally feline world, where strange bipedal* primates have no place.

Because of this difference between domestic cats and domestic dogs, cat-lovers tend to be rather different from dog-lovers. As a rule cat-lovers have a stronger personality bias toward working alone, independent of the larger group. Artists like cats; soldiers like dogs. The much-lauded "group loyalty" phenomenon is alien to both cats and cat-lovers. If you are a company person, a member of the gang, or a person picked for the squad, the chances are that at home there is no cat curled up in front of the fire. The ambitious Yuppie, the aspiring politician, the professional athlete, these are not typical cat-owners. It is hard to picture football players with cats in their laps—much easier to envisage them taking their dogs for walks.

Those who have studied cat-owners and dog-owners as two distinct groups report that there is also a gender bias. The majority of cat-lovers are female. This bias is not surprising in view of the division of labor evident in the development of human societies. Prehistoric males became specialized as group-hunters, while the females concentrated on food-gathering and childbearing. This difference contributed to a human male "pack mentality" that is far less marked in females. Wolves, the wild ancestors of domestic dogs, also became pack-hunters, so the modern dog has much more in common with the human male than with the human female.

The argument will always go on—feline self-sufficiency and individualism *versus* canine camaraderie and good-fellowship. But it is important to stress that in making a valid point I have caricatured the two positions. In reality there are many people who enjoy equally the company of both cats and dogs. And all of us, or nearly all of us, have both feline and canine elements in our personalities. We have moods when we want to be alone and thoughtful, and other times when we wish to be in the center of a crowded, noisy room.

(50)

(55)

(60)

(65)

(70)

(75)

(80)

(85)

(90) *bipedal: having two feet*

The questions should be done in the following order (remember, you should do general questions first and then vocabulary-in-context questions):

24 The primary purpose of the passage is to

(A) show the enmity that exists between cats and dogs

(B) advocate dogs as making better pets than cats

(C) distinguish the different characteristics of dogs and cats

(D) show the inferiority of dogs because of their dependent nature

(E) emphasize the role that human society plays in the personalities of domestic pets

24. Pam's answer is C.

From 2-2-2-F-ing the passage, you should have determined that the passage is about the difference between cats and dogs and their respective owners. If you picked B, you are probably letting your own love of dogs get in your way of understanding what the author is trying to say.

26 In line 17 the word *pseudoparents* means

(A) part-time parents that are only partially involved with their young

(B) individuals who act as parents of adults

(C) parents that neglect their young

(D) parents that have both the characteristics of humans and their pets

(E) adopted parents that aren't related to their young

26. Pam's answer is E.

Read a few lines after the word *pseudoparents*. Lines 17–21 suggest that owners are pseudoparents because "they took over from the real mother at a sensitive age of the kitten's development . . . ."

30 In line 60, *much-lauded* means

(A) vehemently argued

(B) overly discussed

(C) unnecessarily complicated

(D) typically controversial

(E) commonly praised

30. This is a vocabulary-in-context question in which you have to have some idea of what the word means. *Lauded* means praised, so E is Pam's answer. You can also eliminate C *unnecessarily complicated* because it would not fit into sentence from which "much lauded" is taken. Why would *group loyalty* be complicated?

QUESTIONS	EXPLANATIONS

25 According to the passage, the domestic cat can be described as

(A) a biped because it possesses the characteristics of animals with two feet

(B) a pseudopet because it can't really be tamed and will always retain its wild habits

(C) a contradiction because although it lives comfortably with humans, it refuses to be dominated by them

(D) a soldier because it is militant about preserving its independence

(E) a ruler because although it plays the part of a pet, it really dominates humans

25. To answer this question search through the passage for descriptions of the domestic cat. Since this is the first explicit question, Pam will most likely have put her answer in the beginning of the passage. Because of the general nature of the question, your best approach is to eliminate wrong answers.

Choice A is incorrect because cats don't have two feet.

Choice B is incorrect because domestic cats are tame.

Choice C is Pam's answer. Look at lines 1–4 (which you should already have read.)

Choice D is incorrect because cats aren't soldiers.

Choice E is incorrect because cats don't dominate humans. (Remember, you can use some outside knowledge here.)

27 The author suggests that an important difference between dogs and cats is that, unlike dogs, cats

(A) do not regard their owners as the leader of their social group

(B) obey mainly because of their obedient nature

(C) have a more creative nature

(D) do not have complex social organizations

(E) are not skilled hunters

27. Pam's answer is A.

If you look in lines 32–38, you find that "the adult pet dog sees its human family both as pseudoparents and as the dominant members of the pack, hence its renowned reputation for obedience and its celebrated capacity for loyalty. Cats . . . never hunt in packs."

28 It can be inferred from the passage that the social structure of dogs is

(A) flexible

(B) abstract

(C) hierarchical

(D) male dominated

(E) somewhat exclusive

28. Pam's answer is C.

Lines 29–30 suggest that the social structure of dogs is hierarchical.

QUESTIONS	EXPLANATIONS

29 Lines 39–43 are used to stress

(A) the laziness of cats that keeps them from being pack animals
(B) the ignorance of dogs, which makes them more obedient pets
(C) the antipathy that cats feel for humans
(D) a difference between cats and dogs that emphasizes the independent nature of cats
(E) the stubborn and complacent disposition of cats

29. Pam's answer is D.
    This question is asking what purpose lines 29–43 serve. In these lines, the author is emphasizing one of the differences between cats and dogs—that dogs are more willing to be trained and that cats are more independent.

31 The "ambitious Yuppie" mentioned in line 65 is an example of a person

(A) that is power hungry
(B) that craves virtue
(C) that is a stereotypical pet owner
(D) that has a weak personality
(E) that seeks group-oriented status

31. Pam's answer is E.
    To find the answer, you must read five lines before and five lines after the indicated line. The lines before line 65 indicate that a dog owner is more likely to be "a company person, a member of the gang, or a person picked for the squad." The lines after line 65 indicate that the ambitious Yuppie is probably not a cat owner (and thus probably a dog owner). From this we can infer that the ambitious Yuppie is one who seeks group-oriented status.

32 Paragraph 6 indicates that human females

(A) are more like dogs than cats
(B) developed independent roles that didn't require group behavior
(C) had to gather food because they were not strong enough to hunt
(D) are not good owners for the modern dog
(E) were negatively affected by the division of labor of human societies

32. Pam's answer is B.
    You can immediately eliminate choices C, D, and E because Pam would never say anything negative about women. To find Pam's answer you must look at lines 75–79. The author states that "this difference contributed to a human male 'pack mentality' that is far less marked in females."

QUESTIONS	**EXPLANATIONS**

4

33 The author uses lines 84–88 to

(A) show that the argument stated in the passage is ultimately futile
(B) disclaim glaring contradictions that are stated in the passage
(C) qualify the generalizations used to make the author's point
(D) ensure that the reader doesn't underestimate the crux of the passage
(E) highlight a difference between individualism and dependency

33. Pam's answer is C.
To answer this question, you have to know what the author means by "caricatured." A caricature is an exaggerated drawing. So the author is saying that he has exaggerated in the passage. He is thus qualifying some of the generalizations in the passage.

34 The last four sentences in the passage (lines 86–94) provide

(A) an example of the argument that has been made earlier
(B) a summary of the points made earlier
(C) a reason for the statements made earlier
(D) a modification of the position taken earlier
(E) a rebuttal to opposing views referred to earlier

34. Pam's answer is D.
This question is similar to question 33. It is clear from these lines that the author is backpedaling a little on his argument. Thus these sentences are a modification of the position taken earlier.

35 The passage as a whole does all of the following EXCEPT

(A) use a statistic
(B) make parenthetic statements
(C) use a simile
(D) restate an argument
(E) make a generalization

35. Pam's answer is C.
Although this is a general question and we normally do general questions first, it was saved for last because it is an EXCEPT question. The only way to do this question is to search the passage for each of the answer choices. The passage uses a statistic (lines 70–73), makes a parenthetic statement (lines 45–46), restates an argument (lines 84–86), and makes a generalization (The entire passage is one big generalization). Therefore, the answer must be C.

SECTION 5

1 If $2 + a = 2 - a$, then $a =$

   (A) -1
   (B) 0
   (C) 1
   (D) 2
   (E) 4

1. Jim's answer is B.
   This simple equation should present us with little difficulty, although beware: it is on precisely such questions that our guard comes down and we become careless!
$$2 + a = 2 - a$$
$$a = -a$$
$$2a = 0$$
$$a = 0$$

2 In which of the following patterns is the number of horizontal lines three times the number of vertical lines?

   (A)   (B)   (C)

   (D)   (E)

2. Jim's answer is D.
   If you missed this question, you either misread the question or miscounted the lines. Choice D has 6 horizontal lines and 2 vertical ones. Remember, horizontal means side to side, vertical means up and down.

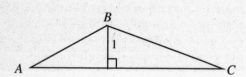

3 If $AC = 4$, what is the area of $\triangle ABC$ above?

   (A) $\dfrac{1}{2}$

   (B) 2

   (C) $\sqrt{7}$

   (D) 4

   (E) 8

3. Jim's answer is B.
   As the instructions to this section remind us, the area of a triangle is given by the formula:
$$A = \frac{1}{2}bh$$
Since the base is 4 and the height is 1, the area is 2.

QUESTIONS	EXPLANATIONS

4 If $\frac{4}{5}$ of $\frac{3}{4} = \frac{2}{5}$ of $\frac{x}{4}$, then $x =$

(A) 12

(B) 6

(C) 3

(D) $\frac{3}{2}$

(E) 1

4. Jim's answer is B.
Translating the word "of" as "times," we get the following equation:

$$\left(\frac{4}{5}\right)\left(\frac{3}{4}\right) = \left(\frac{2}{5}\right)\left(\frac{x}{4}\right)$$

$$\frac{3}{5} = \frac{2x}{20}$$

$60 = 10x$
$x = 6$

5 If $x + y = z$ and $x = y$, then all of the following are true EXCEPT

(A) $2x + 2y = 2z$

(B) $x - y = 0$

(C) $x - z = y - z$

(D) $x = \frac{z}{2}$

(E) $z - y = 2x$

5. Jim's answer is E.
With algebraic answer choices, we should plug in numbers. Let's let $x = y = 2$, which makes
$z = 4$. Plugging these values into the choices, and working from the outer choices toward the center, we'd get the following:
[Yes] (A) $2(2) + 2(2) = 2(4)$
[Yes] (B) $2 - 2 = 0$
[Yes] (C) $2 - 4 = 2 - 4$
[Yes] (D) $2 - \frac{4}{2}$
[No] (E) $4 - 2 = 2(2)$ False!
If you missed this question, you may not have used the EXCEPT trick. (see page 120).

5

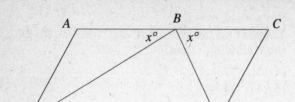

Note: Figure not drawn to scale.

6. In the figure above, *AC* || *ED*. If the length of *BD* = 3, what is the length of *BE*?

(A) 3
(B) 4
(C) 5
(D) $3\sqrt{3}$
(E) It cannot be determined from the information given.

6. Jim's answer is A.
Keep in mind that this figure is not drawn to scale. Since the *AC* || *ED*, we know that the following angles are equal:

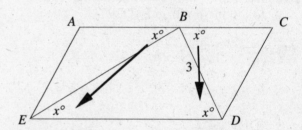

Since $\triangle EBD$ has two equal angles, the opposing sides are also equal. Therefore, *BE* = *BD* = 3.

7. $\dfrac{900}{10} + \dfrac{90}{100} + \dfrac{9}{1000} =$

(A) 90.09
(B) 90.099
(C) 90.909
(D) 99.09
(E) 999

7. Jim's answer is C.
If you missed this question, you should review decimal place values:

$\dfrac{900}{10} = 90$

$\dfrac{90}{100} = 0.9$

$\dfrac{9}{1000} = 0.009$

$$\begin{array}{r} 90 \\ +0.9 \\ +0.009 \\ \hline 90.909 \end{array}$$

8 Fifteen percent of the coins in a piggy bank are nickels and 5% are dimes. If there are 220 coins in the bank, how many are <u>not</u> nickels or dimes?

(A) 80
(B) 176
(C) 180
(D) 187
(E) 200

8. Jim's answer is B.
Twenty percent of the coins are either nickels or dimes, so 80% are neither. Eighty percent of 220 equals 176. Use your calculator!

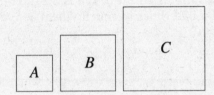

9 In the figure above, the perimeter of square A is $\frac{2}{3}$ the perimeter of square B, and the perimeter of square B is $\frac{2}{3}$ the perimeter of square C. If the area of square A is 16, what is the area of square C?

(A) 24
(B) 36
(C) 64
(D) 72
(E) 81

9. Jim's answer is E.
Estimating first, we'd notice that the area of square C is four or more times that of square A. We'd expect the area of B to be at least four times 16, or 64. That isn't the answer, of course, since we're just eyeballing the squares. This estimation does allow us to eliminate choices A and B as too far out of the ballpark. Anyway, if the area of square A is 16, the length of each side is 4 and the perimeter is 16. We are told that this is two thirds B's perimeter, which we can calculate

$$A = \frac{2}{3} B$$

$$16 = \frac{2}{3} B$$

$$\left(\frac{3}{2}\right) 16 = B$$

$$24 = B$$

Now that we know the perimeter of B, we can calculate the perimeter C:

$$B = \frac{2}{3} C$$

$$24 = \frac{2}{3} C$$

$$\left(\frac{3}{2}\right) (24) = C$$

$$36 = C$$

If the perimeter of C is 36, each side is 9 and so the area of C is 9^2 or 81. If you chose (B), you need to read the question more carefully.

QUESTIONS	EXPLANATIONS

10 A bakery uses a special flour mixture that contains corn, wheat, and rye in the ratio of 3:5:2. If a bag of the mixture contains 5 pounds of rye, how many pounds of wheat does it contain?

(A) 2
(B) 5
(C) 7.5
(D) 10
(E) 12.5

10. Jim's answer is E.
First, by estimation, we know that the mixture contains more wheat than rye; so wheat must be more than 5. So let's eliminate choices A and B.
Use the ratio box.

3	5	2	10
	2.5	2.5	
	7.5	5	

Since the ratio of wheat to rye is 5:2, there is two and a half times as much wheat as rye: $(2.5)(5) = 12.5$

11 If $a^2b = 12^2$, and b is an odd integer, then a could be divisible by all of the following EXCEPT

(A) 3
(B) 4
(C) 6
(D) 9
(E) 12

11. Jim's answer is D.
Note first that this is an EXCEPT question. Now, since $a^2b = 12^2$, and b is an odd integer, let's see what we can come up with. The first value for b that occurs to us is 1, so we get the following:
$a^2b = 12^2$
$(a^2)(1) = 12^2$
$a^2 = 12^2$
$a = 12$
If a equals 12, it is divisible by 1, 2, 3, 4, 6, and 12. So the only choice that remains is D.

12 A coin was flipped 20 times and came up heads 10 times and tails 10 times. If the first and last flips were both heads, what is the greatest number of consecutive heads that could have occurred?

(A) 1
(B) 2
(C) 8
(D) 9
(E) 10

12. Jim's answer is D.
If the first and last flips were heads, we could have 9 consecutive heads followed by 10 consecutive tails followed by the final head.

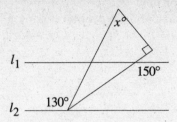

13 If l_1 is parallel to l_2 in the figure above, what is the value of x?

(A) 20
(B) 50
(C) 70
(D) 80
(E) 90

13. Jim's answer is C.
Estimating first, x is less than 90 and more than 20. So we can eliminate choices A and E. Now let's examine the figure:
Since $l_1 \parallel l_2$, $130 + y = 150$ and $y = 20$.
If $y = 20$, and $x + y + 90 = 180$, $x = 70$.

14 Which of the following must be true?

I. The sum of two consecutive integers is odd.
II. The sum of three consecutive integers is even.
III. The sum of three consecutive integers is a multiple of 3.

(A) I only
(B) II only
(C) I and II only
(D) I and III only
(E) I, II, and III

14. Jim's answer is D.
We note before we begin that the question asks for what <u>must</u> be true. Let's start with the first option:
   I. $2 + 3 = 5$
           $3 + 4 = 7$
Option I must be true. Eliminate choice B.
   II. $2 + 3 + 4 = 9$
Option II is false. Eliminate choices C and E. We still need to check the third option:
   III. $2 + 3 + 4 = 9$
           $3 + 4 + 5 = 12$
           $4 + 5 + 6 = 15$
It's a safe bet III must be true.

QUESTIONS	EXPLANATIONS

5

15 Which of the following is equal to .064?

(A) $\left(\dfrac{1}{80}\right)^2$

(B) $\left(\dfrac{8}{100}\right)^2$

(C) $\left(\dfrac{1}{8}\right)^2$

(D) $\left(\dfrac{2}{5}\right)^3$

(E) $\left(\dfrac{8}{10}\right)^3$

15. Jim's answer is D.
This is a fairly simple problem using a calculator.

16 If the average (arithmetic mean) of four distinct positive integers is 11, what is the greatest possible value of any one of the integers?

(A) 35
(B) 38
(C) 40
(D) 41
(E) 44

16. Jim's answer is B.
With average (mean) problems, the first step is usually to compute the sum. If the average of four numbers is 11, the sum can be calculated as follows:

$$\text{average} = \frac{\text{sum}}{\#}$$

$$11 = \frac{\text{sum}}{4}$$

$$44 = \text{sum}$$

If the sum of the numbers is 44, we can now determine the greatest possible value of any one of them. Now, to determine the greatest possible number we should make the other numbers as small as possible. We'd like to make the numbers all 1, since they must be positive, but the problem states they are distinct. So the smallest we can make them is 1, 2, and 3. The greatest possible value of 44 minus these numbers, or 38. If you overlooked the word "distinct," you probably answered D.

For $x = 0$, $x = 1$, and $x = 2$,
Set A = $\{x,\ x + 3,\ 3x,\ x^2\}$.

17 What is the mode of Set A?

(A) 0
(B) 1
(C) 2
(D) 2.5
(E) 3

17. Jim's answer is A.
Plugging in was the appropriate first step.
When $x = 0$, A = $\{0,3,0,0\}$
when $x = 1$, A = $\{1,4,3,1\}$
and when $x = 2$, A = $\{2,5,6,4\}$
Thus, set A has 12 elements—3 of which equal 0. Choice A is the mode of the set.

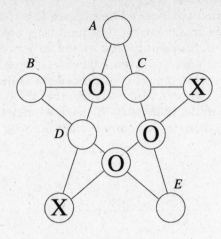

18. If the figure above is filled in so that each row of four circles contains two circles marked with an X and two circles marked with an O, which circle must be marked with an X?

(A) *A*
(B) *B*
(C) *C*
(D) *D*
(E) *E*

18. Jim's answer is E.
This problem is probably best approached by the brute force method of trial and error. (On the SAT, with the clock ticking away, you'll often find that you don't have the time to be logical.) Eventually you'd discover that circle *E* is the answer. If you were logical, you'd notice that rows *BE* and *AE* are identical. That being the case, circle *A* equals circle *B*, and circle *D* equals circle *C*. The odd man out is circle *E*.

19. At the beginning of 1992, the population of Rockville was 204,000 and the population of Springfield was 216,000. If the population of each city increased by exactly 20% in 1992, how many more people lived in Springfield than in Rockville at the end of 1992?

(A) 9,600
(B) 10,000
(C) 12,000
(D) 14,400
(E) 20,000

19. Jim's answer is D.
Take out your calculator:
216,000 + 20% of 216,000 = 259,200
204,000 + 20% of 204,000 = <u>244,800</u>
 14,400
Another route to the answer is to take the difference immediately (216,000 − 204,000 = 12,000) and then to increase that by 20%. On a calculator either solution is equally effective.

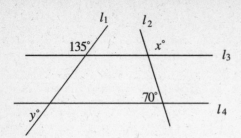

Note: Figure not drawn to scale.

20 If four lines intersect as shown in the figure above, $x + y =$

(A) 65
(B) 110
(C) 155
(D) 205
(E) It cannot be determined from the information given.

21 S is the set of all positive numbers n such that $n < 100$ and $\sqrt{n}$ is an integer. What is the median value of the members of set S?

(A) 5

(B) 5.5

(C) 25

(D) 50

(E) 99

20. Jim's answer is C.
We trust you noticed that choice D is too simple an answer for this question since it can be arrived at by adding the only two numbers we are given. Likewise, choice E is another Joe Bloggs choice. Looking at the figure, we should not assume that the lines are parallel (did you?). Instead, we must use vertical angles to compute the following values:

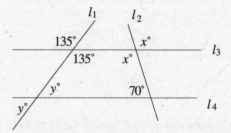

Since the sum of a quadrilateral's interior angles is 360°, we get the following equation:
$135 + x + 70 + y = 360$
$205 + x + y = 360$
$x + y = 155$
By the way, although the figure is not drawn to scale, a brief inspection reveals that the angles as drawn cannot be too far off. So we could have estimated x and y, thereby eliminating A and A as too small.

21. Jim's answer is C.
First, we need to compute all possible values of n:

$\sqrt{n}$	n
1	1
2	4
3	9
4	16
5	25
6	36
7	49
8	64
9	81

Now, careful! The median value for $\sqrt{n}$ is 5, but the median value for n is 25.

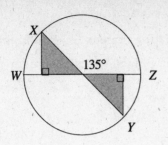

22 If segment *WZ* and segment *XY* are diameters with lengths of 12, what is the area of the shaded region?

(A) 36
(B) 30
(C) 18
(D) 12
(E) 9

22. Jim's answer is C.
Let's see what we can deduce from the diagram:

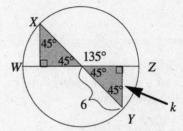

The two isosceles triangles are equal, each with sides of length *k*. Now, the area of each triangle is $\frac{1}{2}k^2$, for a total of k^2. Using the Pythagorean theorem, we get the following equation:
$k^2 + k^2 = 36$
$k^2 = 18$

23 If *c* is positive, what percent of 3*c* is 9?

(A) $\frac{c}{100}\%$

(B) $\frac{c}{3}\%$

(C) $\frac{9}{c}\%$

(D) 3%

(E) $\frac{300}{c}\%$

23. Jim's answer is E.
Plug in 3 for *c*. The question is now asking what percent of 9 is 9. The answer would be 100. Plugging in 3 to give a value of 100. Therefore *E* is the answer. Remember, plugging in good numbers will make your life much easier!

24 Line A has a slope of $-\dfrac{3}{2}$. If points $(-2, 6)$ and $(m, -9)$ are on line A, then $m =$

(A) 3
(B) 4
(C) 6
(D) 8
(E) 12

24. Jim's answer is D.

The formula for slope is $\dfrac{y_2 - y_1}{x_2 - x_1}$. Plugging in our given points, we can solve for x.

$$\dfrac{6 - (-9)}{-2 - m} = \dfrac{-3}{2}$$

$$\dfrac{15}{(-2 - m)} = \dfrac{-3}{2}$$

$$30 = (-3)(-2 - m)$$
$$-10 = -2 - m$$
$$-8 = -m$$
$$8 = m$$

Ugh. Well, what did you expect for problem 24?

25 A researcher found that a certain student's score on each of a series of tests could be predicted using the formula

$$P = \dfrac{310T + (LT)^2}{100}$$

where P is the number of points scored on the test, T is the number of hours spent studying, L is the number of hours of sleep the night
before the test, and where $P \leq 100$. If, before a particular test, this student spent no more than 10 hours studying, what is the least number of hours of sleep she should get if she wants to score at least 80 points?

(A) 6
(B) 7
(C) $\sqrt{56}$
(D) 8
(E) $\sqrt{69}$

25. Jim's answer is B.
Substituting 10 for T and 80 for P, we get the following equation to solve:

$$80 = \dfrac{(3100) + (10L)^2}{100}$$

$$8000 = 3100 + (10L)^2$$
$$4900 = 100L^2$$
$$7 = L$$

Questions 1-13 are based on the following passages.

In Passage 1, the author presents his view of the early years of the silent film industry. In Passage 2, the author draws on her experiences as a mime to generalize about her art. (A mime is a performer who without speaking, entertains through gesture, facial expression, and movement.)

Passage 1

Talk to those people who first saw films when they were silent, and they will tell you the experience was magic. The silent film had
Line extraordinary powers to draw members of an
(5) audience into the story, and an equally potent capacity to make their imaginations work. It required the audience to become engaged—to supply voices and sound effects. The audience was the final, creative contributor to the process
(10) of making a film.

The finest films of the silent era depended on two elements that we can seldom provide today—a large and receptive audience and a well-orchestrated score. For the audience, the
(15) fusion of picture and live music added up to more than the sum of the respective parts.

The one word that sums up the attitude of the silent filmmakers is *enthusiasm*, conveyed most strongly before formulas took shape and
(20) when there was more room for experimentation. This enthusiastic uncertainty often resulted in such accidental discoveries as new camera or editing techniques. Some films experimented with players; the 1915 film
(25) *Regeneration*, for example, by using real gangsters and streetwalkers, provided startling local color. Other films, particularly those of Thomas Ince, provided tragic endings as often as films by other companies supplied happy
(30) ones.

Unfortunately, the vast majority of silent films survive today in inferior prints that no longer reflect the care that the original technicians put into them. The modern versions of silent films
(35) may appear jerky and flickery, but the vast picture palaces did not attract four to six thousand people a night by giving them eyestrain. A silent film depended on its visuals; as soon as you degrade those, you lose elements
(40) that go far beyond the image on the surface. The acting in silents was often very subtle, very restrained, despite legends to the contrary.

Passage 2

Mime opens up a new world to the beholder, but it does so insidiously, not by
(45) purposely injecting points of interest in the manner of a tour guide. Audiences are not unlike visitors to a foreign land who discover that the modes, manners, and thoughts of its inhabitants are not meaningless oddities, but
(50) are sensible in context.

I remember once when an audience seemed perplexed at what I was doing. At first, I tried to gain a more immediate response by using slight exaggerations. I soon realized that these
(55) actions had nothing to do with the audience's understanding of the character. What I had believed to be a failure of the audience to respond in the manner I expected was, in fact, only their concentration on what I was doing;
(60) they were enjoying a gradual awakening—a slow transference of their understanding from their own time and place to one that appeared so unexpectedly before their eyes. This was evidenced by their growing response to
(65) succeeding numbers.

Mime is an elusive art, as its expression is entirely dependent on the ability of the performer to imagine a character and to re-create that character for each performance. As a
(70) mime, I am a physical medium, the instrument upon which the figures of my imagination play their dance of life. The individuals in my audience also have responsibilities—they must be alert collaborators. They cannot sit back,
(75) mindlessly complacent, and wait to have their emotions titillated by mesmeric musical sounds or visual rhythms or acrobatic feats, or by words that tell them what to think. Mime is an art that, paradoxically, appeals both to those
(80) who respond instinctively to entertainment and to those whose appreciation is more analytical and complex. Between these extremes lie those audiences conditioned to resist any collaboration with what is played before them;
(85) and these the mime must seduce despite themselves. There is only one way to attack those reluctant minds—take them unaware! They will be delighted at an unexpected pleasure.

To crack a double passage, 2-2-2-F the first passage first, and then answer the questions that pertain to it. Then 2-2-2-F the second passage and answer the rest of the questions. In this case, the first seven questions pertain to the first passage. For more information on how to attack these passages, see page 96.

1 Lines 14–16 of passage 1 indicate that

(A) music was the most important element of silent films
(B) silent films rely on a combination of music and image in affecting an audience
(C) the importance of music in silent film has been overestimated
(D) live music compensated for the poor quality of silent film images
(E) no film can succeed without a receptive audience

1. Pam's answer is B.
Lines 14–16 indicate that the combination of music and pictures created something that was truly spectacular and affecting.

2 The "formulas" mentioned in line 19 of the passage most probably refer to

(A) movie theaters
(B) use of real characters
(C) standardized film techniques
(D) the fusion of disparate elements
(E) contemporary events

2. Pam's answer is C.
Do this question as if it were a sentence completion: "conveyed most strongly before —— took shape and when there was more room for experimentation. This enthusiastic uncertainty. . ." The word in the blank is the opposite of uncertainty. Therefore, the formulas must mean standardized film techniques. The remainder of the paragraph provides examples of experimentation with film techniques.

3 The author uses the phrase "enthusiastic uncertainty" in line 21 to suggest that the filmmakers were

(A) excited to be experimenting in an undefined area
(B) delighted at the opportunity to study new acting formulas
(C) optimistic in spite of the obstacles that faced them
(D) eager to challenge existing conventions
(E) eager to please but unsure of what the public wanted

3. Pam's answer is A.
The filmmakers' enthusiastic uncertainty led to "accidental discoveries as new camera or editing techniques." Thus, the actors were excited to be trying new things. If you picked D, you went a bit too far. The filmmakers' enthusiasm was conveyed most strongly before there were conventions to challenge.

QUESTIONS	EXPLANATIONS

4 The author uses the phrase "but the . . . eyestrain" (lines 33–35) in order to

(A) indicate his disgust with the incompetence of early film technicians
(B) suggest that audiences today perceive silent films incorrectly
(C) convey his regret about the decline of the old picture palaces
(D) highlight the pitfalls of the silent movie era
(E) argue for the superiority of modern film technology over that of silent movies

4. Pam's answer is B.
In the indicated lines, the author is stating that silent films are today perceived as jerky and flickery because of the inferior prints. But the author contends that huge crowds would not go to see such films. Therefore the films must have been different before.

5 The word *legends* in line 39 most nearly means

(A) arguments
(B) symbolism
(C) propaganda
(D) movie stars
(E) misconceptions

5. Pam's answer is E.
Attack this problem like a sentence completion. The last sentence reads "The acting in silents was often very subtle, very restrained, despite —— to the contrary." A word that would fit in here would be "false ideas."

6 The last sentence of passage 1 implies that

(A) the stars of silent movies have been criticized for overacting
(B) many silent film actors became legends in their own time
(C) silent film techniques should be studied by filmmakers today
(D) visual effects defined the silent film
(E) many silent films that exist today are of poor quality

6. Pam's answer is A.
From the last sentence of the passage, we can figure out that the acting was considered by some people as unrestrained.

7 The word *restrained* (line 39) most nearly means

(A) sincere
(B) dramatic
(C) understated
(D) inexpressive
(E) consistent

7. Pam's answer is C.
Do this problem as if it were a sentence completion. The acting was "often very subtle, very ——." The word *restrained* cannot mean sincere or dramatic, because these words do not express subtleties. The word *restrained* means held back; acting that is held back is understated. Thus the answer is C. Answer choice D was too extreme in this case.

8 The author mentions the incident in lines 47–59 in order to imply that

(A) the audience's lack of response was a positive sign and reflected their captivated interest in the performance

(B) she was forced to resort to stereotypes in order to reach an audience that was otherwise unattainable

(C) exaggeration is an essential part of mime because it allows the forums used to be fully expressed

(D) her audience, though not initially appearing knowledgeable, had a good understanding of the subtlety of mime

(E) although vocalization is not necessary in mime, it is sometimes helpful for slower audiences

8. Pam's answer is A.
If you look carefully in lines 52–58, you will see that the author was explaining that what she at first thought was "a failure of the audience to respond . . . was, in fact, only their concentration . . ." If you picked D, you were on the right track; however, the author seems to believe that some people can get pleasure out of the art of mime by responding instinctively (line 73).

9 . Lines 47–59 indicate that the author of passage 2 and the silent filmmakers of passage 1 were similar because

(A) neither used many props

(B) both conveyed universal truths by using sophisticated technology

(C) for both, trial and error was a part of the learning process

(D) both used visual effects and dialogue

(E) both had a loyal following

9. Pam's answer is C.
This is a question that asks you to know information about both passages. You should have just looked at the lines in question in answering question 8. The author in the second passage is experimenting, trying to find the best way to reach the audience. The other answers are all aspects that apply to only one of the art forms.

10 The sentence "As a . . . life" (lines 63–65) suggests that the author of passage 2 feels mimes

(A) cannot control the way audiences interpret their characters

(B) must suspend their own identities in order to successfully portray their characters

(C) have to resist outside attempts to define their acting style

(D) should focus on important events in the lives of specific characters

(E) know the limitations of performances that do not incorporate either music or speech

10. Pam's answer is B.
The sentence in question refers to the mime as "a physical medium." In this case, a medium is the forum in which an artist works. For example a painter is said to use the medium of canvas. Because the mime is a physical medium upon which "the figures of my imagination play their dance of life," she is allowing her characters to figuratively take over her body. Hence B is correct.

QUESTIONS	EXPLANATIONS

11 Which of the following pieces of information makes mime and silent film seem less similar?

(A) Vaudeville and theatrical presentations were also popular forms of entertainment during the silent film era.
(B) Silent films presented both fictional drama and factual information.
(C) Silent film sometimes relied on captions to convey dialogue to the audience.
(D) Musicians working in movie theaters were usually employed for long periods of time.
(E) Many of the characters in silent films gained wide popularity among movie-goers.

11. Pam's answer is C.
The key similarity between the two passages, is that both describe communication that happens without words. If silent films actually used words to communicate information, then mime and silent films are not as similar.

12 Passages 1 and 2 are similar in that both are mainly concerned with

(A) the use of special effects
(B) differences among dramatic styles
(C) the visual aspects of performance
(D) the suspension of disbelief in audiences
(E) nostalgia for a bygone era

12. Pam's answer is C.
This question can be answered using the process of elimination.

(A) Mimes don't use special effects.
(B) Neither talks about the difference between dramatic styles.
(D) The mime passage discusses the suspension of disbelief, the silent film passage does not.
(E) Only the silent film passage is concerned with nostalgia for a bygone era.

13 Which of the following is an element that figures in the success of the dramatic arts described in both passages?

(A) A successful combination of different dramatic styles
(B) The exaggeration of certain aspects of a character
(C) The incorporation of current events in the narrative
(D) High audience attendance
(E) The active participation of the audience

13. Pam's answer is E.
According to the author, both mime and silent film require the participation of the audience. See lines 12–13 and lines 65–67.

SECTION 7

Price of Buttons in Store X	
Color	Price
Black	$2 per 5 buttons
Blue	$2 per 6 buttons
Brown	$3 per 8 buttons
Orange	$4 per 12 buttons
Red	$4 per 7 buttons

1 In Store X, which color button costs the most per individual unit?

(A) Black
(B) Blue
(C) Brown
(D) Orange
(E) Red

1. Jim's answer is E.
This is an excellent calculator question.

2 Which of the following numbers can be written in the form $6k + 1$, where k is a positive integer?

(A) 70
(B) 71
(C) 72
(D) 73
(E) 74

2. Jim's answer is D.
To answer this just start plugging in values of k until you get into the 70–74 range:
$6(12) + 1 = 73$

QUESTIONS	EXPLANATIONS

3 $\left(\dfrac{4}{5}\times 3\right)\left(\dfrac{3}{4}\times 5\right)\left(\dfrac{5}{3}\times 4\right) =$

(A) 1
(B) 3
(C) 6
(D) 20
(E) 60

3. Jim's answer is E.
A calculator might actually slow you down on this question. Instead, simply reduce the expression before calculation

$= \left(\dfrac{2}{5}\times 3\right)\left(\dfrac{3}{4}\times 5\right)\left(\dfrac{5}{3}\times 4\right)$

$= \dfrac{4\cdot 3\cdot \cancel{3}\cdot \cancel{5}\cdot 5\cdot \cancel{4}}{\cancel{3}\cdot \cancel{5}\cdot \cancel{4}}$

$= 60$

4 For which of the following values of x is $\dfrac{x^2}{x^3}$ the LEAST?

(A) 1
(B) –1
(C) –2
(D) –3
(E) –4

4. Jim's answer is B.
Again, before you reach for your calculator, reduce the expression:

$\dfrac{x^2}{x^3} = \dfrac{\cancel{x}\cdot \cancel{x}}{\cancel{x}\cdot \cancel{x}\cdot x} = \dfrac{1}{x}$

then simply plug in each choice; $\dfrac{1}{-1}$ is the least value. If you selected E you didn't work out each choice.

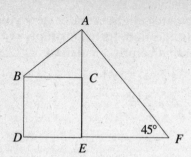

5 If the area of square *BCED* = 25, and the area of △*ABC* = 10, what is the length of *EF*?

(A) 7
(B) 8
(C) 9
(D) 10
(E) 14

5. Jim's answer is C.
First, we can estimate. Since square *BCED* has an area of 25, *DE* equals 5 and *EF* looks to be less than twice *DE*, or in the 7–9 range. Thus, we can eliminate D and E.

Now, we're looking for the length of *EF*. Since angle *AEF* is a right angle, angle *EAF* must be 45°. So we know that *AE* = *EF*.

We know that the area of triangle *ABC* is 10, and that its base (*BC*) is 5. Using the formula for area, we especially can calculate *AC*:

$A = \frac{1}{2}bh$

$10 = (\frac{1}{2}) (5) (h)$

$4 = h$

So *AE* = *EF* = (5 + 4) = 9.

6 The Wilsons drove 450 miles in each direction to Grandmother's house and back again. If their car gets 25 miles per gallon and their cost for gasoline was $1.25 per gallon for the trip to Grandmother's but $1.50 per gallon for the return trip, how much <u>more</u> money did they spend for gasoline returning from Grandmother's than they spent going to Grandmother's?

(A) $2.25
(B) $4.50
(C) $6.25
(D) $9.00
(E) $27.00

6. Jim's answer is B.
First, let's calculate how many gallons are consumed in each direction:

$\frac{450}{25} = 18$

Now each of the 18 gallons cost us $ 0.25 more returning than going.
(18) (0.25) = $4.50

7 If the average measure of two angles in a parallelogram is $y°$, what is the average degree measure of the other two angles?

(A) $180 - y$

(B) $180 - \dfrac{y}{2}$

(C) $360 - 2y$

(D) $360 - y$

(E) y

7. Jim's answer is A.
Let's begin by drawing a parallelogram and plugging in a number for y, say 50:

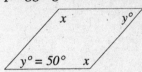

Since there are 360° in a quadrilateral, we know that $2x + 100° = 360°$; or $x = 130°$. So, we're looking for the choice that gives us 130 when
$y = 50°$. We simply plug 50 into the answer choices until we find our answer.

8 A swimming pool with a capacity of 36,000 gallons originally contained 9,000 gallons of water. At 10:00 A.M. water begins to flow in at a constant rate. If the pool is exactly three-fourths full at 1:00 P.M. on the same day and the water continues to flow in at the same rate, what is the earliest time when the pool will be completely full?

(A) 1:40 P.M.
(B) 2:00 P.M.
(C) 2:30 P.M.
(D) 3:00 P.M.
(E) 3:30 P.M.

8. Jim's answer is C.
Let's start by drawing a picture of the situation.

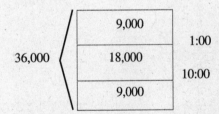

We know that by 1:00 the pool is three fourths full. Three fourths of 36,000 is 27,000. Since we started with 9,000 gallons, we added 18,000 gallons in 3 hours, or 6,000 gallons per hour. To fill the remaining 9,000 gallons at this rate will take 1 1/2 hours (9,000 ÷ 6,000). One and a half hours later would be 2:30.

QUESTIONS | EXPLANATIONS

9 On a map, 1 centimeter represents 6 kilometers. A square on the map with a perimeter of 16 centimeters represents a region with what <u>area</u>?

(A) 64 km^2
(B) 96 km^2
(C) 256 km^2
(D) 576 km^2
(E) 8,216 km^2

9. Jim's answer is D.
This is a tricky question. The answer can't be as easy as 96(6.16) or 256 (16^2).
Let's draw a picture:

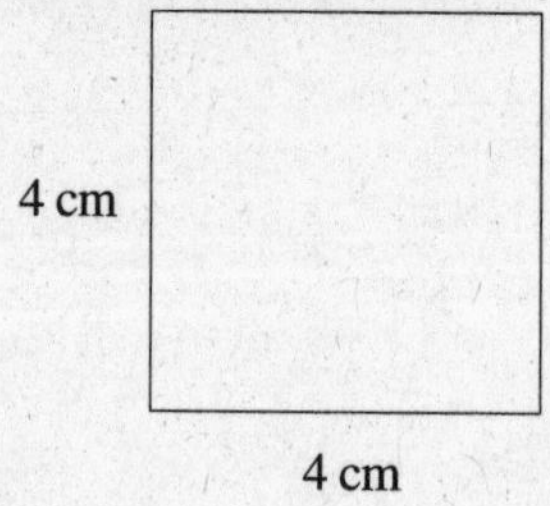
4 cm
4 cm

since 1 centimeter equals 6 kilometers, 4 centimeters equals 24 kilometers:

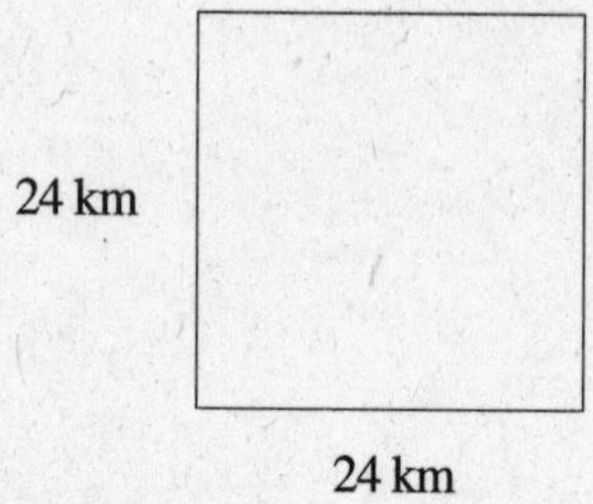
24 km
24 km

The area of this regions 24^4 or 576.

10 If $4 < a < 7 < b < 9$, then which of the following best defines $\frac{a}{b}$?

(A) $\frac{4}{9} < \frac{a}{b} < 1$

(B) $\frac{4}{9} < \frac{a}{b} < \frac{7}{9}$

(C) $\frac{4}{7} < \frac{a}{b} < \frac{7}{9}$

(D) $\frac{4}{7} < \frac{a}{b} < 1$

(E) $\frac{4}{7} < \frac{a}{b} < \frac{9}{7}$

10. Jim's answer is A.
We're looking for the range of the fraction $\frac{a}{b}$, from its minimum to its maximum value. The maximum value $\frac{a}{b}$ would be when a is as large as possible and b is as small as possible. Thus, $\frac{a}{b}$ must be less than $\frac{7}{7}$. Eliminate choices B, C, and E. At the extreme, $\frac{a}{b}$ achieves its maximum value when a is as small as possible and b is as large as possible. Thus, $\frac{a}{b}$ must be greater than $\frac{4}{9}$.

Appendix 1

The New SAT

After promising dramatic reforms in the SAT for several years, the Educational Testing Service and the College Board have finally revised the nation's leading college-entrance examination. The changes took effect in the spring of 1994. You've probably read about these changes in the newspaper, or heard about them from a guidance counselor. If you've already taken or prepared for an older form of the SAT or PSAT and are planning to take the test again, you may be worried that ETS has changed the rules in the middle of the game.

Well, ETS has changed the rules, but you'll probably discover that for the most part the new rules actually work in your favor. The bulk of the test is exactly the same as it has always been, but on the whole the test is even easier to crack. Still, the changes are mostly minor. You'll notice differences when you take the new test, but you won't feel that you've landed on an alien planet.

Even so, you're going to need to pay attention. In order to do well on any standardized test, you need to know what you're up against before your start. That's doubly true on the new SAT. Last year's guides and preparation materials are now out of date. If you want to do well on the new SAT, you're going to have to learn what it's all about.

WHAT HAS CHANGED?

Although you'll still have to answer analogy items in the verbal sections and quantitative comparison items in the math sections, other aspects of the test have changed. Here's a summary of the most important changes, and their significance for you.

1. *The Name:* What used to be called simply the SAT is now called SAT-I: Reasoning Tests. (In this book, we refer to it simply as the SAT.) What used to be called Achievement Tests are now called SAT-II: Subject Tests. The PSAT is still called the PSAT. In addition, *SAT* doesn't stand for Scholastic Aptitude Test anymore; it now stands for Scholastic Assessment Test. The old test was supposed to test your scholastic aptitude; the new test is supposed to assess something that you aren't supposed to refer to as aptitude anymore.

   The name changes are meaningless.

2. *The TSWE:* Between 1974 and 1993, the SAT contained a thirty-minute section called the Test of Standard Written English (TSWE). It didn't count toward your SAT score, and colleges weren't supposed to use it in making admissions decisions, although they sometimes did—usually in ways that didn't do test takers any good. Now the TSWE has joined eight-track tapes, disco, and mutton-chop sideburns in the Smithsonian Institution's permanent collection of dumb stuff from the seventies.

The death of the TSWE is good news.

3. *The Time:* The SAT used to be a three-hour, six-section test. Now SAT-I is a three-hour, seven-section test. The thirty minutes that used to be devoted to the TSWE have been turned into a fifteen-minute math section and a fifteen-minute verbal section. (The five other sections last thirty minutes each.) The test still has an experimental section, which is used to try out new questions and to provide a statistical benchmark in comparing tests from different years. ETS and the College Board say that adding time to the verbal and math sections has made the new SAT less "speeded" than the old SAT was; that is, they say you won't have to hurry as much. Still, most if not all of your "extra" time will be eaten up by item types that are more time-consuming to answer.

The change in timing will not affect you.

4. *Antonyms:* The old SAT verbal sections used to contain quite a few antonym items—items in which you were given one word and asked to pick its opposite from among five choices. Now these items are gone. If you have a big, solid vocabulary, you will no doubt regret the passing of antonyms, but everyone else should be happy, because antonym items were hard to crack: you either knew the words or you didn't.

For most test takers, the disappearance of antonyms is good news.

5. *Sentence Completion:* Some sentence completion items on the new SAT are a bit shorter than their predecessors. As in the past, sentence completions mainly test your vocabulary.

The change in the length of sentence completions will not affect you.

6. *Reading Comprehension*: ETS now calls reading comp critical reading, in an effort to make teachers and college admissions officers think the new test measures more important skills than the old one did. ETS says the new passages are meant to be more "engaging," and to a certain extent they are; fewer of them seem to have been drawn from ETS's vast library of the World's Most Boring Books. There are fewer passages on the test, but each one is somewhat longer and is followed by more questions. In addition, each passage is preceded by a brief introductory paragraph that will help you figure out what the heck is going on. All in all, critical reading is more coachable than reading comp ever was.

The changes in critical reading are a good thing.

7. *Double Passages:* The fifteen-minute verbal section on your SAT will contain a pair of related critical reading passages followed by thirteen multiple-choice questions. In each pair of passages, the second passage will usually support or rebut opinions expressed in the first, and you will have to sort things out in order to answer two or three of the questions. (The other questions are based on only one passage or the other.) These passages are no different from single passages. We have developed good techniques to handle them.

Double passages are no big deal.

8. *Critical Reading Vocabulary:* ETS has added some straight vocabulary items to critical reading questions, to make up for the elimination of antonym items. Instead of being asked merely to infer something about the boring opinions of the author of a boring passage, you may also be asked for the plain old dictionary definition of one of the words the author used.

Vocabulary items on critical reading are great news. These are the easiest critical reading questions ever.

9. *Student-Produced Responses:* This is the change that test takers worry about most, and it's probably the only genuinely significant change in the test. In the past, all questions were multiple choice. In the SAT, ten math questions will require you to come up with your own answer and enter it on your answer sheet by filling in spaces on a grid that can be read by a grading machine. The math questions are straightforward, but the grid is a pain. (We hate the name Student-Produced Responses, so we're going to call these new math items grid-ins.)

Grid-ins seem like bad news, but actually are no big deal.

10. *Calculators:* Students are now allowed to use calculators on the SAT. ETS says the calculators are optional, and they are, but you should view them as mandatory. Calculators can be extremely helpful on some questions, especially grid-ins. Calculators are not supplied. You should bring your own four-function, scientific, or graphing calculator. No, you cannot bring your laptop computer.

Calculators are good news, but don't get carried away.

11. *Essays:* Contrary to popular belief, **there is no essay on the new SAT.** (A twenty-minute essay is part of the SAT-II Writing Test, which used to be known as the English Composition Test with Essay, an Achievement Test.)

The addition of an essay to the SAT is an unfounded rumor, not a change.

12. *The PSAT:* The Preliminary Scholastic Assessment Test (PSAT) changed format about a year before the SAT did. The changes on the PSAT are just like the changes on the SAT, although the PSAT is somewhat shorter. (For one thing, there is no experimental section.) To prepare you for the essay question on the SAT-II Writing Test, some schools will offer a sample essay test, which you will take immediately after you finish the PSAT. This sample essay will be scored by a teacher at your school. Your scores on the rest of the PSAT will be calculated by ETS. You will receive one verbal score and one math score, each reported on the 20- to 80-point scale that ETS has always used on the PSAT.

Like the changes to the SAT, the changes to the PSAT won't affect you very much.

SO?

Is the new SAT different from the old SAT? Yes.

Is it scarier? It doesn't have to be, if you do your homework ahead of time.

Is it harder to crack? Definitely not. In fact, in some ways the new SAT is easier to crack than the old one was—as long as you know the correct techniques.

Appendix **2**
The PSAT

The PSAT/NMSQT is the Preliminary Scholastic Assessment Test/ National Merit Scholarship Qualifying Test. It is usually administered in the fall of eleventh grade, and it has two purposes. First, it gives students some experience at taking a test that is almost exactly like the SAT, which they usually take later. Second, it serves as the first hurdle in the competition for National Scholarships. The great majority of students should look at the PSAT merely as practice for the real thing. Only those receiving a combined score of 130 or so have a chance of winning a National Merit Scholarship, and only those receiving a combined score of 120 or so have a chance of winning a commendation, which is a sort of honorable mention that may or may not catch the attention of a college admissions officer. Most colleges don't even look at PSAT scores.

THINK OF THE PSAT AS PRACTICE

Although you shouldn't feel pressure when you take the PSAT, you should pay attention and try to do as well as you can. The questions in the PSAT are exactly like the questions in the SAT, and both tests are taken under the same conditions. Your PSAT score will give you a good idea of where you stand. (Adding a zero to the end of your math and verbal scores will give you a rough idea of how you would be likely to score on the SAT if you took it tomorrow.) If you have trouble with the critical reading questions on the PSAT, you will have trouble with the critical reading questions on the SAT. Every SAT technique in this book applies equally to the PSAT.

The differences between the PSAT and the SAT have to do with format rather than content. The PSAT contains four sections rather than seven, and the entire test lasts two hours rather than three. There is no experimental section, and there are no fifteen-minute sections. Like the SAT, the PSAT contains ten grid-in questions and at least one pair of dual critical reading passages. You are allowed to use a calculator, and you definitely should.

Pacing is a little different on the PSAT. After taking a practice exam, look at these charts to determine the number of questions you must answer.

MATH PACING CHART FOR THE PSAT

If, on your last diag, you scored between:	Your target score is:	In the 25-question section, you should answer only:	In the Quant Comp section, you should answer only:	In the Grid-in section, you should answer only:
20–28	35	1–10	26–31	41–43
29–35	40	1–13	26–34	41–44
36–40	45	1–16	26–35	41–45
41–45	50	1–19	26–38	41–46
46–50	55	1–21	26–39	41–48
51–55	60	1–23	All	41–48
56–60	65	1–24	All	41–49
61–65	70	All	All	All
66–up	80	All	All	All

VERBAL PACING CHART FOR THE PSAT

If, on your last diag, you scored between:	Your target score is:	Analogies	Sentence Comp.	Critical Reading	
				13 Questions	17 Questions
20–29	35	All	All	1 Passage	1 Passage
30–39	45	All	All	1 Passage	1 + 1/2 Passage
40–49	55	All	All	1 + 1/2 Passage	1 + 1/2 Passage
50–59	65	All	All	Both	Both
60–69	75	All	All	Both	Both
70–79	80	All	All	Both	Both

AFTERWORD

ABOUT THE PRINCETON REVIEW COURSE

The Princeton Review course is a six-week course to prepare students for the SAT.

Students are assigned to small classes (eight to twelve students) grouped by ability. Everyone in your math class is scoring at your math level; everyone in your verbal class is scoring at your verbal level. This enables the teacher to focus each lesson on your problems, because everybody is in the same boat.

Each week you cover one math area and one verbal area. If you don't understand a particular topic thoroughly, some other courses expect you to listen to audiocassettes.

Not so with The Princeton Review. If you want more work on a topic, you can come to an extra-help session later in the week. Classes in extra-help are optional, so usually they are even smaller than regular classes, allowing still more personal attention. If after coming to an extra-help class you still don't understand a concept, or you simply want more practice, you can request free private tutoring with your instructor.

Four times during the course you will take a diagnostic test that is computer evaluated. Each diagnostic is constructed according to the statistical design of actual SATs. Indeed, some of our questions are actual questions licensed directly from ETS.

The computer evaluation of your diagnostic tests is used to assign you to your class, as well as to measure your progress. The computer evaluation tells you what specific areas you need to concentrate on. We don't ask you to spend time on topics you already know well.

Princeton Review instructors undergo a strict selection process and a rigorous training period. All of them have done exceedingly well on the SAT, and most of them have gone to highly competitive colleges. All Princeton Review instructors are chosen because we believe they can make the course an enjoyable experience as well as a learning one.

Finally, Princeton Review materials are updated each year. Each student is assigned a manual and workbook. Each person receives materials that are challenging but not overwhelming.

IS THIS BOOK JUST LIKE YOUR COURSE?

Since the book came out, many students and teachers have asked us, "Is this book just like your course?" The answer is no.

We like to think that this book is fun, informative, and well written, but no book can capture the magic of our instructors and course structure. Each Princeton Review instructor has attended a top college and has excelled on the SAT. Moreover, each of our instructors undergoes several weeks of rigorous training.

It isn't easy to raise SAT scores. Our course is more than fifty hours long and requires class participation, quizzes, homework, four diagnostic examinations, and possibly additional tutoring.

Also, for a number of reasons, this book cannot contain all of the techniques we teach in our course. Some of our techniques are too difficult to include in a book, without a trained and experienced Princeton Review teacher to explain and demonstrate them. Moreover, this book is written for the average student. Classes in our course are grouped by ability so that we can gear our techniques to each student's level. What a 900-level Princeton Review student learns is different from what a 1400- or 1600-level student learns.

WE'RE FLATTERED, BUT . . .

Some tutors and schools use this book to run their own "Princeton Review course." While we are flattered, we are also concerned.

It has taken us thirteen years of teaching tens of thousands of students across the country to develop our SAT program, and we're still learning. Many teachers think that our course is simply a collection of techniques that can be taught by anyone. It isn't that easy.

We train each Princeton Review instructor two hours for every hour he or she will teach class. Each of the instructors is monitored, evaluated, and supervised throughout the course.

Another concern is that many of our techniques conflict with traditional math and English techniques as taught in high school. For example, in the math section we tell our students to avoid setting up equations. Can you imagine your math teacher telling you that? And in the verbal section, we tell our students not to read the passage too carefully. Can you imagine your English teacher telling you that?

While we also teach traditional math and English in our course, some teachers may not completely agree with some of our approaches.

BEWARE OF PRINCETON REVIEW CLONES

We have nothing against people who use our techniques, but we do object to tutors or high schools who claim to "teach the Princeton Review method."

If you want to find out whether your teacher has been trained by The Princeton Review, or whether you're taking an official Princeton Review course, call us toll-free at 1-800-995-5585.

IF YOU'D LIKE MORE INFORMATION

Princeton Review sites are in dozens of cities around the country. For the office nearest you, call 1-800-995-5585.

About Computerized Testing

INTRODUCTION TO COMPUTERIZED TESTING

ETS, CBT, CAT, GRE—WHAT DOES IT ALL MEAN?

In 1990, Howard Wainer, an official of the Educational Testing Service, published a book called *Computer Adaptive Testing: A Primer*, in which he wrote, "There are . . . several aspects of computerized and adaptive testing that raise new issues in the consideration of validity," and went on to admit, "There is, as yet, very little information available about the validity of computerized adaptive tests." The book was co-written by four other ETS functionaries and includes a foreword by ETS Vice President C. Victor Bunderson.

In 1991, despite these reservations, ETS began offering the computer-based GRE. Baffling, isn't it?

Anyway, the world is now graced with two forms of the GRE: the pencil-and-paper (standard) test and the CBT (computer-based test). The CBT has the same format as the standard GRE, except it's on a computer. However, along with its regular (linear) sections, the CBT includes a computer-*adaptive* test (CAT) which, depending on the individual tester's performance, can be used at the program's discretion as either the scored or the experimental section. "Computer adaptive" means that the computer program molds itself to the individual test-taker's performance level. For example, if you answer an easy question correctly, the test will give you a harder one. If you miss an medium question, you'll get an easy one next. Supposedly, this process enables the computer to pinpoint your scoring level more quickly and accurately than a paper-and-pencil test could.

ETS has stated that they plan to eliminate the computer-based test (CBTs) once they are confident of the validity of their computer-adaptive tests. As of November 17, 1993, in fact, all sections of the GRE—math, verbal, and analytic—will be offered in CAT format. However, ETS is not confident enough in its CAT analytic section to let it stand alone; therefore, immediately following the CAT section, there will be two computer-*based* analytic sections. Just in case. Whichever analytic section you score best on will be the one that counts.

While ETS has not yet made any formal announcement about offering other tests in CBT or CAT format, they do have a tendency to keep their tests uniform. Considering this history of homogeneity, it is highly likely that ETS will, at some time in the near future, come up with a CAT option for its other admissions tests.

ENTER REVIEWARE

It looks like we're in for a major CAT proliferation, folks. And we at The Princeton Review feel that the only effective way of dealing with this crisis is to help people start preparing now. That's why we developed the RevieWare Computer Diagnostic, our version of ETS's CBT/CAT, and included it in this book. We have attempted to duplicate precisely the format, style, appearance, and workings of the ETS CBT and CAT tests. Aesthetically, ETS's program is rather unattractive, and it's a bit hard to move around in. So is ours. In mirroring the GRE test's look and feel, we made the decision that an accurate test would be more helpful as an instructive and evaluative tool than a fun, attractive test that bore little resemblance to the barren moonscape that is the GRE. They're bland, so we're bland.

But a discussion of the philosophy behind RevieWare isn't really meaningful without an understanding of exactly what computerized testing means to ETS, and what it means to you as a test taker.

WHAT'S IN IT FOR THEM: CASH AND CONVENIENCE

The big question is, if ETS itself questions the validity of these tests, why do they offer the CBT, let alone a fully adaptive CAT?

For one thing, convenience. The standard paper-and-pencil exams are administered five times per year. For each administration, ETS must rent thousands of rooms worldwide, hire proctors, transport materials, and register and collect fees from walk-in testers. In the case of the CBT/CAT, all ETS needs is a room in one of their or Sylvan Learning Centers' (Sylvan) offices equipped with a couple of computers, and an employee to deal with testers. This room can be open for testing at ETS/Sylvan's discretion, thus eliminating almost all of the hassle associated with administering the paper-and-pencil exam.

Another plus, for ETS and Sylvan, is dollars. The fee for the CBT/CAT is $45 *more* than the fee for the paper-and-pencil exam. At this rate, the expenditure for computer hardware and software will be paid back in very little time. After that, it's straight profit. Or should we say "non-profit"? That ETS might have financial concerns is often overlooked. Most people assume that ETS is some kind of government organ. Actually, ETS is a non-profit association of academic organizations, which means that they're not supposed to make a profit. But if they do, well, oops! It's called an "overage," and can be spent on anything from incredibly high salaries and perks to one of the tennis courts or swimming pools in ETS's Princeton, NJ, compound. Sylvan, on the other hand, is a good old-fashioned corporation. They are in business for the bucks, plain and simple.

WHAT'S IN IT FOR YOU: BIAS, EYESTRAIN, TEARS, AND SWEAT

What seem to be the advantages to the test taker? For one, he or she can take the exam virtually any day of the work week. Also, a computerized test can often take far less time than its paper-and-pencil counterpart. That's what ETS would like you to believe, anyway. Now, let's look at these "advantages" and see how they really play out.

First, fourteen states do not have a single test center that offers the CBT/CAT, and ten others have only one. Also, a sampling of test centers showed that none offers testing on the weekends, so anyone interested would have to be in a position to take a day off if he or she wanted to take the CBT/CAT. This means that if you don't live near a test center or if you go to school or work during the week—situations that apply to a large portion of the country—the first "advantage" does not apply.

Second, who in his or her right mind would not use every minute allotted? If you are told, as you are for the GRE CBT, that you have thirty-two minutes per section, then you are going to use thirty-two minutes. In addition, according to our friend from ETS, Mr. Wainer, ". . . a CAT makes much more stringent demands on its component items than does its paper-and-pencil counterpart. Because the CAT tends to be much shorter . . . each item is more critical. If an item is flawed, its impact on the . . . examinee's proficiency is doubled. Additionally, because not everyone gets the same set of items, a flawed item can affect some examinees and not others. Hence, test fairness, in addition to test validity, can be compromised." So much for the second "advantage."

The difficulties described above begin to bring to light some of the other serious problems with computerized testing. For example, what about the simple, undeniable fact that this test is *on a computer*? Think about the people you know who own and/or spend lots of time with computers and/or video games. Are most of these people members of one gender? Are most of these people members of a specific socioeconomic class? Probably. As Wainer puts it, "It is conceivable that a CAT may be more vulnerable to problems of [bias] than are conventional paper-and-pencil tests, due to the possibility that differences between ethnic groups or genders in familiarity with computers in general may affect scores on computerized tests." In fact, the question of general bias is perhaps the most profound problem facing ETS in creating and administering the CBT/CAT.

For its part, ETS has steadfastly denied that any of its tests exhibit a bias for or against any gender, ethnicity, or race. But for something that doesn't exist, the subject sure does get a lot of attention. In fact, the standardized test-writing community is so worried about bias that its members don't even use the word "bias," opting instead for more comfortable euphemisms. Recently, the term *differential item functioning (dif)* has replaced *item bias* as a less evaluative label. Item bias refers to a specific question that exhibits a bias against a specific group or groups.

Computerized tests, especially computer-adaptive tests like the one that ETS wants to replace the CBT with, are at far greater risk of showing bias than are paper-and-pencil tests. Wainer explains, "Adaptive tests may be more vulnerable to the effects of *dif* on validity than fixed tests. A fixed test may contain items with counterbalancing *dif* that can 'cancel each other out'; however, in an adaptive testing situation, the presence of such [biased] items in the test pool permits the possibility that an unlucky examinee could be administered several items biased against him or her. The resulting test score would not provide a good indication of proficiency." Basically, a paper-and-pencil test is an equal-opportunity bigot, while a CAT can tailor itself to discriminate against you specifically. (See the diagram below for a description of the adaptive flow.)

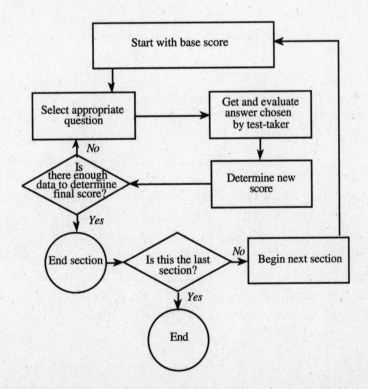

GET IT BEFORE IT GETS YOU

You've been taking multiple-choice, paper-and-pencil, fill-in-the-bubble tests your whole life. So while the prospect of taking another one may not be pleasant, at least it's familiar. But imagine walking into something as completely unfamiliar as a computer-adaptive test. You've never seen anything like it before. You've never practiced on it. You feel like Captain Kirk in that *Star Trek* episode where he has to dress up in a really short toga and act like some live pawn in a game these super-intelligent aliens are playing, but he doesn't know any of the rules.

Well, you don't have to feel that way. RevieWare Computer Diagnostics are here to help. Because adaptive testing is the future, if you don't get familiar with it, you'll regret it. Maybe not today, maybe not tomorrow, but soon, and for the rest of your life. Okay, okay, probably not for the rest of your life. But since you have the option, why not use RevieWare Computer Diagnostics to beat ETS at its own game? Happy testing and good luck!

NOTES

NOTES

NOTES

NOTES

NOTES

NOTES

NOTES

NOTES

ABOUT THE AUTHORS

Adam Robinson was born in 1955. He graduated from Wharton before earning a law degree at Oxford University in England. Robinson, a rated chess master, devised and perfected the Joe Bloggs approach to beating standardized tests in 1980, as well as numerous other core Princeton Review techniques. A free-lance author of many books, Robinson has collaborated with The Princeton Review to develop a number of its courses.

John Katzman was born in 1959. He graduated from Princeton University in 1980. After working briefly on Wall Street, he founded The Princeton Review in 1981. Beginning with nineteen high school students in his parents' apartment, Katzman now oversees courses that prepare tens of thousands of high school and college students annually for tests, including the SAT, GRE, GMAT, and LSAT.

Both authors live in New York City.

The Princeton Review

1.

YOUR NAME: _____
(Print)   Last   First   M.I.

SIGNATURE: _____   DATE: __/__/__

HOME ADDRESS: _____
(Print)   Number and Street

_____
City   State   Zip Code

PHONE NO.: _____
(Print)

IMPORTANT: Please fill in these boxes exactly as shown on the back cover of your test book.

2. TEST FORM
_____

6. DATE OF BIRTH

Month	Day	Year
⊂ ⊃ JAN		
⊂ ⊃ FEB		
⊂ ⊃ MAR	⊂0⊃ ⊂0⊃	⊂0⊃ ⊂0⊃
⊂ ⊃ APR	⊂1⊃ ⊂1⊃	⊂1⊃ ⊂1⊃
⊂ ⊃ MAY	⊂2⊃ ⊂2⊃	⊂2⊃ ⊂2⊃
⊂ ⊃ JUN	⊂3⊃ ⊂3⊃	⊂3⊃ ⊂3⊃
⊂ ⊃ JUL	⊂4⊃	⊂4⊃ ⊂4⊃
⊂ ⊃ AUG	⊂5⊃	⊂5⊃ ⊂5⊃
⊂ ⊃ SEP	⊂6⊃	⊂6⊃ ⊂6⊃
⊂ ⊃ OCT	⊂7⊃	⊂7⊃ ⊂7⊃
⊂ ⊃ NOV	⊂8⊃	⊂8⊃ ⊂8⊃
⊂ ⊃ DEC	⊂9⊃	⊂9⊃ ⊂9⊃

3. TEST CODE   **4. REGISTRATION NUMBER**

⊂0⊃	⊂A⊃	⊂0⊃	⊂0⊃	⊂0⊃	⊂0⊃	⊂0⊃	⊂0⊃	⊂0⊃	⊂0⊃	⊂0⊃
⊂1⊃	⊂B⊃	⊂1⊃	⊂1⊃	⊂1⊃	⊂1⊃	⊂1⊃	⊂1⊃	⊂1⊃	⊂1⊃	⊂1⊃
⊂2⊃	⊂C⊃	⊂2⊃	⊂2⊃	⊂2⊃	⊂2⊃	⊂2⊃	⊂2⊃	⊂2⊃	⊂2⊃	⊂2⊃
⊂3⊃	⊂D⊃	⊂3⊃	⊂3⊃	⊂3⊃	⊂3⊃	⊂3⊃	⊂3⊃	⊂3⊃	⊂3⊃	⊂3⊃
⊂4⊃	⊂E⊃	⊂4⊃	⊂4⊃	⊂4⊃	⊂4⊃	⊂4⊃	⊂4⊃	⊂4⊃	⊂4⊃	⊂4⊃
⊂5⊃	⊂F⊃	⊂5⊃	⊂5⊃	⊂5⊃	⊂5⊃	⊂5⊃	⊂5⊃	⊂5⊃	⊂5⊃	⊂5⊃
⊂6⊃	⊂G⊃	⊂6⊃	⊂6⊃	⊂6⊃	⊂6⊃	⊂6⊃	⊂6⊃	⊂6⊃	⊂6⊃	⊂6⊃
⊂7⊃		⊂7⊃	⊂7⊃	⊂7⊃	⊂7⊃	⊂7⊃	⊂7⊃	⊂7⊃	⊂7⊃	⊂7⊃
⊂8⊃		⊂8⊃	⊂8⊃	⊂8⊃	⊂8⊃	⊂8⊃	⊂8⊃	⊂8⊃	⊂8⊃	⊂8⊃
⊂9⊃		⊂9⊃	⊂9⊃	⊂9⊃	⊂9⊃	⊂9⊃	⊂9⊃	⊂9⊃	⊂9⊃	⊂9⊃

7. SEX
⊂ ⊃ MALE
⊂ ⊃ FEMALE

THE PRINCETON REVIEW

© 1994 The Princeton Review
FORM NO. 00001-PR

5. YOUR NAME

First 4 letters of last name				FIRST INIT	MID INIT
⊂A⊃	⊂A⊃	⊂A⊃	⊂A⊃	⊂A⊃	⊂A⊃
⊂B⊃	⊂B⊃	⊂B⊃	⊂B⊃	⊂B⊃	⊂B⊃
⊂C⊃	⊂C⊃	⊂C⊃	⊂C⊃	⊂C⊃	⊂C⊃
⊂D⊃	⊂D⊃	⊂D⊃	⊂D⊃	⊂D⊃	⊂D⊃
⊂E⊃	⊂E⊃	⊂E⊃	⊂E⊃	⊂E⊃	⊂E⊃
⊂F⊃	⊂F⊃	⊂F⊃	⊂F⊃	⊂F⊃	⊂F⊃
⊂G⊃	⊂G⊃	⊂G⊃	⊂G⊃	⊂G⊃	⊂G⊃
⊂H⊃	⊂H⊃	⊂H⊃	⊂H⊃	⊂H⊃	⊂H⊃
⊂I⊃	⊂I⊃	⊂I⊃	⊂I⊃	⊂I⊃	⊂I⊃
⊂J⊃	⊂J⊃	⊂J⊃	⊂J⊃	⊂J⊃	⊂J⊃
⊂K⊃	⊂K⊃	⊂K⊃	⊂K⊃	⊂K⊃	⊂K⊃
⊂L⊃	⊂L⊃	⊂L⊃	⊂L⊃	⊂L⊃	⊂L⊃
⊂M⊃	⊂M⊃	⊂M⊃	⊂M⊃	⊂M⊃	⊂M⊃
⊂N⊃	⊂N⊃	⊂N⊃	⊂N⊃	⊂N⊃	⊂N⊃
⊂O⊃	⊂O⊃	⊂O⊃	⊂O⊃	⊂O⊃	⊂O⊃
⊂P⊃	⊂P⊃	⊂P⊃	⊂P⊃	⊂P⊃	⊂P⊃
⊂Q⊃	⊂Q⊃	⊂Q⊃	⊂Q⊃	⊂Q⊃	⊂Q⊃
⊂R⊃	⊂R⊃	⊂R⊃	⊂R⊃	⊂R⊃	⊂R⊃
⊂S⊃	⊂S⊃	⊂S⊃	⊂S⊃	⊂S⊃	⊂S⊃
⊂T⊃	⊂T⊃	⊂T⊃	⊂T⊃	⊂T⊃	⊂T⊃
⊂U⊃	⊂U⊃	⊂U⊃	⊂U⊃	⊂U⊃	⊂U⊃
⊂V⊃	⊂V⊃	⊂V⊃	⊂V⊃	⊂V⊃	⊂V⊃
⊂W⊃	⊂W⊃	⊂W⊃	⊂W⊃	⊂W⊃	⊂W⊃
⊂X⊃	⊂X⊃	⊂X⊃	⊂X⊃	⊂X⊃	⊂X⊃
⊂Y⊃	⊂Y⊃	⊂Y⊃	⊂Y⊃	⊂Y⊃	⊂Y⊃
⊂Z⊃	⊂Z⊃	⊂Z⊃	⊂Z⊃	⊂Z⊃	⊂Z⊃

Start with number 1 for each new section. If a section has fewer questions than answer spaces, leave the extra answer spaces blank.

SECTION 1

1 ⊂A⊃ ⊂B⊃ ⊂C⊃ ⊂D⊃ ⊂E⊃   11 ⊂A⊃ ⊂B⊃ ⊂C⊃ ⊂D⊃ ⊂E⊃   21 ⊂A⊃ ⊂B⊃ ⊂C⊃ ⊂D⊃ ⊂E⊃   31 ⊂A⊃ ⊂B⊃ ⊂C⊃ ⊂D⊃ ⊂E⊃
2 ⊂A⊃ ⊂B⊃ ⊂C⊃ ⊂D⊃ ⊂E⊃   12 ⊂A⊃ ⊂B⊃ ⊂C⊃ ⊂D⊃ ⊂E⊃   22 ⊂A⊃ ⊂B⊃ ⊂C⊃ ⊂D⊃ ⊂E⊃   32 ⊂A⊃ ⊂B⊃ ⊂C⊃ ⊂D⊃ ⊂E⊃
3 ⊂A⊃ ⊂B⊃ ⊂C⊃ ⊂D⊃ ⊂E⊃   13 ⊂A⊃ ⊂B⊃ ⊂C⊃ ⊂D⊃ ⊂E⊃   23 ⊂A⊃ ⊂B⊃ ⊂C⊃ ⊂D⊃ ⊂E⊃   33 ⊂A⊃ ⊂B⊃ ⊂C⊃ ⊂D⊃ ⊂E⊃
4 ⊂A⊃ ⊂B⊃ ⊂C⊃ ⊂D⊃ ⊂E⊃   14 ⊂A⊃ ⊂B⊃ ⊂C⊃ ⊂D⊃ ⊂E⊃   24 ⊂A⊃ ⊂B⊃ ⊂C⊃ ⊂D⊃ ⊂E⊃   34 ⊂A⊃ ⊂B⊃ ⊂C⊃ ⊂D⊃ ⊂E⊃
5 ⊂A⊃ ⊂B⊃ ⊂C⊃ ⊂D⊃ ⊂E⊃   15 ⊂A⊃ ⊂B⊃ ⊂C⊃ ⊂D⊃ ⊂E⊃   25 ⊂A⊃ ⊂B⊃ ⊂C⊃ ⊂D⊃ ⊂E⊃   35 ⊂A⊃ ⊂B⊃ ⊂C⊃ ⊂D⊃ ⊂E⊃
6 ⊂A⊃ ⊂B⊃ ⊂C⊃ ⊂D⊃ ⊂E⊃   16 ⊂A⊃ ⊂B⊃ ⊂C⊃ ⊂D⊃ ⊂E⊃   26 ⊂A⊃ ⊂B⊃ ⊂C⊃ ⊂D⊃ ⊂E⊃   36 ⊂A⊃ ⊂B⊃ ⊂C⊃ ⊂D⊃ ⊂E⊃
7 ⊂A⊃ ⊂B⊃ ⊂C⊃ ⊂D⊃ ⊂E⊃   17 ⊂A⊃ ⊂B⊃ ⊂C⊃ ⊂D⊃ ⊂E⊃   27 ⊂A⊃ ⊂B⊃ ⊂C⊃ ⊂D⊃ ⊂E⊃   37 ⊂A⊃ ⊂B⊃ ⊂C⊃ ⊂D⊃ ⊂E⊃
8 ⊂A⊃ ⊂B⊃ ⊂C⊃ ⊂D⊃ ⊂E⊃   18 ⊂A⊃ ⊂B⊃ ⊂C⊃ ⊂D⊃ ⊂E⊃   28 ⊂A⊃ ⊂B⊃ ⊂C⊃ ⊂D⊃ ⊂E⊃   38 ⊂A⊃ ⊂B⊃ ⊂C⊃ ⊂D⊃ ⊂E⊃
9 ⊂A⊃ ⊂B⊃ ⊂C⊃ ⊂D⊃ ⊂E⊃   19 ⊂A⊃ ⊂B⊃ ⊂C⊃ ⊂D⊃ ⊂E⊃   29 ⊂A⊃ ⊂B⊃ ⊂C⊃ ⊂D⊃ ⊂E⊃   39 ⊂A⊃ ⊂B⊃ ⊂C⊃ ⊂D⊃ ⊂E⊃
10 ⊂A⊃ ⊂B⊃ ⊂C⊃ ⊂D⊃ ⊂E⊃   20 ⊂A⊃ ⊂B⊃ ⊂C⊃ ⊂D⊃ ⊂E⊃   30 ⊂A⊃ ⊂B⊃ ⊂C⊃ ⊂D⊃ ⊂E⊃   40 ⊂A⊃ ⊂B⊃ ⊂C⊃ ⊂D⊃ ⊂E⊃

SECTION 2

1 ⊂A⊃ ⊂B⊃ ⊂C⊃ ⊂D⊃ ⊂E⊃   11 ⊂A⊃ ⊂B⊃ ⊂C⊃ ⊂D⊃ ⊂E⊃   21 ⊂A⊃ ⊂B⊃ ⊂C⊃ ⊂D⊃ ⊂E⊃   31 ⊂A⊃ ⊂B⊃ ⊂C⊃ ⊂D⊃ ⊂E⊃
2 ⊂A⊃ ⊂B⊃ ⊂C⊃ ⊂D⊃ ⊂E⊃   12 ⊂A⊃ ⊂B⊃ ⊂C⊃ ⊂D⊃ ⊂E⊃   22 ⊂A⊃ ⊂B⊃ ⊂C⊃ ⊂D⊃ ⊂E⊃   32 ⊂A⊃ ⊂B⊃ ⊂C⊃ ⊂D⊃ ⊂E⊃
3 ⊂A⊃ ⊂B⊃ ⊂C⊃ ⊂D⊃ ⊂E⊃   13 ⊂A⊃ ⊂B⊃ ⊂C⊃ ⊂D⊃ ⊂E⊃   23 ⊂A⊃ ⊂B⊃ ⊂C⊃ ⊂D⊃ ⊂E⊃   33 ⊂A⊃ ⊂B⊃ ⊂C⊃ ⊂D⊃ ⊂E⊃
4 ⊂A⊃ ⊂B⊃ ⊂C⊃ ⊂D⊃ ⊂E⊃   14 ⊂A⊃ ⊂B⊃ ⊂C⊃ ⊂D⊃ ⊂E⊃   24 ⊂A⊃ ⊂B⊃ ⊂C⊃ ⊂D⊃ ⊂E⊃   34 ⊂A⊃ ⊂B⊃ ⊂C⊃ ⊂D⊃ ⊂E⊃
5 ⊂A⊃ ⊂B⊃ ⊂C⊃ ⊂D⊃ ⊂E⊃   15 ⊂A⊃ ⊂B⊃ ⊂C⊃ ⊂D⊃ ⊂E⊃   25 ⊂A⊃ ⊂B⊃ ⊂C⊃ ⊂D⊃ ⊂E⊃   35 ⊂A⊃ ⊂B⊃ ⊂C⊃ ⊂D⊃ ⊂E⊃
6 ⊂A⊃ ⊂B⊃ ⊂C⊃ ⊂D⊃ ⊂E⊃   16 ⊂A⊃ ⊂B⊃ ⊂C⊃ ⊂D⊃ ⊂E⊃   26 ⊂A⊃ ⊂B⊃ ⊂C⊃ ⊂D⊃ ⊂E⊃   36 ⊂A⊃ ⊂B⊃ ⊂C⊃ ⊂D⊃ ⊂E⊃
7 ⊂A⊃ ⊂B⊃ ⊂C⊃ ⊂D⊃ ⊂E⊃   17 ⊂A⊃ ⊂B⊃ ⊂C⊃ ⊂D⊃ ⊂E⊃   27 ⊂A⊃ ⊂B⊃ ⊂C⊃ ⊂D⊃ ⊂E⊃   37 ⊂A⊃ ⊂B⊃ ⊂C⊃ ⊂D⊃ ⊂E⊃
8 ⊂A⊃ ⊂B⊃ ⊂C⊃ ⊂D⊃ ⊂E⊃   18 ⊂A⊃ ⊂B⊃ ⊂C⊃ ⊂D⊃ ⊂E⊃   28 ⊂A⊃ ⊂B⊃ ⊂C⊃ ⊂D⊃ ⊂E⊃   38 ⊂A⊃ ⊂B⊃ ⊂C⊃ ⊂D⊃ ⊂E⊃
9 ⊂A⊃ ⊂B⊃ ⊂C⊃ ⊂D⊃ ⊂E⊃   19 ⊂A⊃ ⊂B⊃ ⊂C⊃ ⊂D⊃ ⊂E⊃   29 ⊂A⊃ ⊂B⊃ ⊂C⊃ ⊂D⊃ ⊂E⊃   39 ⊂A⊃ ⊂B⊃ ⊂C⊃ ⊂D⊃ ⊂E⊃
10 ⊂A⊃ ⊂B⊃ ⊂C⊃ ⊂D⊃ ⊂E⊃   20 ⊂A⊃ ⊂B⊃ ⊂C⊃ ⊂D⊃ ⊂E⊃   30 ⊂A⊃ ⊂B⊃ ⊂C⊃ ⊂D⊃ ⊂E⊃   40 ⊂A⊃ ⊂B⊃ ⊂C⊃ ⊂D⊃ ⊂E⊃

DO NOT MARK IN THIS AREA
⊂ ⊃ ⊂ ⊃ ⊂ ⊃ ⊂ ⊃ ⊂ ⊃ ⊂ ⊃ ⊂ ⊃ ⊂ ⊃ ⊂ ⊃ ⊂ ⊃ ⊂ ⊃ ⊂ ⊃ ⊂ ⊃

Start with number 1 for each new section. If a section has fewer questions than answer spaces, leave the extra answer spaces blank.

SECTION 3

1 ⊂A⊃ ⊂B⊃ ⊂C⊃ ⊂D⊃ ⊂E⊃
2 ⊂A⊃ ⊂B⊃ ⊂C⊃ ⊂D⊃ ⊂E⊃
3 ⊂A⊃ ⊂B⊃ ⊂C⊃ ⊂D⊃ ⊂E⊃
4 ⊂A⊃ ⊂B⊃ ⊂C⊃ ⊂D⊃ ⊂E⊃
5 ⊂A⊃ ⊂B⊃ ⊂C⊃ ⊂D⊃ ⊂E⊃
6 ⊂A⊃ ⊂B⊃ ⊂C⊃ ⊂D⊃ ⊂E⊃
7 ⊂A⊃ ⊂B⊃ ⊂C⊃ ⊂D⊃ ⊂E⊃
8 ⊂A⊃ ⊂B⊃ ⊂C⊃ ⊂D⊃ ⊂E⊃
9 ⊂A⊃ ⊂B⊃ ⊂C⊃ ⊂D⊃ ⊂E⊃
10 ⊂A⊃ ⊂B⊃ ⊂C⊃ ⊂D⊃ ⊂E⊃
11 ⊂A⊃ ⊂B⊃ ⊂C⊃ ⊂D⊃ ⊂E⊃
12 ⊂A⊃ ⊂B⊃ ⊂C⊃ ⊂D⊃ ⊂E⊃
13 ⊂A⊃ ⊂B⊃ ⊂C⊃ ⊂D⊃ ⊂E⊃
14 ⊂A⊃ ⊂B⊃ ⊂C⊃ ⊂D⊃ ⊂E⊃
15 ⊂A⊃ ⊂B⊃ ⊂C⊃ ⊂D⊃ ⊂E⊃

16 ⊂A⊃ ⊂B⊃ ⊂C⊃ ⊂D⊃ ⊂E⊃
17 ⊂A⊃ ⊂B⊃ ⊂C⊃ ⊂D⊃ ⊂E⊃
18 ⊂A⊃ ⊂B⊃ ⊂C⊃ ⊂D⊃ ⊂E⊃
19 ⊂A⊃ ⊂B⊃ ⊂C⊃ ⊂D⊃ ⊂E⊃
20 ⊂A⊃ ⊂B⊃ ⊂C⊃ ⊂D⊃ ⊂E⊃
21 ⊂A⊃ ⊂B⊃ ⊂C⊃ ⊂D⊃ ⊂E⊃
22 ⊂A⊃ ⊂B⊃ ⊂C⊃ ⊂D⊃ ⊂E⊃
23 ⊂A⊃ ⊂B⊃ ⊂C⊃ ⊂D⊃ ⊂E⊃
24 ⊂A⊃ ⊂B⊃ ⊂C⊃ ⊂D⊃ ⊂E⊃
25 ⊂A⊃ ⊂B⊃ ⊂C⊃ ⊂D⊃ ⊂E⊃
26 ⊂A⊃ ⊂B⊃ ⊂C⊃ ⊂D⊃ ⊂E⊃
27 ⊂A⊃ ⊂B⊃ ⊂C⊃ ⊂D⊃ ⊂E⊃
28 ⊂A⊃ ⊂B⊃ ⊂C⊃ ⊂D⊃ ⊂E⊃
29 ⊂A⊃ ⊂B⊃ ⊂C⊃ ⊂D⊃ ⊂E⊃
30 ⊂A⊃ ⊂B⊃ ⊂C⊃ ⊂D⊃ ⊂E⊃

31 ⊂A⊃ ⊂B⊃ ⊂C⊃ ⊂D⊃ ⊂E⊃
32 ⊂A⊃ ⊂B⊃ ⊂C⊃ ⊂D⊃ ⊂E⊃
33 ⊂A⊃ ⊂B⊃ ⊂C⊃ ⊂D⊃ ⊂E⊃
34 ⊂A⊃ ⊂B⊃ ⊂C⊃ ⊂D⊃ ⊂E⊃
35 ⊂A⊃ ⊂B⊃ ⊂C⊃ ⊂D⊃ ⊂E⊃
36 ⊂A⊃ ⊂B⊃ ⊂C⊃ ⊂D⊃ ⊂E⊃
37 ⊂A⊃ ⊂B⊃ ⊂C⊃ ⊂D⊃ ⊂E⊃
38 ⊂A⊃ ⊂B⊃ ⊂C⊃ ⊂D⊃ ⊂E⊃
39 ⊂A⊃ ⊂B⊃ ⊂C⊃ ⊂D⊃ ⊂E⊃
40 ⊂A⊃ ⊂B⊃ ⊂C⊃ ⊂D⊃ ⊂E⊃

If section 3 of your test booklet has math questions that are not multiple-choice, continue to item 16 below. Otherwise, continue to item 16 above.

ONLY ANSWERS ENTERED IN THE OVALS IN EACH GRID AREA WILL BE SCORED.
YOU WILL NOT RECEIVE CREDIT FOR ANYTHING WRITTEN IN THE BOXES ABOVE THE OVALS.

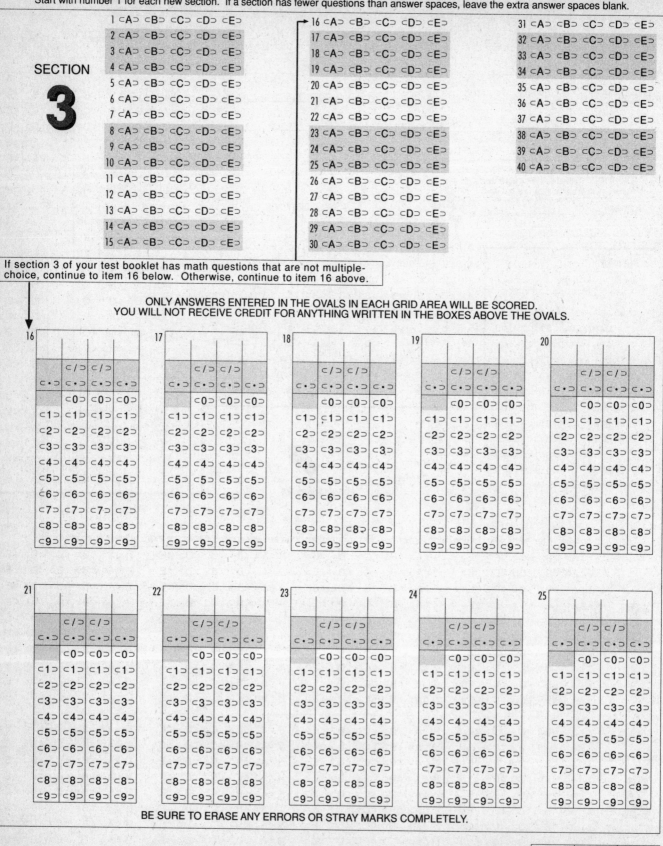

BE SURE TO ERASE ANY ERRORS OR STRAY MARKS COMPLETELY.

PLEASE PRINT YOUR INITIALS

First   Middle   Last

Start with number 1 for each new section. If a section has fewer questions than answer spaces, leave the extra answer spaces blank.

SECTION 4

1 ⊂A⊃ ⊂B⊃ ⊂C⊃ ⊂D⊃ ⊂E⊃
2 ⊂A⊃ ⊂B⊃ ⊂C⊃ ⊂D⊃ ⊂E⊃
3 ⊂A⊃ ⊂B⊃ ⊂C⊃ ⊂D⊃ ⊂E⊃
4 ⊂A⊃ ⊂B⊃ ⊂C⊃ ⊂D⊃ ⊂E⊃
5 ⊂A⊃ ⊂B⊃ ⊂C⊃ ⊂D⊃ ⊂E⊃
6 ⊂A⊃ ⊂B⊃ ⊂C⊃ ⊂D⊃ ⊂E⊃
7 ⊂A⊃ ⊂B⊃ ⊂C⊃ ⊂D⊃ ⊂E⊃
8 ⊂A⊃ ⊂B⊃ ⊂C⊃ ⊂D⊃ ⊂E⊃
9 ⊂A⊃ ⊂B⊃ ⊂C⊃ ⊂D⊃ ⊂E⊃
10 ⊂A⊃ ⊂B⊃ ⊂C⊃ ⊂D⊃ ⊂E⊃
11 ⊂A⊃ ⊂B⊃ ⊂C⊃ ⊂D⊃ ⊂E⊃
12 ⊂A⊃ ⊂B⊃ ⊂C⊃ ⊂D⊃ ⊂E⊃
13 ⊂A⊃ ⊂B⊃ ⊂C⊃ ⊂D⊃ ⊂E⊃
14 ⊂A⊃ ⊂B⊃ ⊂C⊃ ⊂D⊃ ⊂E⊃
15 ⊂A⊃ ⊂B⊃ ⊂C⊃ ⊂D⊃ ⊂E⊃

16 ⊂A⊃ ⊂B⊃ ⊂C⊃ ⊂D⊃ ⊂E⊃
17 ⊂A⊃ ⊂B⊃ ⊂C⊃ ⊂D⊃ ⊂E⊃
18 ⊂A⊃ ⊂B⊃ ⊂C⊃ ⊂D⊃ ⊂E⊃
19 ⊂A⊃ ⊂B⊃ ⊂C⊃ ⊂D⊃ ⊂E⊃
20 ⊂A⊃ ⊂B⊃ ⊂C⊃ ⊂D⊃ ⊂E⊃
21 ⊂A⊃ ⊂B⊃ ⊂C⊃ ⊂D⊃ ⊂E⊃
22 ⊂A⊃ ⊂B⊃ ⊂C⊃ ⊂D⊃ ⊂E⊃
23 ⊂A⊃ ⊂B⊃ ⊂C⊃ ⊂D⊃ ⊂E⊃
24 ⊂A⊃ ⊂B⊃ ⊂C⊃ ⊂D⊃ ⊂E⊃
25 ⊂A⊃ ⊂B⊃ ⊂C⊃ ⊂D⊃ ⊂E⊃
26 ⊂A⊃ ⊂B⊃ ⊂C⊃ ⊂D⊃ ⊂E⊃
27 ⊂A⊃ ⊂B⊃ ⊂C⊃ ⊂D⊃ ⊂E⊃
28 ⊂A⊃ ⊂B⊃ ⊂C⊃ ⊂D⊃ ⊂E⊃
29 ⊂A⊃ ⊂B⊃ ⊂C⊃ ⊂D⊃ ⊂E⊃
30 ⊂A⊃ ⊂B⊃ ⊂C⊃ ⊂D⊃ ⊂E⊃

31 ⊂A⊃ ⊂B⊃ ⊂C⊃ ⊂D⊃ ⊂E⊃
32 ⊂A⊃ ⊂B⊃ ⊂C⊃ ⊂D⊃ ⊂E⊃
33 ⊂A⊃ ⊂B⊃ ⊂C⊃ ⊂D⊃ ⊂E⊃
34 ⊂A⊃ ⊂B⊃ ⊂C⊃ ⊂D⊃ ⊂E⊃
35 ⊂A⊃ ⊂B⊃ ⊂C⊃ ⊂D⊃ ⊂E⊃
36 ⊂A⊃ ⊂B⊃ ⊂C⊃ ⊂D⊃ ⊂E⊃
37 ⊂A⊃ ⊂B⊃ ⊂C⊃ ⊂D⊃ ⊂E⊃
38 ⊂A⊃ ⊂B⊃ ⊂C⊃ ⊂D⊃ ⊂E⊃
39 ⊂A⊃ ⊂B⊃ ⊂C⊃ ⊂D⊃ ⊂E⊃
40 ⊂A⊃ ⊂B⊃ ⊂C⊃ ⊂D⊃ ⊂E⊃

If section 3 of your test booklet has math questions that are not multiple-choice, continue to item 16 below. Otherwise, continue to item 16 above.

ONLY ANSWERS ENTERED IN THE OVALS IN EACH GRID AREA WILL BE SCORED.
YOU WILL NOT RECEIVE CREDIT FOR ANYTHING WRITTEN IN THE BOXES ABOVE THE OVALS.

16   17   18   19   20

21   22   23   24   25

Grid columns for each (16–25) contain:
⊂/⊃ ⊂/⊃
⊂•⊃ ⊂•⊃ ⊂•⊃ ⊂•⊃
⊂0⊃ ⊂0⊃ ⊂0⊃
⊂1⊃ ⊂1⊃ ⊂1⊃ ⊂1⊃
⊂2⊃ ⊂2⊃ ⊂2⊃ ⊂2⊃
⊂3⊃ ⊂3⊃ ⊂3⊃ ⊂3⊃
⊂4⊃ ⊂4⊃ ⊂4⊃ ⊂4⊃
⊂5⊃ ⊂5⊃ ⊂5⊃ ⊂5⊃
⊂6⊃ ⊂6⊃ ⊂6⊃ ⊂6⊃
⊂7⊃ ⊂7⊃ ⊂7⊃ ⊂7⊃
⊂8⊃ ⊂8⊃ ⊂8⊃ ⊂8⊃
⊂9⊃ ⊂9⊃ ⊂9⊃ ⊂9⊃

BE SURE TO ERASE ANY ERRORS OR STRAY MARKS COMPLETELY.

PLEASE PRINT YOUR INITIALS

First   Middle   Last

Use a No. 2 pencil only. Be sure each mark is dark and completely fills the intended oval. Completely erase any errors or stray marks.

Start with number 1 for each new section. If a section has fewer questions than answer spaces, leave the extra answer spaces blank.

SECTION 5

1 ⊂A⊃ ⊂B⊃ ⊂C⊃ ⊂D⊃ ⊂E⊃	11 ⊂A⊃ ⊂B⊃ ⊂C⊃ ⊂D⊃ ⊂E⊃	21 ⊂A⊃ ⊂B⊃ ⊂C⊃ ⊂D⊃ ⊂E⊃	31 ⊂A⊃ ⊂B⊃ ⊂C⊃ ⊂D⊃ ⊂E⊃
2 ⊂A⊃ ⊂B⊃ ⊂C⊃ ⊂D⊃ ⊂E⊃	12 ⊂A⊃ ⊂B⊃ ⊂C⊃ ⊂D⊃ ⊂E⊃	22 ⊂A⊃ ⊂B⊃ ⊂C⊃ ⊂D⊃ ⊂E⊃	32 ⊂A⊃ ⊂B⊃ ⊂C⊃ ⊂D⊃ ⊂E⊃
3 ⊂A⊃ ⊂B⊃ ⊂C⊃ ⊂D⊃ ⊂E⊃	13 ⊂A⊃ ⊂B⊃ ⊂C⊃ ⊂D⊃ ⊂E⊃	23 ⊂A⊃ ⊂B⊃ ⊂C⊃ ⊂D⊃ ⊂E⊃	33 ⊂A⊃ ⊂B⊃ ⊂C⊃ ⊂D⊃ ⊂E⊃
4 ⊂A⊃ ⊂B⊃ ⊂C⊃ ⊂D⊃ ⊂E⊃	14 ⊂A⊃ ⊂B⊃ ⊂C⊃ ⊂D⊃ ⊂E⊃	24 ⊂A⊃ ⊂B⊃ ⊂C⊃ ⊂D⊃ ⊂E⊃	34 ⊂A⊃ ⊂B⊃ ⊂C⊃ ⊂D⊃ ⊂E⊃
5 ⊂A⊃ ⊂B⊃ ⊂C⊃ ⊂D⊃ ⊂E⊃	15 ⊂A⊃ ⊂B⊃ ⊂C⊃ ⊂D⊃ ⊂E⊃	25 ⊂A⊃ ⊂B⊃ ⊂C⊃ ⊂D⊃ ⊂E⊃	35 ⊂A⊃ ⊂B⊃ ⊂C⊃ ⊂D⊃ ⊂E⊃
6 ⊂A⊃ ⊂B⊃ ⊂C⊃ ⊂D⊃ ⊂E⊃	16 ⊂A⊃ ⊂B⊃ ⊂C⊃ ⊂D⊃ ⊂E⊃	26 ⊂A⊃ ⊂B⊃ ⊂C⊃ ⊂D⊃ ⊂E⊃	36 ⊂A⊃ ⊂B⊃ ⊂C⊃ ⊂D⊃ ⊂E⊃
7 ⊂A⊃ ⊂B⊃ ⊂C⊃ ⊂D⊃ ⊂E⊃	17 ⊂A⊃ ⊂B⊃ ⊂C⊃ ⊂D⊃ ⊂E⊃	27 ⊂A⊃ ⊂B⊃ ⊂C⊃ ⊂D⊃ ⊂E⊃	37 ⊂A⊃ ⊂B⊃ ⊂C⊃ ⊂D⊃ ⊂E⊃
8 ⊂A⊃ ⊂B⊃ ⊂C⊃ ⊂D⊃ ⊂E⊃	18 ⊂A⊃ ⊂B⊃ ⊂C⊃ ⊂D⊃ ⊂E⊃	28 ⊂A⊃ ⊂B⊃ ⊂C⊃ ⊂D⊃ ⊂E⊃	38 ⊂A⊃ ⊂B⊃ ⊂C⊃ ⊂D⊃ ⊂E⊃
9 ⊂A⊃ ⊂B⊃ ⊂C⊃ ⊂D⊃ ⊂E⊃	19 ⊂A⊃ ⊂B⊃ ⊂C⊃ ⊂D⊃ ⊂E⊃	29 ⊂A⊃ ⊂B⊃ ⊂C⊃ ⊂D⊃ ⊂E⊃	39 ⊂A⊃ ⊂B⊃ ⊂C⊃ ⊂D⊃ ⊂E⊃
10 ⊂A⊃ ⊂B⊃ ⊂C⊃ ⊂D⊃ ⊂E⊃	20 ⊂A⊃ ⊂B⊃ ⊂C⊃ ⊂D⊃ ⊂E⊃	30 ⊂A⊃ ⊂B⊃ ⊂C⊃ ⊂D⊃ ⊂E⊃	40 ⊂A⊃ ⊂B⊃ ⊂C⊃ ⊂D⊃ ⊂E⊃

SECTION 6

1 ⊂A⊃ ⊂B⊃ ⊂C⊃ ⊂D⊃ ⊂E⊃	11 ⊂A⊃ ⊂B⊃ ⊂C⊃ ⊂D⊃ ⊂E⊃	21 ⊂A⊃ ⊂B⊃ ⊂C⊃ ⊂D⊃ ⊂E⊃	31 ⊂A⊃ ⊂B⊃ ⊂C⊃ ⊂D⊃ ⊂E⊃
2 ⊂A⊃ ⊂B⊃ ⊂C⊃ ⊂D⊃ ⊂E⊃	12 ⊂A⊃ ⊂B⊃ ⊂C⊃ ⊂D⊃ ⊂E⊃	22 ⊂A⊃ ⊂B⊃ ⊂C⊃ ⊂D⊃ ⊂E⊃	32 ⊂A⊃ ⊂B⊃ ⊂C⊃ ⊂D⊃ ⊂E⊃
3 ⊂A⊃ ⊂B⊃ ⊂C⊃ ⊂D⊃ ⊂E⊃	13 ⊂A⊃ ⊂B⊃ ⊂C⊃ ⊂D⊃ ⊂E⊃	23 ⊂A⊃ ⊂B⊃ ⊂C⊃ ⊂D⊃ ⊂E⊃	33 ⊂A⊃ ⊂B⊃ ⊂C⊃ ⊂D⊃ ⊂E⊃
4 ⊂A⊃ ⊂B⊃ ⊂C⊃ ⊂D⊃ ⊂E⊃	14 ⊂A⊃ ⊂B⊃ ⊂C⊃ ⊂D⊃ ⊂E⊃	24 ⊂A⊃ ⊂B⊃ ⊂C⊃ ⊂D⊃ ⊂E⊃	34 ⊂A⊃ ⊂B⊃ ⊂C⊃ ⊂D⊃ ⊂E⊃
5 ⊂A⊃ ⊂B⊃ ⊂C⊃ ⊂D⊃ ⊂E⊃	15 ⊂A⊃ ⊂B⊃ ⊂C⊃ ⊂D⊃ ⊂E⊃	25 ⊂A⊃ ⊂B⊃ ⊂C⊃ ⊂D⊃ ⊂E⊃	35 ⊂A⊃ ⊂B⊃ ⊂C⊃ ⊂D⊃ ⊂E⊃
6 ⊂A⊃ ⊂B⊃ ⊂C⊃ ⊂D⊃ ⊂E⊃	16 ⊂A⊃ ⊂B⊃ ⊂C⊃ ⊂D⊃ ⊂E⊃	26 ⊂A⊃ ⊂B⊃ ⊂C⊃ ⊂D⊃ ⊂E⊃	36 ⊂A⊃ ⊂B⊃ ⊂C⊃ ⊂D⊃ ⊂E⊃
7 ⊂A⊃ ⊂B⊃ ⊂C⊃ ⊂D⊃ ⊂E⊃	17 ⊂A⊃ ⊂B⊃ ⊂C⊃ ⊂D⊃ ⊂E⊃	27 ⊂A⊃ ⊂B⊃ ⊂C⊃ ⊂D⊃ ⊂E⊃	37 ⊂A⊃ ⊂B⊃ ⊂C⊃ ⊂D⊃ ⊂E⊃
8 ⊂A⊃ ⊂B⊃ ⊂C⊃ ⊂D⊃ ⊂E⊃	18 ⊂A⊃ ⊂B⊃ ⊂C⊃ ⊂D⊃ ⊂E⊃	28 ⊂A⊃ ⊂B⊃ ⊂C⊃ ⊂D⊃ ⊂E⊃	38 ⊂A⊃ ⊂B⊃ ⊂C⊃ ⊂D⊃ ⊂E⊃
9 ⊂A⊃ ⊂B⊃ ⊂C⊃ ⊂D⊃ ⊂E⊃	19 ⊂A⊃ ⊂B⊃ ⊂C⊃ ⊂D⊃ ⊂E⊃	29 ⊂A⊃ ⊂B⊃ ⊂C⊃ ⊂D⊃ ⊂E⊃	39 ⊂A⊃ ⊂B⊃ ⊂C⊃ ⊂D⊃ ⊂E⊃
10 ⊂A⊃ ⊂B⊃ ⊂C⊃ ⊂D⊃ ⊂E⊃	20 ⊂A⊃ ⊂B⊃ ⊂C⊃ ⊂D⊃ ⊂E⊃	30 ⊂A⊃ ⊂B⊃ ⊂C⊃ ⊂D⊃ ⊂E⊃	40 ⊂A⊃ ⊂B⊃ ⊂C⊃ ⊂D⊃ ⊂E⊃

CERTIFICATION STATEMENT
    Copy in longhand the statement below and sign your name as you would an official document. DO NOT PRINT.

    I hereby agree with The Princeton Review that the SAT is nothing to fear and certify that I am the person who will conquer it.

_____

_____

_____

SIGNATURE: _____   DATE: _____

FOR TPR USE ONLY	VTR	VTFS	CRR	CRFS	ANW	SCR	SCFS	5MTW	MTFS		5AAW	AAFS	5GRW	GFS
	VTW	VTCS	CRW	ANR	ANFS	SCW	MTR	4MTW	MTCS	AAR	4AAW	GRR	4GRW	
								0MTW			0AAW		0GRW	

DO NOT MARK IN THIS AREA
⊂ ⊃ ⊂ ⊃ ⊂ ⊃ ⊂ ⊃ ⊂ ⊃ ⊂ ⊃ ⊂ ⊃ ⊂ ⊃ ⊂ ⊃ ⊂ ⊃ ⊂ ⊃ ⊂ ⊃ ⊂ ⊃ ⊂ ⊃ ⊂ ⊃

CULTURESCOPE

The

Princeton Review

Guide to an Informed Mind

Has this ever happened to you?

You're at a party. An attractive person who you have been dying to meet comes over and says, "Man, does that woman have a Joan of Arc complex, or what?" and you, in a tone that is most suave, say "Uh," while your mind races wildly, *"Joan of Arc, OK, France, uh...damn,"* as the aforementioned attractive person smiles weakly and heads for the punch bowl.

No? How about this?

Your boss finally learns your name and says, "Ah, good to have you aboard. Do you like Renaissance painting?" You reply with an emphatic "Yes! I do!" to which she returns, "What's your favorite fresco?" You start stammering, glassy-eyed, your big moment passing you by as visions of soda pop dance through your brain.

CULTURESCOPE can help.

If you have gaps of knowledge big enough to drive a eighteen-wheeler through, The Princeton Review has the thing for you. It's called CULTURESCOPE. It's a book that can make people think you've read enough books to fill a semi, even if you haven't.

CULTURESCOPE covers everything: history, science, math, art, sports, geography, popular culture—it's all in there, and it's fun, because along with all of the great information there are quizzes, resource lists, fun statistics, wacky charts, and lots of pretty pictures.

It's coming in October of 1994 to a bookstore near you.

You won't go away empty-headed.